Gender, Race and Religion
in Video Game Music

Studies in Game Sound and Music

Series editors: Tim Summers, Michiel Kamp, Melanie Fritsch and Andra Ivănescu
Print ISSN: 2633-0652 | **Online ISSN:** 2633-0660

Intellect's Studies in Game Sound and Music will publish accessible, detailed books that provide in-depth academic of topics and texts in video game audio. The books will present detailed analysis, historical investigation and treatment of conceptual and theoretical issues related to game audio.

The series aims to: reveal important information about major media texts, investigate game music in a degree of depth and detail hitherto unseen, address major critical issues in game music studies, deploy and evolve approaches of antecedent scholarship and develop new ways examining this media music.

The titles will be significant texts in a blossoming field, at once drawing on the opportunity presented by the growing subject area, and supporting that development through the research they prompt and represent.

The series will not seal game audio into a scholarly suburb, but will instead be outward looking: it seeks to engage game audio practitioners and researchers from a range of disciplines, including anthropology, performance studies, computer science, media studies, psychology, sociology, sound studies, as well as musicology. Recently contracted titles include a companion to music in The Legend of Zelda, a collection on nostalgia and video game music, and a collection on the work of Nobuo Uematsu.

In this series:

The Legend of Zelda: Ocarina of Time: A Game Music Companion, by Tim Summers (2022)
Nostalgia and Videogame Music: A Primer of Case Studies, Theories, and Analyses for the Player-
    Academic, edited by Vincent E. Rone, Can Aksoy and Sarah Pozderac-Chenevey (2022)
The Music of Nobuo Uematsu in the Final Fantasy Series, edited by Richard Anatone (2023)
Gender, Race and Religion in Video Game Music, by Thomas B. Yee (2024)

To Tori and Tsuki.

Gender, Race and Religion in Video Game Music

Thomas B. Yee

Bristol, UK / Chicago, USA

First published in the UK in 2024 by
Intellect, The Mill, Parnall Road, Fishponds, Bristol, BS16 3JG, UK

First published in the USA in 2024 by
Intellect, The University of Chicago Press, 1427 E. 60th Street,
Chicago, IL 60637, USA

Copyright © 2024 Intellect Ltd

All rights reserved. No part of this publication may be reproduced,
stored in a retrieval system, or transmitted, in any form or by
any means, electronic, mechanical, photocopying, recording, or
otherwise, without written permission.

A catalogue record for this book is available from
the British Library.

Copy editor: MPS Limited
Cover designer: Tanya Montefusco
Cover image: BongkarnThanyakij, Wiphop Sathawirawong and terra.incognita
Production manager: Sophia Munyengeterwa
Typesetter: MPS Limited

Hardback ISBN 978-1-78938-993-7
ePDF ISBN 978-1-78938-995-1
ePUB ISBN 978-1-78938-994-4

Part of Studies in Game Sound and Music series
Print ISSN: 2633-0652 | Online ISSN: 2633-0660

To find out about all our publications, please visit our website.
There you can subscribe to our e-newsletter, browse or download our current
catalogue and buy any titles that are in print.

www.intellectbooks.com

Supplementary material available on Intellect Discover.

https://intellectdiscover.com/content/books/9781789389937

This is a peer-reviewed publication.

Contents

List of Figures and Tables	ix
Introduction: Enter the Virtual	1

PART I: NARRATIVE AND PLAY   21

1. Ludo-Narrative Harmony: Interpretative Interactivity   23
   in *Chrono Cross* and *Gris*

PART II: GENDER   45

2. Feminine Themings: The Construction of Musical   47
   Gendering in the *Final Fantasy* Franchise
3. Single Ladies and Herbivore Men: Alternative Femininities   79
   and Masculinities in *Final Fantasy XIII* and *XV*
4. Damsel No Longer: The Empowered Mezzo-Soprano   106
   Voice in *Horizon Zero Dawn*

PART III: RACE   127

5. Racialized Fantasy: Authenticity, Appropriation and Stereotype   129
6. Antiracist Storytelling: Representation and Diversity   163
   in *Civilization VI* and *Overwatch*

PART IV: RELIGION   193

7. Sonic Iconography: The Sacred Music Topic in   195
   Lightning Returns: Final Fantasy XIII

GENDER, RACE AND RELIGION IN VIDEO GAME MUSIC

8. Battle Hymn of the God-Slayers: Troping Rock and   225
Sacred Music in *Xenoblade Chronicles*

Conclusion: Enter the Real   245
Appendix: Audiovisual Media   249
References   253
About the Author   275
Index   277

Figures

I.1	Diagram conceptualizing semiotics.	14
1.1	Pitches produced by each Element colour type.	34
1.2	Screenshots of *Gris*.	38
1.3	Five statues corresponding to Kübler-Ross' five stages of grief.	40
1.4	Differentiated vocal range/registers.	40
1.5	'In Your Hands' vocal duet transcription.	41
2.1	Princess Hilda/Lamia Queen seduces Firion.	53
2.2	Conventionally masculine to the conventionally feminine spectrum of *Final Fantasy* character themes.	60
2.3	Partial musical transcriptions of the character themes analysed.	61
3.1	Partial musical transcription of 'Lightning's Theme'.	88
3.2	Partial musical transcription of 'Noctis's Theme'.	99
4.1	'Sawtooth' machine beast (top left), Aloy's character model (top right), Lantern ceremony (bottom left), Aloy's allies (bottom right).	112
4.2	Appearances of 'Aloy's Theme'.	115
4.3	Partial musical transcription of 'In the Flood' and Zo's song.	123
5.1	Wide angle of Tostarena town (above), Mario wearing sombrero and poncho with a Tostarenan (below).	138
5.2	Wide angle of Bowser's Castle (top left), Stairface Ogre with red *oni* mask, *geta* shoes and *Hanafuda* card stamp (top right), *Jizō* statues in a Zen rock garden (bottom left) Bowser-marked fireworks and Pokio enemy (bottom right).	139
5.3	Partial musical transcription of 'Tostarena – Town'.	141
5.4	Japanese modes used in Bowser's Castle (top), 'Bowser's Castle', strings transcription (bottom).	143

5.5	'Bower's Castle' formal diagram corresponding to *jo-ha-kyū* form.	149
5.6	Wayang puppetry cutscenes (top), Vishnu's Temple (bottom).	153
5.7	Ostinato based on Tzelos' experience in Brahma's temple (top), Kistoor's melody for his wife (bottom).	154
6.1	Segregation – antiracism – assimilation in musical racial representation diagram.	168
6.2	Spectrum of *Overwatch* map musical themes.	185
7.1	Chart of distribution of relevance rankings of 142 games.	202
7.2	Luxerion Cathedral (left), Bhunivelze's character model (right).	212
7.3	'The Ark' hymn, musical transcription (above), 'A Sacred Oratorio', partial musical transcription (below).	214
7.4	Partial transcription of 'Almighty Bhunivelze' (opening).	216
8.1	Partial musical transcription, 'Zanza the Divine'.	234
8.2	Partial transcription of 'The God-Slaying Sword'.	237

Tables

I.1	Table summarizing ludology and narratology perspectives in game studies.	5
1.1	Diagram summarizing a theory of interpretative interactivity for video game music analysis.	31
2.1	Table of conventionally masculine and conventionally feminine musical traits in the *Final Fantasy* franchise.	59
3.1	Table summarizing *FFXV*'s narrative subversions of Japanese hegemonic salaryman masculinity.	98
6.1	Table of leader theme source melodies in *Civilization VI*.	174
6.2	Table of Great Musicians and featured musical works in *Civilization VI*.	177

FIGURES

7.1	Spreadsheet documenting corpus study of video games potentially containing the narrative god-slayer trope, organized according to the trope's degree of relevance and fit.	204
8.1	Parameter comparison of rock and sacred-music topics and their semiotic associations.	229
8.2	A. J. Greimas's modalities as applied in musical semiotics.	230
8.3	Four axes for semiotic analysis of topical troping in music.	235

Introduction:
Enter the Virtual

'New Game?' – Playing with Identity

Allow me to set the scene. I sit in a broadcast studio transfigured into a cutting-edge classroom merged with an interview space that could have emerged straight from Johnny Carson's *Tonight Show*. Livestreaming to the devices of over 700 university students, the course's format exemplifies its subject matter: the intersections of art and technology, focusing on new, emergent art forms enabled by technology. Utilizing a pedagogy that fittingly prioritizes interactivity, this day's session features a hands-on demonstration, aesthetic analysis and social contextualization of contemporary video games. From a couple dozen studio audience members, a few select volunteers play the game examples while the professor and I interview them about their experience.[1] Avery (fictional name) is chosen to showcase *Ori and the Blind Forest* (2015). 'I knew I had to share my story today', Avery speaks with vulnerability and conviction, 'because playing *Ori and the Blind Forest* literally saved my life'.

As a lifelong video game nerd, I resonate with Avery's words, aware that they may strike others as hyperbole. But I see in the student's eyes and hear in the weight of their voice that their statement is true. Avery praises *Ori*'s lovingly crafted visual aesthetics and lush orchestral soundtrack that perfectly echoes every emotional inflection of the story – both elements intensifying immersion and engagement. Interacting with the virtual gameworld as Ori, Avery says, facilitates personal identification with Ori's journey. But first and foremost is the story's human connection, evoked by the game's narrative themes of empathy, grief and companionship. When Avery encountered the game in the midst of isolation, despair and suicidal ideation, *Ori*'s message of hope and portrayal of unconditional caring illuminated a path forward. 'People need people', Avery concludes through tears, 'that has become my life mantra now – and it was a video game that taught me that lesson'.

Transformative. Uplifting. Life-changing. What bestows video games with such incredible power?

Gender, Race and Religion in Video Game Music explores the powerful, meaningful and culturally relevant contribution of music to video games' narrative and thematic meanings. In doing so, it connects the virtual worlds and stories of video games to real-life people and cultures. Researching demographic representation – how recognizable traits, identities or communities are portrayed in a work – is critical, as media shapes audience attitudes and beliefs about others who are different. Each player is a nexus between virtual and real worlds, interpreting a game's messages as relevant to their unique sociocultural context. Far from being cordoned off from the real world, video games speak to crucial and contentious issues of identity in contemporary society. This book explores gender, race and religion as three demographic master categories that affect multiple aspects of an individual's identity and experience. Though video games address countless more salient identities, these three demonstrate video game music's potential to speak to the core of human identity and experience. For each demographic category, video game history presents a rich body of examples of musical representation – from problematic to progressive – worthy of rigorous scholarly study, analysing and revealing the semiotic logic undergirding each case study. By understanding musical representation in video games, we will become more critical players, listeners, interpreters – and more compassionate members of an increasingly diverse world.

This book is ostensibly about analysing musical representation in video games – and it is that. Yet it is equally about meaning-making processes, intersections between art and culture, semiotic politics, the importance of diversity, empathy for the Other and how human beings choose to treat one another. That is to say, it sets out one robust answer to the question: why do video games matter?

Tutorial – Video Games and the Permeable Magic Circle

To begin, what can be learned about video game music from game studies more broadly? What relation do games have to the people who play them and to the real world? These questions require an examination of the relationship of video games to play. Despite their ubiquity in contemporary culture, video games are deceptively difficult to theorize, prompting ample debate among scholars. A good starting point is Johan Huizinga's five characteristics of play listed in 'Introduction: Enter the Virtual' of Huizinga's seminal work *Homo Ludens*, for play is closely intertwined with the nature of games:

1. Play is voluntary;
2. Play is not ordinary life;
3. Play is circumscribed within specific limits of time and place;
4. Play creates order (rules);
5. Play forms social groupings that express identification with the play context as distinct from the common world (Huizinga 1949, 7–13).

INTRODUCTION

Criteria 2, 3 and 5 entail that play generates a conceptual domain different from ordinary life, discussed among game scholars as a 'magic circle'. Though the concept is frequently credited to Huizinga, 'magic circle' only appears a handful of times in *Homo Ludens*, without much fanfare – it is found most prominently in a list of possible play settings (e.g. card table, stage, sports arena) that demarcate play activities from ordinary life (Huizinga 1949, 10). Building on Huizinga's work, game designers Eric Zimmerman and Katie Salen adapted the evocative term 'magic circle' to denote the conceptual domain games create (Zimmerman 2012). In *Rules of Play*, Salen and Zimmerman describe the magic circle as 'enclosed and separate from the real world', accruing special meanings to objects and behaviours (2004, 95–96). For Zimmerman (2012), the magic circle is a discrete context from which new meanings emerge, combining elements intrinsic and extrinsic to the game. Within a magic circle, the rules of ordinary life are temporarily suspended so that mundane actions are imbued with newfound significance in the gameworld. Notably, Salen and Zimmerman consider the interrelation of the gameworld and real world; while the game's rules are bounded by the magic circle, the act of play can be considered an open system in which players 'bring a great deal in from the outside world [... and] a reflection of the players who play them' (2004, 96–97). Paradoxically, depending on one's frame of analysis, a game is both a closed and open system – simultaneously 'powerful' and 'remarkably fragile' as it makes possible the unique affordances of play (Salen and Zimmerman 2004, 98).

A few points are worth emphasizing here. First, a game's magic circle is not impenetrable – it is distinct from ordinary life, but not hermetically sealed off from it. The criticism that a game's magic circle is 'completely divorced from ordinary life' mischaracterizes Zimmerman's (2012) view, as Zimmerman agrees the two are 'inexorably intertwined'.[2] Indeed, one passage from *Rules of Play* sounds remarkably like the porousness advocated by the magic circle's detractors: 'the way has been paved for our entrance into the magic circle. Passing through its open and closed boundaries, we find ourselves in its center' (Salen and Zimmerman 2004, 98). Jesper Juul cites T. L. Taylor (2007), Marinka Copier (2005), Thomas Malaby (2007), and Pargman and Jakobsson (2008) as game scholars understanding Salen's and Zimmerman's magic circle as requiring a strict separation (Juul 2008, 58–59). Huizinga's description of play as 'an activity connected with no material interest' nor motivation for productive outcome is also misinterpreted as requiring strict separation from life, though a majority of *Homo Ludens* explores cases of play embedded within life and society (1949, 13). Juul (2008, 65) proposes a puzzle piece as an alternative metaphor making visible a game's embeddedness within a surrounding social context – however, this updated imagery has not been widely adopted. Edward Castronova describes the boundary between gameworld and

3

ordinary life as a porous cellular membrane, traversed by players who routinely bridge the two domains – a metaphor more likely to ward off mischaracterizations of over-rigidity (Castronova 2005, 145). As a second observation, the discreteness and integrity of the gameworld enable immersion. Because play stands in contrast to ordinary life, it is capable of 'absorbing the player intensely and utterly' into another context or world (Huizinga 1949, 13). Entering a magic circle requires suspension of disbelief and agreement to its rules, no matter how fantastical or supposedly unrealistic (Castronova 2005, 147). Finally, this concept need not be applied only to play or games, but yields productive results in other fields and media – any differentiated context for meaning-making constitutes a magic circle (Zimmerman 2012). Janet Murray writes that stories and games share in common their 'insularity from the real world' – a parallel suggesting that game and narrative are not intrinsically opposed (Murray 2004, 3). Contrary to its critics, the magic circle as set forth by Huizinga, Zimmerman and Salen is remarkably flexible, adaptable and permeable.

What sets the magic circle of video games apart from other games or media? In game studies scholarship, 'virtuality' – along with 'immersion' and 'interactivity' – is frequently credited as a characteristic property of video games, often contrasted with 'reality' or the 'real world'.[3] For example: video game players explore virtual worlds, an avatar in *Second Life* (2003) presents a virtual self and Oculus headsets enable virtual reality experiences. In each case, 'virtual' delineates the video game context from the real world in some way. Marie-Laure Ryan observes three definitions of 'virtual' simultaneously active in video game play: (1) illusory or imaginary, not real; (2) potential, not (yet) actual; and (3) digital, mediated by and dependent upon computers (Ryan 2015, 8). Other games and art forms are often virtual in senses (1) and (2) – e.g. literature as illusory and potential in Aristotle's *Poetics* – but (3) is uniquely characteristic of video games. Though 'virtual' is a specific technical term in computing, in popular culture it has become synonymous with 'the accelerating flight of technology into the unknown' (Ryan 2015, 18). When coupled with influential science-fiction works like *Neuromancer* (Gibson 1984) or *The Matrix* (1999), 'virtual' describes a fictional world – possibly indistinguishable from reality – experienced in an immersive fashion through digital technology. Like the magic circle, virtual and real worlds may affect one another through the players who traverse the permeable boundary between them, since one domain of human life is not cordoned off from all others (Castronova 2005, 7). Because of this, the virtual worlds of video games are rapidly becoming one of the most powerful catalysts for personal meaning-making in the contemporary world, increasingly blurring the boundaries between the virtual and real. Chapter 1 will further explore 'immersion' and 'interactivity', which together with virtuality generates a permeable magic circle – a virtual domain both affected by and affecting its players.

INTRODUCTION

'Level Up' – Video Game Music Between Ludology and Narratology

Vigorous debates between schools of thought aiming to articulate the conceptual and methodological landscape of a field are commonplace in scholarship. Most academic disciplines have been shaped by such discussions, including video game studies. Described by one participant as a 'blood feud' between two entrenched camps, the debate between ludology and narratology probes foundational questions about what video games are and how they should best be understood (Jenkins 2004, 118). Broadly speaking, ludologists hold that video games should be analysed primarily, first or only as games, while narratologists believe examining them as a storytelling medium is also appropriate and productive. Largely occurring in academic conferences and publications from the late 1990s to mid 2000s, the quarrel is somewhat of a historical relic – by 2009, some video game scholars already described it as 'passé' (Crawford and Gosling 2009, 54). However, revisiting this fundamental discourse clarifies the stakes within game studies; are video games' ludic and narrative components complementary, or are they 'different structures that are in effect doing opposite things' (Aarseth 2004, 45)? And how do game and story each relate to music?

Ludological perspectives emphasize gameplay-related components of a video game, including computer programming and implementation, rule mechanics and quantitative parameters, optimal strategies and user play experience. Prominent ludologists include Espen Aarseth, Markku Eskelinen, Jesper Juul and Gonzalo Frasca. Ludologists' main concerns may be summarized as follows (Table I.1):

TABLE I.1: Table summarizing ludology and narratology perspectives in game studies.

	Ludology	Narratology
Values	Video games should be analysed primarily, first or only as games.	Analysing video games as a story-telling medium is productive.
Emphasis	Computer programming, rules, game-play strategy, nature of play.	Narrative, immersion, relationship between ludic and narrative agency.
Major Figures	Espen Aarseth, Markku Eskelinen, Jesper Juul, Gonzalo Frasca.	Janet Murray, Henry Jenkins, Marie-Laure Ryan, Nick Monfort, and others.
Main Points	1) A distinct academic field of ludology is necessary.	1) Most video games are narratives, though not reducible to narrative only.
	2) Video games' unique characteristics relate to gameplay, not narrative.	2) Ludologists critique too narrow a conception of narrative.
	3) Theories from other disciplines are a poor fit for analysing video games.	3) Narrative is a major driver of players' interest in video games.

1. A distinct academic field of ludology is necessary. In 1999, Gonzalo Frasca proposed 'ludology' (from Latin *ludus*, 'game') to name the not-yet-existent academic study of games and play (Frasca 1999). Maintaining a conceptual distinction between ludology and narratology is analytically useful, ludologists argue, to recognize the unique contributions of play to games (Aarseth 2004, 54). Ludologists aimed to correct a perceived deficiency in scholarship by analysing gameplay-relevant factors, instead of approaching games like any other storytelling medium (Frasca 1999). Additionally, ludologists were wary of academic imperialism from other disciplines, including literature and film studies. Aarseth excoriates narratological analysis as humanities scholars' attempts to feel important and relevant by '[reforming] games into a more acceptable form of art' (Aarseth 2004, 49). In this context, ludologists asserted the need for a distinct field studying games as games rather than merely being absorbed into other disciplines.

2. Video games' most unique characteristics relate to gameplay, not narrative. Video games consist of rules, gameplay and a semiotic context (narrative or gameworld); ludologists claim the context is incidental to the 'game itself' (Aarseth 2004, 48). Narratives are ubiquitous – in literature, film, drama and beyond – but what makes video games a unique medium is the interactive gameplay afforded by computing technology. Interactivity is key – unlike other art forms, a video game requires active player participation to access (or even create) its content (Frasca 2004, 86). This interaction is enabled by the game's rules which ground player enjoyment, ingenuity and agency (Juul 2005, 55). Though fictional context is important, '[the] fiction depends on rules' (Juul 2005, 121). For this reason, Frasca prefers to describe video games as simulations rather than narratives, stressing their ability to explore possible outcomes of players' choices and guide them through multiple, alternate perspectives (Frasca 2004, 86, 93). Any narrative reading of video games must account for interactivity and the gameplay that affords it.

3. Theoretical frameworks imported wholesale from other disciplines are a poor fit for analysing games. Ludologists disdained applying narrative theories directly to video games without modification – akin to shoving square pegs into round holes. Aarseth writes that traditional narrative concepts 'are not well-suited to the problems of a simulational hermeneutic' and require adaptation to the particularities of games (2004, 54). Additionally, the term narrative is ill-defined: multiple definitions exist, and narratologists imported overly broad meanings to early video games (Eskelinen 2004, 37; Juul 2005, 156–57). The resulting readings struck ludologists as forced acts of 'interpretative violence' born from narratologists' dogged belief in the relevance of their academic training (Eskelinen 2001). Developers are not immune to this tendency, resulting in 'cinema envy'

INTRODUCTION

from attempts to recreate filmic storytelling in video games (Zimmerman 2004, 157). If scholars, developers and players are to discern narrative in video games, they must tailor their methods to the medium – not approach video games the same as they would a movie or novel.

On the other hand, narratologists affirm that, while gameplay is essential to video games, games may also convey narrative. As a label for a diverse group of interdisciplinary scholars interested in video games, it is more difficult to list narratologists than ludologists; however, Janet Murray, Henry Jenkins, Marie-Laure Ryan and Nick Montfort warrant particular mention. As with ludologists, narratologists' arguments may be grouped into three main concerns (see Table I.1):

1. Although video games are not reducible to narrative, most do constitute narratives. Narratologists never claimed that video games were solely stories – only that they do communicate narratives. 'Games are always stories', writes Janet Murray, 'even abstract games [...] about winning and losing, casting the player as the opponent-battling or environment-battling hero' (Murray 2004, 2). In other words, the player's foregrounded agency, desired goal and opponents/obstacles produce a narrative constructed and fuelled by gameplay actions. Henry Jenkins terms this 'emergent narrative', empowering game players to enact their own stories within a gameworld 'rich with narrative potential' (Jenkins 2004, 129). Because humans are inherently story-constructing, meaning-making creatures, players typically recount their gaming experiences in narrative form – regardless of whether the game is story-driven (Ryan 2015, 164). Rather than replace attention to gameplay, narratology augments it by considering how narrative emerges from ludic agency. Contrary to ludologists' claims, narratologists do not seek to assimilate video games to paradigms of print literature or cinema (Murray 2004, 10). 'We must ... be attentive to the particularity of games as a medium', writes Jenkins, 'specifically what distinguishes them from other narrative traditions' (2004, 120). To analyse video games as stories does not mean they are not also games.

2. Ludologists' critiques operate on too narrow a conception of narrative. Aarseth, Frasca, Juul and Eskelinen each stressed allegedly intractable differences between games and narratives (understood as print literature). Yet their objections presuppose 'too narrow a model of narrative, one preoccupied with the rules and conventions of classical linear storytelling', ignoring twentieth- and twenty-first-century hypertexts and non-linear narratives (Jenkins 2004, 120–21). For example, Juul argues that because the full plot of the *Star Wars* film cannot be deduced by playing the *Star Wars* video game, the game cannot be considered narrative; this is a far too myopic view of transmedial adaptation

7

(Jenkins 2004, 124). Contrary to Eskelinen's objection that narrative requires one or more identifiable narrators, which video games often lack, Marie-Laure Ryan describes games as simultaneous narratives in which the player 'lives the story as she writes it through her actions in the real time of a continuously moving present' (Ryan 2015, 49). Game narratives transcend the game's rules, connecting from the virtual world into the real one – for 'it is the reader who gives a text meaning and life' (Crawford and Gosling 2009, 56). Instead of a narrow definition of narrative, Celia Pearce outlines six narrative modes that manifest particularly well in video games: experiential, performative, augmentary, descriptive, metastory and story system (Pearce 2004, 145). To narratologists, ludologists discard narrative analysis at their own loss, overlooking immense gains from 'meaningful comparisons with other storytelling media' (Jenkins 2004, 119). Narratologists insist that narrative is much more than ludologists assume.

3. <u>Narrative is a major driver of interest in video games.</u> Ludologist writings often dismiss narrative aspirations in video games as irrelevant or worse, a dangerous distraction – Eskelinen (2001) labelled game stories as mere 'marketing tools' and 'a waste of time and energy' to study. Yet for players, narrative engagement is a major motivator for seeking out, enjoying and cherishing video game experiences. It is doubtful that video games would have risen to such mainstream prominence if their narrative contexts never advanced beyond that of *Tennis for Two* (1958) or *Spacewar!* (1962). Immersion within compelling, intricate gameworlds has made video games one of the 'most powerful [sources] of personal meaning in the contemporary world' (Castronova 2007, 207). Ludologists' central error is attempting to completely isolate gameplay from everyday life. However, as with the magic circle, virtual worlds are porous and permeable as their boundaries are traversed by meaning-making players, allowing game narratives to extend beyond the boundaries of the screen (Crawford and Gosling 2009, 62). Murray proposes the label 'cyberdrama' to describe new media forms like video games that blend elements of gameplay and narrative (Murray 2004, 5). The result is an art form that increasingly enmeshes players' real and virtual lives and identities. 'Storytelling and gaming have always been overlapping experiences and will continue to be so', writes Murray, '[human] experience demands every modality of narration that we can bring to it' (2004, 8). To deny the narrative potential of video games is to rebuff the multifarious meaning-making processes that players reify in and through games.

The ludology-versus-narratology debate effectively outlines the ideological landscape within academic game studies. Roughly a decade younger,

INTRODUCTION

'ludomusicology' – the scholarly study of sound and music in games, including video games – owes much to its older cousin, including echoes of ludological–narratological debate. Despite not often invoking the ludology-narratology divide explicitly, ludomusicologists often emphasize on one side of the ludology-narratology spectrum.[4] The following literature review is admittedly abbreviated, selective and somewhat artificial, as I am certain my colleagues would each claim a middle ground between ludological and narratological poles. Additionally, due to the protracted nature of the publication process, it may already be somewhat outdated by this book's publication. Nevertheless, it is useful to observe how prior video game music scholarship parallels existing game studies discourse in its priorities, concepts and methodologies.

Ludology-leaning Ludomusicologists:

Karen Collins: As the first scholarly book published on video game music, Collins's *Game Sound* (Collins 2008) is a landmark that has been described as 'the true establishment of the field' of ludomusicology (Vinzant 2020). *Game Sound* and its spiritual successor, *Playing with Sound* (Collins 2013) theorize interactivity between the player and soundtrack as augmenting a plethora of gameplay functions. Collins argues that two-way interactivity distinguishes game audio from sound in film – actively triggering sound events rather than passively receiving them (2008, 3; 2013, 22). Sound contributes to gameplay in various ways: binding sound to action via kinesonic synchresis, spatializing sound to indicate enemy positions, assisting players in learning gameplay, signifying success or failure at gameplay tasks, guiding player choices through emotional affect and maintaining immersion in the gameworld (2008, 101, 130 133, 134, 148–49; 2013, 32).[5] Of particular interest is interactive non-diegetic music – cues triggered by gameplay choices and therefore manipulatable by players (2008, 126). This interactivity strengthens identification and empathy with virtual characters (2013, 37–38, 58). Interactive audio firmly centres the place of players – for without a player, game audio is merely 'code, lying in wait' (2013, 2).

William Cheng: *Sound Play* (Cheng 2014) is a stimulating phenomenological exploration of how players engage with video game music through gameplay, examining social dynamics that emerge through virtual music-making. Whether synchronizing a nuclear warhead detonation to the Perfect Authentic Cadence of the march 'Stars and Stripes Forever' or watching a gradual in-game sunrise while listening to the world's last Stradivarius violin,

GENDER, RACE AND RELIGION IN VIDEO GAME MUSIC

Cheng demonstrates that video game music is far from irrelevant to gameplay decisions. Especially noteworthy is Cheng's analysis of horror game sound in *Silent Hill* (1999), which obfuscates distinctions between diegetic, non-diegetic and real-world sounds – simultaneously intensifying anxiety and undermining player confidence in the reliability of their 'visual, aural, and cognitive faculties' (98–99). In the MMORPG *Lord of the Rings Online* (2007), players weaponized built-in music-making gameplay actions ('bagpipe spam', 'griefing') to pester fellow players into leaving certain areas (135–37).[6] In a more semiotic interpretation of the famous opera scene of *Final Fantasy VI* (1994), Cheng reads Celes's foregrounded aria and synthesized voice as encoding early video games' aspirations to the cultural prestige of classical art forms like opera (89). Julianne Grasso: Like Collins's work, 'Video Game Music, Meaning, and the Possibilities of Play' (Grasso 2020) focuses on analysing music's influence on gameplay actions – and vice versa. Grasso theorizes affective zones as music that creates affordances for a particular range of gameplay actions by priming players for certain responses (60). A striking example is the disruptive 'hurry-up' music in *Super Mario World* (1990), which interrupts leisurely exploration with a dissonant fanfare followed by a double-time version of the level's music, spurring players to quicken their pace (80). Other examples include the syncopated rhythms and 'blue-note' chromaticisms of *Super Mario Bros.* (1985) – mapping musical instability onto the dangers of an unstable level – or contrasting music affording combat and safety in *The Legend of Zelda* (1986) (57, 163). In the latter, 'Hyrule Field' affords quick, persistent exploration because its rhythms are quick and persistent; 'the sharp musical attacks are Link's attacks, the motion is Link's motion' (89–90). A second gameplay-relevant contribution is habituation, especially well-suited to the looping nature of much game music (148). In *Bejeweled 3* (2010), total habituation to repetitive puzzle-solving music allows players to perceive the dissonant glockenspiel and bass notes signalling impending failure as a marked contrast (168–70). Contrasting tonal relationships in the soundtrack of *Journey* (2012) gently nudge players to seek the next objective, promising a euphoric sonic payoff upon arrival (133). Finally, demonstrating that none of these scholars is wholly ludological or narratological, Grasso proposes a reconciliation between the two camps through 'ludomusical narrativity' (110). Chapter 1 dialogues further with Grasso's work.

While ludological perspectives relate music directly to gameplay actions, narratological ones broaden their scope to narrative, thematic, sociocultural and historical meanings. Representational topics – the focus of this book – typically align more with the interests, questions and methods of narratology.

INTRODUCTION

Narratology-leaning Ludomusicologists:

Tim Summers: Chapter 5 of *Understanding Game Music* (Summers 2016) boldly claims that video game music 'routinely has a greater aesthetic priority, narrative agency and informational content in games than in film' (175). Summers attributes this to interactivity, which incentivizes active engagement with game music and heightens player investment through participating in its discovery and unfolding (2016, 50; 2020, 41). Games encourage players to adopt a hermeneutic orientation, actively seeking to interpret and understand its music as a meaningful entity (2016, 41, 206). Summers' analysis of leitmotif in *Final Fantasy VII* (1997) demonstrates that musical themes do not simply reflect or comment upon the gameplay, but actively shape the perception of character, setting and plot – music is a 'creative, rather than simply descriptive, force' (164). Tiered battle themes blend narrative and ludic function, as 'One-Winged Angel' encodes the battle against Sephiroth as both 'narrative apex and highest point of ludic challenge' (167). Concerning representational matters, Summers observes that video game music is not sealed off from the real world, but rather incorporates 'actual world musical meanings to generate context for a virtual world' – typically cultural or national musical traditions and styles (40, 114). Much of the present book's analyses build on this observation and Summers's overall approach to understanding game music.

Isabella van Elferen: Conceptualizing video game music as a prime opportunity to develop a 'New Drastic Musicology' that centres meaning-making processes grounded in players' actions and experiences, van Elferen proposes 'supra-diegetic' to describe how the act of listening inevitably blends game-specific musical meanings with real-world connotations (van Elferen 2020, 104, 109). van Elferen's ALI model (affect-literacy-interaction) has gained traction in the field as a framework articulating game music's contribution to player immersion (2016, 34, 49). The interplay of these parameters invites players to ascribe 'personal and collective meanings' to game music grounded in their unique phenomenological experience (2016, 35). Literacy – how cultural conventions and discourses shape interpretation – poses special narrative significance, as listeners familiar with musical traditions in film, television and video games will understand a track differently than one hearing a strategy for the first time (2016, 36). In other words, players become sites of intertextual meaning-making, connecting game music to unique sets of previously heard pieces. 'More than any other music', writes van Elferen, 'game music is an event, not a work; its performance is playful, immediate, and interactive' (2020, 106). As a result, musical meaning in video games is not reducible to internal rules and gameplay but presupposes exposure to larger bodies of works.

William Gibbons: It is tempting to think that the genres of classical and video game music have little to no relation; *Unlimited Replays* (Gibbons 2018) shows this could not be further from the truth, as classical music makes appearances in 'even the most unexpected of video games' (114). Intersections of classical music and video games are striking hermeneutic opportunities, a 'transgression [...] that begs for explanation and interpretation' (4). In a video game soundtrack, classical music imports a wealth of 'ready-made perceptions and associations', including pastness, high class, irony or artistic value (22, 81, 114). Games may incorporate pieces for their specific meanings, such as Mozart's 'Requiem Mass' in *BioShock Infinite* (2013) or Chopin's 'Funeral March' and 'Revolutionary Étude' in *Catherine* (2011), producing an intertextually enriched narrative statement (45–49, 105–09). Classical music in games acts as a destabilizing force that challenges cultural boundaries, 'exposing the art in the game, and the game in the art' (138, 157). The unexpected, fruitful combination gestures to 'a future where the artificial distinctions between highbrow and lowbrow are erased' (174).

Sean Atkinson: Musical topics group constellations of musical characteristics into patterns that invoke consistent cultural associations when they appear. Atkinson traces the 'soaring' musical topic from its origins in film to its frequent usage in video games, exploring how its semiotic meanings impact their narrative interpretation (2019, 2). Adopting David Neumeyer's topic-trope continuum, in which topics are conventional and normative while tropes are novel and strategic, Atkinson identifies the soaring topic as an erstwhile trope of martial, transcendent, mechanical and supernatural topics that has since become a standalone topic (4, 18). Melodic ascents (especially ascending leaps), ascending sequences, upward arpeggios or harp glissandi and Lydian-mode inflection are hallmarks of the soaring topic (10, 13, 14, 17). In video games, the soaring topic is nearly always paired with flight-based levels or gameplay – in Grasso's terms, it creates an affective zone affording flight. However, Atkinson connects the soaring topic to robust narrative readings of *The Legend of Zelda: Skyward Sword* (2011) and *Final Fantasy IV* (1991) that foreshadow future narrative events and subvert conventional expectations (23–25). Nonetheless, the narrative is never far from gameplay significance, as Atkinson concludes that musical topics and tropes guide player actions towards particular story outcomes; '[interactivity] adds an additional layer of complexity to narratives that are often already as complex as [...] in film, television, and opera' (29).

In *A Composer's Guide to Game Music* (2014), Winifred Phillips considers both ludological and narratological concerns as essential to successful game music

INTRODUCTION

composition. Ludologically, a sudden striking musical motif can draw a player's attention to a location or object coming into view, or silence can subconsciously prompt the player to move elsewhere (41, 180). An understated defeat stinger can psychologically assuage players' sense of failure, encouraging them to try again (179). Narratologically, music can differentiate plot-significant characters and focus emotional engagement on those for whom players are meant to feel empathy (54, 68). Music that is emotionally and stylistically syncretic with a game's visual components enhances players' holistic aesthetic experience and contributes significantly to worldbuilding and immersion (46, 103). From a game composer's standpoint, the relationship between game and story is not 'either/or', but 'both/and'. In the same way, the field of ludomusicology benefits most from incorporating ludology-leaning and narratology-leaning perspectives, avoiding the overly binary feuds of game studies' past.

'Mission Start!' – Semiotics Harmonizing Ludology and Narratology

In game studies history, ludology and narratology tended to monopolize discussion as their entrenched camps vied for conceptual territory. In actuality, the ludology-narratology binary is unacceptably myopic, presuming that gameplay and narrative are the only interesting or meaningful parameters of video games (Montfort 2004, 310). Adopting a semiotic approach prioritizing meaning-making processes of all kinds harmonizes the ludological and narratological traditions, incorporating a diverse range of other topics of interest. Reflecting on the ludology-narratology debate nearly a decade later, Michalis Kokonis proposes semiotics as an umbrella concept encompassing the study of gameplay and narrative, as well as visual aesthetics, sound/music and interactivity (Kokonis 2014, 176). Presenting players with multiple simultaneous streams of visual, aural, verbal, haptic and cognitive information to decode, playing a video game is one of the most complex multimodal semiotic feats available. As semiotician Gunther Kress writes, a multimodal approach 'assumes that all *modes of representation* are, in principle, of equal significance in representation and communication, as all *modes have potentials for meaning*' (2009, 104, emphasis original). In other words, video game music constructs and communicates meaning comparable to its story, graphics or gameplay. A multimodal, semiotic approach leads beyond a reductionist spectrum of game and narrative into a rich kaleidoscope of multimodal meaning (Figure I.1).

Semiotics equips players and scholars with the tools necessary to analyse the interconnectedness of virtual and real worlds via the permeable membrane of the magic circle. In the process of play, players' demographic identities, social values and interpretative agency are entangled inextricably in the reification of

13

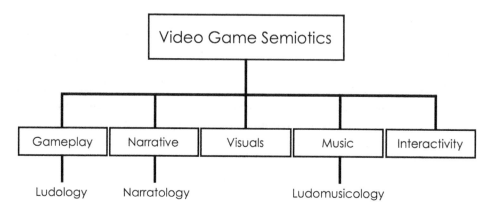

FIGURE I.1: Diagram conceptualizing semiotics as an umbrella concept encompassing various modes of communication in video games (Kokonis 2014, 176–77).

the gameworld. More than any other art form, video games explore interactive play, within which 'the distinction between belief and make-believe breaks down' (Huizinga 1949, 25). Today, our lives are increasingly interwoven with virtuality, as we are entrained to 'live, work, and play' through digitally mediated platforms (Ryan 2015, 28). As we enter the virtual worlds of video games, we discover no realm of pure rules and play, sealed off from our humanity and individual identity. Instead, 'we find human society on either side of the membrane' of the magic circle – for it is we who created it, and we for whom it was created (Castronova 2005, 147–148). This crucial point applies equally to video game music, which is 'no more confinable to virtual worlds than the players are' (Cheng 2014, 14). To listen to game music with semiotic ears is to hear our own aural reflection – entangling our identities, values, cultures, histories and politics within the magic circle.

Gender, Race and Religion in Video Game Music explores the intersection of cultural identity, narrative interpretation and musical meaning. Methodologically, I adopt a thoroughly semiotic approach throughout, which carries certain implications for the present project's scope and execution:

1. Centring interpretation: I explore video games as multimodal, meaningful, communicative artworks that reward interpretative engagement. A semiotic perspective approaches the aesthetic surface of a work with a view towards

INTRODUCTION

its significant design properties which serve as hermeneutic keys to decode its meanings. My primary enterprise in this work is analysis – not history, ethnography, cognition or game development. Each of these is a crucially important domain to examine in its own right, but not this project's focus. For example, a chapter analysing *Super Mario Odyssey* (2017) would prioritize music-theoretical description and interpretation of its soundtrack over a historical survey of a technique's usage in the *Super Mario* franchise or ethnographic interviews with the game's players. Creator intention and audience reception are important sources of corroborating evidence where available, but interpretation is not dependent upon or delimited by knowledge of these. As interpreting, meaning-seeking listeners, players regularly apprehend semiotic significance in game music beyond known developer intention or widespread intersubjective agreement (cf. Barthes 1977). The readings this book presents are exactly that – readings. My readings – or better yet, hearings – of this music may not fully agree with others', nor is my claim that all listeners do or should interpret it as I do. Instead, I model the process of semiotic interpretation so that readers may reach their own conclusions, placing my hearings in dialogue with their own in an ongoing semiotic spiral. As Robert Hatten writes, 'I find merits in each interpretation, and I can hear the piece convincingly in [multiple, seemingly-competing] ways' (2018, 214). This is precisely the advantage of polysemous, interpretative semiotics, such as this book undertakes.

2. <u>Work-focused</u>: My analyses generally prioritize understanding individual works as texts rather than painting broad patterns or trends (Chapter 2 and the corpus study in Chapter 7 are exceptions to this). In the words of Michael Klein echoing Kofi Agawu: 'analyzing comes more easily to me than theorizing' (Klein 2005, ix). As a scholar blending the roles of music composer and theorist, my expertise is explicating how individual works communicate their unique musical meanings. By examining each work in its particularity, I am primarily concerned with the question 'how does this work represent X?' rather than 'how is X represented in video games?' more broadly. No medium speaks univocally between its works, and I make no pretence that these analyses capture the state of the entire video game industry on any topic. My aim is not constructing a theoretical framework of identity representation in video games, but rather analysing significant case studies that illustrate the multitudinous ways that video game music plays with personal identities.

3. <u>Multimodality</u>: As stated at this section's outset, video games are a remarkably multimodal art form, combining aural, narrative, visual, ludic, tactile and social dimensions, to name a few. As the book's title indicates, my analytical focus is on video game music and sound, in dialogue with narrative, ludic and

visual features. The majority of the book is devoted to a detailed analysis of video games' music and sound design. I do not undertake to determine the degree of attention a hypothetical 'average player' devotes to sound relative to other aesthetic and gameplay factors – though it would be a valuable project. My commitment to multimodality entails constant contextualization of audio within a game's narrative, ludic and visual landscape. A game's narrative influences how its music is understood, and vice versa; gameplay actions and sonic events contextualize one another. Severing any of these undercuts the work's holistic aesthetic unity – interpreting game music in constant dialogue with other factors resonates with the work as a multimodal semiotic entity.

4. Social relevance: Each video game soundtrack contributes its meaningful voice in the sociocultural milieu of its developers and players. Rather than divorcing gameworlds from the real world as 'mere entertainment', I read video games as artworks of enormous significance speaking to many of today's most relevant issues. Demographic diversity, mental health, gender identity, racial justice and religious faith – all these topics and more – are encoded in semiotically interesting ways within a game's musical discourse. Each chapter frames its musical analyses with public events and social or historical scholarship situating the game examples within their cultural context. I do this not to reduce a game's meanings to social or political movements, but rather to bring them into dialogue with broader societal factors, which players already relate to their interpretation of the game. The public anecdotes mentioned tend to reflect my own geographic and cultural context in the United States – however, I believe most are widely known or have available parallels in other contexts. In discussing socially relevant topics, my intention is not to be a political provocateur – though the topics covered in this book have often become politicized. As stated above, I do not expect all readers to be convinced of my interpretations; my goal is demonstrating that game music is relevant to a plethora of sociocultural factors, inviting other interpreters to dialogue with my hearings wherever their understandings may differ.

In addition to these commitments, the reader may notice a certain predilection for video games produced by Japanese developers among the book's case studies. This is a result of my specialization as a scholar, the influence certain Japanese-produced games and franchises continue to hold across the video game industry and my personal preferences as a player. I resonate strongly with the narrative, cultural, musical and aesthetic characteristics presented in many Japanese-produced video games, as the book's analyses will demonstrate (particularly Chapters 3, 5, 7 and 8). I do not take this focus to diminish the importance of works produced in other nations but rather to foreground the unique

interpretative opportunities and challenges afforded by approaching this repertoire. Certainly, this complicates the semiosis of these works – speaking their
meanings first to a Japanese audience and cultural context, which is refracted into
other markets – but it also serves to illustrate the interconnectedness of cultures
worldwide. For example, a video game, anime or manga carrying Japanese ideas
of gender, culture or religion may encounter a considerably different context in
Europe or the United States, dialoguing with their perspectives and influencing
those factors' subsequent development in the receiving nations. This, too, is a
prime example of the ongoing, porous, polysemous nature of meaning-making
and interpretation.

Part I explores foundational concepts from game studies scholarship, as this
chapter's discussion of the magic circle and ludology-narratology debate has done.
Chapter 1 builds on the first chapter's content by considering 'immersion' and 'interactivity', two concepts often discussed in game studies literature as characteristic
of video games. Karen Collins applies interactivity to video game sound, theorizing
interactive game audio as the sonification of human action, bidirectional between
player and game system. The discussion then turns once more to ludology and
narratology in video game music, considering Julianne Grasso's proposed harmonization, 'ludomusical narrativity' or 'ludonarrative'. While Grasso's account has
much to commend it, the chapter furthers Grasso's insights by proposing 'interpretative interactivity' as a framework that includes a robust role for players' semiotic
agency, in dynamic dialogue with their ludic agency. The chapter then analyses
the music of *Chrono Cross* (1999) and *Gris* (2018) as case studies exemplifying
interpretative interactivity. The final level and boss of *Chrono Cross* leads players
to hear pitches as tones, using interactive sound prompted by in-game abilities to
reconstruct a previously heard melody. At multiple points, the narrative establishes
an analogy between music and nature to foreshadow the need to think musically
about game sound and bring together narrative and ludic elements. *Gris* presents
an evocative, artistic representation of the protagonist's inner world, depicting
Elizabeth Kübler-Ross' 'five stages of grief' as a visual and musical journey to
self-acceptance and mental flourishing. Story and gameplay flow together into a
playable parable emerging from the player's interpretative interactivity.

Part II explores gender representation in video game narrative and music,
presenting a tripartite trajectory across three chapters. Broadly speaking, Chapter 2
presents musical conventions of gender signification as they have been through
video games' history from 1987 to 2006, Chapter 3 analyses significant subversions of binary gender conventions in games from 2009 and 2016 and Chapter 4
gestures towards non-binary representational possibilities by carving out a third
space transcending conventional femininity and masculinity. Chapter 2 examines gendered musical conventions in the 30-year *Final Fantasy* series, revealing

problematic musical patterns throughout its history. Though a few significant outliers subvert conventionally gendered expectations, the character themes of *Final Fantasy* largely present an uncannily consistent pattern of conventionally feminine and conventionally masculine musical characteristics. Chapter 3 explores alternative femininities and masculinities that meaningfully subvert gendered conventions, illustrating that there can be as many femininities and masculinities as there are individuals. *Final Fantasy XIII* (2009) features a female protagonist embodying the *arafō*, a Japanese alternative femininity that is professionally successful and not defined by marriage or romance; *Final Fantasy XV* (2016) presents its male protagonist as a *sōshokudanshi* who subverts hegemonic *bushidō* and salaryman masculinities, characterized by gentleness, emotional awareness and egalitarianism. Chapter 4 analyses the music of *Horizon Zero Dawn* (2017) and *Horizon Forbidden West* (2022), placing the series' protagonist in a 'third gender' space transcending conventional femininity or masculinity. Using low-register mezzo-soprano voice and melodic cello writing to connect historically to the lost sound of Italian opera's castrati, this approach gestures towards a possible non-binary representation that is aurally present as neither conventionally feminine nor masculine.

Part III turns to the musical representation of nationality, culture and race in video game music – three concepts that blur together in games' musical and narrative discourse, as they frequently do in public discussion. Chapter 5 introduces 'racialised fantasy' – designing a fictional culture with traits associated with a particular real-world culture – to explore racial representation in video game music, and Chapter 6 applies Ibram X. Kendi's segregation-assimilation-antiracism spectrum to musical cultural representation (Kendi 2019). Both chapters closely analyse two case studies, identifying problematic and productive representational features in each. Chapter 5 contrasts the pan-Latin caricature of Tostarena's music in *Super Mario Odyssey* (2017) with the nuanced, hybridity-driven discourse of the score for Bowser's Castle, proposing 'stereotype' as a better litmus test for musical cultural representation than 'authenticity'. Next, the invitational approach of *Raji: An Ancient Epic* (2020) presents a work that invites players to participate in its ongoing cultural practices – not existing for outsiders nor catering to their preferences. Chapter 6 highlights antiracist musical storytelling in *Civilization VI* (2016) and *Overwatch* (2015), two video game scores exemplifying musical racial diversity. Both case studies largely avoid musically segregating or assimilating its characters of colour, charting a third, antiracist course that acknowledges cultural diversity without erasure or exoticism.

Part IV examines religion, introducing the concept of 'sonic iconography' to describe the importation of theological meanings through the use of sacred music in video game soundtracks. Although any religious tradition's music may be invoked in this way, Chapters 7 and 8 focus on the multifaceted interactions between Japanese

INTRODUCTION

culture and sonic iconography of Catholic Christianity. Chapter 7 presents a broad narrative and musical analysis of the god-slayer trope frequently featured in video games, followed by a historical account of anti-Christian policy and rhetoric in Japan during the Tokugawa shogunate and Meiji Restoration. In dialogue with the theology of Jürgen Moltmann, *Lightning Returns* (2013) critiques the Christian classical theist doctrine of impassibility as a parallel to the Japanese philosophy of *sonnō jōi* – worship of a transcendent, inaccessible god-Emperor. Chapter 8 considers the god-slayer trope in *Xenoblade Chronicles* (2010, remake 2020) through a cultural-historical lens, tracing its narrative to the descent of post-war Japan's god-Emperor from divine to human status. *Xenoblade*'s musical troping of sacred- and rock-topic music encodes both the considerable struggle necessary to displace *sonnō jōi* and the egalitarian, populist philosophy modelled by Emperor Hirohito to his subjects after the Second World War.

Chapters 1–8, taken together, envision and develop a theory that situates players as interactive interpreters whose real-world attitudes are influenced by virtual representations of gender, race and religion. Conclusion: Enter the Real concludes with a brief recapitulation of the importance of diversity as a catalyst for engendering 'radical compassion' (Bollmer 2017). As an art form, video games excel at presenting immersive, interactive experiences embodying various narratives and identities that may differ from players' own. Audiences are then confronted with a choice: to consume the other into the player's own subjectivity or embrace their difference as fully human and deserving of dignity. Promoting representational diversity facilitates the latter goal, constituting an ethical vision for encoding gender, race and religion in video game music.

NOTES

1. Foundations of Art and Entertainment Technologies, Professor Jack Stamps, The University of Texas at Austin, Fall 2015–Spring 2019.
2. Zimmerman provides anecdotal accounts of being characterized this way in academic conferences (such as the 'Breaking the Magic Circle' seminar at the University of Tampere's Games Research Lab) as well as in private email correspondence and an invited lecture to a university game studies class.
3. A cross-section of examples include *Exodus to the Virtual World* (Castronova 2007), *Half-Real* (Juul 2005), *Narrative as Virtual Reality* and *Narrative as Virtual Reality 2* (Ryan 2001, 2015), *Reality is Broken* (2010) and *Synthetic Worlds* (Castronova 2005).
4. The most explicit treatment of the ludology-narratology debate in ludomusicological scholarship is Julianne Grasso, 'Video Game Music, Meaning, and the Possibilities of Play' (2020, Ph.D. diss.), Chapter 3, 'Playful Stories: Toward a Ludomusical Narrativity of Video Games'. Grasso proposes to reconcile ludic and narrative perspectives through a ludonarrative account

of music in video games, providing intriguing case studies from *Final Fantasy III* (1990) and *Journey* (2012). Perhaps ludomusicologists' reticence on the topic seeks to avoid reviving – and subsequently, beating – a proverbial dead horse, lest doing so reinscribe the embittered entrenchments present in academic game studies circa 1995–2005. Nonetheless, there is much conceptual clarity to be gained from a historical retrospective on the debate and its impact, considering how its ripples continue to influence the field's perspectives on video game music.

5. Although Collins' interest primarily lies in how audio affects gameplay and vice versa, she mentions musical techniques to enhance narrative structure such as linking related scenes with similar music (2008, 131).

6. Massively multiplayer online role-playing game.

PART I

NARRATIVE AND PLAY

1

Ludo-Narrative Harmony: Interpretative Interactivity in *Chrono Cross* and *Gris*

Orpheus's Lyre: Immersion and Interactivity in Virtual Worlds

In Orpheus's hands, music changed the world. His lyre rendered ravenous lions and tigers docile. Animals flocked to him, entranced by his song. In mythology's first battle of the bands, Orpheus out-performed the notorious Sirens, dispelling their alluring melody with his own. Death itself bent to this musician's will – Orpheus's performance successfully swayed Hades to release his beloved Eurydice's soul from the underworld. Some accounts ascribe to Orpheus outright supernatural powers – trees, rocks and rivers drew nearer to hear his singing, and his dulcet tones stilled the raging seas. The gentle, soft-spoken minstrel able to tame the most perilous domains of nature became emblematic of the civilizing effect of music and the other arts (Robbins 1982, 3). The story of Orpheus epitomizes music's power to impact both the human heart and the external world.

Ancient Greek thought attributed to music immense powers of affecting reality. For this reason, Plato advocated its censorship, permitting only music believed profitable for moral education (Bonds 2014, 21). Music's reality-altering power was understood as part of its 'very essence' – therefore, to produce music was to act directly upon the world (Bonds 2014, 30). Renaissance and Medieval scholars theorized musical harmony as the underlying principle of the universe itself (Bonds 2014, 27). Modelled after Orpheus' harmony with nature – and influence over it – music was thought to possess particular resonance with the natural world and became closely associated with pastoral settings (Monelle 2006, 197). The tales of Orpheus offer an apt mythic parallel to the power of music to affect immersion, interactivity and interpretation in video games. As 'immersion' and 'interactivity' – along with virtuality, discussed in 'Introduction: Enter the Virtual' – are often proposed to distinguish game music from music in film and other media, this chapter applies interactivity to semiotic interpretation, harmonizing the ludology-narratology divide (Summers 2016, 25).

Chapter 1 builds on the discussion of the permeable magic circle in 'Introduction: Enter the Virtual' by considering 'immersion' and 'interactivity', two properties considered characteristic of video games. The chapter then revisits the ludology and narratology debate by way of Julianne Grasso's proposed harmonization, 'ludomusical narrativity' or 'ludonarrative'. While Grasso's account has much to commend it, this chapter furthers Grasso's insights by proposing 'interpretative interactivity' as a framework for theorizing players' semiotic agency, in dialogue with their ludic agency. It then explicates interpretative interactivity with four principles. The chapter then presents two detailed case studies, analysing the musical playfulness of *Chrono Cross* (1999) and *Gris* (2018), which exemplify interpretative interactivity.

Despite their ubiquitous use in game studies scholarship, 'immersion' and 'interactivity' are difficult to define. Nor is their use consistent in the literature – for example, Janet Murray prefers 'agency' to interactivity, citing the latter term's vagueness. Furthermore, the two inform and influence one another, posing challenges to theorizing each independently. Beginning with 'immersion', the concepts of virtuality and the magic circle covered in 'Introduction: Enter the Virtual' offer a convenient foundation, as immersion refers to the experience of entering into or continuing in a virtual world or magic circle. Murray defines immersion as '[the] experience of being transported to an elaborately simulated space' and feeling surrounded by that reality (Murray 1997, 98). Other proposed characteristics include decreased critical distance, increased emotional engagement, the participation of a body in a projected virtual body or receding awareness of the game's control mechanisms and interface (Collins 2008, 133; Phillips 2014, 37; Ryan 2015, 13). Clearly, immersion is a multidimensional phenomenon resisting concise verbal description. It involves both a perceptual component (sense of presence in another place) and a participatory one (acting efficaciously within that domain), often accompanied by a reduced awareness of one's own world and/or body (Mateas 2004, 21).

In video games, enhancing immersion is one of music's primary roles, typically achieved by communicating the setting, mood or gameplay actions appropriate to the moment (Collins 2008, 134; Gibbons 2018, 29). This musical worldbuilding presents players with aural details that make the gameworld more complete and believable (Phillips 2014, 51, 103). Immersion, narrative and gameplay overlap and holistically reinforce one another. Immersion exceeds mere suspension of disbelief – rather, it facilitates belief in the world of the magic circle. Effective game narratives both enhance immersion and depend upon it, creating a feedback loop amplified by interactivity. When interactive agency and narrative engagement are balanced, a high degree of immersion is achieved (Ryan 2015, 226).

Interactivity tricks the brain's frontal lobe into colluding in its own deception, occupying cognitive resources that would otherwise question the veracity of the immersion (Castronova 2007, 29). Fully understanding immersion in video games, then, requires discussion of interactivity.

'Interactivity', complains Zimmerman, 'is one of those words which can mean everything and nothing at once' (2004, 158). If this is so, it is because ambiguity and polysemy are inherently baked into the concept, akin to a blinking question mark awaiting a reply. Interactivity can consist of any action taken by a player in response to a gameworld, whether permitted by its mechanics or not. Using the programmed controls to win the game is interactivity – so too is modding the original game or capturing screenshots to publish on social media. However, in the context of ludomusicology, interactivity typically refers to music or sound design that is triggered or modified by the player's gameplay actions. In *Playing with Sound*, Karen Collins theorizes interactive video game sound as the sonification of human action, where the 'player initiates an event and there is a system-controlled (game-generated) sonic response' (2013, 32). The interactivity between the player and game is bidirectional, as sound informs subsequent gameplay actions. Because responding to the sounds requires coordination with visual and tactile parameters, interactive game sound is multimodal (Collins 2013, 22). Players extend their bodies through virtual avatars, and affecting the sonic environment through the avatar facilitates immersion in the gameworld and identification with the character (Collins 2013, 43). 'We move to the music, and the music moves us', Collins concludes, 'which changes the way that we hear that music' (2013, 63). In other words, interactive game audio is not only ludically significant, impacting gameplay actions, but semiotically significant as well – affecting how we understand and interpret both music and game. Semiotic play is central to the experience of game sound, constituting a 'game within a game', encouraging players to manipulate the musical score through gameplay actions (Phillips 2014, 187). Interactivity also heightens musical affect by semiotically marking player actions; for example, entering an enemy's line of sight may trigger a tense action cue, while defeating or evading the enemy restores calmer music signalling safety. However, if one prefers the adrenaline rush of action music, one could deliberately engage enemy after enemy, making it the norm instead of the exception. Each player's musical journey will be as unique as the player's choices, reflecting the player's individual identity.

Interactivity in video games is closely interwoven with immersion. In most games, players are not located above or outside the unfolding story but participate in it directly (Mateas 2004, 20). This entangles players in the very fabric of the game as co-creators so that its outcome is imprinted with players' choices and personalities. This dynamic is exemplified by interactive game scores, which remain inert and amorphous until player interaction gives them shape. 'More than any other music, game music is an event, not a work', writes Isabella van Elferen, 'its performance is playful, immediate, and interactive; its sound directly influences the perception and phenomenology of the gaming experience' (2020, 106). In other words, gameplay not only generates sound – sound, through player interpretation, generates gameplay. This semiotic feedback loop raises fascinating questions about players' position as both rhetors and interpreters of game music and narratives. It is insufficient to theorize game audio solely in terms of its emotional or psychological affect on players, nor can we account for game music solely in terms of composers' and developers' intended meanings; interactivity and immersion entail that players bring their own unique cultural background, values and identity into the gameworld. Video game music interpretation is never unidirectional, discovering meanings from a fixed musical text.[1] Rather, each and every player's choice is an interpretative act that reconstitutes the gameworld's soundscape around that action. Orpheus's legacy finds its fulfilment in video game soundtracks – through players' meaning-making agency, music truly can change its world.

A Theory of Interpretative Interactivity for Video Game Music

Video game players and observers alike may be tempted to view a game's soundtrack as mere background music – not worth actively listening to while focusing on the gameplay. This perception has been leveraged to dismiss video game music from claims of artistic merit. For instance, when video game composer Nobuo Uematsu (植松 伸夫) began placing in the top 10 of ClassicFM's annual Hall of Fame, music critic Guy Dammann retorted: '[video game soundtracks are] not written to be the central focus of the player's attention … [but] the world of the concert hall makes different, more exacting demands' (Dammann 2015). For many, an artwork's ability to capture its audience's attention and contemplation is essential to its status as art. Accordingly, the argument goes, concert music exhibits the highest artistic potential, followed by film music and musical stage works, with video game music ranked further below. However, this claim overlooks video game music's immense potential to frame, shape and nuance the game's narrative and thematic elements – and, indeed, the meaning-making processes of play. Key to game audio's unique potential is immersion, interactivity and interpretation, each of which invokes the player's semiotic and ludic agency. Collins writes: '[as] the player is no longer a passive listener, but may be involved in invoking sound and music in the game, we must reevaluate theories of reception' (2008, 168). Our attention now turns to constructing such a theory – one that harmonizes ludic, narrative, semiotic, phenomenological and cultural perspectives of analysing video game music.

This runs counter to Dammann's claim that game music is merely sonic wallpaper or that it possesses less artistic merit than concert music. Tim Summers boldly ascribes music 'greater aesthetic priority' and a 'larger role' in video games than in film, citing interactivity as a distinguishing factor (Summers 2016, 175–76). Along similar lines, many ludomusicologists have focused on music's response to or influence gameplay actions. Other scholars – including myself – have studied narrative, semiotic, topical and representational elements in video game music, synthesizing game-specific considerations with analytical techniques from concert and film music. Yet few have theorized the dynamic interplay of narrative semiotics and player agency in relation to video game music. To do so is to revolutionize the putative ludology–narratology dichotomy by demonstrating that, in the medium of video games, semiotic interpretation is ludic, and interactive play is narrative.

The only prior ludomusicology publication in English with explicit, extensive treatment of ludology and narratology is Chapter 2 of Julianne Grasso's 'Video Game Music, Meaning, and the Possibilities of Play' (Grasso 2020). Proposing a harmonization termed 'ludomusical narrativity' or 'ludonarrative', Grasso seeks to reconcile ludic and narrative priorities by focusing on the interactivity of video game music (2020, 110). In Chapter 1 of the work, Grasso argued that 'music informs interactivity by evoking responses that prime the player for certain kinds of interactions' through affective zones and affordances (2020, 60). Winding, mysterious music creates an affective zone fit for cave exploration, driving rock music affords battles against monsters, and so on. Experienced players build conventional knowledge of which musical affective zones suit particular gameplay actions. Developers regularly employ these conventions, or the frustration thereof, to guide players towards narratively appropriate actions – for example, using unsettling music in a town area normally considered safe warns players to proceed with caution (Grasso 2020, 126). Analysing *Journey* (2012) as a case study, Grasso demonstrates that interactive music often encodes narrative structures discovered through gameplay. Surrounded by a vast, infinite desert, *Journey*'s initial soundtrack presents no discernible musical texture – only a mixture of white noise and arrhythmic drone tones – until the player interacts with certain objects that activate motivic pitch fragments or gentle rhythmic layers in the score, providing a sense of progression. If players linger too long without activating the next objective, these layers fade, returning the soundscape to an undifferentiated sonic wash. Maintaining the music's flow and development requires progressing through the game – but there is no cue besides the music to prompt players to do so. The implied musical teleology 'narrativizes play through its own forms of progression' (Grasso 2020, 133). In other words, interactive music, together with players' music-semiotic preferences and expectations, provides a framework that gives significance to gameplay actions. If affective zones create affordances for certain modes of gameplay, ludonarrative creates affordances for certain meaning-making processes.

Grasso's persuasive account of ludonarrative lands quite near this chapter's – yet the present inquiry furthers Grasso's insights in two crucial ways. First, Grasso's conception of player agency is too deterministic. Affective zones may suggest the most expected or appropriate course of action in a gameplay situation, but they do not override player agency. In the previous example, *Journey*'s music presents players with a prompt – the introduction or dissipation of melodic material – but the player must decide how to respond. Perhaps the player, like John Cage, chooses to seek out the beauty in silence and so-called white noise; perhaps one prefers to allow each objective's music to lapse before activating the next. Certainly, this interaction is likely not the response the composer and developers intended – but what of it? By opening its world to player agency, video games' musical meaning becomes multiple. Second, while Grasso's incorporation of musico-narrative factors in *Final Fantasy III* and *Journey* is commendable, it focuses too narrowly on music's impact on gameplay, to the omission of other crucial factors. That *Journey*'s gradually activated melodic layers subtly nudge players towards the next objective is important – but what about the music's thematic, personal significance? What meanings emerge from the discovery of melody from ancient artefacts within a desolate and musically unordered environment? How might players understand the evolution and apotheosis of *Journey*'s primary musical theme as a semiotic analogue to their own life story? Such interpretations are no less part of experiencing a video game – and no less part of understanding its music. The vital element missing from Grasso's ludomusical narrative is interpretation – playing not only with a video game's mechanics but also its meanings. All of a video game's aesthetic modes affect players' understanding of its meanings, which in turn influence player actions that shape the gameworld in an ongoing feedback loop. This chapter proposes and develops 'interpretative interactivity' as a term to describe these ongoing semiotic spirals between player and game text – though 'interactive interpretation' would be just as apt a name.[2]

The remainder of this chapter explores four principles of interpretative interactivity in video game music, followed by two fascinating case studies that illustrate it in play:

1. Interacting with video game music is an interpretative act, reifying a sonic vision of the gameworld.

'The first and most important thing to know about games', writes Celia Pearce, 'is that they center on PLAY' (2004, 144). For video game music, play occurs not only within the game's mechanics but also at the level of realizing its musical score. For all but the most simplistic of games, player choices shape what music is heard at what time, for how long and in what order. Each button press is an interpretative act that decrees how the soundscape shall be for that player's ludonarrative journey. This dynamic resists easy verbal translation; perhaps 'let this music be heard now!' will suffice. Ludomusical interactivity exhibits what Marie-Laure Ryan terms 'ontological interactivity' – enacting lasting changes in the game text itself (Ryan 2015, 162). Because the player does not know ahead of time what action triggers which music nor has total control over when the music starts or ends, the game's rules exercise its own agency over the music, which the player may choose to contest or cooperate with. In this way, interpretative interactivity also carries an evaluative judgement – i.e. 'it is good for the music to take this shape now'. Unlike concert or film music, players can intercept the musical flow, bending it to their desires – and doing so changes the content of the musical text itself. Here, one may object that most game soundtracks are based on pre-rendered music and that changes to the order, duration or frequency of cues have negligible impact. However, this underestimates the semiotic significance of form as a musical parameter. Whether a player lingers in a location or game mode for hours or strives to escape it immediately is phenomenologically significant – and music influences such decisions. As seen in Grasso's *Journey* analysis, hearing melodic fragments compound in a continuous flow state is not narratively equivalent to hearing those same audio cues interspersed with long stretches of white noise.

2. Video game music shapes the player's understanding of both gameplay and narrative, which in turn influences player agency.

Accounting for interactivity in terms of affect and affordance alone overlooks players' agency as active interpreters. Players actively seek meaning from game sound, interpreting the 'music in terms of the gameplay, and vice versa' (Summers 2016, 41). Some deciphered meanings may be ludic (e.g. combat begins); others may be narrative (e.g. sacred music representing combat against a deity). Interpretative interactivity affirms that the narrative meanings heard influence gameplay decisions just as ludic meanings do. In parallel, Juul observes that whether enemies are visually represented as grotesque monsters or benign flowers changes players' assumptions about and actions towards them (Juul 2005, 177). As with graphics, so too with music. Despite primarily focusing on ludic affect, Grasso considers the narrative significance of Golbez's theme in *Final Fantasy IV* (1991), 'Golbez, Clad in Darkness' (黒い甲冑ゴルベーザ; 'black-armored and helmeted Golbez'), quoting the iconic organ piece *Toccata and Fugue* in D Minor (often attributed to J. S. Bach, though this is contested) (Grasso 2020, 157). Its semiotic meanings portray Golbez as a villainous mastermind employing control, subterfuge and manipulation, suggesting players approach the battle differently than one against a wolf or goblin. Musical narrative meaning shapes gameplay decisions in countless other ways – for example, which characters players gravitate towards using, what kind of enemies or obstacles likely populate a particular environment, the difficulty level of a dungeon and what combat tactics an opponent will likely utilize. Accordingly, most game music may be described as 'meta-diegetic' – not occurring in the gameworld, but rather inviting and immersing players into its gameplay and narrative (Roberts 2014, 141–42). In video game music, ludology and narratology are harmonized in the interpretative agency of the player.

3. Players' interpretative agency is indeterminate, personal and plural.

As an interactive medium, video games are rife with multiplicity – of gameplay, of experiences and of meanings. Juul correctly observes: '[the] game designer cannot control the player's interpretation of the game world' (Juul 2005, 139). Though this is true of semiotic interpretation generally, it carries special force when players' interpretative agency impacts the form of the text itself. Video games uniquely '[blur the] boundary between author and audience so completely', casting players as co-creators rather than observers (Pearce 2004, 153). From a narrative-semiotic standpoint, this complexifies narrative analysis of video game music, as Atkinson notes (2019, 29). Objectors to the project of music semiotics typically deride this multiplicity of interpretations as unacceptably vague; however, in an interactive medium like video games, this flexibility is not a bug, but a feature. Ludomusicologists must therefore embrace game music's polysemy, centring players' contributions to its meanings. Video games are less like novels and more like narrative architecture enabling the 'story-constructing activity of players' (Jenkins 2004, 129). The interpretative interactivity of players becomes intensely personal, drawing who they are as individuals into the text's formation and semiosis.

4. The act of interpretation implicates real-world social, cultural and political meanings as it entangles the interpreter's individual identity in the gameworld.

Interpretative interactivity is the reason the magic circle of video games can never be a closed system. '*Interpretation* is central in communication and so, therefore, is the *interpreter*' writes Gunther Kress; the interpreter's cultural values and background join with the text to form 'a new semiotic entity' (2010, 36, original emphasis). In other words, interpretative interactivity entails that players cannot help but bring their selves and identities into the video games they play. We are now positioned to connect play, narrative and interpretative interactivity to musical representation. As Parts II–IV of this book demonstrate, musical meanings transfer from the real world into gameworlds precisely because it is real-world listeners who interpret them. The meanings of the organ *Toccata and Fugue* quote in Golbez's theme do not cease to exist simply because the gameworld of *Final Fantasy IV* contains neither Baroque music nor organs. Because musical meaning in gameworlds signifies in the real world simultaneously, studying its representation of real-world communities, identities and cultures is of paramount importance. As concerning gameplay, interpretative interactivity entails that video games' representational meanings are not deterministic; interpreters play with representational meanings as well as with ludic or narrative ones. Interactivity encourages players to interpret video game meanings as they choose – a heuristic function rather than a didactic one (Anderson-Barkley and Foglesong 2018, 255). Researching demographic representation in video game music is critical precisely because each player is a nexus between the virtual and real worlds, entangling real-world social, cultural and political meanings in the gameworld's permeable magic circle (Table 1.1).

This theory of interpretative interactivity guides the remainder of the book, which presents detailed music-semiotic analyses of video game music that exemplify these four principles. Writing that ludomusicology requires new theories that account for players' interactive agency, Collins concludes: '[we] must work to forge a new theoretical path to explore and explain the many ways in which we play with sound' (2013, 148). Interpretative interactivity is my theoretical contribution in response to Collins's call, and I commend its use and further development within the field of ludomusicology. How players interpret meaning in video game music offers a microcosm into how they understand other people and the world.

TABLE 1.1: Diagram summarizing a theory of interpretative interactivity for video game music analysis.

A Theory of Interpretative Interactivity for Video Game Music		
1	Semiotic Condition	Interacting with video game music is an interpretive act, reifying a sonic vision of the gameworld.
2	Bidirectional Condition	Video game music shapes player understanding of both gameplay and narrative, which in turn influences player agency.
3	Subjectivity Condition	Players' interpretive agency is indeterminate, personal and plural.
4	Social Condition	The act of interpretation implicates real-world social, cultural and political meanings as it entangles the intepreter's individual identity in the gameworld.

Music of the Elements – Ludonarrative
Ear Training in Chrono Cross

The DNA records are poems and music …
Adenine and Thymine … Guanine and Cytosine … Rhythm and Melody …
I wonder if life-forms are just dreaming in an endless flow of music?
Chronopolis Scientist, Chrono Cross (1999)

Imagine that a third, previously unknown Homeric epic starring Orpheus is unearthed. Call it the Orphead. Within its verses, Orpheus returns from his sojourn in the underworld only to discover that ten years have passed, he is presumed dead and nobody believes he is truly Orpheus. Wandering throughout the land, Orpheus discovers humanity torn apart by strife – warring with each other and with nature. Only Orpheus is in harmony with the earth enough to hear nature's song, which reveals to him that the earth is steadily dying. Orpheus journeys to the realm of the Fates to plead humanity's case but learns from them that humanity's own destructive character is driving the world to destruction. Recalling the music he has gathered during his travels, Orpheus weaves together the sounds of nature and humanity into a new melody that revitalizes the land, bringing harmony between them and between warring peoples. Such a narrative would befit the themes, epic scope and mysticism of Orphic mythos. Yet no archaeologists are necessary to excavate this text, for it already exists – the story described as the Orphead belongs to the video game *Chrono Cross*.

The labyrinthine story of *Chrono Cross* (1999) showcases four central themes: fate, prejudice, nature and music. In the idyllic El Nido archipelago, humanity is protected by the supercomputer FATE, which subtly influences individuals' decisions and outcomes. Serge, the game's protagonist, was determined by FATE to drown ten years prior to the game but was rescued by an outsider not subject to FATE. Thwarting FATE's design produced two timelines – one where Serge died and one where he survived – and the early game focuses on FATE's attempts to correct the timeline by eliminating the anomaly. Importantly, three of FATE's satellite systems are named Clotho, Lachesis and Atropos – the fates of Greek mythos – making the intended intertextuality clear. The region of El Nido is riven by war and prejudice in both timelines – Porre and the Acacia Dragoons are at war, humans enslave demi-humans and are mistrusted by them, dwarves and fairies hate and fear one another and the civilizations Chronopolis and Dinopolis were locked in bitter conflict in ancient eras.[3] As Serge assembles a party from a sizable cast of 45 playable characters, virtually every species or major demographic group of El Nido is represented.[4] Nature – and humanity's treatment of it – is one of *Chrono Cross*' primary themes, in harmony or conflict with technology. In El Nido, society relies on Elements – technology that channels one of six forces of nature to produce various effects. Elements coloured red, blue, green, yellow, white and black, respectively, control fire, water/ice, vegetation, lightning/earth, light and darkness. Elements derive from the ancient civilization Dinopolis, whose deified machine the Dragon God controlled nature itself. When Chronopolis, the pinnacle of human technology, defeated Dinopolis, FATE separated the Dragon God into six elemental dragons that give life to El Nido's islands. When Serge destroys FATE, these six fuse to recreate the Dragon God, threatening to raze El Nido with nature's vengeance, comprising the game's penultimate antagonist.

Music is foregrounded multiple times in the game's narrative, suggesting its ludic and aesthetic importance to players. In Marbule, the home island of demi-humans, the song of the land has been stripped – and with it, the land's power – by the enslavement of its people. Though in captivity, demi-humans sing the Song of Marbule in secret – until the musician Nikki persuades the Sage of Marbule to teach it to him, calling it '[a] beautiful song, originating from a beautiful island'. Together, the demi-humans and Nikki's band The Magical Dreamers perform a rock opera based on the Song of Marbule (track name 'Magical Dreamers', ~風と星と波と~; trans. 'wind, stars and waves'). Like a play within a play, the diegetic rock opera 'Magical Dreamers' rivals the famed *Final Fantasy VI* opera scene in aesthetic profundity, foregrounding music's power to bring together communities in harmony. The Song of Marbule renders the phantoms that had taken up residence on the island of Marbule tangible, allowing Serge and his friends to vanquish them and make Marbule habitable by demi-humans again. Another example occurs in the ruins of Chronopolis, humanity's advanced utopia that produced FATE and experimented with technology to control natural evolution and even time itself. The scientists' research logs reveal an obsession with humanity becoming 'like God' through controlling life and time. During these grandiose musings, one scientist says: '[the] DNA records are poems and music | Adenine and Thymine ... Guanine and Cytosine ... Rhythm and Melody ... | Perhaps the DNA of the ones who make contact with the Flame | is recomposed by the sound they generate within? | I wonder if life-forms are just dreaming in an endless flow of music?' Narratively, this links the game's themes of nature and music – in *Chrono Cross*, music is foundational to life itself, encoded into the DNA of all creatures. The third and fourth lines suggest changing the biological telos of all life through resonating with the sounds of nature.

The final level of *Chrono Cross* is Terra Tower (the resurfaced citadel of Dinopolis), headed by Dinopolis' Dragon God and guarded by six elemental guardians: Terrator, Pyrotor, Anemator, Aquator, Gravitor and Luxator. After defeating the Dragon God comes a final encounter with the Time Devourer – this will be examined in detail later. Terra Tower's soundscape is preceded by silence and rushing, atmospheric white noise. The entryway contains the Terrator, guardian of the yellow Element, sonically introduced by ominous cathedral bell chimes on $G\#$. Lugubrious string pads looping a tonic-prolongational D minor progression fade into hearing, subsequently adding faint, ornamented mezzo-soprano vocalise, producing a sombre, fateful mood (track name 'Terra Tower', 星の塔; trans. 'tower of stars'). The musical addition of greatest semiotic significance occurs not in the underscore, but in a gameplay-triggered role typically reserved for sound design. From the Terrator battle through the remainder of *Chrono Cross*, whenever player characters or enemies use an Element skill, an orb of that colour appears at the top of the screen accompanied by a bright, synthesized tone on one of five pitches: B, C♯, E, F♯, A (red and black share F♯; see Figure 1.1).[5] To be clear, players and enemies have been using Elements for the entire game without either visual or audio effect occurring; this phenomenon is unique to the final level and therefore highly semiotically marked along both narrative and ludic axes. Because each of the six Elemental guardians uses only one Element colour – the Terrator uses yellow Elements, the Pyrotor red, the Aquator blue, and so on – players are afforded ample opportunity to hear that each Element colour consistently sounds one pitch and that these pitches differ from one another (except for red and black). The novel sonic element cries out for interpretation – how are these pitches, emerging out of players' gameplay actions, to be understood?

An answer to this question may be posed through analogy to the Aural Skills curriculum, required in most music degree programs. A crucial part of the classically trained musician's core skillset is ear training – the ability to accurately hear and understand heard melodies and chord progressions. In Aural Skills classes, one of the main activities cultivating ear training is melodic dictation – listening to a short melody and notating it by ear on staff paper. The student is confronted with a series of unknown pitches and must make coherent sense of them in relation to each other and to stylistic conventions; this requires identifying the melody's most likely key and tonic pitch in order to contextualize the pitches heard. *Chrono Cross* immerses players in an experience analogous to melodic dictation, presenting

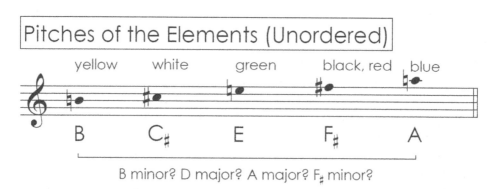

FIGURE 1.1: Pitches produced by each Element colour type.

them with sounds that must be listened to and interpreted to be understood. How do they relate to each other and to the musical score? In what narrative or ludic context are the pitches relevant – in other words, to what key of gameplay do they belong? Semiotically speaking, this is to hear pitch not as merely sound, but as tone – that is, entangled with and implicative of other pitches, with varying congruence or incongruence, tension or resolution. When players first hear the pitches over the D minor string progression of the track 'Terra Tower', several pitches sound out-of-place. While E (green) and A (blue) fit with D minor, B (yellow), C# (white) and F# (red and black) do not. Though B could be interpreted as a Dorian inflection of D minor and C# its raised leading tone, F# certainly clashes with D minor, belonging instead to D major. In the first guardian battle, the Terrator (yellow) always sounds B pitches over the D minor key of 'Terra Tower', signalling from the start that this pitch collection pertains to another context. Approaching these newly introduced sounds from an ear-training perspective attunes players to listen to and interpret them as ludically and narratively relevant.

As players progress through Terra Tower, the narrative encourages players to attend closely to the phenomenon. The spirit of Crono – the protagonist *Chrono Trigger* (1995), the preceding game – tells Serge:

> The Chrono Cross ... The melody and harmony ... | It has the power to cross space and time and unify people's thoughts and feelings ... | By using it as an Element, it has the power to draw on the sounds of the six colored Elements to produce a healing harmony ... | It has the power to combine the sounds of the world into one melody.

If players did not recognize the significance of the Elements' pitches previously, they certainly should now. To make matters abundantly clear, the next room plays the six pitches over white noise, rhetorically marking the resulting melody: B (yellow) – F# (red/black) – E (green) – A (blue) – F# (red/black) – C# (white), looped infinitely. Though six coloured crystals in the room corresponding to the Elements light up as the melody plays, the order does not correspond to that of the melody. Players must understand the phenomenon musically to discern the implied Element order, rather than relying on sight as is typical for puzzle-solving in video games. They must also recognize the sequence's narrative connections to the six Elemental guardians; since red and black Elements both produce F#, the melody alone cannot adjudicate their order. However, realizing that the Pyrotor (red) is fought second and the Gravitor (black) fifth or sixth provides the answer – the Elemental guardians' order in Terra Tower corresponds to that of the melody. By ordering the pitches, players hear them not only as tones but also as a melody.

Serge's party battles the Dragon God at the top of Terra Tower, which uses Element skills in the same order as the melody. This may prompt players to use the melody's sequence in this battle; however, the tonal centres of the combat cue 'Dragon God' (龍神), C minor and B♭ minor, are highly incongruent with the Elements' pitches and produce multiple clashing cross-relations, inveighing against its use here. Indeed, attempting to use the melody in this encounter produces no effect. After defeating the Dragon God, one final obstacle remains: the Time Devourer, a manifestation of humanity's malice and destructive nature capable of destroying all space-time after consuming the Dragon God. Before facing the Time Devourer, Marle – also from *Chrono Trigger* – urges Serge to use a special Element, the Chrono Cross, to unite the tones of nature into a single melody. Accompanying the Time Devourer is the cue 'The Darkness of Time' (時の闇にて; trans. 'in the darkness of time'), consisting solely of dissonant, swirling white noise. As in Terra Tower, when the melody was heard in full, all competing pitches fell away entirely, leaving only the exposed sounds of the Elements. Like silent anticipation for the first note of a music performance, this clears the sonic stage, prompting players: 'what sounds will you create?' Selecting Elements in the order yellow, red, green, blue, black, white and then using the Chrono Cross performs the melody of nature heard in Terra Tower – with the addition of one final note, D. The original six-note loop transfers from the interactive score to the non-diegetic underscore as lush orchestral textures join in (track name: 生命 ~遠い約束~; trans. 'Life -A Distant Promise-'). The violins play a rhythmically augmented melody continuing the seven-note version over the quicker looping texture, climaxing as the Time Devourer dissolves into the void and all space-time is saved. As the game's credits roll, the pop song 'Radical Dreamers -Le Tresor Interdit-' (the track name's French translating 盗めない宝石; 'jewel that could not be stolen') also bases its chorus off of the seven-note melody. Music is the foundation of this game's breathtaking ending.

Chrono Cross presents a striking example of multimodal semiotic synthesis of music, narrative and play. Musically and narratively, it encodes the importance of the Elements' pitches long before they become ludically significant. Players must listen to the music as narratively relevant – not merely as a means to a ludic end – in order to understand its meaning. One could object that the melody is analogous to a puzzle or cheat code, a combination of inputs required to 'win the game'. However, *Chrono Cross* boasts eleven discrete endings, each one with different unlock conditions, and only one ending (though arguably the most narratively satisfying) is reached by reconstructing the melody. Alternatively, players may opt to vanquish the Time Devourer by force, flooding the soundscape with unending cacophonous noise and reaching a narratively ambiguous ending. That most players pursue the more musically, narratively and artistically satisfying route demonstrates that they attend to game music's narrative meanings and sculpt their gameplay decisions according to storytelling considerations. Here, the resolution of the six-note ostinato in B minor to D – the tonic of the relative major – is semiotically significant, encoding the game's narrative meaning. Just as hearing the music of the Elements as a melody frees humanity from its cycles of malice, it re-interprets C♯, the second scale degree of B minor, as a modulating leading tone, lifting the melody to the relative major key. Like the hypothetical Orphead, players choose to reify a world where music makes peace between humanity and nature, and people with one another. The aesthetically compelling finale of *Chrono Cross* exemplifies interpretative interactivity, harmonizing ludic and narrative elements in the player's musical agency.

Self-Harmonization – Songs of Grief and Acceptance in Gris

Gris (2018) is a wordless playable parable exemplifying video games' status as an art form. 'Mesmerizing', 'breathtaking', 'gorgeous', 'soul-stirring', 'arresting', 'transcendent' – these are but a sampling of critics' praise for *Gris*. While catalysing enjoyment and play, its narrative and aesthetic details are profoundly serious. Perhaps best described as an interactive artwork or mediatized meditation, *Gris* offers sublime visual art, musical soundscape and poignant narrative woven into a holistic multimedia tapestry. By omitting in-game dialogue and most on-screen text – an approach modelled by *Journey* and its predecessor, *Flower* (2009) – *Gris* encourages adopting an aesthetic posture, appreciating and interpreting its visual, musical and design elements. From start to finish, *Gris*' watercolour-inspired visual style deriving from the progressive addition of one colour per game chapter and alternatively contemplative, melancholy and soaring soundtrack are utterly enrapturing (Figure 1.2). Speaking in chorus with other critical reviews, Forbes praises *Gris* for its '[w]atercolor skies', 'luminescent caverns' and 'radiant vines and flowers', invigorated by 'an equally gorgeous score' (Kain 2019).

Gris beckons players to traverse an evocative world comprising the titular character's mental and emotional landscape. Describing *Gris* as a 'journey through sorrow', the developer website states: 'Gris is a hopeful young girl lost in her own world' after a devastating, traumatic loss (Nomada Studios n.d.). The opening cutscene depicts Gris singing in harmony with another female voice, as she is held aloft by a statue's cracked hand. Suddenly, the statue's cracks widen and spread, and Gris's voice chokes off abruptly in her throat. The statue crumbles, leaving her plummeting uncontrollably through the sky as all colour fades from her world. Awakening in a greyscale desert drawn in simplistic lines and geometric shapes, the narrative traces Gris' grief process, restoring the colour spectrum to her inner self one by one and rediscovering her song amidst depression and loss. 'Gris' means 'grey' in Spanish (Nomada Studio is based in Barcelona, Spain), which is narratively and aesthetically significant – not only as the absence of colour but also halfway between white and black.

FIGURE 1.2: Screenshots of *Gris* showcasing its visual aesthetics and colour-themed areas.

From the beginning, music encodes great narrative and ludic significance. Diegetic and non-diegetic sound blur together as Gris herself sings the opening cue, marking music's motivating role in the story when she loses her ability to sing.[6] This narrative loss is also ludic – if players prompt Gris to sing in the first three-quarters of the game, only a raspy whisper emerges, bestowing no gameplay effect. Throughout the game, Gris collects musical pitches in the form of glimmering stars, connecting them together to construct musical phrases and bridges to distant locations. Gathering up to six at a time, the pitches, organized in ascending order, are E-G-A-B-D-E – a G pentatonic scale sung from E to E (sometimes termed a 'minor pentatonic scale'). This is multiply meaningful – just as reaching the octave pitch at the top of a scale indicates completion and return to familiarity, Gris uses this pitch collection to restore her song. In music education, scales are ubiquitously used for practice and training, and the pentatonic scale is thought particularly appropriate for beginner improvization, composition and singing. Scales also traverse the octave in various configurations, as Gris reaches her destination using these pitches. Using the relative minor version of the scale is narratively appropriate, as Gris's loss renders her sombre and melancholy. This meaning cannot be reduced merely to gameplay or story – it is semiotic, exemplifying both simultaneously.

Other ludo-narrative examples abound. In the Red chapter, an empty desert scored with pointillistic piano is routinely raked by raging sandstorms, marked by the fade-in of tempestuous organ arpeggios and choral sustains reminiscent of Philip Glass's *Koyaanisqatsi* ('Perseverance', 1982). In the Blue chapter, whenever Gris submerges in water, rainfall and other ambient sounds become muted, and a low-pass frequency filter is applied to the music and sound design – as if hearing underwater. These aesthetic choices, too, are thematic; the winds and sands evoke the ferocity and unpredictability of grief-driven anger, and the psychoacoustics of diving offer a profound analogue to one's altered sensation, cognition and motivation during depression. Gris ends each chapter encountering fragments of a woman's statue – the same whose hand sustained her in the opening cinematic. By mourning and attempting to sing to the statue, one colour is rematerialized throughout Gris's emotional landscape. As each colour spreads, a new musical layer is unveiled in the soundtrack (Red, cello; Green, violin; Blue, choir and percussion; Yellow, soprano solo and string section; Finale: soprano duet and organ).[7] In addition to punctuating the story's organizational movements and signalling a transition to new ludic challenges, this additive progression encodes Gris's personal growth process. The music gradually revealed is the track 'Gris, Pt. 2', a climactic recapitulation of the earlier track 'Gris, Pt. 1' – the song begun by Gris at the game's outset. The soundtrack's diachronic trajectory charts the musical restoration of Gris' lost song.

The recurring statue is established as Gris' mother in a hidden cutscene; thus, its shattering is typically read as her mother's death. Gris's journey processes her bereavement realistically using loss of voice as a metaphor – psychotherapist Viola Nicolucci heartily recommends *Gris* for its nuanced portrayal of grieving (CheckPoint n.d.). The game's chapters parallel the 'five stages of grief' proposed by Elisabeth Kübler-Ross and David Kessler ([1969] 2014.) – Denial, Anger, Bargaining, Depression and Acceptance – ascriptions confirmed by in-game achievements (Figure 1.3).[8] Though commonly critiqued for linearity and rigidity, the stages are intended as a flexible framework with no prescribed progression or order, as unique as each individual's experience (Kessler n.d.). *Gris* encodes this vital nuance in two ways: (1) each stage's colour persists into subsequent stages, and (2) the narrative's primary antagonist, a mass of shadowy creatures conglomerated into various forms, pursues Gris through multiple chapters – including Acceptance (Psych of Play 2020). Appearing first as a blackened mirror image of Gris, the shadows later morph into butterflies, a crow and an eel. Even after the statue has been rebuilt and Gris' world restored to full colour, the shadows return to shatter the statue and consign the world to grey once more. This invokes a difficult reality about grief and depression – just as one seems to have escaped, despair often reappears stronger than ever.

Music-semiotic analysis of Gris's song, contextualized by narrative observations, reveals that her journey concludes in accepting not only her mother's death

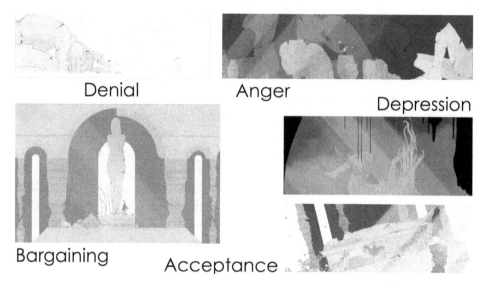

FIGURE 1.3: Five statues corresponding to Kübler-Ross' five stages of grief.

FIGURE 1.4: Differentiated vocal range/registers of Gris (the character) and the opening cutscene statue in 'Gris, pt. 1' and 'Gris, pt. 2'.

but also embracing herself as grieving, vulnerable and flawed – in other words, as human. In each chapter, Gris awakens a narratively appropriate ability, at last regaining her song in Yellow/Acceptance. When she sings, red flowers bloom around her and dormant, helpful creatures awaken. In the game's climax, Gris's song is joined and amplified by a second voice from the now-reconstructed statue ('Gris, Pt. 2') – the same that accompanied her in the introductory scene ('Gris, Pt. 1'). Together, the two voices in harmony dispel the shadowy creature threatening to overwhelm them. The shadows, in the form of a frenzied crow, were earlier shown to dissipate when confronted with music – such as the monumental cathedral bells in the Green chapter – and the voices' duet proves especially potent. Throughout the game, each of these voices consistently occupies a particular register and timbre – the statue's warmer mezzo-soprano from B♭3 to C5, and Gris's brighter soprano from F4 to A♭5 (Figure 1.4). Through the majority of the game, the lower-register voice is conspicuously absent – Gris's song, once regained, sounds wispy and rootless without it. Though two distinct voices are implied by this registrational separation, both are actually performed by the same vocalist: Gemma Gamarra. While this choice is doubtless pragmatically motivated – the composing artist Berlinist is a three-member band with only Gamarra as its vocalist – it is also semiotically significant, communicating continuity or identity between these voices. In music semiotics, registrational changes may indicate shifts in character, perspective, emotional state, resolve or internal/external dialogue, while timbral similarities highlight close relationship, union or intimacy. After the darkness has been overcome, Gris crosses a bridge of connected stars (the earlier-collected pitches), and the two voices sing in joyous euphony, revelling in their reunion. In close, harmonious intervals, the two move *Gris'* home key of F minor to its relative major, A♭ major, encapsulating Gris's transition from sorrow to peace as she ascends into the whitening sky. The track 'In Your Hands' plays as credits roll, intertwining the voices yet more intimately with voice crossings and dovetailing melodies, teasing an anticipated perfect unison with intervals of major and minor seconds (Figure 1.5). A third voice joins next, followed by a cloud of soprano and mezzo-soprano voices in harmonious chorus. Whereas the introduction and re-emergence of the second voice make clear its distinctness, the ending and credit

FIGURE 1.5: 'In Your Hands' vocal duet transcription, illustrating the close intervallic interplay between the voices. Transcription by the author.

tracks blur the voices' identity into unity. A crucial interpretative question now arises: is the voice that joins Gris's the memory of her mother's, or someone else's?

The final hermeneutic key to answer this crucial question is the shadow itself. In the shadow's last attack on the rebuilt statue, the eel emerges from the depths, morphing into an enormous version of Gris's own face, devouring both her and her colourful world. This recalls Gris' first encounter with the entity deep beneath the Red desert, where it becomes Gris' own shadow – her mirror image. To wit, the shadow creature is Gris herself – an aspect revealed through anger in the process of grief. At times threatening to consume her – as within the sea of Depression – at others her shadow propels her onward, such as when she must ride the gust of the crow's screams to reach her next destination. Returning to the five statues shown in Figure 1.3, one might intuitively conclude that they, like the shattered statue, depict Gris' mother. However, these statues, named for the stages of grief, actually correspond to the griever, not the grieved – Gris herself. Indeed, while two poses could fit a dying mother (Denial, Acceptance), the other three do not (Anger, Bargaining, Depression) – rather, these statues display Gris's own psychological state. After the shadow devours Gris, she discovers the Acceptance statue lying in repose floating amidst a pitch black sea and, upon singing to it, red lotuses bloom. Still, Gris sings as the dark waters begin engulfing her once more, no longer running or resisting. Once Gris accepts that this inexorable sorrow and grief, too, is part of who she is, the statue at last opens its lips to sing with her in harmony. To answer the earlier question – the second voice is neither the mother's nor someone else's, but Gris's own. Gris embraces and tenderly kisses the statue's tear-streaked face, weaving its voice with hers into an enriched musical fabric – a new song, befitting one who has experienced loss and been changed by it. And though the statue is completely reformed, it remains cracked – unafraid to openly display its flaws, its vulnerability, its humanity. The statue may well represent memories of Gris's mother, but so too does it embody Gris herself, as the woman she has become. 'Maybe they are two sides of the same coin', concludes Nicolle Lamerichs (2021), '[m]aybe both characters represent you, and the process of accepting death'. This is *Gris*' extraordinary achievement: a compelling, artistic meditation on real mental health experiences, at a time when mental health and neurodiversity visibility is increasingly important. It normalizes patterns of grief, depression and loss, encouraging players to accept these experiences as part of who they are – not as an abnormality to be cured. Gris's journey bridges from her world into ours – one reviewer writes: 'despite being about Gris, it still felt made for me … [it] can be about Gris and her story, but it can also be about you and your story' (Themperor Somnium 2021). In this playable parable, the player, like Gris, may sing in perfect self-harmony.

Like *Chrono Cross*, *Gris* demonstrates the synergistic union between music, play, narrative and interpretation in video game music. In the unified aesthetic of

Gris, academic barriers between story and game melt away in the meaning-making subjectivity of the player. Far from mere background music, game soundtracks wield immense potential to frame, shape and nuance one's experience and interpretation of the work. As this exploration turns to more concrete representative categories of gender, race and religion in video game music, remember the profundity of this playable parable's interpretative interactivity. In music alone, there is meaning – communicating part of what it means to be human.

NOTES

* Supplementary Video 1.1 'Ludo Narrative Harmony: Musical Meaning in the Magic Circle (Semiotic Society of America 2021)' can be found here: https://www.youtube.com/watch?v=fysyvUWCJCE. Accessed 3 June 2024. Standalone colour files of Figures 1.2 and 1.3, and a standalone illustration file of Figure 1.5 can be found under the Front Matter section for *Gender, Race and Religion in Video Game Music's* page on Intellect Discover.

1. Neither, for that matter, is interpretation of a literary text or other type of artwork static or unidirectional. Experiments in hypertexts and non-linear storytelling demonstrate that the interactivity characteristic of video games may be instantiated through the written word as well. However, video games perhaps best exemplify interactivity as a medium, since the selection, pacing, ordering and even content of the artwork are influenced or determined by player response.

2. The question may arise whether interpretative interactivity applies equally to all video games regardless of era or genre. To clarify, no theoretical framework or methodology is equally effective across all examples of a type, not even for those cases the theory claims to cover. For video games with limited audio capabilities, such as *Pong* (1972), the insights gleaned from musical analysis may be fewer. However, here are two points of response: (1) interpretative interactivity is not dependent upon a game utilizing dynamic/user-responsive or non-linear music. Even a looping, linear underscore participates in interpretative interactivity, because player actions may influence how long a cue is heard, in what sequence, how many times in a playthrough and at what point the loop cuts off. (2) Interpretative interactivity is not dependent upon the presence of what is commonly understood as 'plot' or 'story'. I agree with Janet Murray that 'Games are always stories, even abstract games' including *Pong*, *Tetris* and *Candy Crush*, as gameplay affordances narrativize player choices (Murray 2004, 2). Principles 1 and 2 of interpretative interactivity entail that the gameplay – and the soundworld it reifies – is itself narrativized through player interpretative agency.

3. The Dragonians of Dinopolis dispersed into El Nido after their defeat, eventually interbreeding with humans to produce the demi-human races. The ancient war between Chronopolis and Dinopolis is presumed to be the historical basis for hostilities between humans and demi-humans. No living Dragonian is encountered in the game.

4. *Chrono Cross* does not contain a playable dwarf character. Early portrayals of the dwarves as warmongering seem problematic. However, a more sympathetic nuance is introduced after defeating the dwarves, if the player discovers that the highly nature-attuned dwarves' vengeance is spurred by humanity's destruction of their homeland, the Hydra Marshes, and Serge's killing of their deity. Every other species or major demographic group in the game is potentially represented in Serge's party.

5. *Chrono Cross* exists in three versions: PlayStation 1 (1999), a port to the PlayStation Network (2011) and the Nintendo Switch remaster *Chrono Cross: The Radical Dreamers Edition* (2022). In the original 1999 edition, the Element colour icons and accompanying pitches did not occur throughout Terra Tower – only when facing the Time Devourer. In the 2011 PlayStation Network port and 2022 remaster, however, the icons and pitches occur throughout Terra Tower, as described in this chapter. The developers likely implemented this change in order to better foreshadow the importance of the Elements' pitches, prompting players to attend to them musically starting from an earlier point. Even though the sequence of Elements to use in the Time Devourer battle would have been easily accessible through internet guides and walkthroughs written since the original release, the developers considered comprehension of the pitch's narrative rationale significant enough to make more apparent in subsequent releases.

6. In film music studies, diegetic sound is understood as occurring within the narrative world of the film – that is, potentially hearable by on-screen characters – while non-diegetic sound occurs outside the narrative, for viewers' perception and benefit. Frequently, the boundaries between the two are not clear-cut, such as if a character begins humming a tune, using the underscore as accompaniment. These concepts may be applied to video games as well, though games arguably problematize easy distinction between diegetic and non-diegetic more frequently than film.

7. 'Gris, Pt. 1' contains a subdued version of this music, cut off by the statue's destruction. The cues for each chapter transition are: 'Lift' (Red), 'Opaque' (Green), 'Symmetry' (Blue) and 'Sparks' (Yellow). 'Gris, Pt. 2' realizes the material's full texture in the game's climactic scene.

8. David Kessler, who co-wrote two books on the stages of grief with Elisabeth Kübler-Ross, recently proposed a sixth stage of grief, 'Meaning', in *Finding Meaning: The Sixth Stage of Grief* (2019). While Kessler's arguments in favour of this stage are compelling and resonate strongly with my outlook as a semiotician, Kübler-Ross's five-stage model has remained most influential in popular awareness. In any case, *Gris* was released in 2018, prior to the publication of Kessler's book. Thus, only the original five stages are treated in *Gris* – and the present analysis.

PART II

GENDER

2

Feminine Themings:
The Construction of Musical Gendering
in the *Final Fantasy* Franchise

Introduction

[In] the world of traditional narrative, there are no feminine endings.
(McClary 2002, 16)

This chapter explores gender representation in the *Final Fantasy* (*FF*) franchise, warranting an important disclaimer. I am not a woman, which shapes my analysis of gendered elements, musical and otherwise. While I believe that men can productively contribute to gender studies, I acknowledge that my interpretation of gender representation arises from a different lived experience than my women colleagues and readers, who experience the effects of gendered media culture directly. I welcome differing perspectives on the following character analyses and hope to engage in dialogue with them.

Part II of the book takes up the first of three demographic master categories referenced in the book's title: gender. The choice of wording is intentional – the following research and analyses largely explore sociological constructions of gender, with minimal discussion of biological sex (the discussion of castrati in Chapter 4 being the only exception). Following common practice in academia, I take biological sex to refer to medical factors relating to the body – using terminology such as 'female', 'male' or 'intersex' – while gender is a socially constructed, performative and contingent spectrum relating to identity formation and conventional cultural associations, using terminology including (but not limited to) 'woman', 'man', 'non-binary', 'gender-fluid' and 'transgender', with 'feminine'/'femininity' and 'masculine'/'masculinity' used as for cultural conventions of gender.[1] Gender terminology (e.g. 'feminine', 'masculine') will primarily be utilized in this chapter and throughout the book, typically proceeded by 'conventional' or 'conventionally' to emphasize their culturally contingent nature and avoid any hint of essentializing gender as static or monolithic. In reference to fictional characters, sex terminology (e.g. 'female character') is used because characters are typically categorized this way in paratextual sources, without generally providing insight into the characters' gender identification or preferences.

Part II presents the book's argument in a tripartite trajectory across three chapters, tracing gender representation in video game music from the past to the approximate present. Chapter 2 presents musical conventions of gender signification as they have been through video games' history from 1987 to 2006, Chapter 3 analyses significant subversions of binary gender conventions in games from 2009 and 2016, and Chapter 4 gestures towards non-binary representational possibilities by carving out a third space transcending conventional femininity and masculinity. Because Chapter 2 examines established conventions of the past, the analyses in this chapter predominantly feature conventional signification of femininity and masculinity – treatment of alternative and non-binary cases is reserved for Chapters 3 and 4. This narrowed focus is not to reify the very gender binary this project critiques, but rather to contextualize game music's conventionally gendered past to better understand how its representation has developed. Although there are noteworthy exceptions to this pattern (e.g. Terra in *FFVI*), they subvert but do not ultimately replace, the established conventional norms of the time.

Chapter 2 begins by examining Princess Leia and Rey of the *Star Wars* franchise as an illustrative analogue to musical gender representation past and present. The discussion proceeds to explore screen music's participation in gender construction, then transitions to focus on *Final Fantasy* specifically. While the earliest *FF* games featured location- or function-based music rather than distinct character themes, the event- and character-specific music introduced in *FFII* and *FFIII* inaugurated a pattern of gendering the series' female characters in conventionally feminine ways. From *FFIV* to *FFX*, musical themes for female and male characters typically follow conventionally gendered musical roles: conventionally feminine themes according to the 'Feminine Romantic Cliché' theorized by Rebecca Fülöp, and conventionally masculine themes utilizing a heroic or military musical topic. The majority of the chapter undertakes a close music-semiotic analysis of the main character themes from *FFIV–FFXII*, reserving *FFXIII* and *FFXV* to contextualize and analyse in detail in Chapter 3.[2] Though a few significant outliers subvert conventionally gendered expectations, the character themes of *FF* largely present an uncannily consistent pattern of conventionally feminine and conventionally masculine musical characteristics.

A comparative case study of two prominent heroes from the *Star Wars* film franchise serves as an illustrative starting point. The original trilogy's Princess Leia and the recent trilogy lead Rey are strikingly differentiated by multiple aesthetic and narrative factors, including their musical themes. Leia's and Rey's musical themes participate with other factors in conveying crucial aspects about each one's character and narrative role. The iconic 'Leia's Theme', composed by John Williams, contains Romantic-era style and chromaticism, featuring instrumentation of lush strings, flute, oboe and the occasional French horn. Its melody is elegantly lyrical, rising and falling in balanced motivic repetition – except when rapidly ascending via fragmentation to a climax suggestive of an unbridled burst of romantic passion. The cue's initially delicate accompanimental textures yield to a climactic orchestral tutti featuring expressive rubato, a soaring high-string melody and chromatically inflected major-mode harmonies. Narratively, Leia functions 'primarily [as] an enabler for [the] male characters' like Luke Skywalker and Han Solo, serving their development arcs over her own through ceremonial recognition of their achievements (Bruin-Molé 2018, 227). In another example, Diana Dominguez observes that Leia places Luke's grief at the death of his aunt and uncle over her own after the total destruction of her adoptive family and home planet (Harrison 2019, 3). Though Leia repeatedly demonstrates her strength and competence, these feats are often undermined by problematic treatment elsewhere. For instance, Rebecca Fülöp recalls the impact of first witnessing Leia's infamous gold bikini scene at age 15:

> This iconic moment from *Return of the Jedi*, while contributing nothing vital to the plot, sums up quite succinctly the purpose of the character played by Carrie Fisher [...] the infamous gold bikini reminds us that alongside any of her empowering qualities, Leia also functions as an object of sexual desire and romantic pursuit. In this realm she demonstrates little self-contained purpose, for she is largely defined by her relationships to the male characters around her [...] Forced to wear the skimpy gold bikini, she serves as titillating eye candy for the villainous Jabba the Hutt and audience members alike in the final film of the original trilogy.
>
> (2012, 1–2)

Leia's music, like the gold bikini, paints her as an objectified caricature rather than as a nuanced character in her own right, drawing the audience's attention to her 'feminine rather than heroic attributes' (Fülöp 2012, 3). Later, Leia's theme is interwoven with music associated with Han or Luke, subordinating her to the male protagonists as an 'essentially romantic and decorative character' (Fülöp 2012, 4). Though Leia's potential as an empowered female character – as well as actress Carrie Fisher's feminist legacy – is noteworthy, the hopeful glimmers of positive gender representation are ultimately suppressed by narrative and music alike.

Introduced nearly 40 years after *A New Hope*, Rey 'transformed the franchise' as its first female lead protagonist, promising greater demographic diversity to fans alongside protagonists of colour Finn and Rose (Harrison 2019, 1). After Disney acquired *Star Wars* in 2012, the series was 'widely praised for its feminism', with Rey and Jyn Erso (*Rogue One*) being 'hailed as feminist triumphs' (Bruin-Molé 2018, 225). 'Rey's Theme' – also composed by John Williams – strikes a radically different style and tone that contrasts 'Leia's Theme' at every turn. Rather than Romantic-era traits, the style of Rey's music is best described as minimalist in structure and rhythmic drive. Instrumentally, the theme's low-register flute, string ostinato and foregrounded brass-family chorale subvert conventionally feminine patterns. The cue exhibits broadly Dorian-modal harmony, relatively constrained melodic range and an overall lack of chromaticism that differs sharply from Leia's theme. Narratively speaking, Rey is neither sexually objectified nor made an accessory to a male character's development, as Leia repeatedly was. Though Rey does develop a romantic connection with her Sith rival Kylo Ren, the romance does not define her as a character, and the two catalyse each other's development in a reciprocal fashion. Rey thus fulfils the promissory note of Princess Leia, offering a multidimensional female lead with her own unique personality and trajectory, free of musical caricatures of what a woman must be like. This is not to say the modern *Star Wars* trilogy is entirely unproblematic; the initial lack of female characters like Rey or Captain Phasma in The Force Awakens toy product lines and director J. J. Abrams's remarks that *Star Wars* was 'always a boys' thing' sparked the protest hashtag campaign '#Wheresrey?' (Scott 2017, 139, 141, 143). Overall, Rey is regarded as a significantly more positive example of gender representation than Princess Leia. As Megen de Bruin-Molé concludes:

> In popular discussions, *Star Wars*' feminism was reframed as a progression from Leia (a powerful but solitary role model in the original trilogy) to Rey, who takes up the mantle of Jedi hero that previously belonged exclusively to the male protagonist of the films.
>
> (2018, 228)

The musical differences between 'Leia's Theme' and 'Rey's Theme' reinforce the contrasting impact of each character's gendered representation.

The above analytical sketches and the ensuing chapter flow from the broader project introduced by feminist musicology – bringing the analytical resources of musical semiotics to bear on the gendered meanings of musical conventions. Though western music history is steeped in gendered rhetoric and norms, the task of going beyond formalism to interrogate the musical signification of gender was left only to scholars of recent decades (McClary 2002). The scholarship of feminist musicologists, including Susan McClary and many others, explores how music may reinforce and construct gender norms in art, media and society. These findings may be outlined by the following principles:

FEMININE THEMINGS

1. Western musical conventions are gendered.

Since the rise of seventeenth-century opera at the latest, composers strove to develop a consistent musical semiotics of gender – 'a set of conventions for constructing "masculinity" or "femininity" in music' (McClary 2002, 7). These practices musically encoded cultural notions of traits typically exhibited by men and women of the time. 'Masculine' music was thought to possess clarity, order, vigour and rationality, while 'feminine' music embodied softness, roundness, charm and grace (Treitler 1993, 27). Though nearly every musical parameter could participate in this gendered dichotomy, two examples are particularly illustrative: 'masculine' and 'feminine' cadences and sonata form themes. As late as 1970, the *Harvard Dictionary of Music* contained an entry for the 'masculine' and 'feminine' cadence: 'A cadence or ending is called "masculine" if the final chord of a phrase or section occurs on the strong beat and "feminine" if it is postponed to fall on a weak beat' (McClary 2002, 9). McClary elaborates that the 'masculine' cadence was thought to be normative and satisfying, while the 'feminine' cadence was weak, subversive and aberrant (10). As a second example, in 1845, A. B. Marx set the precedent of referring to a sonata-allegro form primary theme as 'masculine' and the secondary theme as 'feminine' – a convention in form theory that persisted until the 1960s (13). This impacted the perception of musical form as narrative; the primary theme 'occupies the narrative position of masculine protagonist', while the 'feminine' secondary theme fuels the tonal arc of the 'masculine' primary theme (19). Because the sonata form demands the triumphant return of the primary theme and the conformity of the secondary theme to the primary theme's key area, McClary writes: '[In] the world of traditional narrative, there are no feminine endings' (16). Dozens of parallel examples could be provided, but these two shall suffice to demonstrate the interweaving of gender and music.

2. Musical character themes communicate gendered information.

In narrative media like opera, film or video games, musical themes presented along with a character's appearance or mention communicate vital information about the character's personality, including gender construction. Film music conveys culturally encoded values that shape the audience's perception of the character's tone, expression and mood (Gorbman 1987, 30). When paired with a narratively foregrounded character, the music seems to speak that character's 'emotions, thoughts and memories' (Laing 2007, 29–30). In other words, the musical score accompanying a character efficiently communicates meanings not yet instantiated in the character's visual appearance or narrative actions. As an operatic parallel, Carmen's 'Habanera' encodes the gypsy's 'unpredictable, maddening' sensuality through the pronounced use of chromaticism in its melody (McClary 2002, 58). It is crucial to note that the creation and/or perception of these musically gendered traits is frequently subconscious. McClary writes: '[When] composing music for a female character, a composer may automatically choose traits such as softness or passivity, without really examining the premises for such choices' (9). This forms a segue to the third principle.

3. Music, media and the arts participate in socializing gender construction.

Music does not exist in an artistic vacuum, but draws on – and, in turn, influences – wider culture. How one acquires a society's gender norms is intrinsically bound up in its narrative, artistic and media culture. Music does not passively reflect social reality, but participates actively in its construction: 'It is in accordance with the terms provided by language, film, advertising, ritual, or music that individuals are socialised: take on gendered identities, learn ranges of proper behaviors, structure their perceptions and even their experiences' (McClary 2002, 21). The arts provide 'public models of how men are, how women are' – and are in turn created by those trained in its conventions (McClary 2002, 37). As a result of this cultural feedback loop, conventional gender representation is notoriously difficult to diagnose and dislodge, since it permeates human experience. Rebecca Fülöp writes: 'Gender shapes our whole reality; it is impossible to disentangle it from other issues in studies of art, culture, history – anything that is part of who we are and how we relate to the world around us' (2012, 334). Video games, like opera or film, culturally construct gender – and their music plays a pivotal role in that gendering.

Damsels and Opera Floozies: The Construction of Musical Gendering in the Final Fantasy Franchise

> *I'm a GENERAL, not some opera floozy!*
>
> (Celes Chere, *Final Fantasy VI*, 1994)

As the 46-year *Star Wars* series marks the progression of gender representation in film, so does the 36-year *FF* franchise in video games.[3] The series' soundtracks are known for their 'discrete [musical] themes associated with characters and locations' (Cheng 2014, 81) which help players 'keep dozens of characters [...] straight' (Gibbons and Reale 2020, 2). These themes musically encode salient traits – including gendered ones – to aid player understanding of a character. As Tim Summers writes: 'Game music does not exist in a musically sealed world, but draws upon a common lexicon from broader culture' (2016, 40). Thus, a character's music constitutes a key determinant of how players perceive and interpret that character.

Yet from the beginning, it was not so. The earliest *FF* games contained few or no musical character themes, owing to hardware limitations on memory available for music – the entire *FFI* soundtrack spans under ten minutes without looping. Debuting on the Nintendo Entertainment System (NES) in 1987, *FFI* features predominantly location-based music such as 'Chaos Temple' or 'Underwater Palace', prioritizing players' sense of sojourning through a vast fantasy world; no character-based themes are included.[4] Similarly, *Final Fantasy II* (1988) contains no character themes but adds a few event-based cues to reinforce important narrative events. Most infamous among these is the seduction of the protagonist Firion by the alluring Princess Hilda (Figure 2.1), scored with a sensual lyrical melody and flowing arpeggiated accompaniment (orchestrated in the Dawn of Souls remake with oboe and harp). 'Temptation of the Princess' is a quotation of the iconic 'Swan Theme' from Pyotr Tchaikovsky's ballet *Swan Lake*, which is a fitting intertextual connection; Hilda is revealed to be the Lamia Queen in disguise, just as the ballet's black swan Odile impersonates the white swan Odette to entice Prince Siegfried. This reference communicates that the imposter Hilda is no chaste maiden, but rather a seductive femme fatale. Even before the *FF* series incorporated conventional character themes, its music participated in gendering a female character, shaping the player's perception of her as an archetypal woman.

Significantly, the first character theme in franchise history is also associated with a woman. *Final Fantasy III* (1990) includes exactly one track attached to a specific character: 'Elia, the Maiden of Water', named for the serene and conventionally beautiful Aria Benett.[5] Though Aria is not a playable character (the

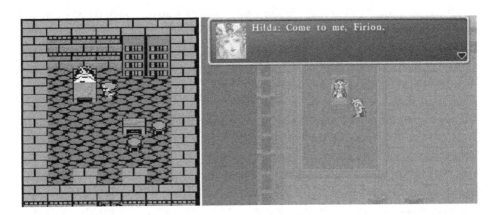

FIGURE 2.1: Princess Hilda/Lamia Queen seduces Firion, *Final Fantasy II*, NES (1988, left), iOS (2010, right).

playable characters in the original *FFIII* are narratively generic and class-based in appearance, similar to *FFI*), her character-specific music is striking and sets a historical precedent for the themes of later main, playable characters. Aria's *dolcissimo*, highly affective theme stands out from the rest of the score, featuring a singing-style melody and gently arpeggiating accompaniment (English horn and harp in the Nintendo DS remake). Its other stylistic features include major mode, periodic phrasing, Romantic-style flourishes and expressive chromaticism. As shall be seen, these are typical signifiers of the feminine in music, marking Aria as the feminized ideal – although Sara is the game's princess character, Aria plays a more conventionally feminine role, supporting the protagonists with healing magic and ultimately sacrificing her life to protect the heroes from harm. Aria's theme establishes a musical archetype that future conventionally feminine themes largely adhered to.

Beginning with the Super Nintendo Entertainment System (SNES) generation, the musical character theme became a staple of an *FF* soundtrack. For example, *FFVI* contains named themes for each of its fourteen playable protagonists – and its two main antagonists – that are heard whenever that character performs an important action or is the centre of narrative attention. For a multimedia demonstration, a video comparison of the primary character themes from *FFIV* through *FFXV* illustrates these themes' pattern of conventionally feminine and conventionally masculine musical features.[6]

A few broad observations are in order before delving into specific case studies. Strikingly, the themes of male characters exhibit greater musical variety than the themes for female characters. What explains this asymmetry? A key concept here is the theory of 'markedness', derived from the field of linguistics and applied to musical semiotics by Robert Hatten. Defined as the 'valuation given to difference', markedness involves an asymmetrical pair of terms – a specific marked term and a more general unmarked one (Hatten 1994, 34). Edwin Battistella explains: 'A marked term asserts the presence of a particular feature, and an unmarked term negates that assertion' (Battistella 1990, 2). In other words, the marked term specifies a distinction from the unmarked term, subsequently modifying the unmarked term's meaning to be opposed to that of the marked term. When the opposition does not need to be invoked, the unmarked term alone suffices. Consider the example of the terms 'cow' and 'bull', where 'cow' is an unmarked term that does not necessarily specify the animal's sex – but when contrasted with the marked term 'bull', which specifies the male animal, 'cow' now signifies the female animal (Hatten 1994, 34). Hatten proceeds to identify marked oppositions in music, including major and minor modes, expressive movement titles, the Picardy third, key relations and musical topics; these observations remain foundational to musical semiotics.[7] However, for present purposes, understanding the broader linguistic concept is sufficient. It is fitting that Hatten's selected examples – 'cow' versus 'bull' and 'man' versus 'woman' – both involve sex or gender, as markedness is also central to the cultural construction of gender.

Musical markedness is analogous to conventional gender dynamics in society via the relationships between masculinity, femininity and hegemonic masculinity. 'Masculinity is everywhere', write Edward Morris and Freeden Oeur, 'at the same time that it is nowhere' (2018, ix). Normative masculinity typically hides in plain view, rendered invisible as the presumed default mode of manhood. In societal gender dynamics, conventional masculinity and conventional femininity are dichotomously polarized in order to render each concept meaningful; normative 'manliness' therefore becomes defined by what it is not, through 'opposition to and/or interplay with a feminine "other"' (Frühstück and Walthall 2011, 60). In terms of markedness, masculinity is unmarked, invisibly generic until contrasted with its negation; femininity is marked and specific, signified by a narrower range of conventional signifiers. Raewyn Connell's seminal concept 'hegemonic masculinity' describes precisely this marked relationship of cultural gendering, defined as the elevation of a particular mode of masculinity over femininity and alternative masculinities.[8] Hegemonic masculinity generates, reinforces and legitimates power differentials 'between men and women, between masculinity and femininity, and among masculinities' (Messerschmidt 2018, 28). Though it may seem that hegemonic masculinity requires a uniform standard of manliness, in reality, approved masculinities may enjoy quite diverse modes of expression – as long as they all are each defined in comparison with another identity considered to be less masculine, whether femininity or alternative masculinity. In parallel to societal gender dynamics, musical gendering exhibits marked relationships between the conventionally feminine and conventionally masculine in music – including in the character themes of *FF*.

The discussion now turns to concrete musical features of *FF*'s character themes. Each theme will later be treated individually; however, some preceding, general remarks are in order. As previously mentioned, the themes of male characters exhibit greater musical diversity than those for female characters, particularly in the parameters of instrumentation, genre/style, phrasing, mode and tempo. When these themes do exhibit common musical traits, they tend to be hallmarks of the 'heroic' musical topic. The heroic topic includes prominent use of brass and percussion, military style, driving rhythms, syncopation and ascending melodic leaps suggestive of great athletic feats. The conventionally masculine themes also tend to utilize full orchestral or ensemble texture, implying a forte dynamic, and often employ the modally borrowed ♭VI and ♭VII chords in major mode, lending the music an 'epic' sound. Particularly noteworthy is the use of the ♭VI – ♭VII – I Picardy-Aeolian cadence, borrowing from Hollywood tropes signifying courageous exploits of conventionally masculine superheroes (cf. Alan Silvestri's iconic 'Avengers Theme' from *The Avengers*) (Lehman 2013, 5.2). Overall, these strategies are designed to present male characters as the central heroes of the story.

In contrast to the themes for male characters, conventionally feminine themes from *FFIV–FFX* bear an uncannily consistent musical profile, patterned after the precedent of 'Elia, the Maiden of Water'. These commonalities shall be explored by way of conventionally feminine musical gendering in the cousin medium of film. Of all art and entertainment mediums, the music of film and television exerts the most direct, tangible influence on video game music. Rebecca Fülöp's work analyses the Feminine Romantic Cliché (henceforth 'FRC') in early film, defined as 'a recurring musical theme [...] [that] acts as a characterising music for a female love interest as well as the love theme for the film's romantic plotline' (Fülöp 2012, 31). The female characters underscored by a FRC typically embody idealized romantic femininity and come to be defined by her romantic potential with a male character (almost always the lead protagonist). To recall an earlier example, 'Leia's Theme' functions as an FRC that 'links [Leia] to other characters rather than establishing her as an individual', contributing to the problematic gendered portrayal previously described (4). Broadly speaking, the FRC functions to strip the female character of agency and individual identity, treating her as a narrative object rather than a subject (34–35). Analysing 100 films from 1935 to 1955, Fülöp (2012) concludes that the FRC typically:

1. reinforces the perception of women as passive, decorative objects to be acted upon by men (18);
2. communicates virginity and moral purity according to Hollywood's ethical Production Code (21);
3. obscures a female character's interior life and complexity in favour of presumed idealization (38); and
4. defines a woman by her 'feminine beauty and romantic potential' (47).

The long-lasting influence of the FRC in musical gender representation is tangible even in twenty-first-century media culture.

Unlike the visual arts, which are capable of representing a female figure directly, musical gender construction relies on 'cultural associations and conventions' thought to be so naturally apropos to femininity that they 'generally go unremarked or unchallenged even in scholarly literature' (Fülöp 2012, 47). These conventions are frequently borrowed from western concert music or operatic traditions, adapted for film music in the early twentieth century. The FRC features a slow tempo and lyrical melodies to convey a 'lilting, unhurried feeling' that Fülöp argues was thought to correspond to conventional femininity's lesser physical vigour and height-ened emotional expressivity (55). Its signature instruments include high strings, woodwinds (especially flute, oboe/English horn) and harp; the FRC usually does not utilize brass or percussion. The accompaniment consists of arpeggiation or chorale textures that serve to foreground the melody. Fülöp also observes that the FRC is typically cast in major mode, to embody the woman's 'positive and love-inspiring nature' (59). Though almost always diatonic in tonal structure, the music of the FRC contains a great deal of harmonic variety through Romantic-style expressive chromaticism (60). Finally, a FRC melody exhibits a balanced contour, alternating between gradual ascent and descent before climaxing on a high note late in the phrase and resolving by descent to a stable consonance (63). Again, 'Leia's Theme' is a striking example exemplifying most of the FRC's musical features. The telltale musical signifiers of the FRC find parallels in the conventionally feminine themes of *FF*.

For the most part, the *FF* conventionally feminine themes share common instrumentation, typically scored with prominent use of flute, oboe or another woodwind instrument over harp or lush strings. Its singing-style melodies employ generally stepwise motion, lyrical character, periodic phrasing, alternation of ascending/descending contour and balancing leaps with a contrary motion by step. The accompaniment consists of arpeggiation or sustained chords, and its mode is nearly always major. Rhythmically, conventionally feminine music adopts a slow tempo and relaxed, on-the-beat rhythmic values and may be further marked by triple or compound meter. Additional features that are either not as prominent or not as ubiquitous include the use of (or allusion to) soprano voice, piano dynamic implied by sparse texture, harmonic rhythm of one chord per measure, circle-of-fifths chord progressions, expressive chromaticism and either Romantic-era or contemporary pop ballad style.[9] With the FRC in mind, the association with Romantic-era style is readily explicable; however, why employ a pop ballad style for several conventionally feminine themes (*FFV*, *FFVIII*, *FFIX*, *FFX*)? In a Japanese context, this calls to mind the music genre known internationally as 'J-pop' – specifically the アイドル ('idol') cultural phenomenon, which primarily features female performers and groups. Minora Kitahara writes: 'In idol culture women are the stars. There may be nowhere else in Japanese society where we're the driving force' (McAlpine 2017, n.pag.).[10] Building on this association, the conventionally feminine themes in *FFVIII* through *X* are instrumental versions of originally composed Japanese pop ballads ('Eyes on Me', 'Melodies of Life', 'Suteki da ne'),[11] which are heard in full during the game's ending credits or romantic scenes. This links a female character with the story's happy ending, calling to mind the problematic, male-hero-centred 'save the world, get the girl' trope common to media and narrative storytelling throughout history (further explored in Chapter 4).

It must be noted that Nobuo Uematsu was the sole composer for the conventionally feminine themes from *FFIV* through *X* (listed and analysed below) which exhibit the greatest similarity to one another. Indeed, as shall be seen, when the series changes composers for *FFXII, XIII* and *XV*, the conventionally feminine pattern described thus far is subverted.[12] Should the similarity solely be attributed to Uematsu as an individual, independently of cultural conventional trends? By no means – due to these traits' resemblance to conventional musical femininity in other art and entertainment media – especially the FRC in film – it is clear that they are not merely due to a personal compositional quirk of Uematsu's, but are rather a symptom of broader cultural practices. Uematsu is a Japanese composer known for drawing deep inspiration from European-American concert music and film traditions, so the pathway for adapting these gendered musical conventions is clear. Combined with the medieval high fantasy settings of the *FF* series – the fantasy genre often perpetuating gendered archetypes – it is little wonder that its music, like its narratives, draws on readily recognizable devices. When paired in marked opposition with heroic, conventionally masculine themes, this musical conventional femininity marks female characters as the feminized 'other', legitimizing male protagonists' masculinity by negation of its supposed opposite. Reminiscent of cadences, sonata form themes and 'Leia's Theme', the music of *FF*'s heroines treads well-worn paths of problematic gender representation in music history (Table 2.1).

The sonic picture the preceding analysis paints admittedly uses too broad a brush. Robust understanding is possible only through semiosis – a detailed and nuanced interpretation of a specific case study. Accordingly, the remainder of this chapter is devoted to remarks on each primary character's musical and narrative gender representation. As *FF* is a Japanese series – and Uematsu a Japanese composer – the analyses will dialogue closely with Japanese cultural scholarship and concepts to facilitate rigorous semiosis. Paired analyses of conventionally feminine and conventionally masculine themes in the *FF* series reveal the marked opposition of conventional femininity and conventional masculinity communicated through video game music.

Musical Narrativizing: Analysing Musical Gendering in Final Fantasy IV–XII

Someday I will be queen, but I will always be myself.
(Garnet Til Alexandros XVII, *Final Fantasy IX* 2004).

For each main series *FF* title starting with *FFIV* through *FFXII*, brief analytical summaries of each main character's narrative role, primary musical theme and gender representation are provided below; unfortunately, there is not ample space to treat either music or narratives with nuance they deserve. Chapter 3 explores *FFXIII* and *FFXV* in much greater detail, so they are omitted from the corpus study below (though included in Figure 2.2). Additionally, *FFXI* and *FFXIV* will be omitted due

TABLE 2.1: Table of conventionally masculine and conventionally feminine musical traits in the *Final Fantasy* franchise.[13]

Parameter	Conventionally-Masculine Themes	Conventionally-Feminine Themes
Orchestration	Brass, percussion, otherwise varied; often *tutti* orchestra or thick texture	Flute, oboe, other woodwinds, harp, lush strings, female voice (soprano); sparse texture
Style	Varied	Romantic-era, contemporary ballad-style
Topics / Genre	Martial, heroic topics; varied genre	Singing-style topic; ballad or aria genre
Dynamics	*Forte* (implied)	*Piano* (implied)
Melody	Active, ascending leaps	Stepwise, lyrical
Phrasing	Varied	Regular, periodic phrasing
Accompaniment	Varied; typically block chord	Arpeggiation, sustained chords
Harmony	Varied harmonic rhythm and chord progressions; flat-VI and flat-VII chords in major.	One chord per measure; circle-of-fifths and other sequential progressions; expressive chromaticism and secondary dominant chords
Mode	Varied	Major
Rhythm	Active, driving, syncopated	Regular, relaxed, on-beat
Meter	Varied; typically quadruple or duple meter	Esp. triple or compound meter
Tempo	Varied	Slow

to their MMORPG nature, lacking clear, centralized protagonists.[14] Main characters are often associated with multiple themes or variations of their theme, developed throughout the course of the game's narrative or presented in significant moments of the story. However, to limit the scope of the present analytical task, only the character's primary (typically eponymous) theme will be discussed, except for a few passing references to secondary themes.[15] This results in a snapshot impression of a character's gendered presentation but does not provide a full picture of the character's musical development over the course of the game's narrative. Nonetheless, focusing on eponymous themes where possible bears distinct advantages, due to their relative clarity of association and potential freedom from narrative event-specific meanings. For example, 'High Summoner's Daughter' (*FFX*) is another candidate for musical

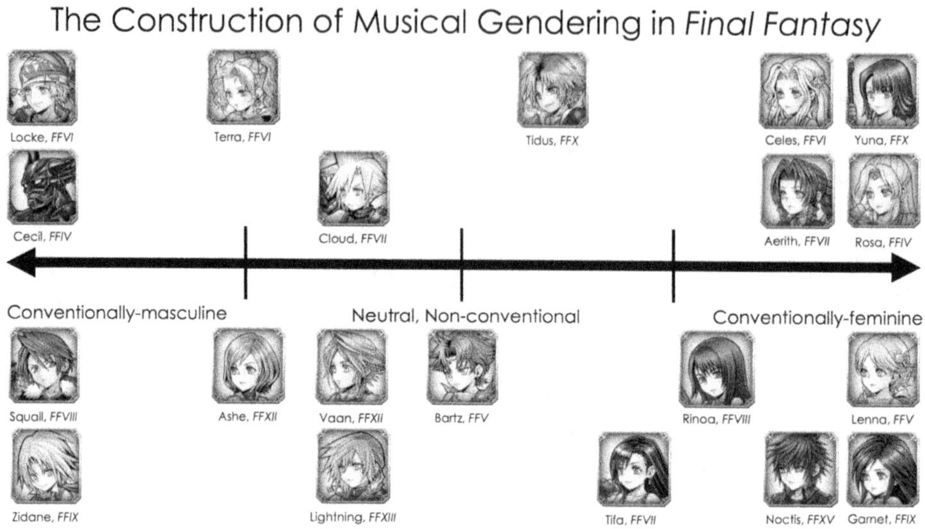

The Construction of Musical Gendering in *Final Fantasy*

FIGURE 2.2: Conventionally masculine to the conventionally feminine spectrum of *Final Fantasy* character themes. Lightning (*FFXIII*) and Noctis (*FFXV*), covered in Chapter 3, are included here for later reference/contextualization.

association with Yuna, as it is heard when she is initially introduced and is melodically related to 'Yuna's Theme'. However, 'High Summoner's Daughter' also plays during narrative events not solely centred on Yuna, and the direct naming of 'Yuna's Theme' serves to disambiguate it as specifically characterizing Yuna. Selection for transludic and transmedial adaptation – such as including 'Aerith's Theme' over 'Flowers Blooming in the Church' in the *Distant Worlds: Music from Final Fantasy* orchestral concerts – may also reinforce perceived links between music and character.[16] Primary character themes participate in communicating gendered expectations for the character due to 'virtual agency', or music's 'capacity to simulate the actions, emotions, and reactions of a human agent' (Hatten 2018, 1). One does not simply hear music, but encounters it directly as a coherent other; as Naomi Cumming writes: 'Music could be thought of as subverting the boundaries between the material and the personal, commanding an attention more familiar in the encounter with other human beings' (2000, 284). Hearing a character's music is akin to an interpersonal encounter, from which one cannot help but glean various kinds of information and character traits, including gendered ones.

My analysis of each theme is diagrammed as a spectrum in Figure 2.2, based on its conformity to masculine or feminine musical conventions. Figure 2.3 provides a transcribed excerpt of each musical theme, followed by a rationale for each character's placement.[17]

FIGURE 2.3: Partial musical transcriptions of the character themes analysed. Transcriptions by the author.

(Continued)

Rinoa — 'My Mind' (*Final Fantasy VIII*)

Zidane — 'Zidane's Theme' (*Final Fantasy IX*)

Garnet — 'Garnet's Theme' (*Final Fantasy IX*)

Tidus — 'Tidus' Theme' (*Final Fantasy X*)

Yuna — 'Yuna's Theme' (*Final Fantasy X*)

(*Continued*)

GENDER, RACE AND RELIGION IN VIDEO GAME MUSIC

Vaan — 'The Dream to Be a Sky Pirate' (*Final Fantasy XII*)

Ashe — 'Ashe's Theme' (*Final Fantasy XII*)

(Continued)

FFIV *(1991)*

Cecil exemplifies the chivalrous masculinity of the samurai tradition of *bushidō* (武士道; 'way of the warrior'). Historically, *bushidō* is Japan's longest-lasting hegemonic masculinity, set forth as Japan's masculine ideal in Nitobe Inazō's *Bushidō: The Soul of Japan*. Inazou portrayed *bushidō* as 'the perfection of Japanese men and the Japanese people', elevating it to a hegemonic ideal to which all honourable Japanese men must aspire (Frühstück and Walthall 2011, 63–65). Cecil embodies *bushidō* masculinity through his profession as a knight, his honourable character and his dedicated loyalty to his lord, the king of Baron – though the integrity of all three is later thrown into question. Cecil's initial theme 'Red Wings' reflects his military origins, featuring brass and percussion, ascending melodic leaps and an intertextual resemblance to Gustav Holst's 'Mars, the Bringer of War'. After Cecil decides to disobey his king's ruthless orders to slay innocent civilians, he is stripped of his command and exiled from Baron in dishonour; he appears to have transgressed the *bushidō* code and must therefore be emasculated as punishment. However, after the warmongering king is exposed as an imposter, the true king's ghost blesses Cecil and names him as his successor – restoring his title, honour and affirming Cecil's loyalty to his true lord. Ultimately, Cecil's story illustrates that true *bushidō* is not blind obedience to one's superiors, but rather loyalty to the principles of *bushidō* itself. This insight is musically encoded in 'Paladin' (associated with Cecil's transformation from Dark Knight into a holy Paladin), which features transcendent-topic harp arpeggiation, broad sustained string chords, and recontextualizes the brass melody from 'Red Wings' in the relative major key

(G minor → B♭ major). Conventionally masculine heroic-topic signifiers in this track, including brass and percussion, ascending leaps and modally borrowed flatted chords, illustrate that it was Cecil – not his more compliant Baron military peers – who carried out the true path of *bushidō* by upholding the honour, and not merely the power, of his lord. Cecil nuances and clarifies, but does not ultimately displace, hegemonic bushidō masculinity.[18]

Rosa's 'Theme of Love' showcases musical gendering at work, exhibiting virtually every common feature of conventional musical femininity. Its lyrical woodwind melody, arpeggiated harp, lush strings, Romantic style, expressive chromaticism and periodic phrasing strikingly parallel the conventions established in 'Elia, the Maiden of Water' and exemplified in 'Leia's Theme' (especially in *Distant Worlds*' 'Theme of Love' arrangement). Rosa is repeatedly sidelined by illness or abduction, prompting Cecil and the others to retrieve a Sand Pearl to cure her from Desert Fever or to rescue her from Kain and Golbez at the Tower of Zot. Even when Rosa acts independently, refusing to be left behind and joining the final battle, Cecil vows to protect her, as he has all along. Rosa encapsulates the 'emphasized femininity' archetype – women who, by exemplifying conventional femininity, function to reinforce hegemonic masculinity's position of power. Both Rosa's character and music conform to hegemonic gender norms, sharpening the conventional standard passed down from Aria for later female characters to follow, subvert or defy.[19]

FFV *(1992)*

The fifth *FF* is an oddity in countless ways, including the character development of its hero, Bartz. Curiously, Bartz does not possess a personal musical theme, reflecting his status as an orphan and perpetual wanderer, drawing his chameleonic identity from wherever he travels rather than bringing his own personality into the story. Though lacking a named theme, Bartz is typically associated with a piece of location-based music. 'Home Sweet Home', the music of Bartz's hometown Lix, does not participate in the conventionally feminine-to-masculine spectrum, since it is not primarily intended for a person. Its Dorian-mode melody, VII-i cadential harmonies, Baroque-era counterpoint and rustic instrumentation suggest ancientness rather than conventional masculinity or conventional femininity. That Bartz develops no canonized romance is perhaps another reason he is not musically masculinized, functioning instead primarily as a surrogate through which players may immerse into the narrative. Providing player characters relatively devoid of individuality is a common technique in a variety of video game genres, from Japanese visual novels to western first-person shooters and sports games. *FFI* and *FFIII* similarly employed this strategy, using class-based player characters rather than ones with character arcs and backstories, each exhibiting an apparently masculine appearance. This approach preserves masculinity's place as the invisible, presumed default, as players are expected to immerse vicariously into a male character's subjectivity – though the reverse is rarely true in games from this era.

Lenna, like many other folklore princesses, does not innovate female representation but rather perpetuates the conventional standards of emphasized femininity. Like 'Theme of Love', 'Lenna's Theme' conforms strongly to conventional femininity, with prominent flute melody, arpeggiation, string chords and periodic phrasing throughout. 'Lenna's Theme' fulfils a similar role to 'Elia, the Maiden of Water', as Lenna's music is the only character theme for a playable protagonist in the game's soundtrack (with the above acknowledgement that Bartz's association with 'Home Sweet Home' is an indirect one). Not even Faris, a supporting character with much more interesting and innovative character development, has music of her own. Considering the precedent of Aria Benett, this fact once more illustrates musical gender construction as a marked opposition, in Hatten's terminology – Lenna's femininity must be musically distinguished, while Bartz's gendering need not be remarked on by the score. In 'Lenna's Theme', hints of a pop-ballad topic emerge via the synthesized electric bass timbre, which foreshadows a feminized musical convention from later entries in the series. Lenna's personality is defined by her compassionate and self-sacrificial nature – classic feminine traits in the West and especially in Japan via the culturally privileged *sengyōshufu* (専業主婦; 'housewife') femininity embodying the traditional ideal of *ryōsaikenbo* (良妻 賢母; 'good wife, wise mother') who sacrifices her time and vitality to meet the needs of the family (Pasaribu 2020, 52–53). Her most memorable narrative moments involve two separate acts of self-sacrifice in order to save a dying dragon: (1) traversing a field of toxic flowers and (2) ingesting grass poisonous to humans in order to persuade an ill dragon of its safety. Though compassion is an excellent character trait, it is far too often considered a conventionally feminine one. Lenna does not notably digress from Rosa's precedent.

FFVI *(1994)*

FFVI is distinctive in gender representation, featuring not one but two lead female protagonists: Terra and Celes. 'Terra's Theme' is the sole outlier to conventionally feminine music in the series' early years, with a 'mournful', 'tragic' A section that contrasts serene, major-mode femininity through its minor-mode melody and military snare drum (Summers 2016, 207). Rather than inspiring romantic love, it establishes a contemplative, mysterious mood for the game's opening. Richard Anatone argues that the track's B section – in the relative major, with rising French horn and string melody, driving staccato chords and rousing percussion – is Terra's true theme (Anatone 2021). If so, it is significant that 'Awakening' – heard when Terra is first introduced by name – lacks this heroic B section, corresponding to Terra's memory loss and traumatization from being mind-controlled by Kefka and the Gestahlian Empire. By the story's end, the heroic B section has swapped places with the tragic A section to occupy the primary position during Terra's portion of the 'Ending Theme'. This triumphant core of 'Terra's Theme' most resembles the signature heroic topic of conventionally masculine themes, since she occupies the position typically held by male characters. Terra is a significant outlier among a predominantly binary gendered pattern, gesturing towards a new path for empowered female characters.

Celes and Terra share a considerable degree of their backstory; each was raised by an empire official as a Magitek Knight,[20] committed war atrocities in the name of the empire, and ultimately defected to the Returners with the aid of Locke. However, the two heroes then diverge dramatically – in both music and gender representation. Celes's musical identity is even further obscured than Terra's, as her introduction is underscored by 'Under Martial Law', which is a location- and narrative-based theme associated with the imperial occupation rather than Celes in particular. It is only through the events of FFVI's narrative that Celes establishes a musical agency independent from the empire. 'Celes's Theme' derives from her iconic opera solo 'Aria di Mezzo Carattere', initially donned as a dramatic persona with the intention of escaping her past and reinventing her identity; its adaptation into a personalized theme suggests Celes's internalization of aspects of her fictional operatic role (Thompson 2020, 124). This instrumental aria closely follows conventionally feminine patterns including major mode, harp arpeggiation, lyrical melody and periodic phrasing. A retransition at the loop point of 'Celes's Theme' utilizing ♭III, ♭II, ♭VI, and ♭VII chords constitutes an exception to the norm, contributing a heroic inflection that somewhat mitigates Celes's musical feminization. However, Celes becomes increasingly characterized by her romance with Locke; her theme plays only when pining for him, and their themes are interwoven in the 'Ending Theme'. While Terra musically defies gendered convention, Celes ultimately embraces it.

The treasure hunter (read: thief) Locke seems an unlikely protagonist – therefore, his music compensates, asserting a clear heroic identity on his behalf. Locke's assertive, outgoing personality and agile, acrobatic combat style is amply encoded in his musical theme. Tim Summers observes that 'Locke's Theme' is replete with 'standard signifiers of heroism' including major mode, rapidly ascending melodic leaps, military brass and percussion, staccato block chords, modally borrowed flatted chords in major and fast tempo (Summers 2016, 207). The tender, bittersweet variant 'Forever Rachel' plays in connection with Locke's tragic romantic backstory, but returns voiced by heroic French horn in the 'Ending Theme'. Musically, Locke is thoroughly, conventionally masculine.

FFVII *(1997)*

Like Bartz, Cloud has no clearly named musical theme; rather, the 'Main Theme of *Final Fantasy VII*' is perhaps his most closely associated music. This attribution is quite debatable, though the ambiguity does not greatly impact the present argument; if one does not associate the 'Main Theme' with Cloud's development, then Cloud lacks any character theme and his musical gender representation simply falls outside the scope of the present investigation. That Cloud has no clear musical identity is appropriate because he has suppressed his memories after traumatization, instead assuming an arrogant false persona as an ex-SOLDIER mercenary.[21] Only after departing from Midgar – the epicentre of SOLDIER operations and the cornerstone of Cloud's assumed identity – is the 'Main Theme' heard, suggesting that the ensuing journey across the gameworld chronicles Cloud's arc of self-discovery and reconstructed individuality. The 'Main Theme' is difficult to categorize according to gendering, as it spans many styles and textures, from lyrical ballad to lush symphonic climax – even a mechanistic, industrial aesthetic gesturing towards the narrative's darker themes. Its core melody is feminine in instrumentation, accompaniment, tempo and style, while its 'epic' orchestration, Picardy-Aeolian cadences ($\flat$VI–$\flat$VII-I) and foregrounded brass seem more conventionally masculine. If associated with the Cloud, the 'Main Theme' signifies his raw potentiality, his identity unfolding and evolving throughout the journey itself. Similarly to Bartz, Cloud's characterization creates a blank slate for players to experience narrative events more personally.

Aerith and Tifa split the position of a primary female character, both involved in a love triangle with Cloud. 'Aerith's Theme' largely conforms to conventionally feminine patterns, particularly through its arpeggiated harp, singing-style oboe melody, Romantic-era style and periodic phrasing. The unusual inclusion of a heroic brass countermelody in the A section's forte consequent phrase somewhat mitigates her theme's conventionality. A variation of 'Aerith's Theme', 'Flowers Blooming in the Church', features the theme's melodic material in a gentle, waltz-like compound meter, reinforcing her feminization. Preceding the appearance of 'Aerith's Theme', 'Flowers Blooming in the Church' is heard during Aerith's introduction, inflecting players' first impression of her towards the feminine end of the spectrum. Like Rosa, Aerith is a frequent damsel-in-distress, and when she acts independently to stop the villainous Sephiroth herself, he impales her in *FF*'s most iconic death scene. Thus, Aerith mostly conforms to conventionally feminine narrative and musical expectations.

The no-nonsense Tifa might be expected to have less conventionally feminine music than Aerith, but this is not entirely the case. Rather, 'Tifa's Theme' displays virtually the same gendered properties as Aerith's, owing to Tifa's characterization as a romantic interest for Cloud. Summers writes: 'Tifa's music conforms to musical stereotypes of a "feminine" theme' with a cantabile melody and arpeggiating accompaniment (2016, 207). Though its primary melodic instruments are flute and oboe – familiar instruments communicating femininity in the vein of Aria's and Rosa's themes – the melody's repetition is played by bassoon, out of step with conventional musical femininity due to its low registration. After Aerith's death, Tifa is increasingly characterized by her romantic potential with Cloud, especially while caring for him after his mako overdose.[22] On the other hand, Tifa does free herself from execution and is named leader of the party while Cloud is unconscious, so she is granted a few empowered narrative moments. This partial subversion of conventionally feminine narrative expectations is musically encoded by the marked presence of tenor-register bassoon, positioning Tifa closer a middleground between conventional femininity and conventional masculinity.

FFVIII *(1999)*

No character theme tries as earnestly to be masculine as Squall's 'Maybe I'm a Lion', combining with his taciturn demeanour to overcompensate for his internal insecurities. Opening with a hypermasculine shout from male voices, Squall's music exudes conventionally masculine stereotypes, blending heavy metal electric guitars and tribal percussion. Heavy metal culture, like that of many hard rock scenes, is 'very much a male-dominated arena', promoting primal, aggressive and hypermasculine attitudes (Vocum Personae 2015). It may be observed that 'Maybe I'm a Lion' is a combat cue, making its heavy metal inflection less surprising. However, Squall's own identity as a mercenary warrior is also inextricably bound up in combat, channelling bushidō warrior masculinity. Despite this masculinist affectation, the track does not succeed in truly channelling heavy metal, due to its slow (for metal) tempo of 110 bpm, rhythmically sparse drum set, non-rearticulated guitar chords and melody generally on synth organ rather than guitar. Accordingly, Squall confesses to a comatose Rinoa that his brusqueness is a front, hiding his anxieties concerning what others think about him. Another track associated with Squall, the sombre string adagio 'The Oath', hints at his inner sensitivity and complexity.

Rinoa represents missed potential as an empowered female hero whose agency is contained via romance with a male character. 'My Mind' features electric guitar and an ambiguous toy piano sound as melodic instruments; neither are musical signifiers of conventional femininity. The melody and accompaniment are rather typical for conventionally feminine themes, and the synthesized strings suggest a pop ballad style. The B section of 'My Mind' is the chorus of 'Eyes on Me', the pop ballad from the credits, inaugurating a trend seen in subsequent *FF* titles of calling to mind Japan's idol culture and linking the female character's identity to the game's 'happy ending'. 'Eyes on Me' is narratively and musically linked to another romance between Laguna and Julia, Rinoa's mother. Julia is much more conventionally feminine, imbuing the recurring melody from 'My Mind' with FRC-like function through romantic associations. Rinoa's initial independence and headstrong leadership of the Forest Owls resistance group transform into an increasing romantic attachment to Squall, and she is rendered a damsel-in-distress for him to rescue several times through capture, possession and even floating adrift in outer space. Once more, romance becomes a vehicle to contain and conventionalize potentially deviant femininities; although Rinoa enters as the hero of her own story, she is increasingly rendered little more than a romantic accessory to Squall's development.

FFIX *(2000)*

To western audiences, Zidane may not seem conventionally masculine; for the original Japanese context, however, the lithe, confident ladies' man is a mainstream conventionally masculine archetype, the *bishōnen* (美少年; 'beautiful young man'). Originating in the seventeenth century as the younger partner in a male-male *nanshoku* (男色; male-male eroticism, lit. 'man colour') pair, the *bishōnen* today has become a confident, popular playboy winning the hearts of his female peers – an archetype exemplified by Tamaki Suō in *Ouran High School Host Club* (2006) (McLelland 2020). The *bishōnen*'s nanshoku associations became predominantly heterosexualized among early 1900s Japanese high school boy culture, where gruff, aggressive *kōha* (硬派; 'manly man', lit. 'hard faction') were known for sexual conquests of younger male *kōhai* (後輩; 'junior') while more emotionally sensitive, romantically expressive *nanpa* (ナンパ, 'to flirt', from a reading of 軟派; 'ladies' man, playboy', lit. 'soft faction') wooed and entered relationships with their female peers (Angles 2011, 17–18). After a period of suppression and 'renewed emphasis on masculine vigor and physique' during the Second World War, the smooth-talking 'pretty boy' *bishōnen* became a mainstream staple of the performing arts (e.g. Miwa Akihiro and Shinnosuke 'Peter' Ikehata, 1950–60s) and manga/anime series (1970s–present), typically portrayed as highly influential, desirable and successful (McLelland 2020).[23] 'Zidane's Theme' encapsulates his flirtatious nature, which is foregrounded in the first half of the *FFIX*. Exhibiting a fast tempo, driving rhythm, military snare drum, staccato accompaniment and leaping melody, the A section embodies confident, optimistic heroism in accord with conventionally masculine themes such as Locke's. The following B section consists of a jaunty swing tune encoding Zidane's carefree attitude and incorrigible flirtatiousness with women, reflecting his nature as a successful *nanpa bishōnen* (Angles 2011, 17). Though Zidane's named character theme presents an unambiguous masculinist façade, Zidane experiences much character development over the story's unfolding. The cue 'Not Alone', prominently featured after Zidane has despaired, but learned to rely on his friends, bears greater musical depth and marks his growth as an individual. While Zidane is a promising case for tracing the development of gender representation throughout a game's narrative, his early musical characterization in 'Zidane's Theme' is classically masculine, reflecting his projected nanpa persona.

'Garnet's Theme' includes conventionally feminine flute and oboe, major mode, slow tempo, triple meter, harmonic sequencing and a simple melody derived from the credits' pop ballad 'Melodies of Life'. Crotales, the main melodic instrument, is not customarily gendered, nor is the pizzicato upright bass or sleigh bells that enter in the B section. The pastoral-topic flute, clarinet and woodwind oscillations recall 'Flowers Blooming in the Church', befitting a serene conventional femininity. Much like 'My Mind' from *FFVIII*, this music's connection to the J-pop idol ballad 'Melodies of Life' reinforces its conventionally feminine signification. Sean Atkinson argues that a fast variant featuring a heroic brass fanfare, playing as Garnet leaps from a castle wall to escape, paints her as independent rather than a stereotypical, damsel-in-distress princess (Atkinson 2022, 143). Indeed, the escape scene leaves quite a strong empowered first impression; however, Garnet's named theme, heard later during extensive dialogue scenes with Zidane, communicates a more conventional, romantic femininity. A handful of other tracks incorporate melodic material from 'Melodies of Life', further enriching its musical significance; like Rinoa, or even Celes before her, Garnet's gendering becomes increasingly bound up in the game's romantic happy ending and her relationship with Zidane, containing her earlier deviations into a conventional love interest role.

FFX *(2001)*

The aspiring blitzball[24] champion Tidus lives in his father Jecht's shadow, who was widely considered an unrivalled blitzball player before vanishing ten years before the game. Tidus often dreams of his father insulting him, demeaning his masculinity and causing Tidus's mother to ignore him in favour of spending time with Jecht. However, Tidus unconsciously mirrors the demeanour and personality traits of the man he loathes most, including his carefree attitude and tendency to run from responsibility. Tidus's mentor Auron, who travelled extensively with Jecht, points out Tidus's similarities in temperament to Jecht, admonishing Tidus on one occasion that he is 'the one running away', just as he believes his father did. 'Tidus's Theme' is a relaxed ballad featuring acoustic guitar and melodica, borrowing the primary instrumentation of 'Jecht's Theme', a twelve-bar blues featuring acoustic guitar and non-distorted electric guitar. The nonchalant timbre of the acoustic guitar in both tracks encodes Tidus's imitation of Jecht's easygoing manner and other qualities. In terms of gendering, Tidus's music exhibits conventionally feminine traits, including arpeggiation, lyrical melody and periodic phrasing, without employing conventionally masculine tropes like the military/heroic topic, brass, percussion, forte dynamic or fast tempo. This subversion encodes Tidus's process of wrestling with his father's legacy and striving to become a different kind of man. Tidus's character and music blur gendered boundaries, as he matures into a masculinity he can call his own, rather than inheriting behaviour patterns that he despises in his father.

Like the preceding two conventionally feminine themes, 'Yuna's Theme' derives from the game's J-pop ballad, 'Suteki da ne'. After a wistful Lydian-mode flute introduction, 'Yuna's Theme' exemplifies conventionally feminine melody and accompaniment, played on a gender-neutral melodica to connect to 'Tidus's Theme' and musically signifying their romantic relationship. This meaning is reinforced when 'Suteki da ne' debuts during the extensive romantic cutscene between Yuna and Tidus at Macalania Spring. Interestingly, 'Yuna's Theme' contains a clear melodic reference to 'Aerith's Theme' from *FFVII*, suggesting that her predecessor's famous self-sacrifice will be echoed in Yuna's giving her own life to defeat the calamity Sin. As in Lenna's case, self-sacrifice like Aerith's and Yuna's is a conventionally feminine trait. The game's narrative trajectory consists of the characters' efforts to discover an alternative means of saving the land of Spira from Sin. Yuna is protected by a team of guardians, kidnapped for ransom, pressured to marry the villainous Seymour and repeatedly instructed to sacrifice her life to restore world peace. However, she does rescue herself from her forced marriage by leaping off a high rooftop and using her summoner abilities to break her own fall, exhibiting more empowered narrative agency – though this is not reflected musically.

FFXII *(2006)*

Of all *FF* protagonists, Vaan is the most forgettable, with a backstory concerning his late brother – a knight and casualty of war – that resolves in the story's first half; accordingly, he, like Bartz and Cloud, has no named musical theme. Instead,

'The Dream to be a Sky Pirate', heard when Vaan shares his dream to become one, is most closely associated with him. This brief track opens with a conventionally feminine piano texture, moving into an adventurous orchestral flourish that leans towards conventionally masculine conventions but evokes a sense of flight and expansiveness more clearly than gender. This void of gender construction points both to Vaan's youth – prior to his coming of age as a man – and providing a narratively empty avatar for players to experience the story's events (as in Bartz's case). Vaan cedes the musical and narrative spotlight to *FFXII*'s true main character – Ashe.

Shortly after her happy marriage, Princess Ashe's homeland is invaded and her new husband slain in battle. The game's narrative traces Ashe's quest to reclaim her throne and decide whether to pursue peace or vengeance. 'Ashe's Theme' defies easy classification, spanning a wide range of textures and reflecting her depth of character. The track consists of three stylistically distinct sections, and only one invokes flute and harp in conventionally feminine ways. The other sections draw on dark, dissonant harmonies and staccato, industrial timbres, contrasting the cheerful innocence of most conventionally feminine themes. Combined with the prominent usage of heroic French horns, 'Ashe's Theme' is unique in following masculine conventions more closely than feminine conventions, as 'Terra's Theme' did. In terms of its expressive range, it is most akin to *FFVII*'s 'Main Theme', suggesting that *FFXII* tells Ashe's story through a variety of circumstances and situations rather than pigeonholing her into an archetype. Though *FFXII*'s antagonists attempt to manipulate Ashe's actions by using her deceased husband's ghost as a guise, Ashe learns to let go of her husband and seize her own decision-making agency. Thus, she stands in stark contrast to Celes, Tifa, Rinoa and the expectations of the FRC, refusing to be contained by a romantic connection to a male character. Overall, 'Ashe's Theme' musically resembles conventional masculinity more than conventional femininity. In both narrative and musical development, Ashe, rather than Vaan, is the game's main character.

To make a few brief analytical remarks on the overarching findings of this study, the majority of *FF* main character themes establish gendered conventions that follow a remarkably consistent pattern – especially for its conventionally feminine themes. Though not demonstrated in a broad longitudinal survey like this one, some characters musically subvert gendered expectations by having multiple themes or via later thematic variation and development. The overall analysis reveals a trajectory towards greater female character agency and more nuanced presentation of femininity and masculinity over time; Cecil and Rosa adhere entirely to traditional gender norms, while Ashe offers a hopeful promissory note for a way forward – and Chapter 3 will demonstrate two of the franchise's subsequent progressive developments. Ashe is a robust, multilayered lead character who drives the game's central narrative and defies easy definition by romance or the will of male characters in her life. Accordingly, this shift is aurally reflected in 'Ashe's Theme' – significantly coinciding with the series' shift away from Nobuo Uematsu as sole series composer towards the talents and perspectives of others. Finally, Terra is a significant outlier in this historical progression, standing as an empowered female lead character who narratively and musically defies conventional femininity.

Uematsu's legacy of musical gendering conventions in the *FF* franchise remains palpable as a normalized voice to which later compositional perspectives respond. In the music of *FF*, Uematsu inherited, adapted and perpetuated traditionally gendered musical stereotypes, particularly in his conventionally feminine themes. Like the FRC in early film, these musical traits mark female characters as the feminized 'other' – secondary to the central narrative, characterized as an idealized woman rather than a unique individual and valued as the object of a male character's romantic affection rather than an empowered agent in her own right. Despite establishing the series' conventionally feminine and conventionally masculine musical archetypes, Uematsu also cleverly subverted that standard in subtle ways, signalling more nuanced depth of character; this is most prominent in the themes of Terra, Tifa and Tidus. However, these notable outliers also highlight the consistency of other main characters' musical gendering. Overall, employing conventionally feminine and conventionally masculine musical strategies reinforces problematic disparities in gender representation. Though beyond the scope of this investigation, Uematsu's music is doubtless one of the most impactful in video game music history – especially to Japanese-produced video games, but likewise in global markets. Though he did not invent gendered musical conventions, his usage ensured their perpetuation in numerous video game scores in the following decades; exploring how other composers adopt or transform Uematsu's precedent in musical gender representation is worth further study. Ultimately, it was necessary to pass the torch to other composers – Hitoshi Sakimoto (*FFXII*), Masashi Hamauzu (*FFXIII*) and Yōko Shimomura (*FFXV*) – in order to innovate and reimagine how the franchise's main character themes could sound.

The *FF* franchise has been present with me through my entire life. Doubtless, it has influenced my and others' perceptions of gender norms throughout Japan, Europe, the United States and the world. Music participates vitally in the societal construction of gender, whether in art, film or video games. Gendered musical conventions inevitably evolve, dancing in a semiotic spiral with the musical culture and the individuals that produce them. Nobuo Uematsu's compositional voice is embedded in my musical soul, shaping how I hear, analyse and create music.[25] As in the *FF* series, that impact cannot change – even as I choose to invite a diversified dialogue of voices into the conversation.

NOTES

* Supplementary Video 2.2 'Feminine Themings — The Construction of Musical Gendering in the *Final Fantasy* Franchise' can be found here: https://www.youtube.com/watch?v=bLth1ov8zrE. Accessed 3 June 2024. Standalone colour files of Figures 2.1 and 2.2, and standalone illustration files of Figure 2.3a–c can be found under the Front Matter section for *Gender, Race and Religion in Video Game Music's* page on Intellect Discover.

1. Even this formulation can and has been problematized in gender studies scholarship. For example, Judith Butler argues that there is no biological bedrock to which 'sex' terminology refers, but rather the terms are themselves idealizations – a performative and political imposition of symbolic order (cf. Butler 2011). Suffice it to say that social and scholarly discussion surrounding these terms remains contested, and this book does not need to settle the ontology of sex in order to analyse the cultural and musical conventions associated with socially constructed gender.

2. This chapter was written in 2020 and revised in early 2023. Though *Final Fantasy XVI* is scheduled to release in June 2023, the book's publication timeline does not permit its inclusion. I look forward to analysing gender construction in *FFXVI* in future scholarship.

3. Year calculations are from 1977 and 1987 to 2023, the year this chapter was written and revised. Though it will appear and be read later, the calculation is correct at the time of composition.

4. Gibbons identifies categories for 'location-based' and 'game-state' cues in the RPG. The former refers to music that accompanies the player's exploration of the gameworld (i.e., castle, dungeon, field), while the latter refers to situations like the game's title screen, the introduction and ending sequence. See Gibbons (2017).

5. The NES version of *FFIII* never received an official English-language translation, leading to ambiguity concerning Aria's name. In Japanese, Aria's name is エリア (lit. e-ri-a), leading to her being known as Elia prior to the worldwide release of the Nintendo DS remake in 2006. In the DS version, her name was localized as 'Aria', most likely to sound more natural as an English name. Because most subsequent English versions of the game (iOS, Android, PlayStation Store, Steam) have been ports of the DS remake, she has been known primarily as 'Aria' ever since 2006. However, the 2022 mobile pixel remaster ports of the NES *FFIII* preserved the Japanese spelling and used Elia once more. Name changes from Japanese to English that are updated in later editions were common in early video games (e.g. Aerith's name initially appearing in English as "Aeris"). I use 'Elia, the Maiden of Water' for Aria's music even though her name is different, as the DS title 'Priestess Aria' is further removed from the linguistic structure and meaning of the Japanese title.

6. See https://youtu.be/KRcJRifpf2U (accessed 22 February 2024) to view the montage video, 'The Construction of Musical Gendering in the Final Fantasy Series'. The video spans the main series *FF* games from *FFIV* to *FFXV*. *FFXI* and *FFXIV* are omitted due to being massively multiplayer online role-playing games (MMORPG), lacking a centralized narrative or main characters. *FFVI* and *FFVII* each contain two main female protagonists, both of whom are shown. *FFXIII* does

not have a clear primary male protagonist, and *FFXV* does not contain any permanent female party characters. Sequel games are not shown. Finally, the attribution of musical themes for Cecil, Bartz and Cloud bears some ambiguity, which is discussed in the game-by-game analysis in the subsection titled 'Musical Narrativising: Male and Female Character Theme Analyses'.

7. See Chapters 2 and 3 of Hatten (1994).

8. At the time of writing, it has become common in broader popular culture to refer to 'toxic masculinity'. I prefer 'hegemonic masculinity' as a term and concept to toxic masculinity (though the two are not identical in meaning). Hegemonic masculinity is a foundational concept in academic gender studies and is value judgement-free and more precise in specifying the relationship between hegemonic masculinity, femininity and alternative masculinities. The crucial insight is that hegemonic masculinity enforces unequal power dynamics on femininity and alternative masculinities – and therein lies its toxicity. Also, not all elements of a culture's hegemonic masculinity may be intrinsically toxic (e.g. the pursuit of honour in Japanese bushidō masculinity); however, when imposed as the ideal standard and discouraging alternative expressions, the normative masculinity perpetuates unequal power relationships between groups of people. Thus, the hierarchical structure itself may rightly be termed 'toxic'.

9. Nobuo Uematsu also composed the soundtrack to *Nakayama Miho no Tokimeki High School* (NES 1987), a dating simulation game that involves Miho Nakayama (a real-life Japanese pop idol), whom the player's avatar tries to date. The soundtrack contains several tracks that incorporate the pop ballad style. See Alan Elkins's chapter in Richard Anatone's (ed.) *The Music of Nobuo Uematsu in the* Final Fantasy *Series* (2022).

10. Daniel Black's study of the virtual idol Hatsune Miku (Galbraith and Karlin 2012) reveals a profound parallel to female characters in video games. The real-or-virtual idol's *kawaii* femininity 'evokes youthful innocence, vulnerability, and meekness, and a lack of remoteness or self- sufficiency' (Galbraith and Karlin 2012, 219). However, unlike real idols – who can betray her fans' adoration by falling from grace into controversy or scandal – a virtual idol like Hatsune Miku can never sully her kawaii purity (Galbraith and Karlin 2012, 224). The conventionally feminine ideal, though 'unlikely to be satisfactorily embodied in any living human being' (Galbraith and Karlin 2012, 219), may be realized as a virtual woman in a paradoxical 'technologised, artificial, endearing, and seductive fantasy of femininity' (Galbraith and Karlin 2012, 225). Thus, the connection between the FFVII–X female protagonists and J-pop idol culture may well bear more pernicious meanings than simply marking them as feminine rather than masculine. Considering the similarity of the FRC in film, idealizing – or, perhaps more fittingly, idolizing – fictional female characters as embodying the perfect femininity that real women cannot fulfil has a long and widespread pedigree.

11. Vocalists include Faye Wong ('Eyes on Me'), Emiko Shiratori ('Melodies of Life') and RIKKI ('Suteki da ne'). That these themes were initially conceived as vocal pieces in a pop ballad genre and then retrojected into earlier parts of the score as instrumental versions is implied by Nobuo Uematsu's interview concerning the creation of 'Suteki da ne' in *Beyond Final Fantasy*: 'Regarding the theme song, my first concern was to find someone to sing it' (Uematsu 2002, 2:02).

Similarly, Uematsu recalls writing ten versions of the song's music in an all-night composing session: 'I completed the melody first so I had [Kazushige] Nojima write the lyrics afterwards. We both celebrated the night it was completed.' Rinoa's, Garnet's and Yuna's instrumental themes should be conceived as musically prefiguring their vocal pop ballad counterparts.

12. As mentioned in note 5, *FFXI* and *XIV* are omitted from this project's scope for a number of reasons: (1) as MMORPG games, the two lack centralized narrative and main characters, making narratological music analysis difficult; (2) Uematsu did compose a number of tracks for *FFXI*, in collaboration with Naoshi Mizuta and Kumi Tanioka. Thus, *FFXII* marks the clearest break from Uematsu's influence and involvement in the series; (3) the *FFXI* and *XIV* scores contain predominantly location-based and game-state tracks rather than character themes. *FFXI* contains unique character creation cues for each race, divided by male and female, but these are not true character themes. *FFXIV* contains character themes for guest character cameos from other *FF* games (e.g. Shantotto, Gilgamesh), which is more of an intertextual quotation or arrangement than a character theme for *FFXIV* per se.

13. The attributes described in table should be understood as properties that cumulatively move a piece of music further towards conventional masculinity or femininity, but none is solely a necessary or sufficient condition for a passage being conventionally masculine or feminine. As in musical topic theory, a theme may exhibit musical masculinity or femininity to varying degrees and by employing different components of the paradigm. As Frank Lehman writes concerning film music cadences, the musical construction of conventional masculinity and femininity is 'best formulated in terms of paradigm cases and attributes', gesturing towards paradigms with fuzzy boundaries rather than a transcendent Platonic form (2013, 3.7– 3.8, original emphasis). My aim in the present project concerning musical gender construction in video games is akin to Lehman's work with cadences in film.

14. Massively multiplayer online role-playing game.

15. Secondary themes mentioned include 'Paladin' (*FFIV*), 'Awakening' (*FFVI*), 'Aria di Mezzo Carattere' (*FFVI*), 'Ending Theme' (*FFVI*), 'Forever Rachel' (*FFVI*), 'Flowers Blooming in the Church' (*FFVII*), 'The Oath' (*FFVIII*), 'Eyes on Me' (*FFVIII*), 'Not Alone' (*FFIX*), 'Melodies of Life' (*FFIX*), 'Suteki da ne' (*FFX*) and 'Blinded by Light' (*FFXIII*).

16. Ultimately, selecting any musical theme as primarily exemplifying a character is somewhat artificial, and other readers or players may hold differing opinions about the themes I have selected in this chapter. I welcome analyses of other character themes – especially detailed case studies that draw together all of a character's associated themes throughout a game – to dialogue with the brief treatment I have provided in this chapter.

17. See Video 2.1, 'The Construction of Musical Gendering in the *Final Fantasy* Series': https://www.youtube.com/watch?v=KRcJRifpf2U. Accessed 3 June 2024.

18. For an in-depth case study of the transformation of Cecil's musical themes, see Atkinson (2019).

19. Rydia and 'Rydia's Theme' are not included because – despite the compelling nature of her development arc – Rydia more closely occupies the 'second woman' position (in operatic terms) than the clear 'first woman' archetype of Rosa. Also, including Rydia would entail including other prominent 'second women' such as Faris and Quistis, further expanding the scope of the project. However, note that 'Rydia's Theme' exhibits clear, conventionally feminine musical traits as described in this chapter, similarly to 'Theme of Love', inflected with a greater degree of innocence corresponding to her youth. Her highly feminized theme repeats verbatim even after reuniting with the party as a fully grown woman and defeating the antagonist that the party could not overcome; thus, Rydia's music likewise genders her in problematic ways and denies her independent agency.

20. Soldiers of the Gestahlian Empire with a rare ability to cast magic and pilot the formidable Magitek armour.

21. An elite super-soldier military force boasting superhuman physique and combat skill.

22. A refined form of the planet's energy and the source of technological and magical power in the gameworld.

23. The Boys' Love (abbreviated 'BL', Japanese 少年愛; *shōnen ai*) genre of *shōjo* manga (marketed towards young women) features *bishōnen* who pursue romance with one another, constituting one of a number of prominent representations of the *bishōnen* in Japanese media culture. Female manga artists in the 1970s (e.g. Riyoko Ikeda, Moto Hagio and Keiko Takamiya) adapted the *bishōnen* as an idealized, romanticized masculinity for heterosexual female enjoyment, which persists in the BL genre today (McLelland 2020). In other words, it is precisely the *bishōnen*'s mainstream success as a nanpa – successful flirtation and desirability with women – that fuelled the *bishōnen*'s adaptation into BL. While 'hard-line' men may deride the *bishōnen* as an insincere seducer leading women astray, the *bishōnen*'s association with homoeroticism in BL does not undermine perception of their masculinity in Japanese culture.

24. A ball-based sport played underwater, providing the gameworld's main source of entertainment.

25. My earliest musical memory is hearing 'Red Wings' while playing *FFIV* on the SNES, and Nobuo Uematsu's music was the primary influence motivating me to pursue music composition.

3

Single Ladies and Herbivore Men: Alternative Femininities and Masculinities in *Final Fantasy XIII* and *XV*

Introduction: Clothes Don't Make the Man

In December 2020, pop music star Harry Styles became the first man featured on the cover of *Vogue* magazine. Rocking a periwinkle ballgown and other dresses throughout the gallery, Styles attracted vociferous critique from conservative commentators like Candace Owens, who declared the need to 'bring back manly men', and Ben Shapiro, decrying Styles's outfit as a 'referendum on masculinity' (Wheeler 2020). A familiar page from the culture wars playbook, such objections cast any transgressive expression of masculinity or femininity as a threat to rigid, hegemonic gender order. However, conservative critics were not Styles's only detractors. Actor Billy Porter – a pioneer of androgynous outfits – questioned whether Styles understood the gravity of wearing the clothes which for Porter, a gay Black man, was a matter of life and death (Blistein 2021). Others alleged that a presumably heterosexual man should not be the representative for gender-nonconforming fashion (Smith 2021). Alok Vaid-Menon appealed to cultural appropriation, arguing that gender-subversive aesthetics were cultivated by transgender models passed over in favour of Styles (Rodgers 2020). While conservative outcry foretold the demise of gender itself, others saw Styles's move as insufficiently radical.

But these objections – though understandable considering the long history of conflating non-normativity and queer sexuality – are misplaced and, at worst, ultimately reinforce conservative pundits' core assumption. By questioning Styles's queer community bona fides or probing his sexual preferences and history, these objections presume a necessary link between non-normative fashion choices and queer sexuality or non-binary gender identity. This merely plays into the hegemonic gendered order's hands, which insists that dresses and other conventionally feminized outfits are off-limits for 'true men'. Rather, for Styles, avoiding any clothing because it is conventionally feminine '[shuts] out a world of great clothes'

(Moniuszko 2020, n.pag.). 'I want things to look a certain way', Styles explained, '[not] because it makes me look gay, or it makes me look straight, or it makes me look bisexual, but because I think it looks cool' (Wheeler 2020, n.pag.). In other words, Styles wearing dresses on *Vogue*'s cover is no coded coming-out statement, but rather an affirmation of diverse fashion choices for men of any sexuality. If this gambit succeeds, it eradicates the very foundation on which Owens and Shapiro stand, for Styles's *Vogue* cover becomes no more marked than any other runway outfit. Affirming alternative expressions of masculinity as no less legitimate than privileged expressions counteracts hegemonic masculinity.

Society vigilantly polices countless minutiae to enforce conformity to hegemonic masculine norms. Clothing and other modes of visual presentation are among the most visible – and therefore most heavily regulated. For instance, British football star David Beckham received ridicule and backlash for donning a sarong – interpreted by objectors as a type of skirt – during the 1998 World Cup (in its originating Indonesia, men and women alike wear sarong). Anything that questions conventional distinctions between men's and women's fashion is decried as a threat to the natural order of gender essentialism (Holland 2004, 78). In western cultures, the result of this dynamic is termed the Great Masculine Renunciation – shoehorning men's fashion options into a restrictive selection of forms and colours defined by restraint rather than individual expression (Holland 2004, 73–74). The narrow clothing choices left to men serve as a straitjacket – an apt analogy to hegemonic masculinity, which likewise validates a few modes of masculinity. Wherever rigid rules exist, however, there are those like Styles and Beckham who defy them, instead embracing alternativity and diversity.

Chapter 3 continues the critical analysis of gender representation in the music of *Final Fantasy* (*FF*) begun in Chapter 2. Where the previous chapter revealed remarkably consistent patterns in conventionally feminine and conventionally masculine musical themes for *FF* main characters, this chapter's analyses explore alternative femininities and masculinities that meaningfully subvert gendered conventions. Contextualizing the findings of the previous chapter, the study begins by explicating the concepts of hegemonic masculinity and emphasized femininity as the presumed default which essentialize conventional femininity and conventional masculinity as polarized opposites. However, the existence of alternative femininities and alternative masculinities challenges established gendered norms, reconstructing gender as individual and multiple rather than prescriptive and singular. Narrative and musical analyses of character themes for Lightning (*FFXIII*) and Noctis (*FFXV*) reveal protagonists that embody alternative femininity and alternative masculinity in a Japanese social context, with musical themes that transcend the conventional patterns established in the series' earlier instalments. *Final Fantasy XIII* (2009) features Lightning, a female protagonist embodying the *arafō*, a Japanese alternative femininity that is professionally successful and not defined by marriage or romance. As Lightning's character arc involves the holistic integration and expression of her emotions without suppression or exaggeration, 'Lightning's Theme' presents a nuanced musical characterization of Lightning's multifaceted personality. *Final Fantasy XV* (2016) presents Noctis as a *sōshokudanshi* who subverts hegemonic *bushidō* and salaryman masculinities, characterized by gentleness, emotional awareness and egalitarianism. 'Noctis's Theme' is remarkable in resembling conventionally feminine themes more than conventionally masculine ones, exemplifying musical alternativity for a new generation of heroes not bound by gendered conventions. These detailed case studies illustrate that there can be as many femininities and masculinities as there are individuals, contrary to the polarized essentialism of hegemonic masculinity. The line between subversion and transcendence is a thin one – for once the entire range of femininities and masculinities have been legitimized, they become fully overlapping, setting the foundation for future non-binary possibilities.

The Importance of Being Different: Alternative Masculinities and Femininities

A central question underpinning gender scholarship may be stated as: 'Are femininity and masculinity singular or plural?' While Chapter 2 explored the established gendered conventions of *FF*'s past, this chapter focuses on those norms' alternatives, subversions and negations. While hegemonic masculinity remains dominant in most societies, alternative modes of being exist. Though feminist and gender studies scholarship has done much to analyse, critique and deconstruct normative masculinity, positive accounts of alternative femininities and masculinities remain underexplored in both academia and popular culture (Carabí and Armengol 2014, 1). The result is that individuals wishing to break away from gendered norms often do not know how, and others interpret critiques of normative femininity or masculinity as assaults on femininity and masculinity itself. Therefore, it is imperative to examine media representation of alternative femininities and masculinities.

Hegemonic masculinity exists in fraught symbiosis both with other masculinities and with femininities. Defined by what it is not, hegemonic masculinity seeks to subjugate or eradicate anything in opposition to its values, even while paradoxically depending on them for existence. To render hegemonic masculinity visible requires naming that which it rejects; similarly, alternative femininities and masculinities may be defined as a subversion of assumed norms. Hegemonic masculinity rests on three premises that, taken together, portray femininity and masculinity as diametrically opposed:

1. **Difference Condition:** Femininity and masculinity are maximally different. If an attribute is considered conventionally masculine, its negation or opposite is conventionally feminine – and vice versa.
2. **Narrowness Condition:** The range of idealized femininity and masculinity is extremely narrow and difficult – even impossible – to attain.
3. **Essentiality Condition:** Gender differences are biologically hardwired in women and men. Thus, alternative femininities and masculinities defy the natural order of reality.

Conservative evangelical figurehead James Dobson expresses this perspective well: 'Males and females differ biochemically, anatomically, and emotionally [...] they are unique in every cell of their bodies' (Du Mez 2020, 82). By unique, Dobson means the opposite – men are rational while women are emotional, men assertive/ dominant and women passive/submissive and so on. Conventional masculinity is associated with 'public space, productive paid work outside the home, mind and rationality' and femininity with 'domestic space, reproductive unpaid house-work, body and emotions' (Rezeanu 2015, 16). In this view, '[w]hat is accepted as feminine cannot be accepted masculine at the same time' – there can be no ambiguity or blurring of boundaries (Buschmeyer 2013, 293). As a result, hegemonic masculinity polarizes perceived gendered differences and solidifies them through social convention. However, alternative femininities and masculinities challenge precisely the three conditions above, modelling other possibilities of expressing an individual's gender identity.

We may now proffer a working definition of alternative femininities and masculinities as any lifestyle 'in contrast with the norms of hegemonic masculinity and emphasised femininity' – hence the descriptor 'alternative' (Pasaribu 2020, 50). In the anglophone world, virtually every facet of society reinforces conventional gender stereotypes, from popular media and product marketing to clothing forms and shopping displays (Holland 2004, 65). These ubiquitous sources of gender socialization ensure that rejecting conventional gender norms for alternative femininity or masculinity – a process Raewyn Connell names 'renunciation' – requires considerable individual agency (Connell 2005 132). The common denominator of alternative femininities and masculinities is the rejection of the status quo, against all the societal pressures invested in maintaining it. As hegemonic masculinity presupposes the subordination of women, alternative masculinities typically subvert or resist this hierarchy. For example, Christian Groes-Green identifies 'philogynous masculinity' as promoting 'agency, security, respect and well-being' for women (Groes-Green 2012, 93). Michael Flood similarly describes men engaged in activism to end violence against women as 'counterhegemonic' (Flood 2014, 39). Other alternative masculinities include the 'New Father' – engaged in active parenting, domestic nurturing, and modelling empathy – and male kinder-garten teachers working in a career typically associated with women (Buschmeyer 2013; Requena-Pelegrí 2014, 117). Since 2000, Japan developed a diverse range of alternative masculinities including the *NEET* (not in employment, education or training), *freeter* (long-term part-time worker), *sōshokudanshi* (草食男子; lit. 'herbivore men'), *ikumen* (育メン; 'man taking an active role in childcare') and house-husband (Pasaribu 2020, 49). Alternative masculinity rejects the singular, normative use of masculinity as a generic account of what men are, instead affirm-ing 'a range of masculinities in society reflecting the differences amongst men' (Pease 2000, 8). In hegemonic masculinity, there are only true men and imposters; in alternativity, there are as many valid masculinities as there are men.

Hegemonic masculinity's counterpart is emphasized femininity (introduced in Chapter 2). Emphasized femininity consists of the negation and opposite of hegemonically masculine traits – for example, if assertiveness and dominance are valued in men, passivity and submission are valued in women. Though describing emphasized femininity in Japanese culture, Pasaribu's words could easily apply to anglophone contexts:

> An unambiguous woman is one who meets the standard of patriarchal values, a woman who supports the belief that men are dominant and have real power and authority [...] Men are expected to be active, exhibit strong leadership, work hard, and have economic and social power. To enable men to meet these standards, there must be binary opposition – a role that is passive and submissive, has no ambition, and less power.
>
> (Pasaribu 2020, 53)

Just as emphasized femininity exists, so too do alternative femininities. Typically, alternative femininities subvert or resist expectations that women will be quiet, submissive, physically weak, emotional, sexually/romantically available, bereft of agency and/or economically dependent on men. Examples in C. J. Pascoe's study of alternative femininities in high schools include the tomboy, honour student, athlete and those initiating romantic relationships (Pascoe 2018). Holland's extensive study of alternative femininities traces meaningful departures in British women's clothing, body type, hair, tattoo usage, career, personality and speaking style. For example, Holland develops semiotics of short hair length, variously signifying progressive politics, 'butch' aesthetics, liberation from normative beauty stand-ards, loss of feminine attractiveness and/or lesbian sexuality (Holland 2004, 62). In Japan, a series of pop culture terms for unmarried, childless working women emerged from approximately 2000–10: 'Christmas cake', 'parasite singles', *'make inu'*, *'ohitorisama'* and *'arafō'* – women deviating from the social script of marriage and domestic childcare (Mandujano-Salazar 2017, 531). However, this is not to say that these alternative femininities are without contestation. The act of labelling alternative femininities can diminish their power, rendering them 'easier to comprehend and less threatening and turning them into symbols of social progress and problems' (Freedman and Iwata-Weickgenannt 2011, 299). In other words, taxonomic labels may provide a target for derision and scorn or a convenient scapegoat for society's ills. As shall be seen, alternatives to prevailing gender norms invariably spawn controversy.

As with Chapter 2, the following analyses focus on Japanese media representation and cultural context. However, the broader themes gleaned are relevant to anglophone contexts. Japan presents a fascinating case study for media representation of alternative femininities and masculinities, as the year 2000 marks a burgeoning of media – particularly films and television shows – featuring alternative lifestyles and less rigid gender roles (Pasaribu 2020, 49). These alternative femininities and masculinities articulate sharp conflicts with hegemonic values, narratively encountered as internal or external naysayers to protagonists' unconventional choices (Pasaribu 2020, 55). Indeed, cultural battles over gender politics are familiar to the West and have yielded far-reaching consequences. For example, Du Mez traces conservative evangelical backlash against U.S. President Jimmy Carter's alternative masculinity – dubbed his 'wimp factor' by detractors – through a two-decade trajectory resulting in the astonishing presidential election of Donald Trump, who exemplified the hegemonic masculine values prized and cultivated by Christian evangelicalism (Du Mez 2020, 102, 268–69). As a recurring theme throughout this book, the stakes of fictional representation are very real – media representation of alternative femininity and masculinity stages real lifestyles and cultural changes for viewers to consider, understand and interpret (Mandujano-Salazar 2017, 540). And just as subverting any conventionally gendered norm potentially signals alternativity, so too does video game music communicate counterhegemonic meanings by defying the norms of its medium. The following case studies of *FFXIII* and *FFXV* explore the semiotics of alternativity in music.

'No One's Slave': Arafō *Femininity and Empowered Agency in* Final Fantasy XIII

I control my fate! … I'm no one's slave!

(Lightning Claire Farron, *Final Fantasy XIII* 2009)

Final Fantasy XIII's director Motomu Toriyama described the 'powerful, cool, calm, and collected' Lightning as the series' 'first female protagonist', elaborating that in *FFVI* 'every person within the party is a main character' (Bailey 2013, n.pag.). Whether or not his assessment of *FFVI* is considered correct, Toriyama's statement demonstrates series creators' awareness of Lightning's distinctive position within *FF*'s history of gender representation.[1] Lightning's popularity propelled her to become *FF*'s highest-rated female character twice (2013, 2017), Dengeki character of the year once (2013) – and even a Louis Vuitton fashion icon. Toriyama's character concept for Lightning originated as the 'strong woman' archetype (Hillier 2011), and artist Testuya Nomura designed her to be cool and strong, like a 'female version of Cloud from *FFVII*' – though producer Yoshinori Kitase downplayed this connection (GameZone 2012). The strong woman archetype stems from the Amazons of Greek mythology, resonating with the confident, independent female action hero of protest feminism such as Lara Croft or Bayonetta (Droumeva 2018, 60). Closer to the Japanese developers' historical context is the *onna-musha* or *onna-bugeisha* (女武者 and 女武芸者, respectively; both 'female warrior'), a tradition of *naginata*-wielding female warriors equally renowned on the battlefield as their male samurai peers. Legendary onna-musha including Empress Jingu, Tomoe Gozen and Akai Teruko constitute a noteworthy mythic precedent for Lightning – Gozen is described in *Heike Monogatari* as having the strength of a thousand warriors, outstripping the feats of her male peers, battling demons and commanding 300 samurai as Minamoto no Yoshinaka's second-in-command (McGee n.d.). Although the onna-musha archetype is seeded in Japanese history and literature as one viable alternative for women outside the domestic sphere, as *sengyōshufu* femininity (専業主婦, 'housewife') – already the primary mode of femininity – became the singular legitimized femininity during modern Japan's bubble economy years, the onna-musha faded into the annals of legend. From the outset, every narrative and aesthetic aspect of Lightning was created to subvert conventional ideals of Japanese emphasized femininity – and her music is no exception.

To contextualize Lightning's portrayal, it is crucial to note *FFXIII*'s release date: 2009. In Japanese society, the 1990s – known as the 'Lost Decade' (失われた十年, *ushinawareta jūnen*) – were years of economic stagnation and social unrest, after Japan's growing bubble economy in the 1980s abruptly burst in 1991. Hegemonic gendered norms that relied on economic success as a path to power such as *sararīman* masculinity (アラリーマン, lit. 'salaryman') and traditional *sengyōshufu* femininity appeared vulnerable and unsustainable as a default standard to which every family must conform. In the same decade, changes wrought by the Equal Employment Opportunity Law (passed in 1985) became progressively more tangible, as droves of women entered Japan's workforce for the first time. The result was a marked renegotiation of gender norms in the 2000s, as alternative femininities and masculinities emerged (including NEETs, *freeters*, *ikumen, sōshoukudanshi*, house husbands and *arafō*). During the 2000s, a range of terms was applied to unmarried working women, culminating in *arafō*'s selection as Japan's top neologism of 2008, coinciding with the airing of the hit television drama, *Around 40 (arafō* is an abbreviation of *araundo fōti*, transliterating 'around forty'). Writing in 2011, Freedman and Iwata-Weickgenannt reported the rise of a new type of female lead protagonist in Japanese media corresponding to the *arafō* – professional, independent, successful and unmarried (Freedman and Iwata-Weickgenannt 2011, 302). Appearing in 2009, Lightning reflects precisely this wave of empowered female heroes.

It is difficult to overstate the importance of marriage and child-rearing to conventional femininity in Japan. Though most cultures similarly associate women with domestic spaces, familial care and marriageability, Japanese femininity enmeshes a woman's identity with these factors (Rezeanu 2015, 16). In anglophone contexts, it is atypical for gender scholars to speak of 'hegemonic femininity', instead preferring 'emphasised femininity' to clarify that hegemonic masculinity ultimately wields the greatest societal power, subordinating femininities as well as other masculinities (Messerschmidt 2018, 47–48). However, Japan scholars can properly speak of 'hegemonic femininity' in Japan, due to the regulatory power that *sengyōshufu* femininity still holds in policing and suppressing alternative femininities. '[Women] are expected to meet the standard of *ryōsaikenbo*' (良妻賢母, 'good wife, wise mother'), writes Pasaribu, 'marriage is essential to Japanese women, because this is the only way they can meet the standard of being a good wife and wise mother' (2020, 52). During Japan's bubble economy years, companies pressured female professional workers to marry and retire early to bear the next generation of economic warriors; *sengyōshufu* femininity 'came to symbolise successful women who had achieved one of the greatest personal and social goals for their gender' (Mandujano-Salazar 2017, 528). In the 1990s, women who defied this norm and continued working were derogatorily labelled 'Christmas cake' (suggesting deterioration after age 25) and 'parasite singles' (Mandujano-Salazar 2017, 531). In the 2000s, two women authors proposed alternative terms to positively reclaim single womanhood: *make inu* (負け犬, lit. 'loser dog') in 2003 by Junko Sakai, and *ohitorisama* (an honorific for a customer eating alone) in 2007 by Chizuko Ueno (Freedman and Iwata-Weickgenannt 2011, 299).[2] Meanwhile, 2005 marked the first time Japan's birth rate dropped below its death rate, which was declared a national emergency by the prime minister. Many cast unmarried working women as the 'main culprits behind Japan's demographic crisis' for 'prioritising personal happiness over that of the family or the nation' (Freedman and Iwata-Weickgenannt 2011, 206–207; Mandujano-Salazar 2017, 526). When *arafō* attained mainstream status in 2008 and Lightning debuted in 2009, the societal stage was set for *FFXIII*'s message. At stake was not simply a different take on female *FF* protagonists; Lightning boldly affirmed a contemporary – and hotly contested – mode of alternative femininity.

The narrative of *FFXIII* centres on the weight of societal expectations, xenophobic scapegoating and individual agency. In the world of Cocoon, l'Cie – beings cursed to fulfil a specific mission termed as Focus, or else mutate into zombified creatures – are feared as renegades who will bring about the downfall of society. Any person suspected of being a l'Cie is summarily exiled to the wilderness world of Pulse, such as the train full of condemned prisoners where Lightning makes her first appearance. From the start, it is clear Lightning is no typical *FF* woman, like the damsel-in-distress Rosa or martyred saint Aerith. In *FFXIII*'s opening cutscene, Lightning frees herself and the exiles, single-handedly dispatching a squadron of soldiers. Lightning quickly takes charge of the ensuing resistance struggle, fending off opponents many times her size with a combination of agility and strategy.[3] The setting and opponents of the train action sequence intertextually invoke the opening bombing mission of *FFVII*, placing Lightning in Cloud's role as an ex-soldier and unstoppable force in battle. As the narrative progresses, Lightning remains the pillar of strength and leadership for her companions – both male and female. When she and the others are branded l'Cie and tasked with becoming Ragnarok to destroy Cocoon, Lightning vows to defy their fate, declaring: 'Maybe Cocoon is past saving, but it's our home. And we'll protect it or die trying! We live to make the impossible possible!' In the *FF* series, such resolute bravado is typically reserved for the male protagonist. Another crucial observation is that Lightning has no canon or implied romantic trajectory, as all the series' past female leads except for Terra had. This contrast is highlighted by juxtaposing Lightning with her sister Serah, who is engaged to marry Snow, comprising one of the main conflicts in Lightning's character development (explored below). Instead, Lightning sustains a successful military career as a sergeant in the Guardian Corps prior to the game's events – though her long hours allow little free time to spend with her sister and brother-in-law-to-be. The stark difference between Lightning's and Serah's femininities powerfully encodes modern Japan's dilemma between *arafō* and *sengyōshufu* femininity, offering an alternative vision for an empowered female protagonist.

Similarly, *FFXIII*'s score, composed by Masashi Hamauzu, departs radically from the lush, neo-Romantic orchestral style of his predecessors Uematsu and Sakimoto. Though not lacking incorporation of the orchestra entirely, Hamauzu leans more heavily on electronic and pop-influenced textures – *FFXIII*'s soundworld is as likely to foreground a melody on synthesized timbres or heavy metal guitar as on violin or piano. Hamauzu's harmonies are typically jazz-influenced 'tall' chords, revelling in intervals of the seventh and second – features less frequent in Uematsu's music. Overall, *FFXIII* presents a darker, edgier soundtrack evoking a more sombre, industrial, contemplative and technological impression than the music of *FF* games past. 'Lightning's Theme' likewise defies prior gendered convention, exemplified by the FRC and the conventionally feminine themes in *FFIV–FFX* covered in Chapter 2 (Figure 3.1). Its introduction, featuring string section and piano chords, would sound at home in a Uematsu *FF* soundtrack if not for the jazzy extended thirds adding harmonic depth and complexity. However, the track's A section (covered in more detail below) introduces Lightning's melodic theme in the piano's right hand over a B bass drone and incrementally shifting cloud of chords in the other strings – immediately, Lightning's sonic first impression is more melancholy and pensive than any past *FF* conventionally feminine theme. Only Terra's and Ashe's themes contain passages with comparable tonal ambiguity or darkness – and both were significant departures from conventional femininity in their own right. The track's core B section is particularly striking, contradicting most expectations of conventional musical femininity. Though not quite martial in this arrangement of the theme, its affect is rousing and anthemic. Its driving rhythm, marcato strings and syncopated melody convey a forthright assertiveness belying the conventionally gentle, lyrical melodic expectation. A further analytical observation suggests the salience of the heroic musical topic – previously reserved for *FF*'s conventionally masculine themes. The A section is set in the key of B Minor, modulating to G Major – the major VI key area – for its anthemic B section; modulation to VI, or emphasis of the ♭VI chord, is a telltale hallmark of the heroic topic. Lightning is musically foregrounded as a new breed of heroic woman.

FIGURE 3.1: Partial musical transcription of 'Lightning's Theme', A Section (above), B Section (below). Transcription by the author.

SINGLE LADIES AND HERBIVORE MEN

Significantly, 'Lightning's Theme' is a subdued arrangement of *FFXIII*'s recurring battle theme 'Blinded by Light', linking Lightning's core identity to combat. This is narratively fitting on two levels, encoding: (1) Lightning's military profession in the Guardian Corps, and (2) her struggle against her fate as a l'Cie and the society that condemns her for it. No other *FF* primary battle theme (recurrent through most standard encounters) is linked to a specific character in this way – suggesting the entire story of *FFXIII* is Lightning's fight to assert individual agency and free her sister Serah in a more personal way than typical save-the-world quests. While 'Lightning's Theme' is rousing and anthemic, 'Blinded By Light' is overtly confrontational, featuring brassy horn and distorted electric guitar in the A section and drum set breakbeat driving the soaring violin melody in the B section. Semiotically, this relationship depicts Lightning empowered, coming most alive in the furore of combat – the conventional domain of men. In the series sequels *Final Fantasy XIII-2* and *Lightning Returns*, multiple variations of 'Lightning's Theme' appear to provide further depth and nuance into Lightning's character, casting her music as one of the main themes of the trilogy.[4] In none of these variations does Lightning's music follow the FRC or conventionally feminine patterns. In sum, Lightning's music is not conventionally gendered – it truly is 'Lightning's Theme', derived from her identity as an individual and constituting a powerful model of alternative femininity.

The confrontational nature of Lightning's musical identity signifies traits common to the semiotics of alternative femininity. Samantha Holland notes that in emphasized femininity, submissive or docile responses to men's gazes are expected; returning eye contact poses a direct challenge to hegemonic masculinity (Holland 2004, 98). Similarly, wearing all-black clothing may constitute another visible sign of alternativity, appearing more 'striking' and 'formidable' than conventional women's dress (76). In mediatized narrative, music acts analogously to modes of dress or comportment, affirming or disrupting subconscious assumptions about characters' perceived traits. Fundamentally, these alternative strategies enact individuals' agency and control over how they are perceived, in contradistinction to how others perceive them (107). Holland's point synergizes with societal dynamics surrounding the reception of the *arafō* in Japan. Just as the *seken* (世間; 'society'), the court of public opinion, scapegoats *arafō* for Japan's declining birth rates – often represented in media by male authority figures such as government workers or corporate executives – Lightning and her l'Cie companions face condemnation from Primarch Galenth Dysley and Commander Jihl Nabaat (religious and military leaders, respectively) (Mandujano-Salazar 2017, 530). Culturally, Lightning's campaign against fate and the gods encodes Japanese women's battle for equal rights in the workplace and public sphere. Lightning's Focus mandates that her only options are becoming Cocoon's downfall or allowing society to execute her and the others; 'Lightning's Theme' encapsulates Lightning's belief in a third way.

A second semiotically significant aspect of 'Lightning's Theme' concerns its treatment of emotion – specifically, Lightning's development arc integrating emotion in a healthy, holistic manner. In the film tradition, the feminine 'other' is musically constructed through 'excessively emotional' Romantic-style expressivity, destined to be contained by rational, 'masculine' music (Laing 2007, 16). 'Women are [conventionally] defined according to their emotions', writes Heather Laing, 'and the effect of the expression of these emotions on themselves, as well as on men and patriarchal society in general' (Laing 2007, 23). If emphasized femininity abounds in emotional expression, alternative femininity mutes or inflects it, as Lightning does throughout the *FFXIII* trilogy. In most of *FFXIII*, Lightning lashes out with anger or violence, especially against Snow, who she outwardly blames for her sister Serah's death. Internally, Lightning is wracked by guilt, fearing that she is ultimately responsible after driving her sister away by berating Serah when she announced her engagement to Snow. Because of this, Lightning initially refuses to display vulnerability to others, only voicing her contrition when alone; as the narration reflects: 'Lightning was suffering. Reaching out to us. But we just couldn't see it.' Lightning's emotional suppression most frequently manifests in aggression or throwing herself into battle, as she confesses to Hope: 'I didn't want to think, so I fought instead. As long as I was fighting, nothing else was real.' Over the course of the narrative, Lightning integrates emotion holistically into her identity, displaying emotional vulnerability in her close relationships (primarily Hope, sometimes Fang). By *FFXIII*'s conclusion, she even forgives Snow and gives him and Serah her blessing to marry. Though analysed in detail in Chapter 7, it is worth noting here that *Lightning Returns* further develops this theme by reverting Lightning to a state incapable of feeling emotion, positioning emotional expression as central to her development throughout the trilogy. For alternative femininity to fight the patriarchy is simple; positively re-integrating conventionally feminine traits is much harder.

As previously mentioned, the A Section of 'Lightning's Theme' is harmonically and orchestrationally unlike the FRC or conventionally feminine theme precedent set in Uematsu's *FF* scores, suggesting the nuanced complexity of Lightning's internal development. The piano plays an active melody and arpeggiated ostinato over a contemplative string pad, inserting expressive, improvisatory comments between phrases. Where previous conventionally feminine themes were based on melodies and chord progressions of simple triads, the jazzy 'tall' chords of Lightning's music contribute realistic timbral and harmonic complexity to her musical identity. The track's ethereal minor mode and relative harmonic stasis create a brooding air that contrasts the stock 'love-inspiring' emotionality of earlier themes' lyrical major mode. Yet concluding that the A section is devoid of emotion would be too quick. Nuanced, realistic emotion is present – but it is not the saccharine sentimentality of Rosa's 'Theme of Love'. Lightning integrates emotion into her identity, but in her own way, conveying her unique psychological experience. Given the typical neo-Romantic mode of encoding femininity and emotionality, it may seem surprising to associate such a different, jazzy musical style with Lightning's emotions. However, historically speaking, music bears a special philosophical relationship with emotional experience and expression, regardless of genre or style (cf. Robinson 2005). Through virtual agency, a musical theme can 'simulate the actions, emotions, and reactions of a human agent' (Hatten 2018, 1) – even give voice to internal 'desires, memories, [...] or points of view' (Robinson 2005, 325). This makes music an ideal medium to convey complex emotions specific to the individual and difficult to express in words alone (Laing 2007, 3). In this way, Lightning's music surpasses visual means of conveying alternative femininity by providing a window into her internal experience. 'Lightning's Theme' models nuanced emotional expression in a character theme that transcends conventionally feminine pathways of emotionality, forging an alternative direction of her own.

Lightning's arc to holistically integrate emotion speaks powerfully to a reality that *arafō* – and alternative femininities and masculinities generally – routinely face. Having rejected the hegemonic paradigms essentializing them to traits approved for their gender, how might they adopt aspects of those paradigms without betraying their alternativity? For *arafō*, this means reckoning with romance – are career women doomed to loveless lives, defined by their career alone? Interestingly, this is the question that 2000s–10s television shows like *Around 40* and *It's Not That I Can't, It's That I Won't* dramatize and aim to answer. In these works, *arafō* cultivate more successful relationships with *sōshokudanshi* men who 'represent a clear departure from the model of hegemonic masculinity' than with the conventionally dominant *sararīman* men – the rejection of these men symbolizes a repudiation of hegemonic masculinity itself (Mandujano-Salazar 2017, 533). Similarly, if Lightning were to find a romantic attachment with anybody, the strongest argument could be made for Hope – an alternatively masculine, *sōshokudanshi* man. More saliently, Lightning models a healthy balancing of emotional expression and vulnerability alongside her leadership and empowered agency. Arriving at the cusp of Japan's crisis of femininity, Lightning constitutes an inspiration for real-life alternative femininity. Like TV dramas, video games may 'educate viewers about real social issues' by virtually staging highly charged discussions taking place at the societal level (Freedman and Iwata-Weickgenannt 2011, 301–02). Holland's respondents reported seeking role models for alternative femininity in literary and media works, since they encountered few in real life (Holland 2004, 86). Narratives like *FFXIII* are necessary to 'present alternative models [of femininity] with a positive and active voice [... and] validate the different choices Japanese women are making in contemporary society' (Mandujano-Salazar 2017, 540). Though the preceding analysis refracts the discussion of alternativity through arafō femininity in particular, the goal is a social landscape in which every individual determines their own mode of femininity or masculinity. As Square Portal writes: '[Lightning] continues setting a standard for other female and male characters – not to be like her, but who they are' (Square Portal 2015, n.pag.).

'More Than I Can Take': Reimagining Salaryman Masculinity in Final Fantasy XV

Remember – these ain't your bodyguards. They're your brothers.
(Cid to Noctis Lucis Caelum, *Final Fantasy XV*, 2016)

When *Final Fantasy XV* director Hajime Tabata announced the game would feature an all-male playable cast, controversy erupted. How could the game possibly constitute positive gender representation with no playable female characters? However, there is more to media representation than headcounts or numerical equity (explored further in Chapter 6) – indeed, as this chapter demonstrates, presenting an alternative account of femininity or masculinity may break down essentializing gendered expectations. Thus, narrative treatments of femininity or masculinity alone may still participate in counter-hegemonic gender representation. Just as Lightning defied Japanese emphasized femininity, *FFXV*'s protagonist Noctis Lucis Caelum advances a positive account of alternative masculinity that subverts Japan's hegemonic salaryman masculinity on its most crucial points. Noctis exemplifies the potential for alternatively masculine video game protagonists to counter-hegemonic masculinity.

The game's narrative centres on themes of duty, friendship, identity and self-sacrifice. Protagonist Noctis Lucis Caelum is the prince of the Kingdom of Lucis, though at twenty years old he has not yet been assigned active political duties. While Noctis journeys with his retainers and friends Prompto, Ignis and Gladiolus to the neighbouring province Tenebrae to marry his fiancée, Lunafreya, the Niflheim Empire invades Lucis and murders Noctis's father, King Regis. With his nation in disarray and while fleeing from imperial forces, the mantle of kingship is abruptly thrust upon Noctis. *FFXV*'s narrative trajectory comprises Noctis's journey to rebuild his kingdom and reach maturity as king apparent. The sudden loss of his father – together with filling his role – poses crucial questions to Noctis's masculinity. Director Tabata explains: 'Noctis has grown up seeing his father both as a father figure and as the king of the country, so during the game he tries to grow as a person and develop … with his father as a role model' (Tabata 2016).

Will Noctis remake himself in King Regis' image – or will he discover a new mode of being both man and king? Will Noctis let the voice of convention dictate his identity in order to weather an international crisis? Such questions render *FFXV* a fascinating case study of masculine representation in Japanese media.

Noctis's quest is a familiar one derived from the *bushidō* samurai masculinity of Japanese history and literature. In coming-of-age narratives, *shōnen* (少年; 'young man') characters frequently learn how to function as men in society from fathers or father figures.[5] However, the upheaval in Noctis's life leaves him bereft of models – Noctis's closest male mentors are the Crownsguard's leader Cor and the cranky engineer Cid – so Noctis navigates his identity formation with only his similar-age peers for guidance. However, Noctis's group does not invent ideas of masculinity from whole cloth; to the contrary, hegemonic masculinity pervades their very socialization as individuals, so that gendered norms are subconsciously ingrained and manifested. As explored in Chapter 2, Japan's most enduring hegemonic masculinity is *bushidō* – the way of the samurai – described by Nitobe Inazō as 'the perfection of Japanese men and the Japanese people' according to which all honourable Japanese men are measured (Mason 2011, 73). Though samurai are no more, the legacy of *bushidō* remains – Nitobe and others invoked *bushidō* as a 'touchstone for Japanese masculinity' to reclaim idealized masculine virtue in the present (Mason 2011, 87). In the mid-to-late 1900s, *bushidō* ideals pervaded Japanese politics, business and society as the iconic salaryman archetype (Frühstück and Walthall 2011, 11). Linking samurai warriors with white-collar office workers may strike western readers as peculiar, but the two narratives align quite robustly, casting Japanese salarymen as corporate soldiers embroiled in economic warfare for the nation's glory. In Japan's post-war bubble economy, salarymen were the national heroes, symbols of immense national pride, leading Japan to prosperity (Napier 2011, 174). 'The main protagonist of this economic success [...] was the so-called *sararīman*', writes Ronald Saladin, 'regarded as the backbone of Japan's economic success [... and] the idealised representative of Japanese manhood' (Saladin 2019, 69; original emphasis). Salaryman masculinity valorized the prioritization of societal duty over individual well-being, suppression of emotional expression, adoption of rigid familial gender roles and absolute conformity to societal expectations (Dasgupta 2013, 34). For a young man, striving towards salaryman masculinity was virtually synonymous with becoming a socially responsible adult (Dasgupta 2013, 2). It is against this backdrop that the meanings of Noctis's coming-of-age journey emerge.

The following analysis organizes the narrative themes of *FFXV* according to Noctis's four significant subversions of *bushidō* and salaryman masculinity:

1. Choosing diversity over conformity by practising inclusive homosociality through close, equal friendship with a range of alternative masculinities.

Hegemonic masculinity presupposes that there is a single most valid mode of manhood; relationships promoting equality between diverse masculinities challenge the presumed hierarchy. Competition for dominance between male friends is a key strategy through which hegemonic masculinity is maintained and alternative masculinities subjugated or eliminated (Bird 2018, 14). Noctis treats his non-royal friends Prompto, Ignis and Gladiolus as equals – despite their serving as his retainers. Eric Anderson terms this dynamic 'inclusive masculinity' – when 'multiple masculinities [may] proliferate without hierarchy or hegemony' (Anderson 2018, 41). Or, as Cid phrases it in-game: 'Remember – these ain't your bodyguards. They're your brothers.' From Ignis's taciturn analyses and Gladio's brash directness to Prompto's cheerful singing antics, Noctis's party certainly reflects the aforementioned post-2000 diversification in Japanese masculinities, like the *ikumen* or *sōshokudanshi*.[6] The implementation of the group's voices throughout *FFXV* – calling out with individual interests, banter and combat directions – communicates aural diversity, as each companion's voice occupies a unique tone and register (Smith 2021, 51). These diverse, equal homosocial relationships hearken to Yoshitsune and Benkei in the *Heike Monogatari* (*ca.* 1330 CE). As the samurai Benkei challenged any man who dared cross Kyoto's Gojo Bridge, Yoshitsune dressed in women's clothing and attempted to cross unmolested. Nonetheless, Benkei battled Yoshitsune and lost, becoming Yoshitsune's loyal retainer and trusted friend as a result. Though Benkei's rugged samurai masculinity could not be more different from Yoshitsune's courtly elegance and androgynous beauty, the two forged a legendary friendship. Just as *Heike Monogatari* celebrates co-existing masculinities, Noctis and his friends portray diverse, equal masculinities free of competition or hierarchy.

2. Wrestling with duty that requires self-sacrifice – as his father had done – instead of finding meaning in the journey itself. [7]

History is rife with examples of the ensuing costs of salarymen sacrificing their well-being to fulfil their corporate or societal duty (Saladin 2019, 79). Japanese corporate culture encourages late working hours, and even after the workday's conclusion, *nomikai* (飲み会; 'drinking party') – eating and drinking with coworkers and supervisors – is expected. Typically, the salaryman's family suffers his protracted absence most acutely. To show loyalty to and find belonging in the corporate family, salarymen become strangers to their own family (Hidaka 2010, 161). Successful employees frequently spend years living and working away from their families in different cities (単身赴任, *tanshin funin*) at their company's behest, deepening the estrangement and familial neglect. With all-consuming work lives and domestic complications, it is little wonder that many salarymen exhibit fear or deep reluctance to return home to their families, inventing reasons to stay out late with coworkers (Dasgupta 2013, 37). The rifts between salarymen and their spouses may become so intractable that they can no longer relate to each other and divorce shortly after the salaryman's retirement (Saladin 2019, 79). Most striking, however, is *karōshi* (過労死, 'death from overwork'), resulting from burdensome work hours and neglect for personal well-being (Dasgupta 2013, 37). *Karōshi* is closely tied to a perceived duty 'to fulfill their workload no matter what, even sacrificing their physical well-being' (Saladin 2019, 79). The responsibility of kingship weighs heavily on Noctis, as he considers whether to emulate his father or cast off the burden placed on his shoulders. Regis's governing often rendered him unavailable to see his own son – including the day Noctis's group left Lucis. Moreover, Regis's self-sacrifice in defence of the kingdom is a clear analogue to *karōshi*. Though Cid and Gladio urge Noctis to embrace his birthright and duty as king, he demurs, questioning his readiness to sacrifice himself as his father had. Ignis and Prompto support Noctis's roundabout route: 'Noctis will take his place, but only once he is ready.' Noctis learns to find happiness in the journey itself – together with his dear friends – diffusing the all-consuming demands of his royal duty. When he does reclaim the throne and surrenders his life in the game's final scene, it is of his own will, on his own terms: 'It took me a while, but I'm ready now.' Noctis's story ends not with his death, but photographs of his travels with friends – the memories and meaning made together along the way, living for more than self-sacrifice.

3. Emotional integration and processing of grief, anger and sadness through close homosocial relationships.

As excessive emotion was thought to characterize women, emotional suppression is a hallmark of hegemonic masculinity. 'Expressing emotions signifies weakness and is devalued', Bird reports, 'whereas emotional detachment signifies strength and is valued' (2018, 17). Especially prohibited is emotional sharing between men, lest one be suspected of homosexuality. Indeed, homohysteria is a powerful barrier to men cultivating emotional intimacy and physical expressions of friendship with one another (Anderson 2018, 41). Hegemonic masculinity avoids behaviours that 'other men might interpret as being effeminate or unmanly', for fear that 'any intimacy between men may sully their sexual identity' (Pease 2014, 28). Connell describes homohysteria and the aversion to emotional vulnerability as the 'classic barrier' to deepening friendships between men (Connell 2005, 133). Though homohysteria is not as pronounced in Japan as in the West (e.g. 1970s–80s in the United States), there have been periods of suppressing nanshoku (male–male eros) in the Japanese military and schools. For example, school administrator Nitobe

GENDER, RACE AND RELIGION IN VIDEO GAME MUSIC

Inazō (the aforementioned author of *Bushido*) sought to eradicate *nanshoku* behaviours among the 'hard faction' *kōha* in his school in the early twentieth century, and increasing national militarization from 1926 through the end of the Second World War produced suppression of *nanshoku* among the military (Angles 2011, 17; McLelland 2020). In modern salaryman culture, the demand for men to be pillars of strength undergirding their families and society dampens the potential for emotional vulnerability and expression. Salarymen often suppress or conceal emotional and psychological distress – even from their own family (Pasaribu 2020, 53). Instead of seeking help, they attempt to endure their struggles alone (Saladin 2019, 80). Noctis at first lashes out at others in anger and grief after learning of Regis's death – including an especially unsightly meltdown in the Lucis kings' royal tomb demanding to know why Regis sacrificed himself.[8] That Noctis does not process his grief healthily is unsurprising, for until recently, Japanese society typically viewed mental health issues as resulting from 'not trying hard enough to endure pain' (Freedman 2011, 306). Over his narrative trajectory, Noctis learns how to embrace, express and process his emotions in ways that depart significantly from salaryman masculinity. After seeing a vision from his deceased fiancée Lunafreya, Noctis openly weeps, mourning his bereavement and voicing his grief. Especially compelling is the post-credits campfire scene, as the four friends process the complexity and enormity of their emotions at the journey's end. 'Knowing this is it, and seeing you here, now', Noctis says falteringly, tears falling once more, 'it's … more than I can take'. With these words, Noctis dispels the unspoken prohibition against emotional vulnerability and affection between men and models alternative masculinity that disintegrates hegemonic barriers.

4. Refusing to degrade or sexually objectify women and not practising aggression in romance.

The sexual objectification of women is another key feature of hegemonic masculinity – a 'base on which male superiority is maintained' – characterizing men as subjects and women as objects (Bird 2018, 16). The logic of hegemonic masculinity casts femininity and alternative masculinities as the subordinated 'other', reinforced by verbal objectification of women within male friend groups (Pease 2000, 76). Assertiveness or aggression in romance is a corollary to sexual objectification, giving men control of the inception or pace of relationships. Noctis exemplifies *sōshokudanshi* masculinity – men who are gentle, not bound by manliness, not aggressive in romance, viewing women as equals and avoiding causing or receiving emotional pain (Morioka 2013, 8–9). Furthermore, *sōshokudanshi* do not prioritize a woman's physical appearance or sexual attributes when determining or expressing romantic interest (Morioka 2013, 10). Noctis and friends do not engage in sexually objectifying women during their travels, despite extended periods travelling with Iris and Aranea – rather, they welcome both women organically into their group dynamic and conversation. Though Prompto forms crushes easily and frequently express attraction to women like Cindy or Aranea, neither he nor the party's responses do so in an objectifying way. When Noctis speaks of his fiancée, he relives childhood memories of their friendship and receives some teasing from his friends – but not at Lunafreya's expense. Noctis also accompanies Iris on a mock date in Lestallum, treating her respectfully without exploiting her clear interest in him. The group as a whole – and Noctis in particular – embodies a philogynous treatment of women as equals, corresponding to the *sōshokudanshi*. The sole exception is Gladiolus, with a reputation for flirting with women – however, Gladio reserves his escapades for when the others are absent unless players choose to follow and eavesdrop.[9] It should also be noted that, while not the narrative focus of *FFXV*, Luna's narrative arc may be interpreted in an agential and empowering way (Smith 2021, 58–59). Iris and Aranea are also independent and competent companions, offering positive female character representation. Though the story focuses on developing alternative masculinity, its treatment of women is also counterhegemonic (Table 3.1).

Though a few prior *FF* heroes like Squall or Tidus evinced some degree of alternativity, none so thoroughly subverts hegemonic salaryman masculinity as Noctis. Like Lightning's anthem of empowerment, Noctis's alternatively masculine identity is aurally communicated by how unlike conventionally masculine themes his music is. Recall from Chapter 2 that, though *FF* conventionally masculine themes exhibited more variation than conventionally feminine themes, most exhibited either military- or heroic-topic traits. In contrast, 'Noctis's Theme' conveys no inkling of conventionally masculine heroism – no brass or percussion, ascending melodic leaps nor fast tempo. Instead, the track presents a lush, warm and legato timbre reminiscent of a relaxed waltz lullaby. Its main instrumentation consists of flowing piano and sustained strings, a combination not foregrounded in any previous male *FF* protagonist's named theme. Rather than a brass fanfare, marching snare drum or hypermasculine shout, 'Noctis's Theme' opens with a solitary, thin violin *flautando* fading gradually in, conveying uncertainty, tenderness and vulnerability. The piano melody is lyrical with predominantly stepwise motion, with gentle arpeggiated accompaniment in the left hand – both hallmarks of the singing style musical topic. Its rhythms are balanced and lacking syncopation, presenting a lilting triple metre in a moderate tempo (110 BPM). After the A section's polite, reserved tone, in the B section the strings join with the piano melody in soaring expressive arcs. Though not overly sentimental, these expressive outbursts encode Noctis's experience and expression of raw, genuine emotion – rather than suppressing or masking his feelings. Like 'Lightning's Theme', emotional expression in 'Noctis's

TABLE 3.1: Table summarizing *FFXV*'s narrative subversions of Japanese hegemonic salaryman masculinity.

	Bushidō	Salaryman	*Final Fantasy XV*
1	Hegemonic masculinity posits one single valid or legitimate mode of manhood.	Noctis chooses diversity over conformity by practicing inclusive homosociality.
2	*Bushidō* and salaryman masculinity demands self-sacrifice as key to manhood.	Noctis finds meaning in the journey itself, wrestling with social duty to self-sacrifice.
3	Hegemonic masculinity prohibits emotional vulnerability between men (Bird 2018); salarymen endure emotional struggles alone.	Noctis integrates his emotions and process grief, anger and sadness through homosocial relationships.
4	Sexual objectification of women maintains hegemonic masculinity and heterosexuality.	Noctis refuses to degrade or sexually objectify women and is not aggressive in romance.

Theme' communicates Noctis's alternativity. Indeed, emotional phenomenology was key to *FFXV* composer Yōko Shimomura's compositional choices:

> There might be a number of people who are a bit surprised [by] what I have chosen for Noctis's theme because it's [a] very soft and melodious piece. All I am really trying to show through this piece is the weight of destiny on [...] Noctis's shoulders, his internal monologue, his real deep feelings about the situation he is in. ... I really wanted you to feel the emotional resonance in the song.
>
> (Square Portal 2016, n.pag.)

'Noctis's Theme' has more in common with prior *FF* conventionally feminine themes than conventionally masculine themes – in instrumentation, lush tone, singing-style stepwise melody, waltz-like triple metre, balanced rhythms and emotional expression. By frustrating conventional expectations of how heroic masculine music should sound, 'Noctis's Theme' presents the prince as a new breed of male protagonist. By making emotion central to Noctis's musical identity, Shimomura completes the game's narrative critique of hegemonic masculinity.[10] As with Lightning's empowered agency, Noctis's alternative masculinity, homosocial bonds and emotional vulnerability are artfully encoded into his musical theme (Figure 3.2).

Narratively, it is significant that 'Noctis's Theme' is first heard when Talcott, a boy Noctis had grown close to, addresses him as king and expresses confidence in his safe return.[11] Till this point, Noctis's attitudes towards kingship consisted

FIGURE 3.2: Partial musical transcription of 'Noctis's Theme', A Section (above), B Section (below). Transcription by the author.

of frustration or uncertainty, primarily directed at others' insistence on duty to his father and people. This time, Noctis affirms Talcott's use of the title and 'Noctis's Theme' is heard at last, revealing Noctis has accepted his identity as king. However, the kind of king he will become contrasts both his father's and society's expectations, encoded in his musical identity. By invoking musical signifiers associated with the series' past conventionally feminine themes, 'Noctis's Theme' characterizes him as a sōshokudanshi man adopting traits considered conventionally feminine. Whereas older men were forbidden from behaviours associated with *otome* femininity (少女; 'maiden'), such as eating cake or enjoying *kawaii* (可愛い; 'cute') aesthetics, sōshokudanshi may appreciate these activities without reservation (Morioka 2013, 16–17). Similarly, Smith observes that 'Stand By Me' – a Florence + the Machine cover of Ben E. King's famous recording – nuances the rough, low-pitch bickering of the all-male cast with female vocals (Smith 2021, 54–55). By commissioning a female vocalist to perform a rearrangement of the original, known for its male vocalist, Tabata and *FFXV*'s creative team bookend the game with suggestions of its subversiveness and alternativity. Just as Florence Welch's voice underscores four men, 'Noctis's Theme' employs conventionally feminine signifiers and Noctis exhibits emotionally intimate friendship via alternative masculinity.

The cast of *FFXV* may heavily skew male, but its music and message perform vital representational work that benefits women by breaking down hegemonic masculinity. 'Men have to be involved in the process of challenging patriarchy', writes Bob Pease, 'it is possible for men to develop a cognizance of their gender privilege and to act in ways that challenge the reproduction of gender inequality' (2014, 22). Artistic and cultural representations of alternative masculinity are necessary to challenge the presumed default standard of hegemonic masculinity. Narratives like *FFXV* provide discursive space for men to re-imagine their individual identities beyond the script of hegemonic masculinity. Only by articulating viable counterhegemonic alternatives may men forge masculinity 'grounded in social justice and respect for difference' (Pease 2014, 31). Noctis stands as a hero for the future by embracing diversity, subverting societal duty, sharing emotional vulnerability and treating women with respect.

Conclusion: Three Principles for Future Musical Gender Representation

> *I am simply myself. No More and no less. And I only want to be free.*
> (Ashelia B'nargin Dalmasca, *Final Fantasy XII*, 2006)

The sweeping scope of this and the previous chapter warrants a few broad observations by way of conclusion, drawing together multivalent threads from gender studies, musical semiotics and narrative analysis. First, as a scholar blending the roles of composer and music theorist, I offer three guiding principles for future musical gender representation that I hope will benefit scholars, composers and listeners of video game music alike:

1. Tailor character themes to the individual, not an archetype.

Music written to sound conventionally masculine or conventionally feminine flattens a character's unique personality into gendered stereotypes. In Robert Hatten's terms, a piece's individual traits are 'strategic', while its conformities to expectations are 'conventional'. From Chapter 2, 'Rey's Theme' exceeds 'Leia's Theme' at conveying meaningful character qualities due to its emphasis on the strategic over the conventional; likewise, Lightning's and Noctis's themes are derived strategically rather than conventionally. However, does this recommendation mean that conventionally feminine and conventionally masculine musical qualities should never be incorporated into character themes moving forward? Not necessarily – if those gendered traits are apropos to the individual, not employed merely to conform to binary gendered convention. The crucial prerequisite is breaking down the hegemony that elevates limited expressions of femininity or masculinity as acceptable while discouraging alternative ones. Cleansing society's gender representation palate in this way would remove the need to suspect that a conventionally feminine character like Rosa or Lenna is generated to conform to cultural expectations. In other words, removing the hierarchical pressure for characters to exhibit hegemonic masculinity or emphasized femininity promotes greater freedom for characters to be their own authentic selves – even if they turn out to resemble conventional archetypes. 'The goal is not a simplistic androgyny in which everyone is the same', writes James Messerschmidt, 'but *difference with relational equality*' (2018, 158, original emphasis). Then the musical signifiers of conventional femininity and conventional masculinity may even be preserved for future usage, co-existing alongside novel conventions for alternative gender expression – without being burdened by assumed value judgements.

2. Gender studies and musicology will benefit from further study of masculinity.

The impact and importance of feminist musicological projects such as Susan McClary's, Rebecca Fülöp's, Naomi André's and many others cannot be overstated. Whether problematizing gendered rhetoric in western music theory or highlighting empowered female characters (historical and modern), the work of feminist musicology is vital to equalizing gender representations in music. However, further study of masculinity – especially alternative masculinities – is also critical, lest feminism's gains be perceived as an attack on masculinity in general (Carabí and Armengol 2014, 1). Connell remarked that gender studies historically 'has overwhelmingly focused on femininity', extending occasionally to masculinity – though the field has doubtless moved towards greater balance in the years since Connell's observation (Connell 2005, 50). The potential for developing a musical semiotics of a range of masculinities is immense. How might alternative masculinities musically distinguish themselves from hegemonic masculinity, as 'Noctis's Theme' does? Which musical characteristics subvert hegemonic masculinity, and through what compositional strategies? How might certain characteristics of conventionally masculine music, such as its adventurous and active tone, be maintained without falling into gendered stereotype? These are questions deserving of further scholarly attention, including in video game music repertoire.

3. Hegemonic masculinity is decentralized by validating alternatives.

The oxygen that hegemonic masculinity breathes is the unquestioned assumption that its traits are ordinary, natural, unproblematic and commonsense (Dasgupta 2013, 7). In the same breath, claims that essentialize a singular mode of masculinity attempt to justify its position of power over femininity and alternative masculinities. Equal representation of women in general and alternative masculinities are both necessary to replace hegemonic masculinity with a 'more varied [...] mass of personae' (Frühstück and Walthall 2011, 165). As explored above, such a diversity of masculinities emerged in twenty-first-century Japan, with several (NEET, *sōshoukudanshi*, *ikumen*, house-husband) prominently featured in recent Japanese media (Frühstück and Walthall 2011, 174). Only by celebrating a range of alternative masculinities may the West join with Japan in saying: '[Today's] young men have broken the spell of "manliness"' (Morioka 2013, 16–17). This requires rethinking how heroic masculine music should sound – as 'Noctis's Theme' did – promising a new breed of masculinity.

Alternative femininities and masculinities demonstrate the possibility of change and model how that change may be achieved (Seidler 2014, 220). Normalizing modes of alternative femininities and masculinities is key to eroding the stranglehold of hegemonic masculinity. Even as individuals discover a meaningfully personalized femininity or masculinity, hegemonic masculinity persists as long as these options remain publicly invisible (Requena-Pelegrí 2014, 124). This is precisely where art and media excel, becoming 'more than mere entertainment' as they guide audiences to 'reflect [upon], question, and rethink' essentialized gender roles by presenting viable alternatives (Pasaribu 2020, 56). Femininity and masculinity are not synonymous with their conventional expressions but encompass every flavour and variety of individuals in the real world. To reiterate an earlier claim – when all expressions of femininity and masculinity are legitimized – these conventionally binary spheres become fully overlapping, setting the foundation for non-binary possibilities. Alternativity in gender construction views femininity and masculinity not as an evil to disavow, but rather as something that everyone has a right to claim (Holland 2004, 158). As Holland writes, her informants 'did not wish to be seen as "alternative", as different' – rather, they challenged culturally bound gender norms (2004, 145). There is space at the representational table to welcome as many femininities and masculinities as there are individuals, discovering that diversity within groups eclipses the presumed differences between them.

NOTES

*   Standalone illustration files of Figure 3.1 and 3.2 can be found under the Front Matter section for *Gender, Race and Religion in Video Game Music's* page on Intellect Discover.

1.   One could offer an argument (perhaps more compelling) that *FFVI* splits the main character position between Terra and Celes, with Terra foregrounded in the first half (World of Balance) and Celes in the second (World of Ruin). Therefore, Lightning's role as female lead protagonist would be more complete than either Terra or Celes individually. Additionally, one could interpret Ashe as *FFXII's* main character – as the previous chapter does – predating Lightning as a female main character. However, Lightning's narrative centrality is

considerably clearer and more indisputed than Ashe's, so it is appropriate that she is marketed and celebrated as a significant milestone for gender representation in the series.

2. It may strike readers as strange that *make inu* ('loser dog') could be regarded with positive connotation – yet that was indeed Sakai's argument. Sakai combined a mix of self-effacing humility with cultural values of self-denial absorbed from Buddhist influences to console unmarried working women. As Freedman and Iwata-Weickgenannt write: 'Sakai proposes that, no matter how happy and successful they are, single women are regarded by the wider society as losers, and they should humbly self-identify as make inu to show that they accept and thereby feel better about this fate' (Freedman and Iwata-Weickgenannt 2011, 299). It makes no difference to this chapter's argument whether readers regard Sakai's reasoning as convincing.

3. Additionally, Sazh – Lightning's male counterpart in this scene – exhibits many traits of 'New Father' alternative masculinity, deferring to Lightning's competence and prioritizing the well-being of his son Dajh. Alternative masculinity frequently pairs well with alternative femininity, as hegemonic masculinity or emphasized femininity tends to suppress alternatives. Some brief remarks exploring this dynamic will follow concerning Hope Estheim and *arafō* romantic dramas.

4. Variations of 'Lightning's Theme' / 'Blinded By Light' in the series include 'Escape', 'Forever Fugitives,' 'The Yaschas Massif' (*Final Fantasy XIII*), 'Lightning's Theme – Unprotected Future', 'Etro's Champion' (*Final Fantasy XIII-2*), 'Lightning's Theme – A Distant Glimmer', 'Lightning's Theme – Radiance', 'Crimson Blitz', 'Savior of Souls', 'High Voltage', 'The Song of the Savior – The Chosen One', 'The Song of the Savior – Grand Finale', 'Last Resort', 'Humanity's Tale', 'Credits – Light Eternal' and 'Epilogue' (*Lightning Returns*).

5. Teachers, mentors or *senpai* (senior peers in schools or organizations) often fill the father figure role in modern narratives, as biological fathers are frequently absent due to *tanshin funin* (working abroad).

6. Specific character observations are based on *Final Fantasy XV*'s Japanese voice track and performances. There are significant differences in characterization between the Japanese and English voice acting. For example, while Gladiolus channels bushidō warrior masculinity and is certainly brash and direct in the original Japanese audio, his English localization comes across as much more aggressive, arrogant and hegemonic. For clarity of interpretation pertaining to *FFXV*'s original audience and sociocultural context, only the Japanese voice track is considered.

7. For a similar, real-world case pertaining to the Japanese Defense Force, see Sabine Frühstück (2011).

8. Throughout Noctis's breakdown scene, he consistently uses the first-person pronoun *ore*, communicating a more direct, disrespectful and aggressive demeanour. In polite conversation, the pronoun *watashi* would be more fitting for a prince. The presence of Cor – a military leader and one of Noctis's mentors – for this conversation would require more decorum. Even if Noctis speaks more informally with his retainers through most of the

GENDER, RACE AND RELIGION IN VIDEO GAME MUSIC

game, this manner of speaking suggests haughtiness when directed towards someone who should receive greater respect.

9. As observed in endnote 5, Gladiolus's English voice characterization is considerably more aggressive, arrogant and hegemonic in affect than the Japanese original, exacerbating English audiences' perception of Gladio as a womanizer. While one could hardly describe Gladio as alternatively masculine in either vocal performance, his English version is more assertive and objectifying in his interactions with women.

10. Jordan Hugh Sam explores suggestions of homoeroticism in the English language dub between members of Noctis's party and the outcry from groups of players critiquing FFXV as 'being too gay' (Sam 2020). Other player communities celebrated the perceived homosexual relationships through the creation of fanfiction and fanart. This is a valuable research project, from which I do not wish to detract any significance. However, it does not complicate my reading of gender representation in FFXV, as my project is thoroughly semiotic in nature, while Jordan Hugh Sam's exists in the domain of fan studies. I am wary of driving too hard a distinction between semiotic analysis and reception history, as I have written elsewhere that communication is not a unilateral proclamation from sender to receiver, but rather a dynamic process integrating meaning-making contributions from the rhetor's selected design and an interpreter's own context, background, and values (Yee 2018). However, after discussing with Jordan Hugh Sam concerning the interaction of his paper and my findings presented in this chapter, two crucial differences emerge:

a. My research focuses solely on FFXV's narrative and musical score as a meaningful text and generates a reading from those features, while Jordan Hugh Sam's explores player reactions and creative paratexts responding to the game-as-text.
b. My findings derive from the original Japanese sociocultural context and language rendering, while Jordan Hugh Sam's examine an anglophone (mostly American) social and linguistic setting.

Proceeding from my reading, Jordan Hugh Sam's analysis of reception history in the anglophone world shows that FFXV's critique of Japanese hegemonic masculinity is not readily apparent when transplanted to international contexts, raises fascinating questions about script and voice-acting localization decisions and highlights how far the United States has to go in order to dislodge hegemonic masculinity. However, these conclusions are not in tension with the reading itself.

11. There is a noteworthy difference between the English and Japanese versions. The English reads:

Talcott: 'Hey! Your Majesty!'
Noctis: 'What's up?'

104

Talcott: 'Please come back soon! We need our king!'
Noctis: 'Yeah. Count on it.'

In Japanese, it reads:

Talcott: 'Ano!'
Noctis: 'Doushita?'
Talcott: 'Kanarazu kaete kite kudasai! Ou-sama!'
Noctis: 'Aa. Wakatta!'

The differences are as follows: (1) in the English line 1, Talcott addresses Noctis with a royal title, while in Japanese he does not; (2) in Japanese line 1, ano expresses hesitance and reservation about the propriety of addressing Noctis, which is not present in English line 1; (3) in Japanese line 3, kanarazu expresses a deeper personal desire for Noctis's return than English line 3; (4) in English line 3, Talcott expresses the people's need for a king, while in Japanese he simply addresses Noctis as king; (5) in Japanese line 4, wakatta is a broader affirmation (lit. 'understood') than Noctis's affirmative promise in the English. Taken together, the nuance I wish to highlight is that in Japanese line 3, Talcott's plea for Noctis's return is based in naming Noctis as his king. Noctis's agreement in Japanese line 4 includes acknowledgement of Talcott's addressing him as king for the first time. In English line 4, Noctis's promise primarily concerns returning.

4

Damsel No Longer:
The Empowered Mezzo-Soprano
Voice in *Horizon Zero Dawn*

Introduction – Gamergate and Troll Mob Rule

No single event is as thoroughly discussed in the field of video game gender studies as Gamergate. A watershed moment in the culture wars over media and video games, Gamergate was, at its core, an internet-driven harassment campaign. Gamergate began with a backlash against a woman game developer, Zoe Quinn, after the release of her work *Depression Quest* (2013). What may have begun as a critique of the game rapidly ballooned into personal attacks against her romantic life and identity as a woman. Within days, the harassment had expanded to target other women developers, analysts or journalists in the video game industry including Anita Sarkeesian, Jenn Frank, Mattie Brice and Brianna Wu – all of whom were compelled to flee their homes or leave the industry entirely from floods of credible threats to their person. A favourite tactic employed against these women is the issuing of death and rape threats – often including specific address and time information – weaponizing millennia of men's violence against women (Dewinter and Kocurek 2017, 60). In a practice known as 'doxxing', a target's home address, personal email, phone number, private photographs or other personally identifying information are publicized on the internet, violating their individual safety and encouraging others to join in the attacks. Another strategy involves the creation of multiple 'sock puppet' dummy accounts on social media, sending the target violent or obscene messages from each to amplify their perceived volume. On other occasions, troll mobs have coordinated similar attacks on film or video game releases to harm their sales and cultural reputation.

Captain Marvel (2019) was poised to make history as film production giant Marvel Studios' first female-character-led superhero film. Pre-release critic reviews were positive, with popular anticipation steadily rising. However, on the influential review aggregate website Rotten Tomatoes, *Captain Marvel* received abysmal audience review scores pushing its aggregated average below 60%, well below the expected performance of a Marvel superhero blockbuster. The catch? These negative reviews flooded in before the film was even released in theatres. Rather than responding to viewing the film, these organized 'review bombing' campaigns had previously impacted other works featuring positive demographic representation: *Ghostbusters* (2016), *Star Wars: The Last Jedi* (2017) and *Black Panther* (2018). Around the time of *Captain Marvel*'s release, Rotten Tomatoes changed its policies to permit audience reviews only after a film's release – likely in response to review bombings (Sims 2019). *Captain Marvel* drew the troll mob's outrage for its feminist significance and messaging – particularly the lead actor Brie Larson's *Marie Claire UK* interview advocating for greater demographic diversity among film critics. Review bombing is not limited to the silver screen, however, as the campaign against the video game *The Last of Us Part II* (2020) demonstrates. A mere few hours after its release, the game's user score averaged a dismal 3.4/10 on Metacritic, in stark contrast to its stellar 9.5/10 critic score. While there are some legitimate gripes about spoilers revealed in pre-release publicity materials, the common logic underlying the reviews is the foregrounding of a same-sex romantic relationship and the game's female main character, Ellie, in contrast to the previous game's male protagonist Joel (Tassi 2020). Considering that scholars have lauded Ellie as an 'extremely capable and heroic' female playable character only held back in the first game by being overshadowed by Joel, the campaign against Ellie's debut as sole lead protagonist is especially pernicious (Gray et al. 2018, 2). Ellie and *The Last of Us Part II*, like Brie Larson and *Captain Marvel*, faced backlash precisely because they were representational milestones for women in mainstream media.

Sadly, such lashing out is not a historical anomaly in video game and media fandom – nor is it a symptom of having a few bad apples. Rather, sexual harassment in video gaming and fandom cultures has long been normalized, minimized or ignored to appease those perceived to be their primary audience – young men (Gray et al. 2018, 4). Since 2017 at the latest, that assumption has been repudiated by statistical data showing approximately equal proportions of male and female video game players. However, an increasingly vocal and organized segment of the gamer population resists this shift, seeking to make gaming culture a masculinist paradise again. That this description resembles a certain politician's (in)famous campaign slogan – 'make America great again' – is no accident. Suzanne Scott connects Gamergate to the 2016 presidential election of Donald Trump in the United States, drawing striking parallels between the disaffected fans of Gamergate and voters from the rust belt who propelled Trump to victory (Scott 2019, 19–20). Other scholars analyse Gamergate as a proving ground for social media activation and coordination techniques employed in Trump's 2016 election – an unsettling foreshadowing of the 6 January 2021 insurrection storming the U.S. Capitol

(Fordyce et al. 2018, 234). There is infinitely more at stake on a cultural level than the success of any single film or video game. Gamergate and the trend of review bombing against media elevating female characters reveal much deeper societal fissures and dysfunctions.

Gray and Leonard's analysis of the societal dynamics fuelling Gamergate could just as accurately describe other backlash incidents: 'Gamergate as a movement [focused] on white men's anxieties over losing ground in a universe assumed to be homogenous' (2018, 11). In other words, central to these controversies are issues of belonging, of who has the right to a seat at the gaming or fandom table. To wit – do women have an equal stake in video games, media and the fandoms that surround them? Or will disaffected men succeed in toxifying the cultural environment so completely that women players are driven out and industry decision-makers capitulate to their demands? Such questions are robustly treated elsewhere in full-length books (Gray and Leonard 2018; Malkowski and Russworm 2017; Scott 2019). However, this chapter gestures towards the beginnings of an answer through a detailed musical and historical analysis of one prominent case study: *Horizon Zero Dawn*. By creating a musical 'third gender' space representing the series' empowered protagonist Aloy, *Horizon Zero Dawn* articulates an inclusive, diversified vision for video game music and narrative.

Chapter 4 completes Part II's tripartite trajectory exploring gender representation in video game music. Chapter 2 established historical conventions of conventionally feminine and conventionally masculine musical themes in the *Final Fantasy* series, and Chapter 3 examined promising new directions for alternative femininity and alternative masculinity in *FFXIII* and *FFXV*, laying the groundwork for considering non-binary gender representation in this chapter. Turning from the Japan-produced *FF* series to one produced by Dutch developer Guerrilla Games, this chapter analyses the music of *Horizon Zero Dawn* (2017) and *Horizon Forbidden West* (2022), specifically its characterization of the series' female lead character, Aloy. A brief history of the damsel-in-distress trope and its use in video game narratives positions the significance of *Horizon Zero Dawn* as a landmark for gender equality in video games. Musically, 'Aloy's Theme' is characterized by the mezzo-soprano register of vocalist Julie Elven, invoking the operatic history of castrati, who existed as a 'third gender' presenting with conventionally feminine and conventionally masculine traits. As the practice of operatic castrati diminished in the nineteenth century, mezzo-sopranos inherited castrati's dramatic and semiotic potential for blurring binary gender boundaries through registral mixing and appearing as male characters in *travesti*. When Aloy's music is not presented vocally, it is given by the cello playing on its highest string; the masculinized femininity of the mezzo-soprano voice and the feminized masculinity of the cello's expressive highest register together articulate a blended 'third gender' space for

Aloy's musical characterization. *Horizon Forbidden West*, like its predecessor, continues this compositional strategy to present Aloy narratively and musically transcending binary gendered conventions altogether.

A Distressing Narrative Trope – A Brief History

When Anita Sarkeesian was targeted by the Gamergate mob, she had just released the latest instalment of her 'Damsel in Distress: Tropes vs Women in Video Games' series. This series of educational videos traced the damsel-in-distress trope through the history of storytelling, from Perseus to *Star Fox*, with special attention to its persistence in twentieth- and twenty-first-century films and video games. Sarkeesian was a popularizer of feminist scholarship and ideas applied to the medium of video games, taking games seriously as bearers of cultural and representational meanings. In bringing feminist critique to the relatively untilled soil of video games, Sarkeesian prompted greater circumspection in public consciousness concerning video games' reliance on the damsel-in-distress trope to provide a convenient framework for gameplay and player motivation. Sarkeesian's work provoked a backlash from those who saw no issue with the damsel-in-distress trope or argued that Sarkeesian selectively picked her examples to make the trope seem more pervasive in video games than it truly was. However, Sarkeesian's findings synergized with scholarly analysis of the damsel-in-distress trope in video game narratives.

The damsel-in-distress trope describes a plot device that places a female character into captivity or danger, from which she cannot escape on her own power. Typically, a male hero rescues the female character from this situation, receiving validation, gratitude or affection from her in return for his heroic efforts. Damsels-in-distress was 'put on a pedestal, considered pure and innocent, and needed the hero (a male, of course), to rescue them' (Summers and Miller 2014, 1037). The story follows the male hero's journey, leaving the damselled female character in a static state for much or all of the narrative. Even if the damselled female character aids the male hero with information or an essential item, she remains an auxiliary in someone else's story. Representationally, this trope strips the damselled woman of the ability to influence her own outcomes; instead, she is at the mercy of others' competence and goodwill. Casting the male protagonist as a heroic subject and the female damsel-in-distress as victim and reward reinforces traditional gender roles, suggesting a separation of public and domestic domains along gendered lines (Summers and Miller 2014, 1028). Two of the highest-selling video game franchises of all time – *Super Mario* and *The Legend of Zelda* – have historically relied on the damsel-in-distress trope to structure their core games' narratives, and numerous other classic video games incorporate the plot device as well. One earlier

GENDER, RACE AND RELIGION IN VIDEO GAME MUSIC

corpus study identified the damsel-in-distress trope used in 21% of a representative sample of video games (Dietz 1998 cited in Summers and Miller 2014, 1030). Another survey of 223 female video game characters found that between 20% and 70% (depending on the year) of female characters from 1988 to 1997 were portrayed as needing rescue by a male hero (Summers and Miller 2014, 1035). However, the prevalence of the damsel-in-distress trope diminished over time. Summers and Miller trace the manifestations and varieties of the damsel-in-distress in video games over twenty years, from 1988 to 2007, finding a statistically significant decrease in damsel-in-distress video games over this period (rate of change: $b = -0.11$). However, they also observed an increase in female characters portrayed in sexualized or revealing outfits over the same period (rate of change: $b = 0.14$). As video games portray women less frequently as victims in need of rescue, they more often become sexually objectified for players' viewing pleasure. While not necessarily rendering female characters dependent and powerless, sexualization has unique effects warranting its own representational analysis.

The damsel-in-distress trope can be classified as 'benevolent sexism' – claiming a chivalrous protectiveness towards women while treating them as a possession. Sexualization, on the other hand, may be termed 'hostile sexism', objectifying female bodies as vehicles for others' sexual pleasure (Glick and Fiske 1997). Both forms of sexism reinforce the privileged position of male power – either women exist for the approval and pleasure of a man, or as a reward for his heroic deeds. Here a careful balance must be maintained, for individual women may find dressing in revealing clothing or actively wielding their sexuality empowering.[1] Similarly, female players may experience empowerment when playing sexually outgoing female characters. However, sexualization in media and video games must also be measured in the context of the widespread culture of violence against women. Hostile sexism correlates with and may engender victim-blaming attitudes – in other words, that what a woman wears or how she behaves explains or justifies sexual violence against her (Chapleau et al. 2007 cited in Summers and Miller 2014, 1037). Alternatively, some men may view sexually empowered female characters as threats to patriarchal social order and condemn such characters – analogous to the backlash against Brie Larson and *Captain Marvel* (Summers and Miller 2014, 1038). Discussing sexualization in media from a representational perspective is always a fraught enterprise with multiple factors and perspectives to consider, and the present discussion makes no claim to settle such issues. It shall suffice here to acknowledge that sexualization, like the damsel-in-distress trope, may be another avenue of diverting female character agency into existing roles within the paradigm of hegemonic masculinity, giving the reason for pause when female characters are portrayed in a sexualized manner – particularly playable female characters.

The stage is now set to consider the context and significance of *Horizon Zero Dawn*. The central flaw of the damsel-in-distress trope is the asymmetry at its core: male characters are the playable heroes while female characters are twice victimized – once via the narrative and a second time through deprivation of player agency. Counteracting this, a surefire way to mitigate damselling is creating a main playable female character – for video games are unlikely to subject their players to spending the entire game captured and awaiting external rescue. Empowerment and subjective agency are key to combatting the medium's legacy of relying on the damsel-in-distress trope. Simultaneously, to focus on the female character's own agency, her character design should not appear crafted for the sake of players' invisible gazes, external to her world. Her sexuality, to the extent that she expresses it, should be her own, rather than for others' consumption. This is a difficult balance to achieve – but also an imperative one to navigate in an increasingly diverse video gaming market.

Horizon Zero Dawn – A Breakthrough for Feminist Gaming

Guerilla Games' *Horizon Zero Dawn* (2017), *Horizon Forbidden West* (2022) and the games' protagonist Aloy constitute a marked achievement for gender representation in video games. In 2017, the year of *Horizon Zero Dawn*'s release, the Entertainment Software Association released the first of its annual 'Essential Facts about the Computer and Video Game Industry' reports, a wellspring of quantitative data about video game developers and players. The report included a then-surprising statistic about video game player gender demographics: 41% of video game players in the United States were women (Entertainment Software Association 2017). Contrary to popular misconceptions in the 2000s and 2010s that video games were primarily a boys' activity, the ESA results demonstrated that women have an equal stake in the video game industry – and women players have risen to 48% since that time (Entertainment Software Association 2022). Yet women certainly do not comprise half of playable video game protagonists, especially in genres considered to be bastions of 'hardcore', masculine gaming – triple-A first-person shooter and action-adventure games. It is within this context that *Horizon Zero Dawn* and its hero Aloy find their significance – for *Horizon Zero Dawn*, a top-quality open-world game blending shooter and action-adventure elements, is exactly the kind of video game thought to be composed of men, developed by men, for audiences of men. In other words, Aloy transgressed the boundary that the trolls of Gamergate sought to maintain.[2]

Video game developers and journalists alike took notice. Review headlines in praise of *Horizon Zero Dawn* include: 'The Feminist Game we Need' (Swann 2017),

GENDER, RACE AND RELIGION IN VIDEO GAME MUSIC

'The Feminist Action Game We've Been Waiting For' (*The Guardian* 2017), 'A Breakthrough in Feminist Gaming' (Brusuelas 2018) and 'The First Legitimate Feminist Hero in a Mainstream Video Game' (Chen 2017). As is clear from these headlines, many understood the significance of Aloy and *Horizon Zero Dawn* as a rebuttal to the widely perceived masculinist gaming culture, channelling positive gender representation messaging. Set in a post-apocalyptic United States nearly 1000 years after a global extinction event occurring in 2066 C.E., the lush landscape of flora and fauna is punctuated by mechanical creatures wielding overpowering weaponry and force (Figure 4.1). Life as Aloy knows it is defined by a continual struggle

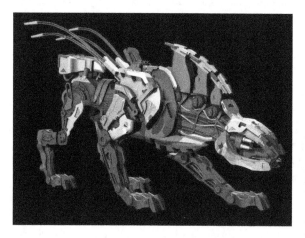

FIGURE 4.1: 'Sawtooth' machine beast (top left), Aloy's character model (top right), Lantern ceremony (bottom left), Aloy's allies (bottom right).

for survival, hunting and foraging for food and resources while avoiding aggressive machines. Aloy's people, the Nora tribe, live within the Embrace – a region naturally protected by mountains that keep out the largest, most dangerous machines. Despite the harmonious, communal society of the Nora, Aloy is not welcomed among them, for she is motherless. Nora's society is matriarchal, led by three High Matriarchs and worshipping the All-Mother as a creator deity. However, Aloy was discovered as a newborn inside the Nora's sacred mountain, where no human was permitted to enter; considered to be motherless, Aloy is exiled to live outside the Nora's main city. Instead, an honourable outcast named Rost agrees to raise Aloy as his own daughter, teaching her how to survive in the wilderness – and even hunt machines. During the coming-of-age trial, the Proving – which Aloy takes part in as a prerequisite to joining the tribe as an accepted Nora – participants may release a floating paper lantern to honour their mother in a blessing ceremony (Figure 4.1). Being motherless, Aloy can instead dedicate the lantern to Rost to honour their found-familial relationship – or if players prefer, to Aloy's unknown mother, or to herself. During the Proving, the Nora are attacked by outsiders and Rost is killed before Aloy's eyes. Having successfully completed her trial, Aloy is named a Nora tribeswoman and designated a Seeker to sojourn outside the Embrace to pursue the truth behind the attack on the Nora and, ultimately, behind the world-ending calamity.

Over the course of her journey, Aloy learns and experiences many things the Nora knew nothing about as she encounters other cultures like the Banuk and Carja, visits ancient ruins revealing the lost past of the Old Ones (our civilization) and gains allies to support her efforts (Figure 4.1). Varl, whose mother is the tribe's war-chief Sona, is a Nora warrior seeking vengeance alongside Aloy for the damage wrought upon their tribe. Erend, an Oseram captain of the guard in service to the Carja nation, joins with Aloy to uncover the truth surrounding his sister's murder. Sun-King Avad rules Carja, the largest nation featured in *Horizon Zero Dawn*; after Aloy saves Avad's life from an assassination attempt, he developed an admiration for her and became her advocate in Carja society. Finally, the enigmatic Sylens seems to know more about Old One technology and the past calamity than anyone other than Aloy, making him alternatively an ally or impediment depending on circumstance. With the exception of Sylens, all these men acknowledge Aloy's competence and treat her with respect, neither expressing jealousy nor undercutting her competency. While these men assist Aloy's endeavours, the spotlight remains entirely hers. Neither is Aloy squeezed into conventional femininity through romance; while any or all of these allies may harbour a romantic interest in Aloy, it never becomes the focus of her story or the game's overarching narrative. Indeed, Aloy's interpersonal relationships are key to her success as a main character – not simply a gender-flipped carbon copy of a typical male video game protagonist.

Kotaku lauds *Horizon Zero Dawn* as 'an unequivocal landmark of gender equality' in the medium, citing Aloy's strength of character, believability and unsexualized design (2020). Key to Aloy's nuanced and realistic personality is her balance of agential resolve and interpersonal empathy, blending conventionally feminine and conventionally masculine traits (Loveridge 2017).[3] As with Lightning's character development arc covered in Chapter 3, Aloy embodies the conventionally masculine strength and heroism reserved for the male playable hero, without abandoning the empathy and emotional intelligence thought conventionally feminine. One minute, Aloy is a badass femme fatale single-handedly bringing down mechanical monstrosities, and the next has the emotional intelligence to counsel her allies through the process of bereavement. Two examples demonstrate these characteristics well. First, Aloy and Erend witness the death of Erend's sister, Ersa, who tells Erend in her final moments that he will need to grow up quickly. Aloy expresses her sincere condolences at the moment and guides Erend through emotional processing in a later conversation. Second, Avad, who harboured romantic feelings for Ersa, finds himself similarly attracted to Aloy after she saves his kingdom. After Avad asks Aloy to become captain of his personal guard, Aloy's response helps him discern his own rebounding interest from Ersa to Aloy. Significantly, though Aloy is a strong, capable protagonist, she allows herself to show emotional vulnerability and grief, such as when Rost bids her farewell with finality before the proving.[4] As the game's Director Herman Hulst explains: '[she's] not a one-dimensional super human, she's Aloy' (Loveridge 2017, n.pag.). Rather than creating another stereotypical action game protagonist who happens to be female, Aloy represents a hero who showcases the full spectrum of realistic humanity in all its raw, paradoxical contradictions.

It is fitting that Aloy's musical characterization is as nuanced and complex as her story and personality. In a post-apocalyptic sonic landscape primarily consisting of synthesized, industrial timbres blended with frenetic percussion, the music associated with Aloy stands as a striking aural contrast. Instead of technological sounds of the environment, the feminine-stereotypical flute or even the more setting-neutral piano, 'Aloy's Theme' and its subsequent leitmotivic occurrences are characterized by the human voice of a woman. In a world dominated by ruthless killing machines, the organic warmth of vocalist Julie Elven is semiotically marked. The human singing voice typically receives our privileged attention when heard in a texture combined with other instruments (Cone 1974, 79). 'The voice', writes Cone, 'is inevitably the most fully human element in any musical texture in which it takes part' (1974, 123). Semiotically, the human voice functions as the basis for musical expression – it is no accident that listeners metaphorically describe even instrumental or electronic melodies as a musical 'voice' (Cumming 2000, 129). Thus, to score Aloy with a vocal melody primes listeners for interpreting the music as revealing some aspect of Aloy's character. *Horizon Zero Dawn*'s composer Joris de Man considered Elven to be Aloy's musical voice, saying in an interview: 'In Julie Elven I found the voice that I felt embodied Aloy best as a person; someone with a gentle strength and determination whilst still retaining a female sensitivity' (MCV/Develop 2017, n.pag.). Though de Man's statement could have been more delicately worded, the sentiment expressed is the same as described above – in Aloy as well as the voice representing her, conventionally feminine and conventionally masculine traits are balanced. Elven's voice type and tone form a fitting analogue to Aloy's character – a crucial observation further explored below. Elven's vocal performance is widely credited as a major contributor to the score's success – including a BAFTA nomination for best score – and Elven names *Horizon Zero Dawn* as one of the favourite performances of her career (Loughry 2018). One review singles out 'Aloy's Theme' and Elven's expressive vocalise for its 'winning combination of simplicity, memorability, and heart' (McMillan 2018, n.pag.). It is no exaggeration to consider 'Aloy's Theme' the heart of *Horizon Zero Dawn*'s musical identity.

Across nine tracks, 'Aloy's Theme' appears in three keys: C minor, A minor and D minor. All of its appearances are presented lyrically and melodically, with little embellishment or variation; each appearance firmly foregrounds Aloy's persona among the rest of the soundscape (Figure 4.2). Of these, the A Minor cues express the widest range, from A3 to B4 in the main melody with an E5 extension for the climax. In the Fach voice classification system, this range corresponds strongly to the

FIGURE 4.2: Appearances of 'Aloy's Theme' leitmotif and their melodic ranges.

mezzo-soprano voice type, and de Man and Elven lean particularly into the mezzo's signature lower register to emphasize that fact. For example, the central leitmotif of 'Aloy's Theme' – a rising perfect fifth followed by an upper neighbour tone a half step above – emphasizes and returns to A3 as the key's tonic and the centre of gravity in the melody. The complete melody follows a large-scale periodic structure with a climaxing coda at the highest tessitura of Elven's voice featured in the score, E5. Just as the melody leads to a high climax at the melody's end, so too do the accompanying orchestration and dynamics crescendo to the cue's finish. 'Aloy's Theme' encodes the phenomenology of lift, flight or rising to fulfil one's complete potential. These musical characteristics resemble the soaring topic, theorized by Sean Atkinson for video game music as having four components: (1) mechanistic (repetitive motions and gestures), (2) martial (large ascending leaps), (3) transcendent (long sweeping gestures, harp) and (4) supernatural (Lydian mode, vi – ♭ VII progression, etc.); all four of these components are present to some degree in 'Aloy's Theme' (Atkinson 2019, 18). The mechanistic manifests in two ways: indexically, with mechanical and synthesized timbres in the track's introduction, and iconically, via the staccato, subdivided string ostinato layer driving the rhythmic motion forward. The martial is instrumentally encoded via booming, tribalistic drums and an overall anthemic tone, which crescendos throughout the track. This interpretation is reinforced by multiple ascending leaps throughout the melody, successively expanding in intervallic span: A3-E4 (P5), A3-G4 (m7), C4-B4 (M7) and E4-E5 (P8) – if one hears the climax's leap originating from arrival on E4, only leaping up to A4 as a jumping-off point en route to E5. This gradually expanding ascending motion is a fitting aural characterization of Aloy's in-game gravity-defying heroics to come. Signifying the transcendent topic, an arpeggiated harp is present in the melody's first phrase prior to the voice's entrance, and cinematic suspended cymbal rolls and brass pad layers contribute to the music's epic scope. Lastly, the transcendent topic is suggested by the ethereal, reverb-laden vocal melody, which seems to emanate from an altogether different realm. Similar to the Celtic/New Age music of Enya or the use of female vocalise in *The Lord of the Rings* film trilogy (composed by Howard Shore), Elven's vocal timbre bears an ethereal quality imparting a fantastical tone. Taken together, 'Aloy's Theme' convincingly invokes semiotic associations of ascent through the soaring topic, weaving together elements of rising flight, fantastical wonderment, technological augmentation and nigh-supernatural heroic feats (Atkinson 2019, 17). All of these characteristics appropriately set the stage for Aloy's narrative agency, musically represented by Elven's voice.

Uncluttered by accompanying instruments competing for aural attention in that register, Elven's voice captivates the player attention, resonating with an expressive depth and richness unique to that register of mezzo-soprano tessitura. That Aloy's musical characterization is marked with a mezzo-soprano voice is no coincidence or simple matter of convenience, but one laden with historical, cultural and gendered meanings through the conventions of opera. To understand why mezzo-soprano voice is an effective, meaningful choice to characterize Aloy, we must look to lost legends and icons of the operatic world – castrati.

Castrati, Travesti and the Empowered Mezzo-Soprano Voice

A precedent for Aloy's musical gender representation is found in the castrati – young male singers surgically castrated before puberty to retain aspects of their pre-pubescent singing voice. So far, this book's analyses have omitted much discussion of biological sex in favour of focusing on the social construction of gender; however, exploring the castrati necessitates discussion of medical aspects of biological sex, and some conflation of sex and gender is present in the literature cited on the topic (though I shall avoid doing so in my own remarks). Renowned in opera for their inimitable vocal timbre, castrati were the conventional male lead vocalist in serious opera from approximately 1680 to 1830 – by the early 1800s, the practice had virtually disappeared (Rosselli 2001). The prevention of hormonal changes in puberty preserves castrati's soprano-sized vocal cords, while their breath capacity matches a typical adult male's (Travén 2016, 4). Castrati had some female physiological traits as well as male ones, lacking an Adam's apple, lacking typically male body hair and possibly developing breasts (Travén 2016, 8). However, as sought-after and celebrated as castrati were for their vocal performance, society was not necessarily accommodating of their liminality. For '[transgressing] the limits of acceptance for the male [norms] at the time', journalists ridiculed castrati as effeminate, impaired and even immoral (Travén 2016, 8–9). However, the castrato voice – powerful and brilliant, 'strange and rare', 'fabulous and other' – beguiled the ear, considered most suitable to portray heroic, royal and divine characters (Reynolds 1995, 137). The castrato voice defied easy gendered classification, producing 'a sound that encompassed the heroic, masculine, and feminine all at the same time' (André 2006, 43). Though people frequently attempt to identify a speaker's sex from their voice, castrati frustrated these aims, defying societal expectations (Smith 2021, 44). Physically, socially and musically, castrati were considered 'a gender of their own', drifting in gendered limbo while bearing a befuddling 'combination of male and female traits' (Travén 2016, 8). Contemporary observers described castrati with alternating wonder and criticism as neither male nor female – or perhaps partially both (Travén 2016, 10).

The castrati's third gender space was rendered plausible by the medical philosophy of sex at the time; as Raewyn Connell writes, referencing Thomas Laqueur's *Making Sex* (1990):

> Historians of the period have noted a shift in medical ideologies of gender, from an earlier period when gender anomalies were freely attributed to hermaphroditic bodies, to a later period when a clear-cut dichotomy of bodies was presumed ... The requirement that one must have a personal identity as a man or a woman, rather than simply a location in the social order as a person with a male or female (or hermaphroditic) body, gradually hardened in European culture.
>
> (Connell 2005, 188)

In other words, medical theories of human bodies as dichotomously and immutably sexed female and male gradually evolved from earlier ideas of sex more permissive of liminalities. Laqueur's influential account of sex in medical history proposes 'one-sex theory' as founded on classical Greek philosophy and medicine (Aristotle, Galen), holding that female and male bodies are physically inversions of one another determined by body temperature, while 'two-sex theory' casts female and male bodies as 'fundamentally different' and 'altogether different [creatures]' (King 2013, 2, 26). Lacqueur and others dialoguing with his ideas identified a date range from the 1670s to 1820s during which European medical philosophy shifted its emphasis from the one-sex theory to two-sex theory, roughly corresponding with the Enlightenment period. If Lacqueur's account is correct, it is striking that this date range also matches the heyday of castrati, including the practice's decline and disappearance by 1830, when the more rigid two-sex theory had become standard (Rosselli 2001). While Lacqueur's central thesis is vigorously contested in the field of medical history today – such as in Helen King's *The One-Sex Body on Trial* – it is noteworthy that Lacqueur's critics do not typically dispute that European medical theory shifted emphasis from a one-sex to a two-sex model. Rather, they critique Laqueur's characterization of one-sex theory in Greek thought postulating the male sex as original/prototypical, point to greater viewpoint diversity during a particular period (such as the medieval period) or propose a different date and historical catalyst for inaugurating the shift (King 2013, 11, 14–15). For present purposes, it suffices to observe that, by the early-nineteenth century, medical philosophies of sex tended to emphasize two-sex theory – a rigid female-male binary that 'gave little room for the castrati's third gender' (11). What space for liminal gender expression castrati had carved out for themselves vanished into the annals of history, living only in the operatic roles written for their voices.

By the late eighteenth century to early nineteenth century, castrati had become rare, owing in part to the popularization of the two-sex theory and partially to bans on the surgical castration procedure. The operatic roles written for these lost castrato voices were given instead to female mezzo-sopranos, who shared similar range and tessitura (Blackmer and Smith 1995, 10). The vacuum left by castrati's disappearance enabled mezzos to perform celebrated heroic roles, usually in *travesti* – that is, dressed as a man (Jander et al. 2001). Because mezzos filled castrati's roles, the semiotic possibilities and meanings aurally encoded in the castrato voice were 'transferred onto the female *travesti* singers' (André 2006, 33). This includes attributes not considered conventionally feminine such as the castrato voice's 'heroic masculinity' and blurring of gender boundaries (André 2006, 47). Described as a liminal operatic archetype, the mezzo in *travesti* could conduct conventionally masculine business or behaviours on-stage with a voice and body known to be female (André 2006, 56). Through the practice of *travesti*, the mezzo-soprano, like the castrato, mystified and beguiled opera audiences with voices signifying as 'male or female or, ... both male and female simultaneously' (André 2006, 88). Through the curious historical circumstance of the 'rise and demise of the castrato', mezzo-sopranos today claim a number of classic heroic roles in the operatic canon – and the potential to blur gendered musical boundaries (Reynolds 1995, 133). To sing as a mezzo-soprano today is to carry the legacy of the castrati into musical culture and convention, down to the present day.

In Romantic opera, the practice of *travesti* became less common – but mezzo-sopranos, now visibly as women, retained the ability to blend gendered boundaries from the castrati and *travesti*. As renowned mezzo-soprano Marilyn Horne once quipped: 'I'm either the girl who doesn't get the guy, or I *am* the guy, and that's fine with me' (Blackmer and Smith 1995, 1, original emphasis). Though Romantic opera most prominently celebrated its virtuoso soprano roles, several mezzo-soprano roles have emerged as iconic, empowered women – Bizet's Carmen, Verdi's Princess Eboli, Saint-Saëns' Dalila and others. Instead of playing male characters, mezzos transitioned to the 'second woman' archetype – typically a secondary female character who contrasted the leading soprano role in some way, whether as a love rival, world-wise mentor or mother. However, these female character roles still blurred conventional femininity and conventional masculinity to an extent. Listeners were primed by the *travesti* tradition to readily hear and accept the mezzo-soprano's voice as 'both a male and a female voice' (André 2006, 9). Even the term 'mezzo-soprano' originally referred to castrati, whose range most closely matches the modern mezzo (Jander et al. 2001; Travén 2016, 5). Recalling the lost mystique of the castrati, the mezzo-soprano simultaneously voices aspects of conventional femininity and conventional masculinity, inheriting a vocal legacy that simultaneously encodes 'masculine *and* feminine without different aural markers' (André 2006, 44, 48). The historical progression from castrati to *travesti* and finally to the second woman makes the mezzo-soprano the ideal voice type to signify Aloy's musical identity, with her blurring of gendered roles and meanings.

Damsel No Longer – Auralizing Third Gender in Video Game Music

The present cultural-semiotic analysis is now well-positioned to return to the music of *Horizon Zero Dawn* and its sequel, *Horizon Forbidden West*, revealing further meaningful points of resonance between Aloy and the castrati. To clarify, this analysis does not claim that Aloy identifies as a non-binary character, but rather that de Man's score presents Aloy in a musical 'third gender' space on account of her narrative liminality as the empowered female hero of an action-shooter role-playing game. 'Aloy's Theme' and its vocal variations are typically heard in scenes clearly foregrounding Aloy's actions or character development such as the Nora discovering her as an infant or her training montage for the Proving. However, video game scores, like film or opera music, often recall earlier semiotic associations by utilizing leitmotif – a partial recapitulation, re-orchestration or similar textural/harmonic context to previously heard music. This strategy proves especially effective during dialogue scenes when a foregrounded melody or human voice would distract from the spoken voices. When 'Aloy's Theme' is revisited non-vocally, the cello is usually the instrumental proxy for Elven's voice – sometimes on its highest string, sometimes in its lower, idiomatic tessitura within the bass staff. De Man's instrumentation choice is semiotically significant, for the cello, a predominantly bass clef instrument, typically suggests conventional masculinity in contrast to the much higher register of the violin, which signals conventional femininity.

Moreover, the cello, on its highest string, occupies precisely the lower register of the mezzo-soprano's tessitura. In this range, the cello's timbre is plaintive, soaring and passionate, embodying a musical third gender that blurs the boundaries of treble and bass voices. This property is prominently displayed in the track 'Years of Training', which features the melody of 'Aloy's Theme' in the exact key and register of the vocal original, performed expressively on the cello's highest string. Whereas 'Aloy's Theme', when sung low in a mezzo-soprano's register, could be heard as a masculinized feminine voice, 'Years of Training', performed in the cello's highest register, articulates the opposite dynamic – a feminized masculine instrument. This cue is heard during a montage of Aloy's combat and survival training as she matures from a child to an adult, honing the skills players will virtually embody through the remainder of the game. In other words, this pivotal scene is when Aloy shoulders the narrative mantle of the hero, hitherto typically reserved in video games for male characters. This is why de Man's use of the cello, traditionally a bass instrument, in its highest register is significant – this compositional strategy aurally encodes the conventionally masculine hero role occupied by Aloy, blurring conventional femininity and conventional masculinity in her narrative individuality. In the full sonic profile of *Zero Dawn*'s score, whether Aloy's music is thought of as a masculinized femininity or a feminized masculinity is inconsequential – it is both simultaneously a blended hybridization of conventions too long kept apart. The gendered meanings of the cello in this range recall the lost liminality of the castrato inherited by the mezzo-soprano voice. The instrument chosen to represent Aloy could easily have been a flute, violin or another conventionally feminine instrument, performing her melody an octave higher in a soprano tessitura. Instead, the high-register cello strains of 'Years of Training' frustrate conventionally binary musical gendering, crafting a blended, non-binary sonic identity that uniquely corresponds to Aloy's narrative role.

Horizon Forbidden West, the second game in the series, has not been the focus of this chapter, but some brief concluding remarks about the sequel are in order. Aloy's character development in *Forbidden West* complicates and nuances her trajectory in *Zero Dawn*, but does not fundamentally alter its representational merits. Immediately after successfully saving Meridian and the tribes encountered in *Zero Dawn*, Aloy embarks to find a backup of Gaia, the supercomputer that can bring the machines dominating the landscape into proper order. In the process, she encounters her allies – Varl, Erend and Avad – who offer their assistance in her mission. Aloy refuses their help, insisting on carrying the burden of saving the world alone. However, as Aloy encounters new antagonists and challenges, she realizes that she must allow others to support her mission however they can, covering her own blind spots and limitations. This does not place Aloy in a position of helplessness as a damsel-in-distress but rather acknowledges that even the most capable, independent individuals cannot succeed entirely on their own – rather, every person needs the support of a network of individuals who they can trust. Musically, 'Aloy's Theme' and its primary leitmotif are used in ways consistent with their usage in *Zero Dawn*. The track 'Aloy's Theme – Forbidden West' builds on the original's existing foundation with added acoustic guitar, electric bass, percussion and synthesizer layers. Further enhancing the intertextual continuity, the original recording of Elven's voice from *Zero Dawn* is used as the basis for the new track. An expanded introduction, outro and transition further inflects the *Zero Dawn* track's signification with associations of the frontier (strummed acoustic guitar, shaker percussion), technological (synthesizer, sequencer layers) and the supernatural through an otherworldly, ephemeral delay effect used on the last note of Elven's melody, transitioning to the track's extended outro.

Similar strategies to *Zero Dawn* recur throughout *Forbidden West*'s score. As the game's opening credits play over a montage of Aloy's travels, the folk-influenced song 'In the Flood' (Oleksa Lozowchuk feat. vocals by Ariana Gillis) plays, emphasizing finger-picked steel-string acoustic guitar, cello playing reminiscent of the fiddle tradition and light shaker/hand percussion. Like 'Aloy's Theme' and its updated reprise, 'In the Flood' is set in the key of A Aeolian-Minor. Just as the cello echoed Elven's voice in 'Years of Training', prominent tenor-register cello melodies alternate with the vocal phrases. Most importantly, vocalist Ariana Gillis, like Julie Elven before her, articulates a clear mezzo-soprano register, ranging from G3 to C5 (Figure 4.3). The opening scenes of *Forbidden West* aurally demonstrate that Aloy's empowered agency and non-binary gender construction continue unabated into the new game. Throughout *Forbidden West*, Aloy encounters additional allies on whom she can rely, including the Utaru Gravesinger, Zo. Zo is another excellent example of positive female character representation, though with a demeanour that contrasts Aloy's. Like Aloy, Zo's identity is tightly bound up in music, reflecting her chosen profession as a ritual singer. When Aloy first meets Zo, the gravesinger is in the process of singing for Re, one of the tribe's fallen Land-Gods (benevolent machines terraforming Utaru land for agriculture).[5] Zo's song, reminiscent of folk traditions, spans a range from A3 to G4, presenting a B Aeolian-Minor melody over a tonic B drone (Figure 4.3). Significantly, this range is almost identical to the iconic lower register outlined at the beginning of 'Aloy's Theme'. Another empowered female character is musically characterized by a mezzo-soprano voice, reinforcing the music-semiotic argument advanced in this chapter.

The mezzo-soprano voice exemplified by Julie Elven fits Aloy narratively and thematically, in a manner consistent with the mezzo's semiotic associations from opera. The average player may not think of the legacy of castrati and *travesti* when hearing Elven's voice in-game but can hear her low register blurring the binary boundaries of female and male voices. The score's use of mezzo-soprano and cello signals a more nuanced presentation of Aloy's character, where a conventionally feminine timbre like flute or soprano voice would lead players to expect a traditional female romantic lead, like countless operatic soprano roles. The shaping of sound encodes subjective qualities akin to an individual's conscious experience, providing listeners a window into the perspective of another (Cumming 2000, 26). In other words, to listen to Aloy's musical voice during gameplay is to encounter who she is as a person. Like the mezzo's voice, Aloy is a heroine who synthesizes conventionally feminine and conventionally masculine characteristics in a single semiotic package.

One final statement deserves mention, elegantly bringing the present analysis full circle. *Horizon Forbidden West* also suffered from review bombing, though

FIGURE 4.3: Partial musical transcription of 'In the Flood' and Zo's song, *Horizon Forbidden West* (2022). Transcription by the author.

not as total or organized a campaign as against *Captain Marvel* or *The Last of Us 2*. The reason? Pre-release promotional footage showed Aloy's *Forbidden West* character model and outfit, updated for higher realism and resolution on the PlayStation 5. However, some viewers complained that Aloy's new outfit and design were insufficiently 'feminine', alleging that developers had hardened her facial features, increased her body weight or reduced her curves (Greenbaum 2022). As seen above, where female characters cannot be contained as damsel-in-distress via benevolent sexism, some may instead turn to hostile sexism, demanding female bodies exist for the consumption and pleasure of men. Fortunately,

Horizon's developers did not listen to these complaints, leaving those disgruntled to take out their frustration on the game's reviews. Where Gamergate would see women banished from centre stage in a bid to revitalize masculinist gamer culture, *Horizon Zero Dawn* unapologetically foregrounds Aloy as a model of female representation needed in today's video game industry. Where the damsel-in-distress trope sequesters women into helplessness, and more recent trends cast female characters' bodies as existing solely for men's viewing pleasure, Aloy falls into neither pitfall. Musically, 'Aloy's Theme' encodes her occupying the hero role traditionally reserved for male characters, blending conventionally feminine and conventionally masculine characteristics just as the mezzo-soprano's semiotic associations did. This is why *Horizon Zero Dawn* – and the kind of hero Aloy represents – matters (Chen 2017). Through the lasting influence of *Horizon Zero Dawn* and its sequel *Horizon Forbidden West*, Aloy powerfully advances positive female representation. Narratively and musically, '*Horizon* is unapologetic about putting a woman in a position of power and prestige: no ifs, ands, or buts required' (Williams 2020, n.pag.). Through empowered lead women like Aloy, the future of positive gender representation in video games appears auspicious.

Though this book now moves on from its discussion of gender into matters of racial representation, the principles established in Chapters 2–4 continue to hold true when discussing matters of race and culture. Societies typically elevate one demographic identity, one mode of being over others, and judge non-normative expressions against that standard. Nonetheless, forms of resistance or subversion to the norm persist, employing a variety of ingenious strategies to signal their alternativity. Finally, while historical video game examples from past decades establish and cling to convention, contemporary case studies gesture towards promising new and more equitable directions.

NOTES

*   Supplementary Video 4.1 'Damsel No Longer: The Empowered Female Voice in Horizon Zero Dawn' can be found here: https://www.youtube.com/watch?v=qiqyaF5pMLY. Accessed 3 June 2024. Standalone colour file of Figures 4.1, and standalone illustration files of Figures 4.2 and 4.3a–b can be found under the Front Matter section for *Gender, Race and Religion in Video Game Music's* page on Intellect Discover.

1.   Bayonetta constitutes a salient case study here, as a female character who openly wields and flaunts her sexuality as an aspect of gameplay – including during combat. Players' intuitions typically do not cast Bayonetta as disempowered by her sexual design, though perspectives may differ. As mentioned at the end of the section, perhaps the distinguishing factor is whether the female character's clothing and mannerisms come across as an expression of

her own sexuality rather than something imposed upon her for external viewers' pleasure. Another example, covered in Chapter 7, is Twintelle from ARMS. Twintelle's figure and mannerisms include features that could be considered exaggerated or sexualized, yet some players – particularly Black women players – report feeling empowered while playing as Twintelle in part because of her body. When discussing sexuality and gender representation in media, there are no easy categorical answers, but rather a few clear cases on the edges with a mire of grey area in between.

2. This should not be taken to imply that Aloy is the first female main character in a triple-A video game series. Far from it – any discussion of female main characters in video games would need to include Lara Croft, Bayonetta, Samus Aran (*Metroid*), Jodie Holmes (*Beyond: Two Souls*), Heather Mason (*Silent Hill 3*), Lightning (covered in Chapter 4), Velvet Crowe (*Tales of Berseria*), Ellie (*The Last of Us 2*) and Senua (*Hellblade: Senua's Sacrifice*) – to list only a few. However, the present purpose is not to be exhaustive, and a treatment of all these exceeds the scope of this research. Though preceded by other female protagonists worthy of study in their own right, Aloy's arrival was perceived as a milestone indicative of a sea change in video game female character representation. Whether or not that perception bears out in the long term remains to be seen.

3. As will be explored further below, the sequel *Horizon Forbidden West* complicates this balance achieved in the first game. However, it does not do so in a way that negates the nature of Aloy's character, but rather sketches opportunities for Aloy's further growth and character development throughout the *Horizon* series.

4. The analysis is somewhat complicated by interpretive player agency, as players often have the opportunity to influence Aloy's responses during pivotal story moments. These response choices are divided into 'confrontational', 'insightful' and 'compassionate' responses. For example, when Rost explains that he and Aloy must never see each other again in order for Aloy to become a full member of the tribe, the abbreviated response choices include: 'Then good riddance' (confrontational), 'But I will find you' (insightful) and 'I understand' (compassionate). The confrontational response in these interpersonal conversations often does not demonstrate empathy or vulnerability, whereas the insightful and especially compassionate responses are more likely to do so.

5. As another musical tie-in within Utaru culture, the Land-Gods are named after the real-world musical system of *solfege* in the major mode – Do, Re, Mi, Fa, So, La and Ti.

PART III

RACE

5

Racialized Fantasy:
Authenticity, Appropriation and Stereotype

Introduction – Racebending in Hollywood

It begins like a joke set-up: 'what do film stars Mary Pickford, John Wayne, Marlon Brando, Mickey Rooney, Yul Brynner and Emma Stone have in common?' Yet the answer is no punchline: all these (and more) appear on the silver screen in yellowface – the practice of portraying characters of Asian-American/Pacific Islander (AAPI) descent using White actors,[1] often using cosmetics in a haphazard attempt to sell the illusion. Yellowface is at least as old as theatrical arts circa 1850, when the chinoiserie fad in decorative arts spurred theatre companies to produce musical and plays set in China and performed by White casts (Moon 2004, 11). In the film, the practice of yellowface is as old as the medium itself, spanning from Mary Pickford's *Madame Butterfly* (1915) to the present day. Particularly notorious is Fox's casting of the Swedish-American Warner Oland as detective Charlie Chan, the first hero of Chinese descent in American film.[2] Another common Hollywood practice is Whitewashing – erasing a character's markers of non-White descent, culture or appearance for a White actor to play – including in recent films *21*, *Prince of Persia*, *Argo*, *Doctor Strange* and *Ghost in the Shell*. Keith Chow of *The Nerds of Color* writes that Whitewashing 'results in the dehumanization of people of color; and, in the specific case of yellowface, in the dehumanization of Asian people' (Fang 2018, n.pag.). Yet an unlikely source spawned the Whitewashing controversy that catalysed a protest movement: the animated television series *Avatar: The Last Airbender*.

The beloved, critically acclaimed *Avatar: The Last Airbender* (2005–2008) occurs in a fantasy world suffused with elements from real-world East Asian and Inuit cultures.[3] Show creators Michael DiMartino and Bryan Konietzko researched East Asian mythology, history, religion and art, collaborating with cultural consultants on the show's scripts, martial arts choreography and Chinese calligraphy (Nickelodeon Asia 2005). However, M. Night Shyamalan's live-action adaptation *The Last Airbender* (2010) faced denunciations of racism and Whitewashing from fans and Asian-American advocacy groups over the film's all-White casting of its three main protagonists Aang, Katara and Sokka. Shyamalan also reworked the dark-skinned Water Tribe as all-White to match, leaving antagonists Zuko and the Fire Nation as visibly non-White others. Casting calls for the Fire Nation 'explicitly requested [...] Near Eastern, Middle Eastern, Far Eastern, Asian, Mediterranean, and Latino' applicants, making the intended juxtaposition clear (Demby 2010, n.pag.).

In response, a staff member of the original show – using the pen name 'Aang Ain't White' – launched a letter-writing protest movement that evolved into the Racebending website, which derived its name from the series. Advocacy groups Media Action Network for Asian Americans (MANAA) and the East-West Players wrote open letters to Paramount Pictures condemning the casting. However, Paramount returned all letters without response, and in an interview Shyamalan retorted: '[m]aybe they didn't see the faces that they wanted to see but, overall, it is more than they could have expected' (MANAA 2010, n.pag.). *The Last Airbender* was released in 2010 with an unchanged cast but imploded under its abysmal quality and critical panning (5 per cent positive reviews on aggregate website Rotten Tomatoes). However, Racebending – as an organization and a term – outlasted the film that brought it into being, continuing to advocate for equitable racial representation in film casting. 'It is the height of White privilege to think a White person is better equipped to play an Asian character than an Asian person', declares actor Sun Mee Chomet, 'Asian-Americans are [...] demanding a permanent seat at the creative table. We have the power to render racist representations of ourselves as obsolete' (Fang 2018, n.pag.). After enduring over a century and a half of yellowface and Whitewashing, AAPI activists' voices make clear that representation of AAPI cultures and communities must be held to a higher standard.

But why should the race of real-world actors portraying fictional characters within an animated fantasy setting – like that of *Avatar* – matter?[4] Indeed, typical counter-arguments to racial representation objections frequently appeal to fantasy in two ways:

1. fictional settings are, by definition, irrelevant to real-world representation; and
2. fantasy is trivial entertainment not worth protesting about (Shaw 2010, 207).

The following two chapters refute both assumptions. In actuality, it is precisely within fantasy that diversity in racial and other forms of representation is most critical since storytelling subtly shapes audience attitudes and beliefs about real-life communities in ways not easily prevented by cognitive or cultural safeguards. Contrary to the fantasy defence, human beings are inherently meaning-making interpreters whose boundaries between reality and narrative are not rigidly defined.

Whenever a fictional world's cultures or populations are designed with traits associated with a particular real-world culture or population, it becomes a 'racialized fantasy'. A plethora of video game worlds qualifies as racialized fantasy, providing provocative case studies for analysing racial representation in these gameworlds – both musical and otherwise.

Chapters 5 and 6 make up Part III of the book, which explores musical representation of nationality, culture and race in video game music. Broadly speaking, Chapter 5 examines case studies that construct fictional cultures with traits associated with a particular real-world culture, introducing the concept of 'racialized fantasy' to describe such cases. Chapter 6 applies Ibram X. Kendi's segregation-assimilation-antiracism spectrum to musical cultural representation, analysing two examples that exemplify antiracist storytelling. Chapter 5 begins by establishing foundational context for the book's analyses of racial representation, including the #BlackLivesMatter and Stop AAPI Hate movements in the United States, backlash against Philip Ewell's 'Music Theory's White Racial Frame' SMT keynote presentation and an abbreviated history of racialized terminology and pseudo-scientific theories. The discussion then considers the music of *Super Mario Odyssey* (2017), contrasting the pan-Latin caricature of Tostarena with the nuanced, hybridity-driven discourse of the score for Bowser's Castle – even though each world's music is shown to be 'inauthentic'. After problematizing and interrogating the concept of 'authenticity' by way of historical precedents including the sale of Turkmen carpets, the world music genre and so-called 'Indianisms', the chapter proposes 'stereotype' as a better litmus test then 'authenticity' for discerning positive or negative musical cultural representation. Finally, the invitational approach of *Raji: An Ancient Epic* (2020) presents a work that invites players to participate in its ongoing cultural practices – not existing for outsiders nor catering to their preferences. By participating in the musical traditions of the communities represented and relaying them in the game's racialized fantasy in non-stereotypical ways, *Raji* and composer Linos Tzelos construct a discourse that honours the culture whose music, architecture, mythology and spiritual traditions infuse the game's narrative and aesthetics.

'It's Complicated' – the Shifting Landscape of Race Discourse

On 25 May 2020, Minneapolis police officer Derek Chauvin pinned George Floyd to the ground, kneeling on Floyd's neck for eight minutes and forty-six seconds until death. Floyd was Black. Chauvin was White. Together with the unjust killings of Breonna Taylor and Ahmaud Arbery (both Black) earlier that year, Floyd's murder resulted in a worldwide outcry for racial justice. It was an all-too-familiar story, one increasingly visible since the 2013 formation of the #BlackLivesMatter movement following the murder of Trayvon Martin. However, this time the zeitgeist felt palpably different. Perhaps it was the three deaths occurring within months of each other. Perhaps it was the chilling video footage documenting each excruciating second of Floyd's final minutes of life. Or perhaps it was the onset of the COVID-19 pandemic bringing the world to a virtual standstill, making news of Floyd's death unavoidable and arresting. Whatever the reason, the protests coalesced into a summer of racial reckoning, as the United States' racist past and present of police brutality, racial inequity and extant Confederate monuments captured centre stage in the public consciousness.

Simultaneously, academic music theory in the United States experienced its own racial reckoning. It began with Philip Ewell's plenary address at the Society for Music Theory's November 2019 conference, titled 'Music Theory's White Racial Frame'. In it – and the expanded *Music Theory Online* adaptation – Ewell challenged academic music theory to acknowledge its white racial frame, citing the overwhelmingly White SMT membership and composers used in music theory textbooks, the inclusion of White supremacist Blackface composer Stephen Foster in all but one major textbook and the racism of German music theorist Heinrich Schenker, whose ideas exert disproportionate influence in American music theory.[5] Debates in academic music theory rarely cause ripples in other disciplines, let alone in society at large – however, the resulting controversy was covered by *National Review*, *NPR*, *The Dallas Observer*, *Inside Higher Ed*, *New York Times*, *New Yorker* and *Fox News*. What prompted this public attention? In July 2020 – as #BlackLivesMatter protests continued unabated – the *Journal of Schenkerian Studies* published a symposium issue aiming to defend Schenker and refute Ewell. This might have constituted healthy scholarly dialogue, had some articles not included racist tropes and ad hominem attacks on Ewell. The journal also failed to meet academic publishing standards: the editors included an anonymous entry, did not invite Ewell himself to participate and did not vet the fifteen essays via standard peer review. For these reasons, the Executive Board of SMT condemned the journal as '[failing] to meet the ethical, professional and scholarly standards of our discipline', and an open letter of 900+ international SMT members echoed the board's sentiments (Society for Music Theory 2020, n.pag.). The fortuitous simultaneity of racial reckoning in American society and academic music theory underscores this conclusion: examining racial representation in every avenue – including in video game music – is a critical enterprise. To that end, proceeding to an abbreviated survey of concepts, terminology and history within the field of race studies will prove beneficial.

A frequent mantra of *NPR*'s podcast *Code Switch* sums up the shifting landscape of race discourse well: 'it's complicated'. This complexity is evident from the terminology used to talk about race and identify individuals of different demographic groups. For starters, why frame discussion in terms of race rather than another concept like ethnicity? In race scholarship, race is a master category that profoundly shapes an individual's social, political, medical and educational outcomes (Omi and Winant 2015, 106). On the other hand, ethnicity refers to people groups with elements of shared immigration history, language, foodways, religion, art or folklore. For Ibram X. Kendi, race collects and organizes perceived differences – including ethnic and cultural ones – into stratified social hierarchies (Kendi 2019, 35). In other words, race results when race-makers make perceived ethnic, cultural or physical differences the basis for social inequities. Though not interchangeable, ethnicity and race are tightly intertwined – particularly within European and American contexts – for when an ethnic group enters a racialized society, it too becomes racialized. First comes counting, the recognition of a population's presence; then comes naming, when race-makers situate the group within the existing hierarchy; last comes characterization, identifying traits purportedly representative of and inherent to the group (Treitler 2013, 7–8). Video games commonly represent ethnicity and culture in ways that become racialized in the context of broader social, political and evaluative meanings.

The terms employed in this book to denote racial demographics are White, Black, Indigenous (to the Americas or Australia), AAPI (Asian-American/Pacific Islander), Middle-Eastern and Latina/o.[6] When describing racial groups that are not White, I use non-White over an acronym like BIPOC or BAME.[7] Note that this terminology is constantly in flux, and these are indexed to my cultural context in the 2020s United States. Though the labels used for demographic groups continuously change, the underlying history and reality of racialization remain as a constant. I take up these words not as ontological categories, but as dialectic tools – ways to talk about social constructions of race reified in communities' lived experiences.

One disclaimer remains before launching the investigation. Though this section centres on racial representation, it does not directly analyse the representation of Black communities in video game music – though it references scholarly literature on Black media and cultural representation. This may strike the reader as an egregious oversight since race theory has traditionally centred around social constructions of White and Black. This omission is due to my lesser scholarly expertise analysing music genres originating from and associated with Black communities – of which there are many. The contributions of Black musicians to American music are too often erased or overlooked (a process Ewell terms 'colorasure'), permeating virtually every popular music genre. Examining Black representation in video game music is crucial work that requires foregrounding these innovations, theorizing musical criteria for interpreting Blackness in a game's score and analysing relevant case studies situated in their narrative and social context – and I am not currently equipped to do so.[8]

However, I am a third-/fourth-generation Chinese-American scholar devoted to analysing racial representation of a broad spectrum of demographics in media and culture, expanding beyond the traditional Black-White binary. Non-White, non-Black communities also experience racialized hate crimes, inequities, stereotypes and misrepresentations – including Latina/o, Indigenous, AAPI and Middle-Eastern communities. For example, *Stop AAPI Hate* was launched in March 2020 to document 'incidents of hate, violence, harassment, discrimination, shunning, and child bullying against Asian Americans and Pacific Islanders' resulting from the rise in xenophobia following the onset of the global COVID-19 pandemic. To date, Stop AAPI Hate documented 10,000+ reports of anti-AAPI activity across the United States, with more occurring in 2021 than in 2020 (Stop AAPI Hate 2021). The deaths of Vicha Ratanapakdee, Yao Pan Ma, Michelle Go, six AAPI women in the March 2021 Atlanta spa shootings and many others from anti-AAPI hate crimes cry out for an adequate response. As someone who experienced racial bullying and discrimination in childhood, I know firsthand the importance of unveiling racism in all its forms, against various communities.[9] As the video game industry establishes an increasingly global presence, understanding the racial representation of cultures worldwide is essential. Today, as in the past, racist ideas are not quarantined by national borders – especially when digital media like video games permeate the globe.

From their inception, theories of race aimed to categorize and structure the world's people groups, attributing to racial others immutable biological or cultural attributes supposedly validating their oppression. Though identifying a definite chronological genesis of racialization is impossible, owing to race's chameleonic conceptual identity that constantly reinvents itself in order to construct hierarchy from socially perceived difference, medieval Europe contains many seeds of racialized policies or ideas (Heng 2018, 19). These include tagging and herding of communities, expulsions of ethnic groups from a nation, state-sanctioned killing of racial others, theological transvaluation of skin colour, anti-miscegenation practices and attribution of monstrous or deformed physical features to bodies of marginalized others (Heng 2018, 16; Ramey 2014, 2). Medieval thought primed European cultures to 'question the very humanness of the Other', justifying their treatment as things and prefiguring trans-Atlantic chattel slavery (Ramey 2014, 31). In a chilling foreshadowing of Germany's Third Reich, thirteenth century England required Jews to wear badges on their chests, monitored Jewish businesses and wealth, limited Jews' areas of residence and ultimately expelled Jews from the nation altogether (Heng 2018, 15, 29). Just as religious differences were racialized, ethnic differences like skin melanation were spiritualized – the colour black symbolized damnation, sinfulness, sensuality, demon-possession and political opposition, stigmatizing Black bodies in the medieval imagination (Heng 2018, 16, 42, 44). The racially fuelled classification of medieval Others demonstrates that racism is no unfortunate accident or mistake, but rather that '[scientific] racism was the inevitable outcome of the centuries of thought that preceded it' (Ramey 2014, 37). As Heng warns, not to identify policies and ideas in the medieval period as participating in racism risks '[destigmatizing] the impacts and consequences of certain laws, acts, practices, and institutions' that upheld racialized regimes and paved the way for overt systemic racism in the centuries to follow (2018, 23).

Pseudo-scientific racial taxonomies such as Carolus Linnaeus's 'White, Red, Yellow, Black' (1735) and Johann Friedrich Blumenbach's 'Caucasoid, Mongoloid, Negroid' (1775) claim to group all humankind into fixed groups with essentialized characteristics designed to justify White superiority and rule (Ramey 2014, 9). Gomes de Zurara (1453) and Leo Africanus (1526) described Africans as bestial and innately subservient for the same reasons, attempting to justify the colonization of Africa and the eventual establishment of the trans-Atlantic slave trade during the Age of Exploration. Similarly, medieval pseudo-scientific treatises falsely claimed Jewish bodies emitted a unique odour (*foetor judaicus*), required consumption of Christian blood for sustenance (blood libel) and even possessed horns and tails (Heng 2018, 15). Thirteenth-century Europe's project of constructing a *mappamundi* (map of the world) is racially fuelled, visualizing communities' distance from Europe as indicative of their degree of humanity, depicting distant peoples as 'part-human, misshapen, deformed, and disabled' (Heng 2018, 34–35). These projects illustrate the link between racial theory and representation of global Others, fuelling the conquest programmes of imperialist Europe throughout the colonialist era. In the United States, race shaped immigration restrictions since 1790 – the infamous Chinese Exclusion Act of 1882 and the Immigration Act of 1924 excluded immigrants of predominantly AAPI and Middle-Eastern descent. Let this be blamed merely on the racism of centuries past, the 2017 Presidential Proclamation 9645 targeted eight Middle-Eastern, African and Asian countries for total or partial immigration bans. The history of imperialism, pseudo-scientific racial taxonomies and immigration politics shows that racialization has global stakes, long after it has become clear that the world's communities and individuals have more in common than what divides them.

A final word about intersectionality: the following analyses focus on racial identity, but race cannot be fully disentangled from other identity markers, including gender (cf. Crenshaw 1989). Racialized discourse frequently employs gendered rhetoric, such as sports media's emasculation of AAPI males suggested by its exaggerated surprise over Taiwanese-American basketball star Jeremy Lin's athleticism (Park 2015). Edward Said explores metaphors used by European writers describing the so-called 'Orient' as a veiled, virgin bride ripe for the taking (Said 1978, 222). The video game *Resident Evil 5* (2009) interleaves racism and sexism, depicting Sheva Alomar – a Black woman – as sexualized, inarticulate and subordinate window-dressing for the White male main character (Brock 2011, 443). As Michael Park writes, 'hegemonic masculinity is also a racialised masculinity' (Park 2015, 372). Thus, the current exploration of race resonates with the book's previous discussion of gender.

A Tale of Two Kingdoms – Racialized Fantasy in Super Mario Odyssey

Nintendo's iconic *Super Mario* franchise may seem an unlikely candidate for a racialized fantasy. What does the whimsical world of Goombas and Koopas, Yoshis and Toads have to do with real-world race or ethnicity? At first glance, the series appears to exemplify both prongs of the typical 'fantasy defence' presented above: (1) representation in fictional worlds is irrelevant to the real world; and (2) representation in trivial play or entertainment is not worth analysing critically. However, the series' latest instalment *Super Mario Odyssey* (2017) generated accusations of racism and cultural appropriation from Latina/o communities over its controversial Mexico-themed level Tostarena.

Producer Yoshiaki Koizumi describes the theme of *Super Mario Odyssey* as 'world travel' – hence the title's allusion to Homer's epic. Throughout the game, Mario pursues Bowser, circumnavigating a vaguely Earthlike planet in his hat-shaped airship Odyssey and visiting various kingdoms along the way. *Mario* series games are no strangers to traversing a range of settings, from the worlds of *Super Mario Brothers*, paintings of *Super Mario 64* or galaxies of *Super Mario Galaxy*. However, *Odyssey* is unique in that several of its kingdoms are inspired by real-world locations: New Donk City by New York City, the Luncheon Kingdom by Italy, Bubblaine by France, Lake Lamode by Scotland, Shiveria by Russia, Bowser's Castle by Japan and Tostarena by Mexico. Koizumi intended this kaleidoscopic approach to evoke the combined awe and alienation of travelling to new, unfamiliar places and encountering a culture for the first time (Byford 2017). By including specific references to the language, architecture, art, artefacts, clothing, cuisine, lore and music of real countries, *Odyssey* creates a racialized fantasy, offering an illuminating case study of cultural representation in a fictional gameworld. Some references are rather a slant – in the Luncheon Kingdom, Italian influences include the volcanic Mount Volbono (read: Vesuvius), Greco-Roman architecture, 'street café' music featuring accordion and *mandolino* and abundant references to gourmet cuisine (the resident Volbonans are sentient forks wearing chef hats).

When developers desired to create a food-themed kingdom, they chose Italy as an inspiration for its culinary reputation (Nintendo UK 2017). Two other kingdoms – Tostarena and Bowser's Castle – bear more obvious cultural footprints.

The Sand Kingdom containing Tostarena became [in]famous before *Super Mario Odyssey* ever launched. Pre-release box art and early trailer footage – especially in the 10 June 2017 E3 trailer – showcased Mario donning a *sombrero* and *poncho* in the Mexico-inspired Tostarena. The town's colourful architecture, *nopales* and *calacas* (skeletons inspired by *Dia de los Muertos* sugar skulls) wearing sombreros, ponchos and holding *maracas* are clear references to Mexican culture (Figure 5.1). In the trailers, Tostarena and New Donk City are the only kingdoms shown to have clear real-world parallels – the Luncheon Kingdom's Italian elements are obscured (showing Mount Volbono's culinary-inspired elements without its clear Roman and Italian references), and the other worlds shown were culturally generic.

While some Latina/o writers praised the inclusion of Mexican elements (Palacios 2018), others objected to the depiction as stereotyping and cultural appropriation (Xataka 2017). Exasperation was specifically directed at Mario's sombrero-poncho outfit, which critics described as a 'caricature of a stereotype' and 'like a thoughtless college student at Halloween' (Muncy 2017, n.pag.; Shimomura 2017). Sombreros and ponchos have long histories as caricatures of Mexican culture in American media, making their ubiquity in Tostarena especially egregious (Garcia 2018). Two months after E3, Nintendo removed the image of Mario in a sombrero from *Odyssey*'s box art, possibly due to poor publicity. Additionally, the Sand Kingdom containing Tosatrena was clearly conceived as a desert level, another odd choice considering that less than a third of Mexico's area consists of desert climate. Wired's Julie Muncy calls Tostarena a 'clumsy mashup' of Mexican stereotypes and a failure to recognize that real communities are being represented by these exoticized symbols (2017). Taken together, Tostarena comes across as a tourist's surface impressions or preconceptions of Mexico rather than a faithful or creative portrayal.

Tostarena is usually considered in isolation, but a fuller understanding requires comparison to another case of cultural representation within the game. *Odyssey*'s penultimate kingdom Bowser's Castle stands in striking contrast to Tostarena, presenting a tableau of Japanese culture eliciting widespread praise. This conclusion may seem obvious – since Nintendo is a Japanese developer, is it not natural to represent Japan authentically? Is it possible for Japanese creators to appropriate Japanese culture? These are more complex questions than they initially appear – ones that shall be problematized later in the chapter. At present, it is beneficial to explore Bowser's Castle's Japanese influences. If Tostarena's Mexican elements were easily recognizable caricatures, Bowser's Castle is an intricate quilt woven from various complementary patterns, communicating a multifaceted vision of

GENDER, RACE AND RELIGION IN VIDEO GAME MUSIC

FIGURE 5.1: Wide angle of Tostarena town (above), Mario wearing sombrero and poncho with a Tostarenan (below).

Japanese culture (Figure 5.2). In fact, the layered Japanese influences are so prevalent and detailed that it is impossible to describe them all. I will provide a representative sample and refer the curious to an excellent video series on the topic (Gaijin Goombah 2017a, 2017b).

Bowser's Kingdom is constructed as a Japanese castle from the *sengoku jidai* (戦国 時代; 'Warring States period'), making Bowser its *daimyō* (大名; 'feudal

RACIALIZED FANTASY

FIGURE 5.2: Wide angle of Bowser's Castle (top left), Stairface Ogre with red *oni* mask, *geta* shoes and *Hanafuda* card stamp (top right), *Jizō* statues in a Zen rock garden (bottom left), Bowser-marked fireworks and Pokio enemy (bottom right).

lord'). Mario's encroachment re-enacts an assault on Bowser's territory from the samurai of an opposing clan. Its residents include Goombahs wearing *jingasa* (陣笠; 'commoner's straw hat'), Stairface Ogres resembling red *oni* (鬼; 'demon') wearing *geta* (下駄; 'traditional wooden sandal') and the Pokio, a swashbuckling bird based on the *aogera* (緑啄木鳥; 'Japanese Green Woodpecker'). The level's puzzles and obstacles include a Zen Buddhist rock garden, Japanese *hanabi* (花火; 'fireworks'), a *byōbu* (屏風; 'folding screen') and a photorealistic koi pond. Its décor and architecture include statues of the bodhisattva *Jizō* (地蔵), golden Bowser statues portrayed as *Raijin* and *Fujin* (雷神 and 風神; 'gods of thunder and wind'), *Hanafuda* (花札) cards and stamps alluding to Nintendo's signature product before video games, a *Kofun jidai* (古墳時代; 'Kofun period') gift shop, ancient *koban* (小判) coins, the *Sanada* clan's *rokumonsen* (六文銭; lit. 'six coin') helmets and *karakuri* (絡繰り; 'mechanical puppets') dolls. Nearing the level's conclusion, *nobori* (幟) flags and *chōchin* (提灯; 'paper lantern') bear *kanji* proclaiming 寿空覇 (*kotobuki kuppa*, lit. 'long life, heavenly rulership'), in which the last two characters play on Bowser's Japanese name, producing the reading 'long live Bowser'.[10] The sheer density and interlocking synergy of these Japanese elements render players and cultural analysts alike awestruck, offering obscure references to uncover on every subsequent playthrough. However, one crucial domain not typically mentioned in such commentaries is music. Though these two kingdoms' soundtracks remain underexplored, detailed musical analysis yields fruitful results. It is to music that our focus now shifts, for music explains the world of difference between Tostarena's and Bowser's Castle's racial representation.

The analysis first considers the music of Tostarena and Bowser's Castle according to the criterion of 'authenticity' – here taken to mean its degree of correspondence to the musical practices of the culture represented. Though authenticity (or 'accuracy' and 'faithfulness' of reproducing the original culture) is a commonsense metric used to assess cultural representation in media, this chapter will probe whether authenticity alone is sufficient as a criterion for differentiating productive and problematic cultural representation. First, the music of Tostarena is considered. Considering Tostarena clothes its residents in sombreros and ponchos, the music used to broadcast Mexican identity is, predictably, mariachi. Mariachi is well-known as a 'visual and sound symbol of Mexico' – but is *Odyssey*'s mariachi authentic (Henriques 2006, 1)? The area's main musical cue, 'Tostarena – Town', signals mariachi through its melody, played in alternation on two trumpets and two violins; alternation of trumpet and violin melodies is standard mariachi practice, though typically trumpets and violin would play the *entrada* in unison, while the track's contains only trumpets (Pearlman 1988, 218). The trumpet duo sound is particularly characteristic of mariachi, as popularized by Mariachi México de Pepe Villa (Sheehy 2006, 21). Additionally, the guitar features a percussive hit resulting from stopping the strings with the strumming hand as part of a *mánico* pattern (Sheehy 2006, 25). This technique is characteristic of mariachi, though the guitar part contains other elements deviating from tradition (Figure 5.3). A second cue, 'Dancing with New Friends!' plays if Mario dons sombrero and poncho and plays the guitar with the Tostarenans. This thirteen-second snippet also evokes mariachi through its two-trumpet melody and foregrounded guitar. Both tracks feature grace notes and slides in the trumpet and violin, a technique that is present in mariachi – but used here in excess. These factors make clear that composer Naoto Kubo intended to reference mariachi music in both cues.

However, Tostarena's music diverges from traditional mariachi practice in multiple ways. Authentic mariachi is primarily characterized by its instrumentation – trumpet, violin, *vihuela*, guitar and *guitarrón* (Henriques 2006, 1; Pearlman 1988, 200). Three guitar-family instruments comprise the core mariachi rhythm section, known as the *armonía*: guitarrón, nylon-string classical guitar and vihuela (from largest to smallest) (Pearlman 1988, 202; Sheehy 2006, 25). In 'Tostarena – Town', an electric bass substitutes for the guitarrón and a contemporary steel-string guitar for the much smaller vihuela. The steel timbre is likely meant to approximate the brighter, higher-tension sound of the vihuela – but steel strings are not used in the mariachi guitar, and mariachi groups rarely if ever double

RACIALIZED FANTASY

FIGURE 5.3: Partial musical transcription of 'Tostarena – Town'. Transcription by author.

guitar as 'Tostarena – Town' does (Pearlman 1988, 203). Lacking both vihuela and guitarrón, two instruments considered especially essential to mariachi and representative of Mexican identity is a devastating omission (Sheehy 2006, 22). The track also adds percussion (bongos, tambourine) and accordion, instruments not typically found in mariachi. While some groups experiment with expanded instrumentation as a reference to the style's past history (such as Mariachi Vargas de Tecalitlán including harp), accordion and percussion are not likely candidates (Sheehy 2006, 26). Traditional ensembles also include three to eight violins, while this track has only two – far too few for the classic mariachi violin section sound and three-part harmonization (Pearlman 1988, 201; Sheehy 2006, 21). The second track, 'Dancing with New Friends!', reduces its instrumentation to classical guitar and two trumpets, but still adds percussion (bongos, castanets). This is likewise anomalous, as the most reduced mariachi ensemble recognized consists of violin, trumpet, guitarrón and vihuela – once more, the signature armonia instruments are absent, as is the necessary alternation between trumpet and violin (Pearlman 1988, 85). These instrumentation deviations are significant for, as Sheehy writes: 'The instruments and the way they are played are essential to the mariachi sound' (Sheehy 2006, 22). As previously mentioned, the slides and grace note ornamentation in the trumpet and violin melodies are exaggerated and used too frequently for stylistic conventions, revealing the tracks' underlying orientation of exoticism.

Finally, while the tracks' harmonic progressions would be acceptable in mariachi, 'Dancing with New Friends!' abruptly cadences from V to i, cutting short the expected eight-measure melodic phrase to six – an odd formal structure for the style.[11] These departures from mariachi tradition – especially its signature instrumentation – demonstrate that Tostarena's music is far from authentic, despite integrating some of mariachi's most recognizable elements.

Like Tostarena, Bowser's Castle communicates cultural associations through its music. Bowser's Castle features three location-based musical cues, each referencing a different Japanese genre or musical function. 'Bowser's Castle' prominently features the three instruments of the *sankyoku* ensemble, *koto* (琴), *shamisen* (三味線) and *shakuhachi* (尺八), together with *taiko* (太鼓; lit. 'big drum') accompaniment. 'Before Bowser's Castle – Main Courtyard' consists of a taiko ensemble of high and low drums with a texture reminiscent of introductory gestures for *kabuki* (歌舞伎) theatre. Finally, 'Bowser's Castle – Main Courtyard' (henceforth 'Main Courtyard') adds *kane* (鐘; 'bell') to the taiko, featuring *shinobue* (篠笛; bamboo flute) and occasional shamisen. Shinobue is also characteristic of kabuki, enhancing the track's dramatic, theatrical tone. However, these tracks' Japanese musical connections go beyond instrumentation, as their primary melodies are organized according to conventional Japanese modes. The A section of 'Bowser's Castle' contains a string chord progression outlining a *min'yō* mode (associated with folk melodies), and the shakuhachi and shamisen solos likewise operate according to *min'yō* (Hynes-Tawa 2021, 27). In 'Main Courtyard', the shinobue presents a pure *miyakobushi*-mode melody emphasizing *chi* and *shō* scale degrees (the fifth and second scale degrees of Phrygian mode, if conceived according to western medieval church modes) (Hynes-Tawa 2021, 5, 16). The traditional melodic material performed on Japanese instruments enhances the music's cultural identity (Figure 5.4).

At this point, the argument may seem clear-cut: Bowser's Castle's music is authentic while Tostarena's is not – hence their differing reception. But that conclusion would be too hasty, as the music of Bowser's Castle also contains elements equally uncharacteristic of traditional Japanese music. Most obvious is the inclusion of European string and brass sections in both tracks and English horn in 'Main Courtyard'. The brass in 'Main Courtyard' plays an especially active role, with commentary and chordal stabs reminiscent of a jazz big band. The strings establish harmonic chord progressions that sound especially atypical in 'Bowser's Castle', for sankyoku music is traditionally heterophonic or polyphonic (independent, interwoven voices) rather than monodic (distinct melody and harmony). Additionally, the European instrument parts include pitches or chords not included in the melodies' corresponding Japanese modes. In 'Bowser's Castle', the strings and brass emphasize the ♭II chord and lowered-second scale degree not found within *min'yō* mode; in

RACIALIZED FANTASY

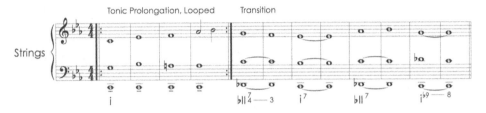

FIGURE 5.4: Japanese modes used in Bowser's Castle (top), 'Bowser's Castle', strings transcription (bottom). Transcriptions by author.

'Main Courtyard', the strings include the III chord built on the lowered-third scale degree, a pitch not part of *miyakobushi* mode. The European brass and string parts thus complicate any reading of pristine musical authenticity.

What shall we say, then? Is the music of Bowser's Castle as problematic as Tostarena's faux-Mariachi on account of its own inauthenticities? But this would flout widespread reception patterns and intuitions that the former truly is more representationally positive than the latter. To grapple with the fascinating case of *Super Mario Odyssey*, an alternative criterion is necessary for evaluating musical cultural representation that better articulates the crucial difference between these case studies. Interrogating the conceptual and cultural history of the term 'authenticity' will clarify the trajectory of the present argument.

Interrogating Authenticity, Cultural Appropriation and Stereotype

From so-called 'oriental' carpets and musical 'Indianisms' to contemporary chinoiserie and the world music genre, the literature on exoticism and orientalism reveals that discourse over authenticity often contributes to dynamics of commodification, appropriation and power. Brian Spooner's seminal study of Turkmen carpets problematizes the concept of authenticity, demonstrating that fixation on genuine cultural or aesthetic features fuels their commodification. For example, one Iranian carpet tradition features *pardis* (*royal garden*) imagery, reflecting a desire for refreshment in nature within human-constructed spaces (Spooner 1988, 212).

Though significant in many Turkmen carpets,[12] not all utilize pardis imagery – and those that do may instead employ abstract, geometric garden symbolism (213).[13] However, equating authentic Turkmen carpets with pardis imagery led western buyers to dismiss works lacking such features as 'inauthentic' (214). A truly authentic element became commodified as a marker of racial difference – in this case, as proof of marketable Turkmen identity. Spooner warns: 'we look for authenticity according to *our* cultural concepts, not *theirs*. Authenticity is our cultural choice' (223, original emphasis). Consequently, Turkmen weavers predominantly produced carpets with pardis imagery to remain competitive, 'both [frustrating] and [fueling] our search for authenticity' (229). Spooner's insights give reason for pause before leveraging authenticity alone as a criterion for positive cultural representation.

A parallel dynamic undergirds various exoticist cultural practices in music. 'Indianism' refers to a set of musical conventions developed in the late nineteenth through early twentieth centuries to signify Indigenous North American populations. In film and concert music, Indigenous identity was evoked by 'stable and unambiguous musical conventions' including a tom-tom-like drumming rhythm accenting the first of four equal beats, perfect fifth bass drones, pentatonic melodies emphasizing falling thirds and a pervasive short-long rhythm (Gorbman 2000, 235). Composers drew these traits from transcriptions of Indigenous songs made by ethnographers in the Indianist movement, who sought to 'salvage disappearing Indian culture' by preserving Indigenous songs in European music notation (Deloria 2004, 194). However, despite originating from Indigenous communities, these transcriptions petrified living music-making traditions in a westernized snapshot, collected for easy use by White composers (Deloria 2004, 204). These Indianist tropes then facilitate problematic racial representation or even overt racism (Deloria 2004, 223). In this way, genuine Indigenous music is flattened and commodified to the detriment of the originating community. Contemporary chinoiserie – the use of non-western instruments and musical characteristics within twentieth-century concert music – presents a similar case (Corbett 2000, 172). Just as the Indianist movement's appeal was its manufactured primitivism, non-western elements ostensibly delivered the 'shock of the ancient' to western ears (Corbett 2000, 167). This is a common orientalist strategy: (1) segregating supposedly 'oriental' traits from western ones; (2) characterizing the oriental as static and primitive while the western is evolving and advanced; (3) embracing oriental elements in the name of rediscovering ancient, forgotten authenticity (cf. Said 1978). As with Indianism, composers then draw selectively upon non-western traditions entirely on western terms (Corbett 2000, 177). Within contemporary chinoiserie, 'the Oriental object can never represent itself, but is essentialised and represented as a [...] reassertion of [western] control' as western composers claim to realize the latent potential of another culture's musical traditions (Corbett 2000, 168). Once again, authentic musical elements become commodified for western adaptation and consumption.

There is perhaps no greater example of commodified authenticity than the world music genre. Rather than specifying a particular musical tradition, the 'world music' label functions as a broad umbrella category, purporting to encompass every non-western musical tradition. Furthermore, Timothy Taylor identifies a musical topic or genre, also dubbed 'world music', that conglomerates aspects of multiple non-western music simultaneously. Its musical characteristics include female vocalise, children's or women's choir, drums and wooden flute, melodic sequencing and modal harmonic organization (Taylor 2007, 185). Though the title 'world music' seems inclusive, it is systematically exclusive, marking and packaging non-western cultures as 'other' (Frith 2000, 306–07). In the rhetoric of world music, authenticity – understood as geographic and cultural distance – equals quality and commercial value (van Klyton 2016, 106).[14] Thus, world music keeps non-western music otherized, unequal and unheard in its individuality (Taylor 2007, 183). Additionally, by focusing on traditional music, authenticity essentializes non-western music as static, precluding living musicians from interpreting and innovating their own traditions (van Klyton 2016, 120).

In contrast, inauthenticity can empower artists pigeonholed into a narrow conception of world music such as the hybridity movement in Punjabi-British *bhangra* music (Taylor 2007, 153).[15] In another example, the Asian Dub Foundation hybridized tabla, James Brown and 'Joshua Fit the Battle of Jericho' to create an intertextual antiracist anthem (Taylor 2007, 159). Taylor proposes the term 'third space' for these works, describing the multivalent semiotic play at work in artists' innovative creative agency (Taylor 2007, 160). A final similar case is the music of the Romani people, engaged in constant hybridization with surrounding musical cultures (Brown 2000, 129). With few occupational options available, Romani musicians developed their craft by integrating Hungarian music, reciprocally influencing it in turn (Bellman 1998, 81–84). Several Romani innovations including emphasized augmented seconds, melodic perfect fourth leaps and dotted rhythms became characteristic of Hungarian music in general (Bellman 1998, 86–87). Significantly, Romani performers often amplified stereotypes of themselves as 'musicians of sublime, God-given talent' to their economic advantage, emphasizing features with no basis in their own music (e.g. augmented second) as a noble fiction (Bellman 1998, 79). It was inauthenticity that empowered both bhangra artists and Romani musicians to transcend the economic and artistic constraints imposed upon them.

If authenticity cannot adequately ground the assessment of cultural representation, perhaps 'cultural appropriation' can. Cultural appropriation may be defined as the taking of a valuable element of another culture for one's own benefit, where its usage is contested by the culture it is taken from (Balint and Lenard 2020, 338–40). Cultural appropriation typically causes profound offence – such as the desecration of a religious symbol – or involves an existing power differ-ence between the appropriator and the appropriated (Brunk and Young 2012, 5). However, to conclude one should never borrow from or represent a culture other than one's own would be far too hasty, as many positive examples from literature, art and media rely on cross-cultural representation. Subject appropriation – when creators from one culture represent elements or people of another culture – may produce positive representational outcomes when done sensitively and empathet-ically (Haley and Young 2012, 268). Is *Odyssey* guilty of blameworthy cultural appropriation? This is difficult to affirm. On one hand, Japan's and Mexico's historical relationship involves complex power differentials that are not as straight-forward as that of colonizer-colonized. On the other, *Odyssey*'s poncho and sombrero certainly caused offence from Latina/o communities – though arguably short of profound offence.[16] Rather, *Odyssey*'s blunder lies more in the manner, rather than the fact, of its appropriation.

The preceding discussion has laid the conceptual foundation for an alternate criterion to evaluate cultural representation: 'stereotype'. Lenard and Balint iden-tify stereotype – a false or misleading representation of a culture or people – as frequently the underlying problem involved in cultural appropriation objections (Lenard and Balint 2020, 336). For example, a clumsy appropriation of a culture's artistic style could lead outsiders to form a low opinion of the culture's art (Brunk and Young 2012, 9). Stereotyping is often the fundamental issue in appropriation or authenticity objections – as seen in the preceding case studies. Media stereotypes have been known to produce grave real-world consequences, including justifying discrimination against racially otherized communities (Haley and Young 2012, 273). Too often, non-White individuals' treatment depends on White individ-uals' perceptions, which is significantly influenced by media stereotyping (The Opportunity Agenda 2011, 15). Research on racial representation in video games shows that stereotypical portrayals of non-White communities influenced White players' real-world beliefs and judgements about them (Behm-Morawitz and Ta 2014, 4). Stereotyping also harms non-White individuals' self-esteem and perfor-mance (The Opportunity Agenda 2011, 28). Due to ubiquitous media exposure in the digital age, these stereotypes often stand in for real interpersonal relation-ships when making judgements about other communities (Behm-Morawitz and Ta 2014, 6). The crucial harm of stereotyping is the obliteration of diversity, for every community is endlessly diverse. Adrienne Shaw writes that misrepresenta-tion inherently obscures diversity, since it presents an 'alternate and unrealistic version of reality' (Shaw 2010, 206). Though not all negative cultural representa-tion is reducible to stereotyping, it is stereotyping – rather than authenticity – that grounds our core intuitions about problematic media representation. The stereotype is the antithesis of diversity, and the denial of diversity is the fuel of discrimination.

Super Mario Odyssey *Revisited*

We are now well-equipped to complete our analysis of cultural representation in *Super Mario Odyssey*'s racialized fantasy. The soundtracks of Tostarena and Bowser's Castle each contained a mix of authentic and inauthentic musical elements. But not all inauthenticity is equal – just as authenticity can be co-opted in dynamics of power, commercialization and appropriation, music external to a style may be adapted to forward a particular rhetorical point or argument. Discovering the semiotic logic underlying each kingdom's music is key to understanding their stark difference in impact. First, in 'Tostarena – Town', consider the bass line and guitar strum pattern, which emphasizes a dotted-eighth + dotted-eighth + eighth note rhythm (<u>1</u> e & <u>a</u> 2 e <u>&</u> a), which is atypical to mariachi style. This rhythm can be traced instead to Cuba's *son cubano* style – specifically, the three sides of the *son clave* – commonly found in bass lines and popularly known as *tresillo*. When this syncopated bass line rhythm entered mariachi via the adoption of Cuba's *boleros* into the mariachi-hybrid *bolero ranchero*, the syncopation was 'squared off' to a more typical bass line of quarter + eighth + eighth (1, 2 & ...), or on beats 1, 3 and 4 in 4/4 time (Pearlman 1988, 232; Sheehy 2006, 33–35). In other words, while the track's primary instrumentation signifies Mexican mariachi, its underlying rhythmic skeleton points to another musical tradition entirely. Cuban influence also explains the presence of bongos (anomalous to mariachi), as they are part of the core rhythm section of son cubano. The incorporation of other stylistic elements is not necessarily inauthentic to mariachi, as many classic mariachi pieces originate from other genres including *tejano*, Cuban *danzón* and Columbian *cumbia*. However, innovations in mariachi's musical characteristics are vigorously contested in the performer and listener community and must be deemed as a 'natural development' for mariachi's trajectory (Henriques 2006, 159–60). The most likely explanation in these tracks is that composer Naoto Kubo conflated different Latin-American musical styles, possibly exposed to Cuban elements during research without sufficiently distinguishing them from Mexican Mariachi. What mattered most to Kubo was not that the music be Mexican per se, but rather that it signal Latin-American associations to hearers. From across the ocean, distinguishing Cuban musical elements from Mexican ones may have seemed unnecessary – they were 'Latin enough' to play the role, as far as Japanese (and, too often, American) audiences were concerned.

Additionally, there is the very choice of mariachi music to represent Mexican culture. Out of the plethora of traditional Mexican musical genres, why pick mariachi? Answer: mariachi most clearly and immediately communicates Mexican cultural identity to players. Or, to rephrase: mariachi is stereotypical Mexican music, the musical analogue to Mario's poncho and sombrero outfit. Though mariachi is genuinely Mexican music with a rich history and tradition, from a non-Mexican perspective it is also the most surefire means to encode Mexican associations in music. In the early 1940s, post-revolutionary Mexico carefully curated mariachi to promote national identity as a 'sound symbol of "the people"' – a unified symbol externally adopted and repackaged as a convenient stereotype for Mexican identity (Henriques 2006, 154–57). While one can argue that mariachi – if accurately manifested – is authentically Mexican, its authenticity in no way diminishes its ubiquitous usage as a stereotype. Historically, ponchos, sombreros and mariachi are commonplace choices to represent Mexico, to the extent that they become caricatures (Garcia 2018). Like the commodification of Turkmen carpets or the discourse surrounding world music, it is precisely the perceived authenticity of mariachi that grounds its convenience to outsiders as a stereotype. The stereotype flattens multifaceted Mexican musical culture into an aural calling card, just as conflating Mexican and Cuban elements reduce distinct Latina/o cultures into a single pan-Latin conglomerate. Here lies the crucial problem with Tostarena's music, as well as its overall cultural representation – not inauthenticity per se, but stereotyping. As Garcia writes, 'we, as Mexican people, are not ponchos and sombreros' – or, for that matter, mariachi music (2018, n.pag.). Cultures are complex entities, and any representation not reflecting that nuance is bound to alienate real individuals from that community.

But how – creators may object – could anyone capture the complexity of a culture in a single representation? Does this not set the bar prohibitively high? After all, composers and developers are not ethnographers. In response, two recommendations drawn from the music of Bowser's Castle gesture towards a way forward. As with Tostarena, examining musical elements previously identified as inauthentic reveals the hermeneutic premise for Bowser's Castle's tracks. In both 'Bowser's Castle' and 'Main Courtyard', the European brass and string instruments are conspicuously non-Japanese and play pitches not included in the traditional Japanese modes established by the shamisen, shakuhachi and shinobue melodies. However, it is precisely this tension and juxtaposition between Japanese and European instruments and pitch organization that musically encodes Kubo's underlying cultural argument. This becomes especially evident when analysing the music of 'Bowser's Castle' through a narrative lens, interpreting Japanese and European instruments as emblematic of their respective cultures. The introduction presents a complex chord using female vocalise, combining the pitches of the *min'yō* mode built on C with a D-flat to C progression

RACIALIZED FANTASY

(♭II – i) in its lowest voice. What appears at first to provide little more than mysterious atmosphere in actuality foreshadows the musical drama of the entire track. The following music can be analysed in terms of a traditional Japanese formal structure, *jo-ha-kyū*, in which a stable texture (*jo*) is destabilized by continually rising and quickening tension (*ha*), resulting in a climactic tearing away or scattering gesture (*kyū*) before a rapid denouement. In the A section (*jo*), the strings provide a cyclical ostinato outlining the *min'yō* mode while shakuhachi and shamisen improvise expressively above, also using *min'yō*. Near the section's end, the strings break the ostinato, rising to D-flat, the lowered second scale degree external to *min'yō* mode (*ha* begins). This transitions to the B section (ha continued), introducing the brass in syncopated unison with taiko drums and articulating the same ♭II – i chords hinted at in the introduction. Approaching the end of the B section, the brass chords become increasingly chromatic and distant from traditional *min'yō* mode, leading to a frenzied, jagged unison run in the shamisen, taiko and strings (*kyū*). This returns directly to the string ostinato at the start of the A section, functioning as the track's loop point (Figure 5.5).

In terms of musical narrative theory, the above sequence encodes an encounter between Japanese and European musical elements, each vying to exert influence – even dominance – over the eventual outcome. In the A section, Japanese instruments and mode predominate, but the insertion of a pitch foreign to the *min'yō* mode (D♭) in the European strings destabilizes this homeostasis. Next, European instrumentation and harmony prominently feature that very D♭, with brass and taiko unisons suggestive of military conflict. Finally, Japanese and European instruments combine in a climactic flourish atypical for Japanese music alone – a musical gesture resulting from this intercultural encounter to become greater than the sum of its parts. However, due to the looping nature of most video game music tracks, Japanese and European musical elements coexist in continual dialogue, each defining and being defined by each other in turn. What Kubo presents in the music

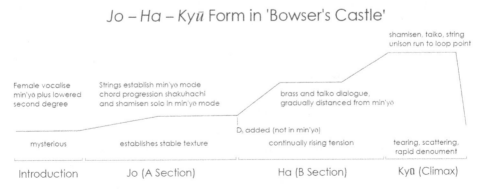

FIGURE 5.5: 'Bower's Castle' formal diagram corresponding to *jo-ha-kyū* form.

of Bowser's Castle is nothing less than a virtual staging of Japan's history in relation to Europe, including its catastrophic outcome in the Second World War and subsequent reconstruction. Musically, the cue encodes Japan's ongoing project to incorporate European harmony and instrumentation while maintaining its distinct heritage and traditions; only holding the two in tension can represent the reality of contemporary Japanese music. The resulting sonic cocktail provides traditional Japanese instruments a globalized, larger-than-life stage on which to perform.

If 'Bowser's Castle' remains agnostic about the outcome of balancing Japanese and European elements, 'Main Courtyard' reaches a more certain conclusion. Its melody encodes Japanese musical identity that does not bend or assimilate to hegemonic European standards. To reveal this discourse, recall that the melody of 'Main Courtyard' is in *miyakobushi* mode centred on E (E-F-A-B-C-E; *kyū-shō-kaku-chi-u-kyū* in Japanese *gosei*). *Miyakobushi*-mode melodies are among Japan's most globally recognizable (e.g. the iconic melody 'Sakura') as a courtly mode associated with the capital city Edo, making its use appropriate for Bowser's seat of power (Hynes-Tawa 2021, 15). Yet there is typically a disjunction between which note Japanese and western-trained ears hear as central to the scale. Japanese scale theory (following Fumio Koizumi) is based on two disjunct tetrachords of the same intervallic content, rendering E out of the aforementioned pitches as the clear scale centre (Hynes-Tawa 2021, 29). However, western-trained listeners often hear this pitch collection as implying an A Minor scale running from *sol* to *sol*; this results in quite different conclusions concerning when and whether a melody has reached closure. In Japanese theory, *kyū* and *chi* (E and B, respectively) are both frequent goal tones for *miyakobushi* melodies. As Rokushirō Uehara writes: 'Pieces generally announce their endings on *kyū*. But also, there are quite a few pieces that end with *chi*. In contrasting pieces that end on *kyū* and those that end on *chi*, we might say that in the totality of their habits they are equal' (Hynes-Tawa 2021, 18, original emphasis). In other words, unlike western tonality's impetus towards melodies ending on the tonic pitch, a *miyakobushi* melody can end well on *kyū* or *chi* (Hynes-Tawa 2021, 29). In 'Main Courtyard', the *shinobue* melody vacillates around less-stable tones *u*, *kaku* and *shō*, teasing arrival on *kyū* before rising to a chi ending. In a westernized A Minor hearing, that final pitch would be the tonic's upper neighbour B, ending the melody unresolved – an unlikely reading inveighing against a western interpretation. Historically, ending on *kaku* (A in this pitch collection) became associated with adapting Japanese melodies to fit western tonality; the *shinobue*'s cadence on *chi* invokes a more ancient, Indigenous tradition (Hynes-Tawa 2021, 30). But as in 'Bowser's Castle', the European musical influences are already present in 'Main Courtyard' – in the big band-like brass section stabs, the English horn countermelody and the strings articulating an implied i-♭II-III-♭II-i chord progression – and that influence cannot be erased, just as in modern Japan. Yet even so, the *shinobue* melody encodes a vibrant Japanese spirit that reifies its own unique cultural identity unassimilated to western listener expectations. The hybridity-driven discourse of 'Main Courtyard' achieves the opposite semiotic effect to Tostarena's music; instead of conflating and commodifying multiple musical styles for convenient listener recognition, this *miyakobushi* melody stands unassimilated in defiance of external cultural expectations.

As is now evident, the rhetorical dynamics of 'Bowser's Castle' and 'Main Courtyard' vastly exceed easy categorization as authentic or inauthentic. Perhaps such a chimerical mixture of Japanese and European elements is the most authentic representation of modern Japanese culture possible. From this analysis, the first principle of positive cultural representation can be articulated:

1. Productively and creatively combine elements internal and external to culture to advance a broader rhetorical, cultural or narrative argument.

The music of 'Bowser's Castle' elicits awe rather than ire because its fusion of Japanese and European instruments and styles is semiotically intentional, producing an artistically satisfying result. In contrast, the irregularities in Tostarena's soundtrack testify to a low-resolution view of Latin-American cultures, presenting a clumsy pan-Latin caricature rather than, for instance, a celebration of lasting Cuban influences on Mexican music. This leads to the second principle:

2. Draw from multiple diverse, non-stereotypical sources to present a multidimensional picture of a culture.

Even if Tostarena's sombreros, ponchos and mariachi had been completely accurate and authentic, they would remain predictable, eye-roll-worthy caricatures. What if Tostarena instead channelled the incredible regional diversity of Mexico in its music, fashion, architecture, climates, customs and lore? Likewise, the taiko drums or samurai costume in Bowser's Castle could have become caricature if those were the sole markers of Japanese identity present. However, its music includes references to two traditional Japanese modes, aesthetic formal principles (*jo-ha-kyū*), theatre instruments, court music and sacred music. Depth of cultural sources also matters – an influence as obscure as a green woodpecker native to a specific Japanese prefecture is unlikely to become a stereotype. With virtual libraries of information accessible in a few clicks, there is no excuse for developers' cultural research – musical or otherwise – to rely on staid stereotypes like mariachi or ponchos. If media representation in a racialized fantasy can capture a portion of the breadth and depth of a real-life culture – as the original *Avatar: The Last Airbender* did – both the culture and work would be celebrated.

Raji: An Ancient Epic – *An Invitational Approach*

The United States and Japan split the majority of the video game industry's market share, measured by revenue and developer influence. However, India may be the 'hottest emerging market' for video gaming, with a 300 million gamer population already eclipsing the United States and Japan (Thapliyal 2020). The India-based development studio Nodding Heads Games aimed to 'put India on the game development map' with its debut title *Raji: An Ancient Epic* (2020), which embodies Hindu traditions, art, culture and mythos in immersive, interactive form (Game Developer 2020, n.pag.). In contrast to the previous example, *Super Mario Odyssey*, *Raji* models an invitational approach that exemplifies positive racial representation in a globalized market.

While *Odyssey* assumed a traveller's outside perspective, *Raji* invites players to experience Hindu culture and folklore from within. If *Odyssey* is like a packaged main street designed to attract tourists, *Raji* is like a local festival that a visitor stumbles upon by accident in medias res. The visitor may inquire what the festival is called, what meanings its rituals and symbols contain – yet the surest path to understanding is to experience it firsthand. The festival does not exist for the visitor or cater to the visitor's preferences; rather, it invites the visitor to participate in ongoing traditions, to see through the subjectivity of another community. *Raji* earned widespread praise for its visual aesthetics, architectural design and cultural representation, including multiple awards at Dev Play 2019, The MIX 2020, and Taipei Game Show 2021. Growing up, Avichal Singh and others among *Raji's* developers never saw a video game feature India's stories and culture, compelling them to create the experience they never had – a goal celebrated by players of Indian descent worldwide (Substance 3D 2020; Vice 2020). GameByte calls *Raji* 'a shining example of what gaming can – and should – be for marginalised and underrepresented groups' (2020, n.pag.). The developer team selected Rajasthan, a region in northwest India with an ancient history dating to 3000 BCE, as *Raji's* unifying premise, stressing the importance of '[giving] prominence to Rajasthan traditions' in every aspect of its aesthetics and narrative (Linos Tzelos, private correspondence, December 2021). Nodding Heads hoped to prove that there is more to India than the Taj Mahal; *Raji* convincingly accomplishes that mission.

Raji's most acclaimed virtues are its architecture and visual aesthetics, including Rajput palaces, Gujarati step-walls, Pahari temples and *wayang* shadow puppetry (Vice 2020). The story predominantly unfolds through cutscenes animated in wayang style (Figure 5.6). Though wayang is a Javanese/Balinese art form, it originated in south India and traditionally depicts Hindu epics including *Rāmāyana* and *Mahābhārata* (Gamebyte 2020). Even the core combat choreography is closely modelled after traditional Hindu dance and martial arts (Substance 3D 2020). Game

RACIALIZED FANTASY

FIGURE 5.6: Wayang puppetry cutscenes (top), Vishnu's Temple (bottom).

settings include replicas of real-world locations including the Jaisalmer Fort and Ajanta Caves, further enriching *Raji*'s cultural connection (Martens 2020). Especially noteworthy is Vishnu's Temple (see Figure 5.6), 'resplendent with floating lotuses and waterfalls' and featuring picturesque water-themed puzzles and level design (Chhibber 2020, n.pag.). As summarized by Christian Donlan: '[*Raji* is] transporting [...] this game gave me a window into another culture and I want to know more' (Donlan 2020). *Raji* exemplifies the potential of video gaming as a medium for cultural immersion.

153

FIGURE 5.7: Ostinato based on Tzelos' experience in Brahma's temple (top), Kistoor's melody for his wife (bottom). Transcriptions by author.

Raji musically encodes Rajasthan as a place through homage to the *Bhopa*, migrant singer-priests hailing from the region. Historically considered part of India's lowest caste, Bhopa are prohibited from holding standard employment and subsist as itinerant musicians and storytellers (Henry 2001). To nurture society's spirit through music and narrative is considered the Bhopa's role, performing for occasions of ritual significance such as sickness or childbirth. Because nomadic Rajasthani communities including the Rabari or Raika could not consistently visit temples, a mobile temple visited them, represented by a Bhopa (Pradeep 2017). A travelling Bhopa carries a *phad*, a long-painted cloth scroll depicting the Pābujī epic, and sings its stories over five nights from dusk to dawn (Henry 2001). Metonymically, Bhopa rhythms, melodies, lyrics and instruments are understood as musical manifestations of the phad and, by extension, the tale of Pābujī. Significantly, though the text remains the same, the melodies and styles used vary widely – every Bhopa performance is unique to the performer and occasion.

In *Raji*'s soundtrack, Bhopa culture is signified by the *ravanhatta*, a signature instrument of Bhopa music and Rajasthan generally (Dick 2001). The Bhopa self-accompany their singing on ravanhatta, typically with bells affixed to the bow to provide a rhythmic dimension to the sound (Sorrell 2001). This highly resonant bowed instrument is not sold commercially, has little publicly available information about it and is near extinction – its existence is 'a surprise even for Indian people' (Tzelos 2021, n.pag.). Composer Linos Tzelos received the ravanhatta heard in *Raji* from a close friend who visited Rajasthan, and Tzelos sojourned to Rajasthan to meet the Bhopa artisan Kistoor, who crafted it by hand. For twenty days in the Pushkar desert under the tutelage of Kistoor and other Bhopa, Tzelos studied the ravanhatta technique, Bhopa music and the community's way of life.

Years later, when *Raji*'s developers asked Tzelos to compose a musical representation of Rajasthan, Tzelos's pilgrimage to Bhopa provided the ideal creative conduit. Compositionally, *Raji*'s tracks are based on Bhopa melodies, rhythms or music that Tzelos encountered and recorded in Rajasthan. Though Bhopa melodies are bright and jovial, in what westerners might consider an Ionian or Lydian mode, Tzelos adapted them to Locrian or Phrygian mode to create an intense atmosphere suitable for combat. Here and following, the terminology of medieval church modes corresponds to Tzelos's language in describing the sound of the Bhopa's ravanhatta and sung scales; Tzelos reports that scale collections of other regions in India, such as Hindustani *raga*, are a poor fit for theorizing Bhopa music, which arose from independent oral tradition and pedagogy, rather than via written systematization (Tzelos 2021). Just as Bhopa musicians improvise phad performances, improvisation was key for Tzelos's ravanhatta and sitar melodies as well as the percussionists he collaborated with in recording sessions. For example, the ravanhatta riff and melody in 'The End' are based on a recurring mistake Tzelos made during lessons with Kistoor, turning a beginner mistake into the premise for a compositional idea. Analysis of two case studies demonstrates the thorough integration of Bhopa aesthetics and style in *Raji*'s music.

Vishnu's Temple is widely considered a highlight of *Raji* for its visual aesthetics – and its music is equally compelling. Considered the most memorable by the developer team, 'Hiranyanagari' features sitar as a melodic instrument, which Tzelos acquired and began learning on a second visit to Rajasthan and the Bhopa. One of the most notable features is a two-measure kalimba ostinato which repeats throughout nearly the entire eight-minute track (Figure 5.7). This is based on Tzelos's experience visiting Brahma's temple, during which an unidentified metallophone arpeggio underscored the whole three-hour ceremony as a foundation for vocal or instrumental improvisation – the kalimba is meant to approximate this instrument, though it would have been better for Tzelos to have identified and recorded the instrument he originally heard. This textural idea is replicated at the piece's end, when the kalimba loop supports Tzelos' improvisation on ravanhatta as other percussion instruments gradually join in. As Raji traverses Vishnu's Temple, players are immersed in a musical experience parallel to Tzelos' in Brahma's temple – as if transported through the composer's sonic memory.

Heard in *Raji*'s penultimate level, 'Mystics Realm' is the composer's favourite piece from the soundtrack, as it combines every instrument, technique and aesthetic feature used thus far in the game. Its percussion accompaniment and sitar, ravanhatta or violin melodic layers sound maximally improvisatory, constantly influencing one another, as if channelling a Bhopa family's phad performance. This sense is reinforced by bass and ravanhatta accompanimental patterns articulating a Locrian mode that Kistoor loved improvising over. The cue's melody holds special significance to Tzelos, as it is Kistoor's composition rather than a traditional Bhopa melody (Figure 5.7). Kistoor dedicated the piece to his wife, who was extremely ill with typhus, setting it in a melancholy Phrygian mode instead of the Bhopa's typical celebratory sound. For Kistoor, this unusual choice musically translated his call to the stars for guidance and healing. Tzelos strategically places this melody in a moment when the protagonist Raji seeks physical and psychological healing – the player's narrative experience of this music corresponds to Kistoor's semiotic intentions, mediated through his student. In *Raji*'s soundtrack, Tzelos encoded Bhopa's passion for improvisation and expression, his pedagogical relationship with Kistoor and experience of Rajasthani religious ritual.

Tzelos's musical fusion of the sacred and cultural through Bhopa music is an ideal semiotic fit, for in India, religion and culture are inseparable. Though this is true of cultural studies generally, India's religious traditions are thoroughly entangled in its ethnic and national identity to a degree few others are (Japan and Shinto come to mind as another example). The developers selected Rajasthan because it is the setting of Hindu mythology's most ancient stories and site of the only temple to Brahma, the creator of India. Accordingly, *Raji*'s narrative themes and semiotic meanings reinforce the spiritual – even devotional – scope of the game. This requires a brief primer on Hindu religious traditions. While none of the world's religions is monolithic, India's traditions are especially malleable and pluralistic, with no unified founder, spokesman or prophet (Dehejia 2007). Rather than institutional orthodoxy, individual experience and communal engagement are most highly prioritized (Chhibber 2020). Any of India's 33 million deities provides a suitable focus for devotion. Principal deities may vary between regions or even villages – yet all are considered manifestations of one divine Brahman, exemplifying the paradox that is Indian spirituality. Hindu religious praxis guides devotees to realize their inherent connection to Brahman. The primary devotional practice cultivating this awareness is *darshan*, meaning 'seeing' (Eck 2002, 171). Darshan consists of beholding the sculpted image of the deity and standing in the deity's presence. The seeing that then occurs is bidirectional – the deity embodied and awakened in the image sees the devotee, just as the devotee sees the deity (Frazier 2014, 25.6). As Diana Eck writes: 'The central act of Hindu worship [... is] to see and be seen by the deity' (Eck 2002, 172). Though typically practised in a home or temple, darshan does not require physical proximity. To a greater degree than most religious practitioners, Hindus embrace digital media and incorporate them into religious devotion (Plate 2002, 163). For example, viewing film or television works featuring one or more deities also constitutes darshan, suggesting a natural extension to the medium of video games. Video games' integration of player agency and personal identity powerfully synergizes with the aims of Hindu devotion – an ideal catalyst for darshan. 'Hindu devotional arts make us receptive, transforming the personality through emotion', writes Jessica Frazier concerning art's essential spiritual role, 'art functions not as a window onto the divine, but a door by which to let it in' (Frazier 2014, 25.9). This is precisely the ludic-spiritual affordance *Raji* achieves.

In *Raji*'s first moment, the goddess Durga speaks: 'This is the heart of our story.' This divine invocation establishes from the outset that Hindu religious themes are central to *Raji*'s semiotic meaning. Soon joined by the god Vishnu, the two deities narrate and comment upon the eponymous character Raji's quest to rescue her brother Golu from demon lord Mahabalasura.[17] Playing a character watched, guided and empowered by Durga and Vishnu invokes interactive darshan, as the player's gameplay actions are seen by the deities – analogous to living one's own life. Additionally, ornate murals narrated by Vishnu depict the origins of Durga, Shakti, Garuda, Vishnu's avatars and Shiva's avatars, demonstrating *Raji*'s pedagogical value and purpose. By the game's end, players experience an overview of Hindu mythology, serving as a gateway to Hindu theology and lore. Three game settings are holy sites of Durga, Vishnu and Shiva, respectively – invoking the Hindu divine triad, the Trimurti – and Raji is bestowed weapons associated with Durga and Vishnu (Chhibber 2020).[18] The design of Vishnu's Temple corresponds to the four-part structure of a typical Hindu temple: *gopura* ('gateway'), *mandapa* ('hallway'), *gabra griha* ('inner shrine') and *shikhara* ('tower'). The gabra griha (lit. 'womb chamber') houses the deity's image in the heart of the temple; in *Raji*, it instead holds Vishnu's sword and shield for Raji's use. Raji does not enter the gabra griha to practise darshan, for Vishnu already watches over and blesses her. As an interactive media text, *Raji*'s invitational approach beckons players to experience Hindu religious traditions, exemplifying darshan for the digital era.

Raji: An Ancient Epic is by no means a perfect creation. The core combat gameplay grows repetitive, and the final boss is far too easy using the game's final weapon (Chhibber 2020). The narrative's climax and ending are abrupt, and some reviewers criticized the 'tell, don't show' exposition via puppetry cutscenes and Durga's and Vishnu's third-person narration – however, the above discussion justifies those storytelling choices as valid, semiotically significant cultural differences. As part of ongoing sociopolitical conversations, Adesh Thapliyal objects that *Raji*'s Hindu-mythology-immersed world portrays a fantastical India that erases Islamic influence in a region filled with Islamic cultural traces (Vice 2020). Additionally, Tzelos' score would benefit from a more thorough and long-term study of ravanhatta with Kistoor and other Bhopa musicians, perhaps transmitting a portion of Rajasthan's unique musical heritage in writing. On balance, however, *Raji* is a breathtaking model of positive cultural representation more akin to interactive art than a typical video game. As Eck writes: 'India must be seen to be known' (2002, 174). Released during the global COVID-19 pandemic, *Raji* offered players exactly the transportive, horizon-expanding experience prohibited in real life (Martens 2020). And for players of Indian descent, this landmark holds special significance: 'it's the first time I've seen a piece of my world in a video game', reports Polygon's Preeti Chhibber, 'and now all I want is more' (2020, n.pag.). Like a Bhopa singing through a digitized phad, *Raji* invites audiences into a robust celebration of India's culture, art, music and spirituality. Or, in Tzelos's own words – the music of *Raji* is the phad he carries from the Bhopa to the world.

Conclusion

Following extensive analysis of two complex case studies and a panoply of sociological and scholarly contextualization on matters of race and culture, some brief concluding thoughts are in order. I aim to synthesize the various threads raised in this chapter and clearly articulate their significance to vital contemporary issues of racial representation. However, race and culture are notoriously tricky topics to navigate, and I do not offer any final answers in such a pithy format. Rather, I hope to provide conversation-starters and conceptual tools to facilitate further discussion.

Super Mario Odyssey and *Raji* provide examples of racialized fantasy, which occurs whenever a fictional world's cultures or populations are designed with traits associated with a particular real-world culture or population. Human minds continuously seek meaning and intelligible patterns, relating new experiences and content to their own background knowledge and social context. Therefore, from a semiotic perspective, fictional worlds are never hermetically sealed off from the real world, since interpretations of the former map meaningfully onto the latter. Music establishes a powerful sense of place, linking gameworld locations to real ones by utilizing conventional cultural associations. Accordingly, video games and other multimedia rely on music to construct a convincing racialized fantasy and communicating real-world meanings. For example, scoring Tostarena with stereotypical mariachi music (even if poorly replicated) encoded Mexican identity into *Odyssey*'s fantasy world. Any music composed by people in the real world inevitably carries echoes of real-world styles and traditions, rendering purely fictional music an impossibility.

We are now well-positioned to refute the aforementioned 'fantasy defense' directly. The fantasy defence claims that fictional worlds are incapable of representing anything real. First, any resemblance *Odyssey* has to Mexican culture is irrelevant, argues the defence, because it occurs in Tostarena, in a gameworld. Second, representation in fantasy settings is thought trivial and not worth objecting to (Shaw 2010, 196). Why subject the whimsical world of Mario to critical analysis – aren't video games just about having fun? This perspective on representation in fiction is hopelessly naïve. Just as fictional music devoid of real-world signification is impossible – because real-world listeners hear and interpret it – neither can a fictional world be wholly detached from real-world meanings. Rather, fantasy is significant precisely for its immersive and imaginative power, catalysing learning about ourselves and our own world. We shape our lives according to the stories we tell – including how we view and treat others. Young and Haley write concerning literature: 'In the process of communication between cultures, literature has a vitally important moral role to play. It is through literature that readers undertake to imagine what it would be to be someone else, someone perhaps completely different' (2012, 286–87). As with literature, so too with video games – if not more so. Gaming centres player interactive agency, affording an ideal medium for cultivating intersubjective understanding and compassion for the Other.

But what does this contribute to conversations about race specifically – not just culture? It is difficult, if not impossible, to discuss race without involving culture at some level. Recall that culture and race are tightly intertwined, and that race results when perceived cultural differences become the basis for social inequities or hierarchies. Linnaeus's and Blumenbach's race theories were preceded by European judgements (by Zurara, Africanus and others in the medieval period) of African culture as inherently primitive or inferior. Put succinctly, the hierarchization of cultures produces a racialized society – the foundation of racial representation is cultural representation. This is why antiracist cultural representation in all facets of human experience – including digital media – is vitally important. At its core, cross-cultural representation, interpretation and participation are about how we treat individuals and communities that are different from us. Do we treat their traditions and culture with nuance and respect? Or do we instead essentialize, exoticize and stereotype them, resulting in the impression that other cultures – and the people that comprise them – are lesser? Only through informed, charitable and sensitive representation can we erode cross-cultural prejudices that reinforce longstanding racial discrimination.

One final clarification to deflect potential misinterpretation is in order. After presenting this material at multiple academic conferences, I was frequently asked whether developers should only present content from their own culture. Should Nintendo stick to Japanese settings, Nodding Heads to Indian folklore and so on? After all, cross-cultural representation is fraught with potential blunders. However, this stay-in-your-lane approach is misguided; *Odyssey*'s error was not its attempt to represent Mexican culture, but rather representing it poorly. This is precisely why I cited *Avatar: The Last Airbender* and the music of *Raji*, for Michael DiMartino and Bryan Konietzko are not AAPI individuals, and Linos Tzelos is not of Indian descent. Yet by engaging in rigorous cultural research with the requisite humility and openness, each crafted an artwork that honoured its source communities and was celebrated by many of the ethnic and/or cultural heritage depicted. Rather, it

NOTES

* Supplementary Video 5.1 'Racialized Fantasy – Authenticity, Appopriation and Stereotype in Super Mario Odyssey (Ludo 2021)' can be found here: https://www.youtube.com/watch?v=cNrU3J8mnA8. Accessed 3 June 2024. Supplementary Video 5.2 'Video Game Composer Interview – Linos Tzelos (Raji: An Ancient Epic)' can be found here: https://www.youtube.com/watch?v=kXVdgxmnhgg. Accessed 3 June 2024. Standalone colour files of Figures 5.1, 5.2 and 5.6, and standalone illustration files of Figures 5.3, 5.4 and 5.7 can be found under the Front Matter section for *Gender, Race and Religion in Video Game Music*'s page on Intellect Discover.

1. 'Actor' here is used as a gender-neutral term for a film or stage performer.

2. This is not to deny positive influence resulting from Charlie Chan as a character – famously, Warner Oland was widely celebrated on a 1933 Shanghai trip for improving portrayal of Chinese people in American films, and Yunte Huang (2010) offers a nuanced, cautiously optimistic reading of the trailblazing detective. However, it is nonetheless worth foregrounding that producers did not cast an actor of Chinese or other East Asian descent, constituting yellowface. Furthermore, after co-starring in *The Jazz Singer* (1927) – a film using blackface, though Oland does not – Oland's career consisted primarily of yellowface roles, including the infamous Dr. Fu Manchu.

3. East Asian and Inuit cultural elements include philosophy, aesthetics, material culture, social organization, written language, names, music, clothing, architecture and martial arts styles.

4. Qualifying praise for *Avatar: The Last Airbender*, one could offer the counterpoint that show creators Michael DiMartino and Bryan Konietzko are White, not AAPI – an observation the analysis returns to by chapter's end. Similarly, the *ATLA* voice cast is primarily White. Regarding the former point, I find the demographic identity of who created an artwork less interesting and impactful than how the work represents its subject matter and what semiotic messaging it conveys about the communities referenced. A creator sharing cultural identity with the represented community makes deep, charitable representation of its source more likely, but is not a prerequisite for positive representation (as *ATLA* and its reception among AAPI communities demonstrates). Regarding the latter point, the casting of non-AAPI actors to voice *ATLA* characters is considerably less egregious than the live-action film's doing so on-screen, where the Yellowface effect is visible, since reliably discerning an actor's ethnicity from voice alone is nigh impossible. Taking a strict stance regarding matching a character's and voice actor's ethnicity could entail odd, far-reaching consequences. For example, in recording English dubs for Japanese anime, must the vast majority of voice actors be Japanese-American, or even Japanese nationals? What ramifications

would this stance have for English film dubbed into languages worldwide – must they be performed by voice actors who match the mostly-White characters shown on-screen? Nonetheless, I agree that ethic diversification is sorely needed among the voice acting, as well as for on-screen actors, to better reflect the demographic diversity of the world.

5. Each of these points and Ewell's experience as a flashpoint for White backlash in academic music theory are well documented in *On Music Theory: And Making Music More Welcoming for Everyone* (Ewell 2023, University of Michigan Press).

6. There is perhaps no racial terminology more fraught at present than those describing ethnicities originating from Central and South America or the Caribbean Islands, often from majority-Spanish-speaking countries. In the United States, historically-popular terms 'Hispanic' and 'Chicano' continue in usage, with 'Latino' emerging as the most prevalent identifier. Many in this group identify as White, or use nationally- or regionally specific terms like 'Mexicano', 'Cubano' or 'Tejano'. 'Latinx' has been proposed as a gender-inclusive term, but it has not received widespread adoption among the communities it describes. This is because 'Latinx' does not synergize well with the Spanish language and has been viewed by many in the community as an external imposition from White academics. With much consideration, discussion and provisionality, I adopt 'Latina/o', which has usage precedent in Latina/o communities and scholarship. Though Latina/o does not explicitly include transgender and non-binary individuals, it is my hope that a maximally gender-inclusive term that better integrates into Spanish language and communities – perhaps 'Latine'? – will arise.

7. My reasons for preferring 'non-White' are threefold: (1) international consistency, as BIPOC (Black, Indigenous and People of Colour) is most common in the United States while BAME (Black, Asian and Minority Ethnic) is in the United Kingdom; (2) BIPOC and BAME problematically flatten and roll multiple demographic groups into the 'POC' and 'ME' parts of the acronym; (3) in the context of race discourse, what groups together various non-White demographics is precisely that they are not White – that is, racially otherized from hegemonic Whiteness in some capacity. 'People of Colour' is a good alternative, but I prefer the stark clarity – and deliberate discomfort – of 'non-White' in these conversations. Additionally, there is much scholarly discussion around whether to keep 'White' uncapitalized to emphasize its socially-constructed and contingent nature and attempt to correct the imbalance of Whiteness' historical valorization. I choose to capitalize 'White' for consistency with other racial labels utilized throughout the book, though I take the aforementioned points quite seriously.

8. Some helpful resources exploring Black representation in video games generally include Malkowski and Russworm 2017, Brooks and Hébert 2006, Burgess et al. 2011 and The Opportunity Agenda 2011.

9. This paragraph, along with the following attention to AAPI and Latina/o representation in this chapter, is intended to be expansive and additive, building cross-cultural coalitions for racial justice, rather than replacing or distracting from attention to anti-Black racism, such as in the #BlackLivesMatter movement. As the group Asians 4 Black Lives states: 'We must recognise that the scapegoating of Asians as the harbingers of disease, and the state

violence against Black people (via systemic policing and state response to the pandemic) are two sides of the same coin. [...] This moment makes it even clearer that we must radicalise our communities for cross-racial solidarity' (#Asians4BlackLives 2020, n.pag.).

10. This is the first instance of rendering Bowser's Japanese name Koopa (*katakana*:クッパ) into traditional *kanji*, which could be interpreted as imparting Bowser a measure of Japanese identity befitting his characterization in the *Odyssey* level. In contrast, neither Mario, Luigi nor Princess Peach have *kanji* names. If so, Bowser's characters 空覇 would bear the lofty meaning 'heavenly rulership'.

11. Most likely, the rationale for this choice is an accommodation to the scene's visuals, to correspond to the duration of Mario's playing animation. Nonetheless, the resulting music is atypical for Mariachi.

12. Turkmen carpets featuring ornate *pardis* imagery are characteristic of the Sassanian court in third–seventh centuries CE.

13. E.g. Beshir carpets.

14. As an illustrative example, world music concert organizers introduced Bill – born in Ghana but living in the United Kingdom for 30 years – as hailing 'all the way from Ghana', a commonly-reported experience among musicians performing in world music spaces (van Klyton 2016, 111).

15. It must be noted that Taylor documents ways that 'hybridity' as a concept may function similarly to authenticity discourse. The industry hegemons (record labels) are endlessly creative in keeping global Others on the margins, whether the descriptor used is world music, authenticity, or hybridity. Taylor writes: 'Thus hybridity has become a marketing term... one that reproduces old prejudices and hegemonies' (2007: 143); 'The "hybrid" can be recoded as "authentic", finding itself back in the "savage slot"' (145); 'Hybridity has become ... another way that musics by people from western Elsewheres are relegated to the world music category and denied access to the more prestigious category of rock' (160).

16. Examples of causing profound offense include wearing an Indigenous headpiece traditionally reserved for community spiritual leaders or drawing the prophet Muhammed in a comic.

17. Mahabalasura, like Raji and Golu, is original to *Raji: An Ancient Epic*. However, Mahabalasura's backstory and role in *Raji* parallel the *Ramayana*'s demon king Ravana in several ways, including early life as a sage, turn to evil, rebellion against the gods and subsequent punishment/imprisonment by crushing.

18. The Trimurti ('three forms') refers to a triad of supreme Hindu deities: Brahma, Vishnu and Shiva, respectively, representing creation, preservation and destruction. However, while Vishnu and Shiva are widely worshipped in India, very few temples are dedicated to Brahma. Thus, a more popular deity – often a major goddess like Durga, who is a principal aspect of the great goddess Shakti – may be substituted for Brahma. The Trimurti's exact composition in Hindu tradition is neither as dogmatic nor immutable as, for example, the Christian Trinity of Father, Son and Holy Spirit.

6

Antiracist Storytelling:
Representation and Diversity in
Civilization VI and *Overwatch*

Introduction: Choose Your Character

Who would win in a duel between Mario and Sonic the Hedgehog? Or if Pikachu clashed with Mega Man? Where might Cloud Strife encounter Ryū or Solid Snake? These are a miniscule fragment of the possibilities afforded by Nintendo's *Super Smash Bros.* franchise, reifying many gamers' wildest crossover fantasies. With 65 million games sold, *Smash* is the world's best-selling fighting game series, and its latest instalment *Super Smash Bros. Ultimate* (2018) is the best-selling individual fighting game with 23.84 million sales (Nintendo 2022).[1] Boasting 83 playable characters and three customizable Mii avatar classes, *Ultimate* delivers players an intertextual stage worthy of the game's tagline: 'everyone is here'! Of particular interest are the 16 characters not created by Nintendo, licensed from major developers including Sega, Capcom, Square Enix, Microsoft and Disney. Usually announced as downloadable content (DLC) via widely publicized broadcasts, which character would next join the roster became the nexus of considerable anticipation, speculation and contention within the gaming community. However, one specific character announcement engendered controversy among communities of colour, alleging that Nintendo missed a prime opportunity for Black representation.

In March 2020, Nintendo announced that *Ultimate*'s seventh DLC character would hail from *ARMS*, a popular family-friendly fighting game. Debate immediately erupted over which of its fifteen playable characters would be selected. Nintendo Life conducted a poll with 12,000+ votes – Min Min scored first with 25% and Twintelle was second with 21% (no other character came close). On 10 June 2020, *ScreenRant* published an article titled 'Smash Bros Ultimate DLC Could (And Should) Introduce Its First Black Character', arguing that Twintelle, as a Black woman, should be chosen as a 'big step towards inclusion', since *Smash*

163

contains no playable Black character (Jones 2020). On 22 June, Min Min – rather than Twintelle – was revealed as the selection, which many in Anglophone nations considered a missed opportunity for Black, female character representation in a mainstream series (Gramuglia 2020).

The discussion is further muddled by the typical complexity surrounding topics of race and culture. For crucial nuance, Min Min is *Smash*'s only playable Chinese character – and the first solely female DLC character – rather than a White character, as some have claimed (Chan 2017).[2] In addition to Min Min's overall popularity, *ARMS* producer Kosuke Yabuki specifically nominated her for *Ultimate*, which was the deciding factor for her selection. However, a confluence of socio-cultural factors contextualizes the swell of support for Twintelle:

1. The murder of George Floyd (covered in Chapter 5) occurred less than a month prior to Min Min's announcement, heightening awareness of *Smash*'s lack of Black representation. Many analyses of this controversy link it to the racial reckoning of Summer 2020 and #BlackLivesMatter movement.
2. Twintelle's pre-existing contributions to Black female representation were well known. The day after Twintelle's reveal for *ARMS* – over three years before ScreenRant's article – Xavier Harding argued for her inclusion in *Ultimate*, mentioning her significance in mainstream video gaming as a non-White female character. Non-White women writers from Black Girl Nerds, NerdMuch? and Paste reported feeling empowerment when playing as Twintelle (Benne 2017; Daniels 2017; Garcia 2019), and CBR described her as 'distinct and memorable' (Jones 2020). Players widely praised Twintelle as a fan favourite and highlight for Black representation – though others have voiced concerns.[3]
3. Playable Black female characters in video games are exceedingly rare – Alisha Karabinus' 2019 corpus study tallied around 30 playable Black women in all gaming history. For Black women gamers, being unable to play any character who resembles them is a 'disturbing, yet familiar' experience (Starkey 2019). Though typical of most developers, the lack of Black characters in Nintendo franchises is especially conspicuous (Jones 2020). *ARMS* producer Yabuki described Twintelle as a rarity for Nintendo – most likely a slant nod to her racial identity (Hilliard 2017). Thus, Paste described non-White youths cheering for and looking up to Twintelle in *ARMS* as 'surreal', comparing her influence to tennis star Serena Williams (Daniels 2017).

Such sociocultural complexity engendered by a video game character announcement may appear surprising, even unwarranted. However, representation and diversity in gaming relate directly to social justice and community belonging – of histories of marginalization and hegemony. To understand our media culture, we must first investigate the racialized society within which it is embedded.

Chapter 6 continues the book's critical examination of cultural and racial representation in video game music, applying Ibram X. Kendi's segregation-assimilation-antiracism spectrum to musical cultural representation (Kendi 2019). Just as in real life, segregationist and assimilationist strategies in video game music preserve the hegemonic status quo by exoticizing or erasing the distinctiveness of the racialized Other, while antiracist ones avoid segregationist and assimilationist poles by elevating and celebrating diversity. Sid Meier's *Civilization* franchise is rightly critiqued for assuming European/American-centric imperialist values, spurring any civilization the player adopts to achieve victory through military domination, religious conversion, technological supremacy or cultural monopoly. The soundtrack of *Civilization IV* (2005) assimilates all nations' musical journeys to a fictionalized, anachronistic reading of European classical music; on the other hand, *Civilization V* (2010) exoticizes its non-European, non-American nations with exaggerated, stereotypical features, segregating them through sonic signifiers of difference. The series' latest instalment, *Civilization VI* (2016), musically bridges these extremes, developing a culturally significant or representative melody over the trajectory of each nation's development, in dialogue with the themes of other nations. Blizzard's *Overwatch* (2015) was released to widespread acclaim for its demographic, cultural and ludic diversity, envisioning a future world where diversity is the norm. Its score exemplifies antiracist storytelling by incorporating each character's cultural identity into the location-based theme associated with them, balanced by pervasive technological elements appropriate to the game-world's futuristic narrative. This chapter concludes Part III by probing the concept of 'representation' itself, specifying 'quantitative equity' and 'representational diversity' as two commonly conflated facets of representation. While both are vitally important, they are not identical – in addition to how many individuals of marginalized identities are represented on a video game's cast or development team (quantitative equity), celebrating diversity as an end in itself via every aesthetic parameter, including music, is equally crucial (representational diversity). Embracing musical semiotics of diversity is essential to producing antiracist storytelling in video games.

Fundamentally, the tone and trajectory of this chapter's readings offer a hermeneutic of hope, presenting its case studies as models of improvement or progressive trends in game music's cultural and racial representation. To praise *Civilization VI* and *Overwatch* as antiracist storytelling is not to claim that either game score is free of problematic aspects – indeed, each section's analysis highlights avenues for further representational improvement. As Kendi writes: 'racist and antiracist are not fixed identities. We can be a racist one minute and an antiracist the next'

(Kendi 2019, 10). Just as no person is entirely racist or antiracist, neither is any artwork created by such people. Furthermore, the work of antiracism is not a goalpost to be reached but is a continually ongoing enterprise in each person's life – even for a race scholar and activist like Kendi (Kendi 2019, 10). As in Chapters 3 and 4 concerning gender representation, positive models are necessary to show that changing the status quo is possible and to inspire developers to move towards antiracism. So too does Kendi's work end with a hopeful exhortation, though no one could accuse Kendi of Whitewashing the world's past and present racism: 'Believe all is not lost for you and me and our society. Believe in the possibility that we can strive to be antiracist from this day forward' (2019, 238). A hermeneutic of hope neither ignores persistent problems out of uncritical optimism nor aborts the project of social justice once progress is 'good enough'. Rather, hope continually highlights steps towards better representation as harbingers of an equitable future, manifested through meaningful creative decisions in the present.

The Anatomy of Racism – Segregation | Assimilation | Antiracism

June 2020 was a month unlike any I had experienced. Amidst the unprecedented convergence of the global COVID-19 pandemic, the murder of George Floyd and a contentious United States presidential election, it seemed that the status quo could not hold, particularly concerning racial injustice and inequity. The earnest hope that the world could never be the same after 2020 seemed imminent for many – though only future readers can adjudicate to what degree this turbulent year was a catalyst for lasting change. However, June did occasion a surge in interest in books that unflinchingly interrogate racialized systems. Two in particular – Robin DiAngelo's *White Fragility* and Ibram X. Kendi's *How to Be an Antiracist* – topped multiple best-selling book lists in the United States, including *The New York Times* Bestseller List, for approximately a year. Kendi's work is especially crucial to our present endeavour, as it develops an insightful, penetrating framework for contextualizing the subsequent musical and cultural analyses.

Among Kendi's most productive contributions is clearly defining 'racist' – a fraught term easily misunderstood and distorted in public discourse – along with its opposite:

RACIST: One who is supporting a racist policy through their actions or inaction or expressing a racist idea;

ANTIRACIST: One who is supporting an antiracist policy through their actions or expressing an antiracist idea (Kendi 2019, 13).

There is some lurking ambiguity due to 'racist policy' including the term under definition, so an additional pair of definitions is necessary:

RACIST POLICY: any measure that produces or sustains racial inequity between racial groups;

ANTIRACIST POLICY: any measure that produces or sustains racial equity between racial groups (18).

Two critical points are worth highlighting here. First, as alluded to in the titles of Kendi's book and this chapter, the opposite of 'racist' is 'antiracist' rather than 'not racist'. Second, complementing this insight, Kendi uses racist and antiracist as adjectival modifiers of a noun (e.g. 'racist policy', 'racist idea') or as a person's state of being – not as an immutable label to categorize people. Thus, to be antiracist is not to be against people labelled racists, but rather to support racial equity. My usage of these terms throughout this book follows Kendi's.

Kendi develops a tripartite conceptual framework of 'segregationism', 'assimilationism' and 'antiracism' to describe racialized dynamics in society:

SEGREGATIONISM: the racist idea that a permanently inferior racial group can never be developed, supporting policy that segregates away that racial group;

ASSIMILATIONISM: the racist idea that a racial group is culturally or behaviorally inferior, supporting cultural or behavioural enrichment programs to develop that racial group;

ANTIRACISM: the antiracist idea that racial groups are equals and none needs developing, supporting policy that reduces racial inequity (24).

Note that Kendi casts assimilationism as another form of racism – not as a supposedly neutral middleground. 'Assimilationist ideas are racist ideas', Kendi writes, because the dominant culture becomes 'the superior standard that another racial group should be measuring themselves against, the benchmark they should be trying to reach' (29). There can be no comfort zone of disinterested neutrality – claiming merely to be 'not racist' only functions to mask racism (9). In the United States, the cultural drive towards 'colourblindness' – ignoring centuries of racist history and their continuing consequences – constitutes the nation's most threatening racist movement, claiming impartiality while preserving systems designed to perpetuate racist outcomes (20).[4] Colourblindness is textbook assimilationism.

Recently, objections characterizing antiracist initiatives as divisive – or even racist by making race visible – have suffused public discourse. In the United States, conservative backlash and legislation aimed at censoring or banning Critical Race Theory for daring to foreground racial inequity in public consciousness have proven quite influential in certain regions. What the 'post-racial myth' of colourblindness disregards is the necessity of using racial categories to illuminate racial inequity and challenge racist policies; without naming race forthrightly, the result is 'a world of inequity none of us can see, let alone resist' (54). Highlighting racial diversity only appears divisive from the standpoint of hegemony, as it disputes the centrality of the dominant monoculture. Whereas hegemony normalizes a slim range of narratives, diversity decentralizes any single perspective, celebrating various identities and experiences. This conclusion draws together antiracism, antisexism and advocacy for all marginalized communities – as Kendi writes, 'to truly be antiracist is to be feminist, to truly be feminist is to be antiracist' (2019, 189). This is the core insight of intersectionality, a concept raised in Chapter 5; because diversity is antithetical to monoculture, dissolving hegemony across multiple demographic parameters disarms the conforming pressure of assimilationism. Like the alternative femininities and alternative masculinities in Chapter 3, diversity is the antidote to hegemony.

Using Kendi's framework, Philip Ewell traces the history of academic music studies in the United States from segregationism to assimilationism, where it remains today (Ewell 2020) (Figure 6.1).[5] Before the mid-twentieth century, non-White musicians were largely disbarred from conservatories and schools of music. When Jim Crow racism became untenable, non-White students and faculty were admitted to the academy on the unspoken condition of performing and studying repertoire predominantly composed by European/American composers who were both White and male. Today, the 'classical music' genre remains shorthand for a canon

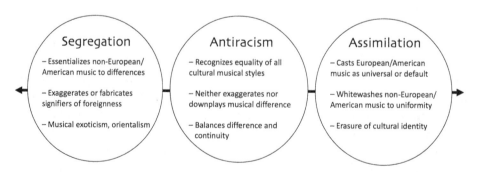

FIGURE 6.1: Segregation – antiracism – assimilation in musical racial representation diagram.

of works written by such composers, and music schools have only just begun to grapple with the assimilationist state of the discipline. In musical representation, segregationism manifests in previously mentioned tropes including exoticism, Indianism, orientalism, minstrelsy, the world music genre and musical stereotyping – the non-European/American music is essentialized to its differences, which are exaggerated or fabricated to communicate foreignness (cf. Chapter 5). Assimilationist strategies are more subtle, establishing European/American musical styles as default or universal, Whitewashing unique cultural identities to uniformity. Examples of musical assimilationism will follow, but one illustrative case comes from the film score of *Broken Arrow* (1950). Sunseeahray, an Apache woman, is introduced using typical Indianisms, but after marrying a White man, becomes associated with a fully European/American romantic theme – musically, 'the union of white and Indian is white' (Gorbman 2000, 243). Both segregationist and assimilationist modes are racist; this chapter proposes a third, antiracist path.

One final, essential exhortation from Kendi: racist and antiracist are never static labels, and most people exhibit an ever-shifting mix of racism and antiracism. 'We can be a racist one minute and an antiracist the next', Kendi declares, '[what we say and do about race] in each moment determines what – not who – we are' (2019, 10). Rather than a good-and-bad-person dichotomy, Kendi provides a heuristic framework for self-assessment that spurs us continually towards antiracism. Such journeys are never fully finished – just as our conversations on racial representation in video game music continue to the present day.

Decolonizing Music History in Civilization VI

Sid Meier's Civilization series stands among the most illustrious video gaming achievements, arresting attention from scholars and laypeople alike. With six instalments and numerous expansions selling over 50 million copies over its 30-year history, *Civilization* is firmly embedded in popular media culture (Longreads 2016) *IGN* ranked *Civilization IV* the 26th best video game of history just behind industry landmark including *The Legend of Zelda: Ocarina of Time*, *Minecraft* and *Halo: Combat Evolved* (2019). From 2010 to 2016, statistical extrapolations estimate the series' total play time at over a billion hours, equivalent to the time spent visiting the world's six largest museums over the same timespan combined (Mol et al. 2017, 214; Mol and Politopoulos 2021, 44). The comparison to museums is especially apt, as pedagogical studies using *Civ* in high school curricula found it productively fostered deep learning and critical thinking about counterfactual history (Majewski 2021, 71). The recurring 'civilopedia' feature historically contextualizes objects, locations and people encountered, enhancing the game's real-world meaning (Majewski 2021, 75). The *Civ* franchise has taught millions of players about history, politics and culture through 'a playful and interactive engagement with the past' (Mol et al. 2017, 218). For some players, *Civ* was a 'genuinely transformative' experience inspiring a lifelong fascination with history—even influencing their career choices (Majewski 2021, 79). Yet precisely because of its unparalleled influence and scope, *Civ*'s cultural representation deserves scrutiny.

To understand *Civ*'s present state, we must examine its past. Kacper Poblocki delivers its most enduring critique: 'the fetish object of [Sid] Meier's fantasies is the ultimate empire, the state that resembles most the end product of all human advancement, namely the United States of America' (Poblocki 2002, 167). In other words, by requiring military domination, religious conversion or other empire-building strategies that resemble European/American colonization for victory, *Civ* squeezes all cultures into becoming the West (Poblocki 2002, 172). Its ludic premise emphasizes technological advancement, urban development and military expansion as criteria of cultural success, instilling a 'distinctively Western view of the world' (Vrtačič 2014, 94). Those that do not aspire to imperialism or cannot achieve it – such as the 'barbarian' populations intended as early-game antagonists – are destined for extinction, their presence literally erased from the world map (Martino 2021, 35). Additionally, *Civ* has been susceptible to various representational blunders. The civilizations and leaders selected to represent the Near East, like Assyria or Sumer, are predominantly ancient and do not correspond to modern countries – conveying that the region's significance lay only in the past (Mol and Politopoulos 2021, 47). Detailed analysis of the series' representation of Persia reveals a focus on: (1) war, (2) gold and (3) monarchy or other authoritarian forms of government, conforming to common orientalist tropes (Mol and Politopoulos 2021, 50). *Civ*'s archaeology feature perpetuates exploitative Victorian practices of claiming any artefacts found, revelling in the glory of discovery to the detriment of ethical excavation methods (Martino 2021, 41). As Eva Vrtačič observes, the series' hegemonic legacy is 'perhaps best exemplified in its name – Civilization. Not Civilizations, Civilization [... only] one path leads to civilization and the player following that path is in fact re-enacting the Western phantasms of history, culture and science' (Vrtačič 2014, 99). The music of *Civilization I* through *IV* similarly conveys 'Western imperialist, colonial, and culturally hegemonic ideologies' (Cook 2014, 179).

Karen Cook analysed the music of *Civilization IV* (2005) with detailed historical precision, concluding that its musical choices support its underlying hegemonic cultural ideology. *Civ IV* contains two soundtrack types, termed by Cook the 'terrain soundtrack' and 'diplomatic soundtrack'. The terrain soundtrack marks the in-game progression of time from Classical to Modern eras, while the diplomatic soundtrack communicates people and place with unique musical themes for each leader. The terrain soundtrack is heard as actions are taken on the world map, constituting the majority of gameplay, and consists primarily of pre-existing music. The 'overwhelming majority' of these pieces hail from the European/American art music tradition; the four exceptions are originally composed cues for the classical era (Cook 2014, 170). Named 'Ancient Soundtrack 1–4', these tracks draw indiscriminately on musical stereotypes of pan-African, Native American or Aboriginal cultures – regardless of which civilization the player selects (Cook 2014, 173). The game's Medieval era presents Medieval and Renaissance pieces for voices or recorders, its Renaissance era instrumental works by Johann Sebastian Bach, Wolfgang Amadeus Mozart and Ludwig van Beethoven – none of whom are Renaissance-era composers – and the Industrial era features significantly louder orchestral works from eighteenth- to nineteenth-century European composers. Curiously, the Modern era solely consists of nine John Adams pieces – as if Adams is the only living composer of significance. Beethoven's repertoire is divided across Renaissance and Industrial eras; this anachronistic placement suggests the developers 'using the "wrong" music' to conform to when players likely assume the music originates (Gibbons 2018, 31).

The diplomatic soundtrack plays when entering negotiations with a civilization leader, playing a unique theme for each leader (Cook 2014, 173). Some of these pairings are fairly obvious – 'La Marseillaise' for Napoleon, Beethoven's Symphony No. 3 for Otto von Bismarck or 'Rule Brittania' for Queen Victoria – but others are specially composed for *Civ IV*. Tellingly, over two-thirds of the original themes belong to non-European/non-American leaders; the only two leaders with arrangements of pre-existing melodies are China's Qin Shi Huang and Japan's Ieyasu Tokugawa. *Civ IV* composer Jeffrey Briggs states: 'in many cases, there simply is not a well-known tune to represent a culture, so we make it up' – an admission most indicative of developer bias and laziness, and a claim that *Civilization VI* later refutes (Cook 2014, 174). Both terrain and diplomatic soundtracks instantiate *Civ IV*'s musical Eurocentrism, imposing a 'fundamentally Western understanding' of music history and ignoring 'equally rich (and often much longer)' non-western musical traditions while substituting exoticized simulacra (Gibbons 2018, 30). Whether you select Napoleon, Gandhi or Montezuma, the musical development of your culture will be that of western classical music from Bach to Beethoven to Adams – the musical analogue to Poblocki's objection concerning imperialism. Returning to Kendi's framework, *Civ IV* exemplifies an assimilationist approach to video game music, enshrining western music as a cultural standard – for 'making a cultural standard and hierarchy is what creates cultural racism' (Kendi 2019, 83). As Cook concludes, *Civ IV* '[equates] Western(ized) music with cultural advancement, leaving stereotypes of non-Western music to represent only prehistoric sound' while excluding actual non-western music entirely (2014, 177).

Civilization V (2010) showcases a transitional approach that foreshadows the developments of *Civilization VI*. No longer are all civilizations pigeonholed into a singular, predominantly European terrain soundtrack. Rather, the terrain soundtrack is grouped according to the continent to which the real-world nation belongs, utilizing a blend of original and pre-existing music thought representative of the real-world continental region. For example, European leaders may be scored with a Claude Debussy piano prelude, an Asian leader with Ravi Shankar's concerto for sitar and a North/South American leader with R. Carlos Nakai's music for cedar flute. Europe still claims the most pre-composed pieces, while the Americas contain the fewest. *Civ V*'s true innovation is the incorporation of individualized musical themes into the terrain soundtrack. Each leader is represented by a musical theme with two versions: 'peace' and 'war'. The theme of the player's selected leader is frequently featured in the terrain soundtrack – the peace version while at peace with other nations, the war version while at war. Other leaders' themes and other continental pieces do not penetrate the terrain soundtrack; like *Civ IV*, they are only heard during diplomatic negotiations with that leader. Typically this is the theme's peace version – the war version appears only during a leader's declaration of war and any diplomacy while the war continues. Unlike *Civ IV*'s assimilationism, one's aural experience of *Civ V* may greatly vary by selecting a different civilization or leader.

Civ V incorporates a greater degree of melodic source material originating from the represented cultures than *Civ IV*'s haphazard approach but orchestrates them in representationally problematic ways. The perceived distinctive characteristics of each culture's music are exaggerated, rendering non-western cultures semiotically marked and exoticized; in contrast, the themes of western leaders like Elizabeth I ('I Vow to Thee, My Country') and George Washington ('America the Beautiful') sound unmarked. Consider Korean leader Sejong's theme, derived from 'Arirang' – a folk song UNESCO records as 'universally sung and enjoyed' by Koreans (UNESCO 2012). Martino observes the developers faced 'considerable pressure' from South Korean's strong gaming market to represent their culture well, prompting them to vet design choices with Korean cultural consultants and focus groups (Martino 2021, 37). Nonetheless, though the theme's Korean instrumentation of *haegeum* and *gayageum* stringed instruments and *moktak* wood blocks are legitimate, they are employed in an exaggerated manner indicative of musical orientalism – a marker of racial difference. Another prime example is the music associated with Hawai'i's King Kamehameha ('Hole Waimea') dripping with gratuitous lap steel guitar bends and light *ukulele* strums better suiting a beach resort than a head of state. Its war version adds tired stereotypes of Polynesian music including *haka* chant and *pahu* drums – yet still foregrounds lap steel guitar bends to eradicate any doubt that this music represents Hawai'i. Though *Civ V* mitigates its predecessor's assimilationism via greater variety in leader themes and terrain soundtrack, it instead exhibits musical segregationism by exaggerating differences between cultures, exoticizing non-western civilizations.[6] Recalling Blumenbach's rigid taxonomy 'Caucasoid, Mongoloid, Negroid', each leader and continent hears only its own sound, siloed away from the diversity of musical others.

Civilization VI (2016) charts a new musical course, rejecting the series' prior assimilationist and segregationist approaches for an antiracist one. Critics praised *Civ VI*'s soundtrack as an 'impressive game score' and 'the best soundtrack in the series' (Marks 2016; Mol et al. 2017, 215). Two strands of innovation facilitate this tangible change: implementation and representation. First, *Civ VI* unifies *Civ IV*'s terrain and diplomatic soundtracks by using the leaders' unique musical themes for the majority of the underscore during overworld map actions. While there is an ambient soundtrack indexed to the player's civilization, with 1–2 short tracks per era selected to complement the leader theme, it occupies much less aural space than in previous instalments. In a crucial alteration from *Civ V*, themes of all civilizations involved in the match – not only the player's – comprise the game's underscore. This soundtrack presents a multicultural vision of a world with cultures inevitably influencing and shaping one another – an ongoing dialogue instead of triumphalist propaganda. Representationally, *Civ VI*'s leader themes demonstrate vast improvement over *Civ IV* and *V*. Each theme derives from a culturally significant or representative melody (only a few of the 54 leader themes are original compositions), evolving alongside the world's civilizations from the Ancient to the Atomic (Modern) eras (Table 6.1). The Ancient version presents the source melody alone on a solo instrument, thickening in instrumentation and compositional complexity as time progresses. While the terrain soundtrack of *Civ IV* similarly presented an aural progression through time, its sources were entirely European/American, semiotically encoding western musical history as the only possible progression; in *Civ VI*, any musical tradition, any culture can flourish to full potential. Notice the United States and European civilizations undergo the exact same musical evolution – in other words, western music is not centralized as more sophisticated or the standard to which other cultures must aspire (the involvement of orchestra for the Industrial and Atomic eras shall be discussed below). Although the diplomatic soundtrack's leader themes in *Civ IV* also develop diachronically in three versions, they are heard only during negotiation with that leader, comprising much less of the musical underscore than in *Civ VI*. In *Civ IV*, musical culture is semiotically marked as 'Other', while the player's default terrain soundtrack is solely European/American. In *Civ VI*, each playthrough's sound-scape is a unique product of the nations involved in the match. The multicultural, progressive approach of *Civ VI*'s soundtrack is justly extolled as one of the best features in a widely acclaimed game (Marks 2016).

TABLE 6.1: Table of leader theme source melodies in *Civilization VI*.

Civilization	Leader(s)	Source Melody
Arab	Saladin	'Tala Ma Ashku Gharami'
Australia	John Curtin	'Waltzing Matilda' (Banjo Paterson)
Aztec	Montezuma	Original composition
Babylon	Hammurabi	Original composition
Brazil	Pedro II	'Brejeiro' (Ernesto Nazarath)
Byzantium	Basil II	Kontakion of the Mother of God
Canada	Wilfred Laurier	'Vive La Canadienne'
China	Qin Shi Huang (秦始皇)	'Mō Lì Huā' (茉莉花; Jasmine Flower)
Columbia	Simón Bolívar	'Velo que Bonito'
Cree	Poundmaker	'Grass Dance Song'
Egypt	Cleopatra	'El Helwa Di'
England	Victoria; Eleanor of Aquitaine	'Scarborough Fair'
Ethiopia	Menelik II	'Tizita'
France	Catherine de Medici, Eleanor of Aquitaine	'Quand je bois du vin clairet'
Gaul	Ambiorix	'La Brabançonne' (François van Campenhout)
Georgia	Tamar	'Shen Khar Venakhi'
Germany	Frederick Barbarossa	'Ich hab die Nacht geträumet'
Greece	Pericles, Gorgo	Epitaph of Seikilos
Hungary	Matthias Corvinus	'Hej, Dunáról fúj a szél'
Inca	Pachacuti	'Siempre Macho' (Monica Gomez)
India	Mohandas Gandhi, Chandragupta	'Vaishnava Jana To' (Narsinh Mehta)
Indonesia	Gitarja	'Rejang Dewa', 'Bapang Selisir'
Japan	Tokimune Hōjō	'Itsuki no Komoriuta' (五木の子守唄)
Khmer	Jayavarman VII	'Khmer Rourm Sam Mawgee'
Kongo	Mvemba a Nzinga	'Banaha'

(*Continued*)

Civilization	Leader(s)	Source Melody
Korea	Seondeok	'Arirang'
Macedon	Alexander	'Tino Mori'
Mali	Mansa Musa	'Mali Sadio', 'Masana Seesay'
Māori	Kupe	'Ka ate, Ka mate' (Te Rauparaha)
Mapuche	Lautaro	Traditional melody (attributed)
Maya	Lady Six Sky	'Xtoles'
Mongolia	Genhis Khan, Kublai Khan	'Urtiin Duu'
Netherlands	Wilhelmina	'Gaillarde L'esmerillonne' (Pierre Phalèse)
Norway	Harald Hardrada	'Gjendines bådnlåt'
Nubia	Amanitore	'Allah Musau'
Ottoman	Suleiman	'Ey Büt-i Nev-eda'
Persia	Cyrus	'Kereshme' (Majid Derakhshani)
Phoenicia	Dido	'Hurrian Hymn to Nikkal'
Poland	Jadwiga	'Hej ide w las'
Portugal	João III	'Fado Menor' (Maria Emilia)
Rome	Trajan	'Magna Mater'
Russia	Peter Alexeyevich	'Kalinka' (Ivan Larionov)
Scotland	Robert the Bruce	'Scotland the Brave'
Scythia	Tomyris	Original composition
Spain	Philip II	'Recuerdos de la Alhambra' (Francisco Tárrega)
Sumeria	Gilgamesh	Original composition
Sweden	Kristina	'Helan går'
United States of America	Theodore Roosevelt	'Hard Times Come Again No More' (Stephen Foster)
Vietnam	Bà Triệu	'Lý Kéo Chài', 'Trống Cơm' 'Giăng Câu'
Zulu	Shaka	'Uthe Ubhuti Asizomlanda'

GENDER, RACE AND RELIGION IN VIDEO GAME MUSIC

Additionally, *Civ VI* expands the role of 'Great Musicians' – special units that boost a civilization's culture and tourism scores. Great Musicians may be drawn to civilization with plentiful performance venues or patronized using gold or faith. Of eighteen total Great Musicians, nine are male European composers like Antonio Vivaldi or Pyotr Ilyich Tchaikovsky. The other nine consist of non-White and/or female musicians including Black-American 'King of Ragtime' Scott Joplin, German pianist and composer Clara Schumann, Japanese 'Father of Modern Koto' Yatsuhashi Kengyō, Chinese *erhu* composer and virtuoso Liu Tianhua, Mexican waltz and polka composer Juventino Rosas and Hawai'i's last ruling monarch Queen Lili'uokalani, a distinguished poet and composer (Table 6.2). There is no civilization-based probability algorithm for recruiting Great Musicians, so players using Japan or Ethiopia are equally likely to attract Ludwig van Beethoven as one playing as Germany. Each Great Musician can create two 'Great Works of Music' corresponding to their real-world repertoire, pausing gameplay to perform an excerpted recording of the work. The Civilopedia further contextualizes each musician's biography, career and legacy. Though the Great Musicians roster still skews White and male, this is remarkable diversification and research for a series that once claimed no extant music could represent Egypt, India or Greece.

Case study analysis of two leader themes will elucidate *Civ VI*'s representational virtues and the musical development of a source melody across eras. Qin Shi Huang (始皇), the first emperor of China, is represented by *Mō Lì Huā*, known in English as 'Jasmine Flower'. The folk song, recognized as the official song of the city Yangzhou, is widely known in China and internationally, featured in Giacomo Puccini's opera 'Turandot' and the 2008 Beijing Olympic Games. The Ancient era version presents the melody monophonically on *guzheng* (古筝, lit. 'ancient *zheng*'), one of China's most enduring instruments. In the Medieval era, guzheng tremolos lead into *luo* tam-tam with accompanying violins. The melody occurs on guzheng, violin and erhu, adding *pipa* arpeggiation and light *jiangu* drum pulses. The Industrial era version broadens in orchestration and scope, introducing brass section swells augmenting the guzheng's *glissandi*. After a three-octave unison exposition of the melody in guzheng, flute and cello, mixed choir and brass accompaniment joins for a soaring rendition of the melody in the violin sections. Unlike *Civ V*'s 'Arirang', at no point do the Chinese instruments seem exaggerated or orientalized but are instead featured against the backdrop of the orchestra. Finally, the Atomic era track reimagines the guzheng, jiangu and orchestra layers with synthesized and cinematic percussion layers for twenty-first-century flavour. Nevertheless, the music's heart remains the guzheng melody, which remains a consistent presence throughout – reinterpreting Jasmine Flower as a concerto for guzheng and orchestra.

The sixteenth-century Kongolese King Mvemba A Nzinga (or Afonso I) is represented in-game by '*Banaha*', a folksong sung by Kongolese soldiers in

176

TABLE 6.2: Table of Great Musicians and featured musical works in *Civilization VI*.

Great Musician	Nationality	Musical Works
Antonín Dvořák	Czech	Symphony No. 9, Op. 95 'From the New World'; Serenade for Strings, Op. 22
Antônio Carlos Gomes	Brazil	*Fosca*; 'Alvarado' from *Lo schiavo*
Clara Schumann	Germany	Prelude and Fugue No. 3, Op. 16; Soirées musicales No. 1, Op. 6
Dimitrie Cantemir	Romania	Pesrev Adjem Yegiahi, Prince of Moldavia, Uzzusule Beresvan
Franz Liszt	Hungary	Études d'exécution transcendante, S. 139; Mephisto Waltz No. 1, S. 110
Frédéric Chopin	Poland	Nocturnes No. 2, Op. 9; Grand valse brillante, Op. 18
Gauhar Jaan	India	Raga Kharnaj Jogiya, Raga Bhairavi
Johann Sebastian Bach	Germany	Fugue in G Minor, BWV 581; Cello Suite No. 1, BWV 1007
Juventino Rosas	Mexico	Sobre las Olas; Vals Carmen
Lili'uokalani	Hawaii	'Lili'uokalani's Prayer'; 'Sanoe'
Liu Tianhua	China	Liáng Xiāo (良宵); Kōng shān niǎo yù (空山鸟语)
Ludwig van Beethoven	Germany	Symphony No. 3, Op. 55 'Eroica'; Symphony No. 9, Op. 125
Mykola Leontovych	Ukraine	'Carol of the Bells'; Prelude for Choir
Pyotr Ilyich Tchaikovsky	Russia	This Year 1812, Solemn Overture, Op. 49; 'Danse des petits cygnes' from *Swan Lake*, op. 20
Scott Joplin	United States	'The Entertainer'; 'Maple Leaf Rag'; 'The Easy Winners' (all from *The Sting*)
Wolfgang Amadeus Mozart	Austria	*Eine kleine Nachtmusik*, K. 525; Symphony No. 40, K. 550
Yatsuhashi Kengyo	Japan	Rokudan no Shirabe (六段の調); Hachidan no Shirabe (八段の調)

the Second World War and recorded by the Belgian priest Guido Haazen in the 'Missa Luba', a Catholic mass sung entirely in Congolese languages and musical styles. Its cheerful melody is introduced in the Ancient era version in octaves on *kalimba*, an instrument popularized in the 1960s by English ethnomusicologist Hugh Tracey adapting the sound of the *mbira*, which is over 1000 years old. Aurally, kalimba and mbira are very close in timbre; because the *Civ VI* recording lacks the mbira's distinctive percussive buzz, it is best identified as kalimba rather than mbira. The Medieval era track adds string quartet and *djembe* and *shekere* percussion accompaniment, alternating the melody between kalimba and violins. Especially striking is a 2:3 polyrhythm that emerges when all instruments but the kalimba drop out – polyrhythmic layering is a signature feature in much African music – which transitions the metre from simple (4/4) to compound (12/8). As with *Mō Lì Huā*, the Industrial era arrangement incorporates the African instruments over an orchestral texture, remaining audible throughout most of the piece. A trumpet fanfare heralds a bold melodic statement of Banaha in the horns over soaring arpeggiation before trading fragments of the tune to the strings. The Atomic era begins with foregrounded synthesized arpeggiation suggestive of *marimba*, another percussion instrument originating in Africa. Melodic motives are initially presented by a timbral cocktail of marimba, kalimba and synthesizer, foreshadowing the melody in flute, strings and brass. The powerful brass and string climax is carried over from the Industrial version, amplified by driving cinematic percussion. Representationally, the latter two arrangements could be improved by retaining a melodic role for the kalimba rather than ceding the melody to European instruments – particularly in their softer moments. Overall, however, these variations on Banaha envision a dynamic kingdom of Kongo leading the world on a grand scale.

The use of orchestra accompanying each civilization's melody in the Industrial and Atomic eras is the remaining echo of *Civ IV*'s assimilationist rhetoric. By presenting more developed music in orchestrated form, does *Civ VI* not also reduce all cultures to the progression of western music history? Is the orchestra itself not an icon of cultural assimilation? These questions have more complex answers than a simple affirmative. Certainly, the standard European orchestra is composed of many instruments that did not originate in Europe (e.g. the string section, various wind instruments and percussion section). Nonetheless, the orchestra today is not merely a symbol of cultural assimilation, but a medium that living composers of any nationality or ethnicity regularly use to create innovative musical expression that goes beyond stylistic conventions imposed by Europe or the United States. Much like the reclamation of derogatory labels originally invented to insult a community, contemporary composers worldwide have infused the orchestra with fresh meanings, redefining it from an instrument of oppression to a catalyst for creative empowerment. Though the orchestra is by no means a 'universal' vehicle for musical expression – an assimilationist line of reasoning – it is also true that in the diverse landscape of today's living composers, virtually every nation has become a stakeholder in the orchestra as a means of musical expression. Additionally, in accordance with the earlier metaphor of these orchestrated tracks as a concerto, there are arrangements that keep the cultural melody firmly foregrounded so that the orchestra seems rather incidental, such as the Māori's 'Ka Mate' and the Cree's 'Drums of Poundmaker' (though the latter's orchestration does participate in stereotypical Indianisms). While this is not always the case – Japan's *Itsuki no Komoriuta* (五木の子守唄; 'Itsuki Lullaby') in Industrial and Atomic eras is an example that assimilates the harmonic characteristics of the cultural melody to European/American expectations – it would be too hasty to dismiss all the Industrial and Atomic orchestral arrangements as European/American assimilations. This music must be adjudicated case by case, and many tracks – such as the China and Kongo themes – maintain strong cultural individuality even while accompanied by an orchestra.

Civ VI's leader themes model the musical semiotics of antiracism, forging a third path between assimilating all musical identities to one monoculture and segregating them into exoticized caricatures. Cook critiqued *Civ IV*'s terrain soundtrack for not drawing musical elements from any specific real-world culture – as *Civ VI* does for nearly every theme (Cook 2014, 177). For people of diverse backgrounds to hear melodies and instruments from their cultural heritage across simulated history is an experience uniquely afforded by *Civilization*'s ambitious premise and scope. *Civ VI* players flocked to message boards, expressing gratitude for the inclusion of so many diverse cultures and significant pride at having their own ancestral or resident nation represented (Majewski 2021, 77). Other writers have noted the latest instalment's improvements in representing Persia or other Near Eastern civilizations and the distribution and naming of unique structures termed 'Wonders' (Mol and Politopoulos 2021, 51; Mol et al. 2017, 217). Representing a multitude of civilizations equally and charitably allows players to project their cultural identities into counterfactual world history. Indeed, historian John Majewski observes that the pedagogical value of *Civilization* is not imparting specific historical facts, but rather leading players to realize that all historical readings are interpretations (Majewski 2021, 81). The semiotic play of interpretative interactivity is central to the meaning-making potential of a video game like *Civ VI*. As Diane Carr writes: 'because of play, interactivity and agency, the "reading position" of the player is more multiple and contesting, more critical and assertive, than that offered to viewers, gazers, or readers' (2007, 234). In other words, *Civ VI* constructs a malleable stage upon which players may reify their vision of the world – where the Māori haka 'Ka Mate' flourishes to epic scale along with its civilization, or 'Lili'uokalani's Prayer' floods global airwaves instead of Beethoven's ninth symphony.

As mentioned in the chapter's introduction, no person or work is entirely antiracist, and the work of antiracism is perpetually ongoing (Kendi 2019, 10). Although the preceding analysis emphasizes *Civ VI*'s improvements from previous instalments, utilizing a hermeneutic of hope, the game is not above reproach and has room for further improvement. On a broad gameplay level, *Civ VI* still squeezes all nations into an imperialist-leaning playstyle, whether in military, religion, science or culture. Even the newly introduced Diplomatic Victory feature leans into privileging western imperialism – owning more territories boosts a nation's diplomatic favour, diplomacy points can be traded for gold and building the United States' Statue of Liberty awards the highest possible diplomacy points. When recording Poundmaker Cree's theme with Cree singer Clyde Tootoosis, composer Geoff Knorr obtained permission from the artist, but not the nation's headman-counsellor, who objected to their nation's behaving similarly to colonialist cultures in the game (Martino 2021, 39–40). On the other hand, a player belonging to the Cree nation reported elation that the player's own people were represented in a global video game franchise (Majewski 2021, 77). Two further musical critiques of *Civ VI*'s score could be raised: the use of orchestra as *telos* for each civilization's melody and the mitigation of unique musical features in later eras. Most leader themes begin in the Ancient era with more distinctive instrumentation, then become predominantly orchestral in the Industrial and Atomic era versions. What if the latter eras instead utilized iconic instrumental ensembles or music genres developed within each culture, culminating in arrangements by living composers of that community – as developers commissioned a New Zealand artist to design the Māori leader Kupe (Martino 2021, 37)? This would diffuse the impression that the symphony orchestra is the 'teleological pinnacle of musical civilization' (Cook 2014, 177). Additionally, the unique stylistic features of a civilization's musical traditions – such as microtones, pitch bends and ornaments in the Indian, Ottoman and Japanese Ancient-era themes – tend to diminish in later eras to better fit with the orchestra. A better approach would seek ways to adapt the accompanying instruments to each culture's stylistic conventions, creatively imagining what an alternate music history based on that tradition could be.

Musical diversity in *Civilization VI* consists of enabling the sound of every culture to flourish in its own unique way – without exoticism or assimilation. Poblocki alleged that players could not easily distance from the game's imperialist ideology due to its immersive properties (Poblocki 2002, 174). However, when cultural representation is well-executed, that same interpretative interactivity transfigures video gaming into an ideal medium for antiracist storytelling. The point is not to teach us about the past, but who we are in the present and who we could become (Longreads 2016). The meanings of *Civ VI* are not static or fixed, but are 'generated by or [emerge] through play' (Carr 2007, 233). Through virtual narrative, we can realize a world where all the Earth's diverse peoples – and musics – are equal.

The World Needs More Heroes: Musical Diversity in Overwatch

Blizzard's *Overwatch* (2016) stands as a landmark of innovation and representational diversity in the video game industry. 'Whoever you want to be', reads the game's website, 'there's an *Overwatch* hero for you' (Blizzard 2021, n.pag.). Loosely classified as a team-based first-person shooter game, *Overwatch* brings together two teams of six players in competitions that emphasize teamwork and a diverse cast of characters. Starkly contrasting the gritty realism of typical competitive shooter games, *Overwatch*'s colourful aesthetics and collaborative philosophy are refreshingly bright and optimistic (Starkey 2016). In its first week alone, *Overwatch* grossed a tremendous $269 million and drew 7 million players, topping industry bestseller charts in multiple countries. A departure from Blizzard's staple fantasy and science-fiction settings, *Overwatch* envisions Earth 60 years in our future, rebuilding after a cataclysmic *Terminator*-like scenario known as the Omnic Crisis. Featuring narrative themes of artificial intelligence, technological ethics and the heroism of every individual, *Overwatch* stages encounters between the resurrected international peacekeeping force Overwatch, the enigmatic terrorist organization Talon and any third party or bystander in the crossfire. With the world's tenuous, newfound peace at stake, confrontations across the globe involve individuals with various backgrounds, talents and motivations.

Overwatch has been lauded as 'one of the most diverse video games in history', with a cast exhibiting an exceptional degree of diversity in nationality, ethnicity, economic class, neurodiversity, age, physical condition, gender and sexual orientation (Downey 2018). Founding director Jeff Kaplan, in his D.I.C.E. Summit 2017 keynote, revealed that *Overwatch* was born out of great despair. After their previous project *Titan* was scrapped, Kaplan's team was granted six weeks to propose a new franchise or be disbanded. From this hopelessness, the *Overwatch* team strove to envision a hopeful future, crafting their gameworld around the philosophy: 'never accept the world as it appears to be; dare to see it for what it could be' (Kaplan 2017, n.pag.). The game is set in our own future – not as post-apocalyptic dystopia, but rather foreshadowing a world working together for peace, justice and equity. With its global scope and expectant outlook, *Overwatch* foregrounds diversity as key to our future (Downey 2018). In a Polygon interview, Kaplan described the developers' paradigm shift from thinking of Earth as a boring setting compared to fantasy or sci-fi to seeing an opportunity to celebrate the unique differences that make it amazing (Campbell 2017). From its 2016 launch, *Overwatch* has been widely praised for centring diversity in a mainstream, big-budget video game. *Den of Geek* described *Overwatch* as 'diversity done right' for its 'accessibility, relatability, heroism, and diversity' (Hardgrave 2015), and *HPCritical* credited its 'vast and deep world [...] built on inclusion' (Fiore 2019, n.pag.). *Overwatch's* success and dedicated fanbase may establish both precedent and pressure for other major video game franchises to emulate. Diverse representation is neither a sales gimmick nor a result of progressive policing, but rather a 'moral imperative' for digital media creators today.

Though the game itself is extremely sparse on narrative exposition, *Overwatch's* world and character backstories are rigorously developed in its transmedial sources (10 animated short films, 11 origin story videos for added characters, 23 comic book issues and 5 short stories at the time of writing), each of which spotlights a specific character or important narrative event. Incorporating transmedia enables the treatment of important identity topics with more nuance than is typically available to competitive shooter games; for example, the comic 'A Better World' and short story 'Stone by Stone' provide insight into Symmetra's experience as a person on the autism spectrum from a first-person perspective, with the requisite subtlety unsuited to *Overwatch's* core gameplay (McMillen 2017). While one could view reserving identity exploration for these sources as hiding or de-centralizing them, I consider the choice appropriate to handle personal identity with the high-resolution care it deserves and avoid tokenism – though integrating transmedia content as viewable/readable from within the game would be a welcome improvement (Villarreal 2017). Three brief case studies – out of over a dozen possible – demonstrate *Overwatch's* commitment to centring marginalized identities and subverting stereotypes:

1. Tracer: The cheerful time-manipulating Overwatch agent Tracer is an irrepressible force for good. The comics 'Reflections' and 'Tracer – London Calling' depicted Tracer's relationship with her girlfriend Emily, which Kaplan described as 'normal things being normal' (Kaplan 2017, n.pag.). Featuring a canonically lesbian hero on *Overwatch's* cover is a significant queer representation, one that disrupts the frequently homohysterical competitive video game culture (King 2021).
2. Lúcio: a music producer, inventor, freedom fighter and social justice activist, Lúcio embodies the grassroots heroism of *Overwatch*. As an Afro-Brazilian, Lúcio represents an important liminal identity often overlooked in media culture (Sánchez 2018). *Geeks of Color* identifies Lúcio's courage to resist corrupt systems and desire to channel his musical talent for social change as themes resonating with Black communities (Willis 2016).
3. Sombra: The savvy, independent and unflappable Mexican hacktivist Sombra 'breaks almost every Latina stereotype' (Sánchez 2018, n.pag.). As an

intelligent, competent and non-sexualized woman, Sombra also constitutes positive gender representation (Fiore 2019). Sombra provides a powerful model for Latina/o children to enter STEM fields, in which Latina/o individuals are consistently underrepresented. Sánchez concludes that Sombra, together with Lúcio and Reaper, makes *Overwatch* an outstanding headliner of Latina/o representation.

Overwatch's emphasis on diversity permeates its gameplay philosophy along with its character design. A flagship in the burgeoning team shooter genre, cooperation with teammates is ludically rewarded above individualistic achievement or high kill-to-death ratio (Colp 2021). Balanced teams each consisting of two 'Tank', 'Damage' and 'Support' players encode diversity into the game's competitive premise, and each role includes heroes that achieve their goals in unconventional ways or hybridize their role with another. Even at launch, reviewers acclaimed *Overwatch*'s 'staggeringly diverse' characters, each offering a unique playstyle unlike any other – and 11 more characters have been added since (Frushtick 2016). In a multiplayer game, play dynamically generates semiotic meaning through ongoing 'ludic dialectic' between players, 'constantly proposing and counter-proposing theories of optimal play' (Colp 2021). In other words, a game's values are embedded in its systems, as ludic diversity is imperative to success in *Overwatch*. Unorthodox heroes like Reinhardt, Winston, Reaper, Mercy and Lúcio allow players to 'feel like a superhero' even when aim – the holy grail skill of most shooting games – is not their strong suit (Webster 2016). This decentralizes aim's hegemonic position in a genre that has been defined by that specific skill for decades. The roster's global diversity is also essential to *Overwatch*'s success as an Esport – especially the Overwatch League, comprising twenty professional teams based in major cities across Europe, Asia and the United States (e.g. Shanghai Dragons, Dallas Fuel). Like the Olympics, Overwatch League matches are not merely about individual or team performance but also a matter of national pride (Turtiainen et al. 2020). Building such a global ethos would be arduous if, for example, the heroes skewed heavily American. Just as heroes emerge from any nation in *Overwatch*'s world, so too may the next Overwatch League champion.

The music of *Overwatch* is as diverse and globally oriented as its cast and Overwatch League teams. *Overwatch*'s music is considered one of its hallmark strengths for its versatility, memorability and immersive function (Holt 2020). While *Overwatch* matches themselves are relatively light on music – providing musical cues only to signal the end of a match or a rapidly depleting timer – each map is introduced with its own unique theme that generally incorporates musical elements associated with the location. For example, the American Route 66 features country blues electric guitar riffs, while Australia's Junkertown foregrounds the iconic sound of the didgeridoo. The location's music sounds for approximately 30 seconds over the loading and character selection screens before gameplay begins – music establishes players' sense of place, carrying with it semiotic and ludic implications. 'The memorable refrains are burned into my mind', reports one reviewer, describing how the music psychologically transports players into the ludic setting (Cardy 2020, n.pag.). These location-based map themes form the majority of *Overwatch*'s soundtrack and the crux of its musical cultural representation. Although these location themes are not, properly speaking, character themes, most location themes are linked to a particular hero (additionally, individual musical themes for each hero are rumoured to be composed for *Overwatch 2* at the time of writing). For example, Hanamura, Japan is the birthplace of Hanzo and Genji, and Dorado, Mexico is the elusive Sombra's hometown. Other maps correspond to nations represented by heroes, such as Paris and Widowmaker (France) or Eichenwalde and Reinhardt (Germany); only 6 out of 30 playable maps are not linked to a particular character. The transmedia content – such as the short film 'Dragons' or Orisa's and Doomfist's origin story videos – musically characterizes certain heroes further, integrating musical references to their cultural backgrounds. In the music of *Overwatch*, cultural representation therefore translates to a personal identity – just as individuals are indelibly shaped by their place and culture of origin.

Analysing musical topics and topical troping in *Overwatch* elucidates how its diversity permeates its soundtrack. Musical topics strategically 'locate music in history and in culture' by forging conventional associations between certain musical parameters and cultural meanings (Monelle 2006, 29). For example, the pastoral topic links recognizable musical features – including slow harmonic rhythm, horn and woodwind instruments, simple melodies, major mode and parallel thirds or sixths – to concepts including peace, spiritual grace, harmony with nature, simplicity and innocence (Hatten 2004, 56). The primary musical topics of *Overwatch*'s location themes may be broadly divided into two types: technological and cultural. The 'technological' topic encompasses features generally characteristic of electronic dance music, including synthesized timbres, danceable percussion beat (especially when electronically generated) and digital music production hallmarks like pan automation, filter sweeps or dubstep-style bass drops. 'Cultural' is an umbrella subcategory for any musical elements associated with a particular culture or tradition; the map themes' explicit connection to cities enables easy identification of culture-specific sounds. Each topic corresponds to a crucial theme of *Overwatch*'s narrative – the technological to its futuristic setting, the cultural to its diversity – and the interplay between them reveals the game's musical meaning. When two or more topics exist simultaneously in a musical passage, the juxtaposition results in a topical trope – a process by which 'new meaning emerges from atypical or even contradictory associations' between musical topics (Hatten 2004, 2).

Robert Hatten theorizes four axes of topical troping – compatibility, dominance, creativity and productivity – as concepts to analyse how multiple topics synergize and interact (2014, 515). 'Compatibility' describes how similar topical components of a trope are, 'dominance' describes which topical component is foregrounded or given more structural weight, 'creativity' describes the novelty and salience of a topical combination and 'productivity' describes the trope's potential for generating expressive discourse over a section or piece. While all four axes will be utilized in Chapter 8, only compatibility is necessary to the present analysis, as it assesses how harmoniously two musical topics are integrated. Figure 6.2 visualizes *Overwatch*'s location themes according to the compatibility exhibited between its technological and cultural topics, with outer extremes reserved for cues that manifest solely one or the other (Figure 6.2).

Two detailed musical case studies illustrate *Overwatch*'s remarkable fusion of the technological and cultural.[7] 'Hanamura' blends Japanese harmony and instrumentation with synthesized timbres. The track opens with shimmering synth pads and a very faint clap on beats 2 and 4. Then, a synth string bass enters, supporting an arpeggiated *koto* riff outlining the pitches C – D♭ – F – G – A♭ (with neighbouring B♭), corresponding to the Japanese *miyakobushi* mode (previously covered in Chapter 5). After a transitional crescendo interweaving synth electric bass eighth-note pulses, rising horn gestures and a torrential filter sweep, an animated electronic percussion beat drives the track's momentum. In a contrasting B section, the technological topic overtakes the *koto* and horns, climaxing in a drum break reminiscent of the famed, oft-sampled break from 'Amen Brother'. The cue ends by reincorporating the koto in alternating octaves over the busy break

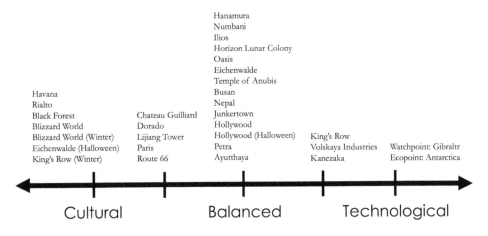

FIGURE 6.2: Spectrum of *Overwatch* map musical themes organized by degree of topical troping.

beat; the *miyakobushi*-mode inflection remains, though transposed up to D instead of C. The result is an energetic, intense track that privileges neither technological nor cultural topic while foregrounding each in turn.

'Numbani' characterizes the fictitious utopia constructed near Nigeria known as the 'City of Harmony', where humans and the artificially intelligent Omnic race coexist as equals; accordingly, its music most exemplifies the balance between the technological and cultural. Its opening blurs the boundaries between organic and synthetic by utilizing marimba and synthesized textures in close counterpoint – as noted in the previous section, marimba is a prominent modern instrument of African provenance. Synthesized metallophones evocative of computer sounds punctuate the contrapuntal equilibrium. The track's full orchestration emerges suddenly, blending the marimba and digital layers with call-and-response-style vocals (on fictitious syllables intended to suggest African languages), droning low brass pedals and complex electronic rhythmic elements. The marimba riff and techy beat are foregrounded one final time, ceding to the vocal chorus for the final flourish. Throughout the piece, pervasive panning, dynamic swells and filter sweeps accentuate Numbani's unique identity as the techno-paradise best integrating Omnics into society. The high compatibility of technological and cultural topics musically encodes *Overwatch*'s central hope for harmony between communities as different as human and Omnic.

In *Civ VI*, navigating between essentialism and erasure of a culture's musical elements was key to communicating an antiracist message; similarly, the balance between technological and cultural is key to *Overwatch*'s musical argument. Its location themes predominantly exhibit a balance between technological and cultural musical topics, producing a synthesis greater than its individual components. Its characters walk the same tightrope between technology and personality, as all heroes except Hanzo and Cassidy substantially rely on advanced technology for their abilities.[8] As with real individuals, *Overwatch*'s heroes carry their unique cultural formation wherever they travel, which cannot be ignored or erased. Conversely, they are three-dimensional beings that cannot be defined by or reduced to their national heritage – as would be conveyed by musical themes stereotypical of their culture. *IGN*'s reviewers echo this observation, writing that each location theme 'perfectly fits the setting without venturing into caricature' (Cardy 2020, n.pag.). Resonating with the preceding analysis of *Civilization*, balanced integration of cultural elements is key. If all location themes used only cultural topics, the result would be segregationist; if solely technological, assimilationism would erase heroes' racial identities entirely. Instead, *Overwatch* cultivates an antiracist approach that allows the cultures of its people and places to exist harmoniously in the same musical universe – embracing a future worth fighting for.

Thanks to its public prominence and commitment to diversity, *Overwatch* is a lightning rod for controversy and criticism calling out representational blunders and needed improvements. As with *Civ VI*, *Overwatch* and its sequel are far from perfect, including in their cultural representation. Pharah's 'Raindancer' and 'Thunderbird' skins, featuring unmistakable Indigenous North American designs, and Symmetra's 'Devi' and 'Goddess' skins, casting her as the great Hindu goddess Devi, kindled backlash for their cultural insensitivity (D'Anastasio 2017; Fahey 2016). Though the transmedia comic 'Reflections' later canonized Pharah as multiethnic Egyptian and Indigenous Canadian, it came across as post-hoc justification and a missed opportunity for multiethnic representation (the *Overwatch* website references only Pharah's Egyptian ancestry). Sigma is a horrendous representation of neurodivergence for multiple reasons – most egregiously his bare feet, chosen to 'sell the "asylum" look' (Lawver 2019). Anita Sarkeesian and others have observed the lack of body diversity among most of *Overwatch*'s female characters – though Zarya and Mei are notable exceptions (Geier 2019; Totilo 2015). While *Overwatch* features two queer characters, their orientations were revealed through transmedia comics and short stories, an approach that seems ancillary, convenient and safe rather than a bolder embrace of queer identity (Lacina 2019). Many have excoriated *Overwatch*'s 'catastrophically negligent' absence of playable Black women – a deficiency only remedied by Sojourn's arrival in *Overwatch 2* (González 2021). The Overwatch League reflects broader Esports as a male-dominated industry, and hegemonic masculinity and toxic verbiage often manifest in text and voice chat due to the 'online disinhibition effect' (Choi et al. 2020, 1129; Gandolfi and Antonacci 2020, 2). Musically speaking, certain European location themes ('Rialto', 'Black Forest', 'King's Row') are unmarked relative to non-European themes, giving the impression of Europe as the default. Additionally, 'Dorado' and 'Lijiang Tower' exhibit a degree of musical stereotyping, and their cultural and technological topic elements are not as thoroughly integrated as 'other tracks'. Despite numerous representational blunders, *Overwatch* is committed to breaking down longstanding demographic barriers in the video game industry; as Villarreal summarizes: 'while Blizzard still has some work to do, the game is an important example' of diverse representation in video games (Villarreal 2017).

Additionally, as a real-world company comprised real human individuals, Blizzard has fallen drastically short of the diversity-driven vision of the future celebrated in *Overwatch*. In July 2021, California's Department of Fair Employment and Housing sued Activision Blizzard, Inc. for 'equal pay violations, sex discrimination, and sexual harrassment' (Department of Fair Employment & Housing 2021, 1). The DFEH determined reports of sexist culture, pay inequity and sexual harassment against Activision Blizzard's female employees to be credible. After a tone-deaf initial response from the company, employees began months of group petitions, walkouts and collective labour bargaining – a first for the video game industry. After months of turbulent corporate back-and-forth, industry protests and high-profile executive resignations, Activision Blizzard announced its purchase by the gaming industry giant, Microsoft. At this time, it is unclear if Microsoft intends to implement the radical changes needed to address Activision Blizzard's toxic culture, or if the acquisition is purely a business gambit aimed at absorbing a lucrative asset during its moment of economic vulnerability. Also unclear is whether Bobby Kotick, CEO of Activision Blizzard who covered up and enabled the company's abusive culture during this period, will have a continued role at the company after its acquisition, or if the acquisition will even proceed due to injunctions and anti-competition court hearings in multiple countries. While these issues of unequal access and unchecked abuses are important to acknowledge as revelations of systemic injustice and hegemonic culture at Blizzard – both symptomatic of the video game industry in general – they do not negate the narrative and artistic message of *Overwatch*'s gameworld. The underlying meanings of its story and gameplay remain, even if the humans who produced it did not embody the ideals they manifested in *Overwatch*.

Like *Civ VI*, *Overwatch* models antiracist storytelling, both narratively and musically. It champions the representation of marginalized communities and centres stories and identities beyond the panoply of White and male video game protagonists, inviting players worldwide to find themselves reflected in its virtual humanity. In *Overwatch*'s hope-filled vision, the world needs more heroes of all kinds – 'regardless of race, sex, creed, or attraction' (Lee 2016, n.pag.). Its music honours and acknowledges the cultural heritage of its heroes and cities without defining them solely by it – these are three-dimensional, living people and places. By presenting a nuanced view of the world's cultures, *Overwatch* subverts the racist strategy of exoticizing and essentializing populations outside of the dominant culture. As Kendi writes: '[just] as racist power racialises people, racist power racialises space' – and representation of culture entails representation of the people and place that produced it (2019, 169). *Overwatch* dares us to see the world as it could be, pointing to a 'happier, brighter future for [video games]' where any player may feel welcome (Starkey). And that is heroism worth celebrating.

Conclusion: Why Diversity?

Recently, diversity has been the subject of much discussion in the spheres of video games, music, academia, journalism and wider culture. But what precisely is diversity – and why is it important? At diversity's core is the inclusion of people considered different from a group's traditional members and the creation of 'an

ANTIRACIST STORYTELLING

inclusive culture that values and uses the talents of all would-be members' (Herring and Henderson 2015, 12). Diversity is the embrace of difference – precisely the antithesis of segregationism and assimilationism, which attempts to exclude or erase heterogeneity. Therefore, diversity is a key ingredient to counteract racism, for '[to] be antiracist is to conquer the assimilationist consciousness and the segregationist consciousness' (Kendi 2019, 34). However, discussions about diversity are often fraught with misunderstandings – for example, characterizing diversity as focused on quotas, ratios or 'reverse discrimination' (Herring and Henderson 2015, 23). Representational controversies – such as in *Smash* or *Overwatch* – sometimes confuse representational diversity with quantitative equity, so it is worthwhile clarifying the nature of diversity in relation to video games.

Adrienne Shaw's research considers two accounts of the importance of diversity in media:

1. people want to see people who are like them;
2. it is important that people see people unlike them (Shaw 2010, 11).

The first corresponds to quantitative equity and the second to representational diversity. Pro-equity arguments frequently assume that video game players must share demographic identities with characters as a prerequisite for identification, but Shaw's findings show that players can identify with characters based on a multitude of factors that the player may or may not share (Shaw 2010, 146). Shaw's informants stressed the importance of greater representational diversity across the board over simply playing as characters that looked or lived like them (261). In other words, diversity benefits everyone – not just marginalized communities – by breaking down hegemonic culture that centres certain stories over others (248). Diversity is imperative because the world is diverse, and any representation not reflecting its diversity presents a distorted alternate reality (206). As Shaw concludes: '[representation] is important in a social sense, not the individualistic sense stressed by market logic' (207). Diversity matters crucially as a cultural parameter – not primarily or necessarily as a quantitative one.

The music of *Civ VI* and *Overwatch* exemplifies the semiotics of diversity in a cultural, representational sense rather than a numerical one. The *Overwatch* team's guiding vision was 'a world where everybody felt welcome' – a philosophy of inclusion, not strict quantitative equity (Kaplan 2017, n.pag.). Diversity done right is not about quotas or optimal identity ratios, but enabling each player to embrace who they are. Even if one's nationality, culture, lifestyle or identity is not currently represented by a *Civ VI* leader or *Overwatch* hero, the possibility is easily imaginable on account of the games' representational diversity. However, this does not detract from the crucial importance of equity, particularly when transitioning from representational analysis in art to quantitative equity in industry hiring and leadership. Quantitative equity is its own worthwhile goal, especially considering the video game industry's history of predominantly White, male protagonists and developers. A company board comprised solely by White men does not reflect a culture of diversity, but reveals systemic discrimination – inequity warns of lurking cultural non-diversity. Conversely, if not in dialogue with equity, the concept of diversity is hollow (Herring and Henderson 2015, 22). However, the two must not be conflated; it is possible to achieve quantitative equity without dissolving underlying monoculture (tokenism), just as works may express cultural diversity without including every demographic identity.

Neither this chapter nor the book can settle all questions concerning racial and cultural representation, even limited to video game music; however, these case studies demonstrate that the narrative can be changed for the better. Hegemony can be dethroned; antiracist storytelling can be achieved. Employing cancer as a metaphor, Kendi declares: '[racism] has always been terminal *and* curable' (2019, 223). Though it is tempting to believe the racist status quo cannot change, incremental improvement should be named and celebrated. By believing that the semiotic promise of *Civilization VI* and *Overwatch* is both desirable and possible, we can reify a world founded on hope and diversity.

This book's focus now turns from analysing the representation of race to that of religion, another important facet of demographic diversity. Chapters 7 and 8 explore the use of sacred music in video game soundtracks to communicate nuanced theological meanings to players. The musical semiotics of religious representation in game scores is especially significant, as attributes of sacred music can be drawn into dialogue with contrasting musical styles to produce productive and often surprising combinations. Through the incorporation of sacred music and religious narrative themes, video games have much to teach about some religious traditions' most dearly held spiritual beliefs.

NOTES

*   Supplementary Video 6.1 'Antiracist Storytelling: Representation and Diversity in *Civilization VI* and *Overwatch* (GSC 2021)' can be found here: https://www.youtube.com/watch?v=xyS29WWFMk8. Accessed 3 June 2024.

1.   Whether *Super Smash Bros.* is in actuality a fighting game is a contentious, much-debated topic. This is partly due to international differences, as Japan classifies the franchise as a 'battle-action game' (対戦アクションゲーム)' rather than fighting game. In anglophone markets, no such designation exists, so *Smash* is generally categorized as a fighting game. Series creator Masahiro Sakurai consistently denies that *Smash* is a fighting game – citing

its broader audience and arguing it transcends existing genres – describing it instead as a fighting-inspired party game. This ongoing discussion is more than can be settled here – for our purposes, I opt to analyse *Smash* as a fighting game.

2. Ascribing Chinese descent to Min Min may puzzle readers, as her family runs the Mintendo Noodle House, a ramen restaurant, and Min Min's design and arms are ramen-themed. In anglophone countries, ramen is considered a quintessentially Japanese dish. In actuality, ramen originates in China and was popularized through Yokohama's Chinatown in 1910, where it was marketed as *shina soba* (支那 そば, lit. 'Chinese noodles') and only nationalized and embraced by Japan after the Second World War. Thus, to Japanese developers and players, ramen can have as much association with Chinese culture as Japanese. See George Solt 2014, *The Untold History of Ramen: How Political Crisis in Japan Spawned a Global Food Craze* (University of California Press). Min Min also speaks Chinese voice lines, confirming her Chinese heritage.

3. DePass extensively criticized Twintelle's 'weaponized hair' (Mic 2017), arguing that natural Black hair is simultaneously scrutinized and erased in media and society (for women especially, but also for men). Others critiqued Twintelle's sexualized design and presentation, arguing that it perpetuated problematic femme fatale tropes about non-White femininity. However, Shonte Daniels interpreted Twintelle's hair as an 'act of resistance', fighting alongside her hair to great advantage rather than against it (Daniels 2017). Similarly, Janet Garcia argued that sexualization does not entail disempowerment if there is narrative and agential justification for it – which Twintelle possesses as a top celebrity and actress (Garcia 2019). Unsurprisingly, with so few playable Black women in video games, each one is a veritable lightning rod for debate and semiotic politics.

4. Another fatal flaw of assimilation is disallowing the expression and celebration of historically marginalized communities. Claiming 'I don't see race' ignores a vital dimension of individual personal identity, barring it from mainstream cultural discourse. To say to a Black person, 'I don't see you as Black', is to erase part of that person's unique experience – part of who that person is. It also entails that to be seen as Black (or another non-White identity) would be disadvantageous, presupposing the hegemonic position of White identity. This is explained via markedness theory (previously explored in Chapter 3), in which unmarked Whiteness is the perceived default over and against marked non-White identities. Where segregation purges the marked populations, assimilation grants provisional access to Whiteness, but thereby preserves its status as the unmarked default. The logic of colourblindness sustains racial inequity; only illuminating, respecting and celebrating diverse racial and cultural identities will validate each individual experience.

5. Cf. Philip Ewell, *On Music Theory, and Making Music More Welcoming for Everyone* (2023). While this book cites Ewell's presentations given to various music schools and departments from 2020 to 2021, Ewell's account of antiblackness in academic music education is detailed more thoroughly in *On Music Theory*.

GENDER, RACE AND RELIGION IN VIDEO GAME MUSIC

6. It may strike readers as odd to describe *Civilization V*'s musical strategies as segregationist after classifying *Civilization IV*'s as assimilationist, since assimilation has often followed segregation in real-world racialized societies. However, the relationship of segregationism, assimilationism and antiracism is not one of linear progression; societies, communities and individuals can move fluidly from one domain to the other and back again. The history of race is not unidirectional. In the United States, AAPI communities have generally experienced segregation (e.g. the Chinese Exclusion Act) moving towards assimilation (e.g. the 'model minority' myth). Many Latinx communities have experienced the opposite change, from early assimilation (e.g. White-passing, conflation with White identity on the U.S. Census) to recent segregation (e.g. nativism, 'border wall' rhetoric, attempted elimination of DACA). More importantly, assimilationism must not be construed as better or less racist than segregationism – both are racism. Segregationism may generally be more visible than assimilationism, but that does not thereby make assimilationism the lesser evil. The belief in linear progress – often accompanied by the presumption that reaching assimilationism is satisfactory – is the *coup de grace* of the post-racial myth of colourblindness.

7. These detailed analyses used the location theme versions from the soundtrack album 'Overwatch: Cities & Countries'. The *Overwatch* game uses 30-second excerpts (typically taken from the ending) of the album tracks (averaging two minutes).

8. The cowboy gunslinger Cole Cassidy was formerly known as Jesse McCree, named after an upper executive of Blizzard. When the real-life McCree was found to be complicit in Blizzard's abusive, misogynistic corporate culture in a highly visible set of official reports, journalism and protests, the *Overwatch* character was renamed to Cole Cassidy.

PART IV

RELIGION

7

Sonic Iconography: The Sacred Music Topic in *Lightning Returns: Final Fantasy XIII*

Introduction – Sacred Symbols and Semiotic Politics

On 1 June 2020, U.S. President Donald Trump held up a Bible. No words, no smiles – just a Bible. Standing before a boarded-up St. John's Episcopal Church at Lafayette Square in Washington, D.C., Trump intended the photo-op to send the nation a message of 'resilience and determination' against the racial reckoning movement following the death of George Floyd (Chalfant 2020, n.pag.). 'Is that your Bible?' a reporter asked. 'It's a Bible', Trump replied. With a sign reading 'all are welcome' in the background, police and National Guard cleared the area of peacefully protesting clergy and citizens using pepper balls and rubber bullets (Ward 2020). After five minutes spent being photographed individually and with close advisors, the Trump caravan departed St. John's. Within hours, the White House disseminated a video of the triumphal march to the church, omitting any signs of force used against protesters. A few days later, Washington, D.C. mayor Muriel Bowser christened the plaza between St. John's and the White House 'Black Lives Matter Plaza' (Dwyer 2020).

Despite Trump's assertion that 'Christians think it was a beautiful picture', the photographs drew critique from all but the staunchest Evangelical supporters (Singman 2020, n.pag.). Many journalists and commentators expressed bewilderment at Trump's use of the Bible – a collection of apolitical, non-partisan texts – to rally his right-wing, nationalist base. Republican Senator Ben Sasse lambasted Trump for '[treating] the Word of God as a political prop' (Warren 2020, n.pag.). The president came neither to pray, worship nor listen to religious community leaders, but rather to assert government and military authority over a local place of worship. Reverend Mariann Budde, bishop of the Episcopal Diocese of Washington, D.C., condemned Trump's 'symbolic misuse of the most sacred texts of our tradition' for purposes 'antithetical to the teachings of Jesus' (Brito 2020, n.pag.). For many Christians, a deeply unsettling contradiction lay at the heart of using the same Bible that declares 'blessed are the peacemakers' to reinforce a law and order message against peaceful protesters of racial injustice. As Episcopal Reverend Gini Gerbasi summarized: 'You want to be living your life by the words in that book, not toting it around as a photo opportunity' (Jenkins 2020, n.pag.).

How can one symbol convey such drastically divergent meanings? Is the Christian Bible an emblem for justice and liberation, or domination and authority? This is not the proper avenue to unpack the sociopolitical and religious dimensions of this publicity stunt, which warrants a book of its own. However, this anecdote is a fascinating case study of semiotic politics – significant public disagreement and debate concerning a symbol's meaning. And while virtually everything surrounding President Trump is controversial and polarizing, this division of interpretative meanings is also characteristic of religious iconography in general. The same Christian crucifix may signify self-sacrificial love, altruism, glorification of anti-Semitic violence against Jews or an assertion of patriarchal triumph and authoritarian traditionalism – all depending on who one asks. This hermeneutic indeterminacy is commonplace in matters of representation – recall the debates over the alternative femininities and masculinities in Chapter 3, or the complexity surrounding matters of racial representation, appropriation and stereotype in Chapter 5. Yet such interpretative politics takes on special gravitas when applied to a religion's sacred symbols. The lines between devotion and veneration versus sacrilege and blasphemy are thin and blurred, as Trump's Bible photo-op illustrates. In the same way, representing religious symbols or ideas in video games invokes a vast network of semiotic associations that transcend any single game and generates complex, profound meanings.

Part IV of the book turns to an analysis of religious representation in video game music, drawing on familiar analytical methodologies previously applied to the representation of gender, race and culture. Just as video game music can sustain semiotic discourse about gender, race and culture, so too can it communicate theological meanings. It is important to state from the outset that, despite the sweeping scope suggested by the book's title, I possess neither the space nor expertise to cover the representation of every religious tradition. Instead, I focus on a detailed analysis of a salient and fascinating interaction between Catholic Christianity and Japanese social/spiritual history, leaving to other scholars the work of analysing musical representation of Islam, Judaism, Hindu spiritual traditions, Buddhism, Sikhism and many more religious/spiritual traditions than I can list here. To reiterate, this is not to oversimplify the complexity of the world's diverse religions or treat Christianity as the only religion of import – rather, it is aimed at modelling semiotic analysis by tracing one significant narrative thread throughout video game history. Chapters 7 and 8 comprise a two-part trajectory rigorously analysing the 'god-slayer' trope in video game narratives and music, probing its theological and sociocultural meanings. First, Chapter 7 proposes 'sonic iconography' as a concept describing music associated with religious functions, ideas or traditions. It then introduces the god-slayer trope, analysing its traits and variations across its appearances in over 30 years of video games – especially in Japan-produced video games – warranting historical contextualization of Christianity in Japan. Kiri Paramore's monograph on anti-Christian ideology in Japan provides an incisive, nuanced account of Japanese-Christian dynamics that illuminates the historical backdrop of the god-slayer trope. The chapter concludes with a detailed musical and narrative analysis of *Lightning Returns: Final Fantasy XIII* (2013), which offers rich religious commentary in dialogue with the theology of Jürgen Moltmann to critique the Catholic doctrine of impassability as a proxy for the abolishment of *sonnō jōi*, Japan's nationally instated practice of Emperor worship.

Sonic Iconography in Video Game Music

Why explore the representation of religious communities and ideas in video games? Like gender and race, religion is another demographic master category warranting detailed scholarly study – including by musicologists. The CIA World Factbook estimates 84.4% of the world population is religious.[1] In media studies, more attention is typically directed to demographic attributes like gender, race or sexuality than religion – perhaps because these are considered more intrinsic to a person's core identity. If this conclusion is based on a belief that religion is significantly more changeable or self-determined than these other factors, consider that the vast majority of religious practitioners retain their religious identity throughout their lives. In a quantitative analysis of 40 countries, most populations had a conversion rate of less than 10% (including religious to non-religious or vice versa), with only Canada, Chile and the United States having over 10% conversion rate – the highest, Canada, with 17% (Barro et al. 2010, 25).[2] Furthermore, statistical demographic analysis of religions worldwide projects remarkably stable distributions of religious populations in the future, accounting for rates of births/deaths, conversions/defections and emigration/immigration (Johnson 2004, 15). For most, religion is a consistent hallmark of identity akin to culture, shaping one's life decisions, expectations and outcomes. Additionally, religious representation is inseparable from cultural representation while also distinct from it, as seen in Chapter 5's discussion of *Raji: An Ancient Epic* – Jewish, Shinto and Hindu religious traditions exemplify this dynamic. Religion is a major factor of identity corresponding to a diverse range of individuals and communities, warranting scholarly attention exploring its representation in video games.

Though religion and video games may initially seem a peculiar match – the former the domain of tradition, spirituality and texts, the latter concerned with innovation, entertainment and multimedia – there is a significant history of scholarship exploring fascinating intersections between the two. 'Fantasy is part of religion and religion is part of fantasy', notes Hodge, concluding that the immersive, imaginative mythologies of video game worlds may present a non-traditional pathway for discovering and understanding God (Hodge 2010, 171, 175). Religion scholar William Sims Bainbridge identifies in video games many of the same narrative, participatory and communal affordances typically offered through religion (Bainbridge 2013, 24). Pedagogically, video games may participate in moral formation, leading players through ethical dilemmas requiring critical thinking (Schut 2013, 48). Representationally, video games do not merely reflect religious norms, but rather interpret and inform religious praxis in active and creative ways (Campbell and Grieve 2014, 16). And when players encounter religious ideas or perspectives that contrast their own, a variety of interpretational responses may ensue: Rejecting (refusing to play or engage with a game conflicting with their worldview), Debunking (dismissing religious discourse of a game as fictional, fantastical or trivial), Debating (engaging in active interpretation of and dialogue with the game's religious ideas) and Connecting (actively seeking out games with contrasting worldviews to challenge the player's existing beliefs) (de Wildt 2017). Of these, Connecting proves especially productive, affording players the opportunity to '[internalise] other ways of thinking and believing – be it temporarily or lastingly' (de Wildt 2017, 472). Like other forms of digital media, video games offer fertile soil for the exploration, representation and interpretation of religious concepts and communities.

Video games that feature religious themes partake in the tradition of 'iconography', leading players to contemplate, challenge and immerse deeper into their own spirituality. In Christianity, an icon is a visual representation of a person or narrative from a sacred text or tradition that draws practitioners deeper into meditation and worship (Plate 2002, 54). Indeed, religious icons are the earliest form of media in the truest sense of the word, for they mediate another domain of existence to our own. A religious sculpture, painting or illuminated text thus functions analogously to a video game, mediating participants' imaginations deeper into narrative immersion, identification and meaning-making. Iconography – the study of the history and interpretation of God and other sacred subjects in art – has been a core feature of Christian teaching and devotion since its inception (The Catholic Encyclopedia 1910). In Orthodox denominations, icons are regarded as direct manifestations of the divine, blurring the sacred and mundane realms (Plate 2002, 56). Another hallmark of iconography is the imaginative engagement of the viewer, making icons ideal for meaning-making processes and personal devotion. The artwork functions as a channel through which the divine and transcendent may be approached, focusing and catalysing the worshiper's devotion (Fortescue 1910).

By way of analogy, this chapter proposes the term 'sonic iconography' to describe music that invokes religious associations or traditions, particularly when embedded in narrative media. Sonic iconography typically consists of sacred music that encodes religious meanings into a narrative moment or scene. Though the terminology of 'iconography' may seem to skew towards Christian religious praxis, the study of religious iconography is not limited to Christianity – for example, *darshan* and temple architecture in Hindu religious traditions discussed in Chapter 5, or studies of Paleolithic, Islamic, Jewish, Chinese, Indian, secular, erotic, political, scientific, imperial, feminist and musical iconography in the medieval period (Hourihane 2017, 1, 3, 251, 267, 295, 310, 356, 425, 479). Artistically, iconography occurs whenever artwork or image is imbued with meaning, along with the process of interpreting what meanings are conveyed through such icons (Hourihane 2017, 1). In video games, sonic iconography often signifies the presence of religious themes pertinent to a character or event where, in the absence of such music, religious associations may be overlooked. This enables music to participate in shaping and communicating a myriad of spiritual or theological meanings. Jeremy Begbie and Steven Guthrie describe sonic iconography as a 'resonant witness', 'bearing testimony to the richness' of religious praxis and theological truths (Begbie and Guthrie 2011, 11). J. S. Bach claimed 'the aim and final end of all music should be none other than the glory of God', and the German Reformer Martin Luther attributed to music immense potential to communicate theological truths on par with public reading of scripture. For instance, a triad provides a musical icon of the Christian doctrine of the trinity, and music's temporal unfolding teaches the acceptance of life's transience and finitude (Begbie 2000, 25–26, 85, 92). Cadential expectation, delay and frustration suggest a parallel to the eschatological concept 'already and not yet', in which religious ideals are only partially realized in the actual world until God perfects its final state (Begbie 2000, 99–100). As Begbie writes: 'music can serve to enrich and advance theology, extending our wisdom about God, God's relation to us and to the world at large' (Begbie 2000, 3). Like virtually any spiritual practice, the iconography tradition is not without its opponents, iconoclasts, particularly within the Protestant denomination. Iconoclasts historically did not oppose iconography by denying icons' efficacy, but precisely because their populist appeal and power are 'not fully controllable and conformable to the institution of the church' (Plate 2002, 57). Just as icons invite the devotee's imaginative engagement with sacred texts and figures, so too may video games employ sonic iconography to catalyse profound, challenging and subversive player interpretations of religious doctrines.

Video games, as participants in iconography, may shape players' experiences in accord with religious devotion such as *Raji: An Ancient Epic*. However, games also regularly offer challenging or subversive narratives that critique, subvert or reimagine a religious doctrine. For example, the god-slayer narrative trope, featuring the death of a gameworld's god, hardly seems compatible with devotional aims. How, then, can they be considered iconography? What religious meanings emerge from this unorthodox approach – and what contribution does music make to their interpretation? To answer these questions, we must first explore the history of the god-slayer trope in video games.

Thirty Years of God-Slaying in Video Games

'God is dead', declared Friedrich Nietzsche in 1882, 'and we have killed him' (Nietzsche 1974, 181). This provocative statement has been thoroughly explored in the writings of philosophers, but it could also be aptly said by numerous video game protagonists by the journey's end. The vast majority of video games require a final boss to be overcome, whether a king, machine, demon or deity. Naturally, this ultimate opponent ought to be the most potent antagonist the player has yet faced. The striking narrative 'god-slayer trope' casts the gameworld's god as the final boss, to be slain by players in an act of deicide. In one sense, the god-slayer trope can be seen as a function of the trajectory of increasingly elaborate video game plotlines and technical capabilities. Where simpler games may pit players against a powerful human enemy or rival as a final boss, other games raise the stakes by making the final boss a monster, a demon – even a god. Additionally, as game console hardware improves in graphical and processing capabilities from generation to generation, game developers seek to showcase the platform's potential by portraying the grandeur and apocalyptic power of a deity being unleashed on the player. While there is truth in this proposed teleological narrative, it overlooks significant semiotic and narrative motivations for developers to employ the god-slayer trope, inviting potential connections to real-world religious ideas. The god-slayer trope invokes an interlocking web of narrative, musical, sociocultural and theological meanings that enables video games to communicate artistically compelling, theologically nuanced and subversive messages about religion.

First, a provisional definition of the god-slayer trope is necessary. Succinctly put, a god-slayer narrative is one in which the final boss or mastermind that the protagonist(s) must defeat is the god of the gameworld.[3] The classic god-slayer trope typically involves the overthrow of a singularly powerful entity associated with light, holiness, goodness and/or order, usually receiving veneration from the gameworld's residents and portrayed in more traditional roles of a deity within the gameworld's mythos such as creation and maintenance of the universe. The protagonists' decision to oppose and defeat the god is often highly surprising to the gameworld's residents, representing a disruption of the received social order. Other variants of the trope – including the 'evil god', 'seizure of divinity', 'advanced alien' and 'divine pantheon' variants – present a spin on the classic trope to further nuance its range of meanings. The evil god variant typically features a dualistic conflict between a good and an evil god, with the good god entreating the protagonist(s) to defeat the evil god. For example, *Persona 5* (2016) pits players against Yaldabaoth, a malevolent god. Overtones of Nietzschean deicide are greatly attenuated, as the god slain is considered morally evil and deserving of overthrow. The seizure of divinity variant involves a non-divine character seizing, usurping or illegitimately acquiring enormous power from a divine or transcendent source – usually during the events of the narrative – becoming a god-like entity that the protagonist(s) must defeat. Kefka of *Final Fantasy VI* (1994) is an excellent example, as he ascends to god-like powers after betraying the story's first antagonist, Emperor Gestahl. This variant does not convey the same degree of social upheaval in defeating the usurper, who was never supposed to possess divine power in the first place. In the advanced alien variant, the slain deity is a technologically advanced entity from another planet or dimension – even if it plays the traditional role of a god by overseeing the world's structure or receiving worship from the gameworld's residents. The classic exemplar of this variant is Lavos from *Chrono Trigger* (1995), an advanced alien power resting dormant deep within the gameworld. As an extra-terrestrial rather than spiritual being, the advanced alien entity embodies Arthur C. Clarke's third law: 'Any sufficiently advanced technology is indistinguishable from magic.' The pantheon variant depicts a polytheistic world in which many entities with near-equal power share oversight and rule of the gameworld, and only one or a subset is defeated or killed by the game's protagonist. For example, *God of War* (2018) features Baldur, one of the Norse pantheon of gods, as primary antagonist. Killing one out of many gods does not bear the same theological or narrative gravity as slaying the gameworld's sole deity.

Overarching trends in the vast repertoire of video games cannot be established by individual case studies alone, no matter how detailed – latitudinal, quantitative analysis is required. Since life is too short for any one individual to play every video game, creating an exhaustive list of games featuring the god-slayer trope is impossible. Nonetheless, a latitudinal study of an approximate corpus of god-slayer video games proves productive. To chart the ubiquity of the god-slayer trope, I crowdsourced a data set of 142 video games from 1989 to 2018 potentially featuring the god-slayer trope from a variety of video game websites, discussion forums, online lists and my own playing experience (see Table 7.1). Responses to my queries came from discussion forums on the video game community websites IGN, Gamespot, GameFAQs and Reddit. Pre-populated lists of god-slayer games were sourced from websites Huffington Post, TV Tropes, All the Tropes, Cheat Code Central, the Escapist, GiantBomb, GameFAQs and the Game Theory YouTube channel. After compiling all nominated god-slayer games into a single spreadsheet, I researched each entry via plot/character synopses and recorded gameplay footage where possible. I ranked these findings in three tiers based on how strongly each entry exemplified the narrative god-slayer trope (summarized in Figure 7.1). A rating of zero indicates no presence of the god-slayer trope; a rating of one marks the game as a weak example of the god-slayer trope, usually exhibiting one of the variants described above. Ratings of two and three indicate the strongest examples of the god-slayer trope, with three reserved for games that exhibit all of the classic god-slayer trope's core characteristics.

The trope occurred most frequently in the role-playing game (RPG) genre – especially RPGs produced in Japan.[4] I conducted a music-semiotic analysis on tracks from the 76 games featuring the trope strongly or very strongly, revealing

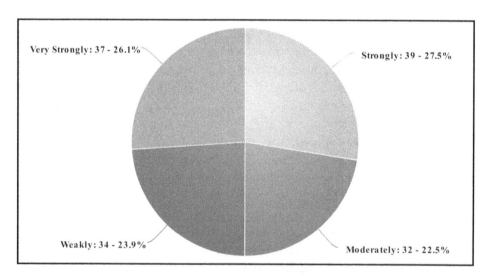

FIGURE 7.1: Chart of distribution of relevance rankings of 142 games potentially featuring the narrative god-slayer trope.[5]

a pattern of common compositional techniques or strategies employed (Table 7.1). Particular focus is warranted by a gameworld deity's musical themes – typically either character themes or battle themes. Overall, the classic god-slayer trope typically features the instrumentation and musical characteristics of the sacred music topic, which shall be unpacked below, in its soundtrack. Moreover, the prevalence of sacred-music features is directly correlated with the games' god-slayer relevance rating, with games ranked with a three exhibiting the most complete sacred-music features. These examples feature a significant preponderance of choir, organ and solo voice along with melodic, harmonic and contrapuntal features of sacred music. Musically, these features are characteristic of Christian liturgical music – especially Catholic plainchant or choral/instrumental mass settings and Lutheran organ or chorale hymnody. Other religious traditions such as Judaism, Islam, Buddhism or Hinduism of course reflect quite different musical characteristics – the present analysis abbreviates the traits described to 'sacred-music topic' primarily for brevity, so as not to reiterate each time that Catholic/Lutheran chant, choral, hymnic, and/or organ styles are in view.

The sacred-music topic is an apt musical calling card for a gameworld's god due to its religious connotations. The sacred-music topic features both contrapuntal polyphony and chorale-like homophony; though these are on opposite ends of the textural spectrum, each is characteristic of European Christian liturgy in different times, denominations and liturgical functions (Sánchez-Kisielewska 2018, 98). Olga Sánchez-Kisielewska identifies the classic sacred topic instrumentation as solo voice, choir and/or organ – all three of which are frequently employed in the music of classic god-slayer games (138). Sacred-music chorales generally utilize simple, stepwise melody for ease of congregational singing and recall (103). Other musical features include a harmonic rhythm of roughly one chord per beat, generally major mode, soft dynamic and slow tempo. Its cultural meanings include archaism, ceremonial order, collectivism, devotion, solemnity, self-control, association with the divine, spirituality and transcendence. The sacred-music topic invokes associations with the Christian religion via synecdoche with liturgical worship and may invoke divinity itself via metonymy of worshippers' veneration of the deity (17, 87). In other words, the sacred-music topic in video game soundtracks is a prime example of sonic iconography – along with all the semiotic and theological possibilities for meaning-making, subversion and play contained therein.

As in Part III, there are considerable cultural complexities at play in the largely Japanese use of Catholic liturgical music signifiers for the god-slayer trope. Therefore, a historical survey of Catholicism's relationship with Japan is beneficial before a detailed case study analysis.

TABLE 7.1: Spreadsheet documenting corpus study of video games potentially containing the narrative god-slayer trope, organized according to the trope's degree of relevance and fit.[6] (*First half of columns*)

Relevance	Game Title	Year	Console(s)	God-Slayer?	Classic?	Evil God?	Seizure?	Alien?	Pantheon?
3	Aquaria	2007	PC	x	x				
3	Arc Rise Fantasia	2009	Wii	x	x				
3	Asura's Wrath	2012	PS3, 360	x					x
3	Bayonetta 1	2009	PS3, 360	x	x				
3	Bayonetta 2	2014	Switch, Wii U	x	x				
3	Bomberman 64: The Second Attack	1999	N64	x	x				
3	Bravely Second	2015	3DS	x	x				
3	Breath of Fire	1993	SNES	x	x				
3	Breath of Fire 3	1997	PS1	x	x				
3	Dark Souls I	2011	PS3, 360	x	x				
3	Shin Megami Tensei: Devil Survivor 2	2009	DS	x	x				
3	Digital Devil Saga: Avatar Tuner 2	2005	PS3	x	x				
3	Dishonored: Death of the Outsider	2017	PS4, XB1	x	x				
3	Dragon Quest VII	2000	PS1	x	x				
3	Elder Scrolls: Skyrim	2011	PS3, 360	x	x				
3	Epic Battle Fantasy 4	2014	PC	x	x				
3	Final Fantasy Legend I	1989	Gameboy	x	x				
3	Final Fantasy Tactics	1997	PS1, PSP	x	x				
3	Final Fantasy VII: Crisis Core	2007	PSP	x	x				
3	Final Fantasy X	2001	PS2	x	x				

(Continued [second half of columns])

Boss Name	Battle Track 1 Title	Rock?	Sacred?	Battle Track 2 Title	Rock?	Sacred?	Battle Track 3 Title	Rock?	Sacred?
The Creator	Worship	x	x						
Eesa	[Untitled]		x	[Untitled]		x			
Chakravartin	Aurora Borealis		x	One Who Spins Samsara					
Jubileus	The Greatest Jubilee		x						
Aesir	Aesir		x						
Angel of Light and Shadow	The Second Attack - Angel								
Providence	Aurora of Darkness	x	x	Battle of Providence	x	x			
Myria	Black Dragon								
Myria	Self Determination	x	x						
Gwyn, Lord of Cinder	Gwyn, Lord of Cinder								
Polaris	Akashic Record		x						
Brahman	Brahman	x							
The Outsider	[Non-Battle Resolution]								
Numen/God	World of the Strong								
Alduin/ Akatosh	Final Battle		x						
Godcat	Fallen Blood	x	x						
The Creator	Furious Battle								
Ultima	Ultima, Nice Body			Ultima, Perfect Body					
Minerva	The Summoned	x							
Yu Yevon	Decisive Battle		x	Summoned Beast Battle		x			

(*Continued* [*first half of columns*])

Relevance	Game Title	Year	Console(s)	God-Slayer?	Classic?	Evil God?	Seizure?	Alien?	Pantheon?
3	Final Fantasy XIII-1	2009	PS3, 360	x	x				
3	Final Fantasy XIII-3	2013	PS3, 360	x	x				
3	Fire Emblem: Radiant Dawn	2007	Wii	x	x				
3	God of War	2005	PS2	x					x
3	God of War 2	2007	PS2	x	x				
3	God of War 3	2010	PS3	x	x				
3	God of War 4	2018	PS4	x					x
3	Shadow Hearts	2001	PS2	x	x			x	
3	Shin Megami Tensei 2	1994	SNES	x	x				
3	Shin Megami Tensei 3	2003	PS2	x	x				
3	Star Ocean: Till the End of Time	2003	PS2	x	x				
3	Super Smash Brothers 64	1999	N64	x	x				
3	Super Smash Brothers Ultimate	2018	Switch	x	x	x			
3	Tales of Symphonia	2003	Gamecube	x	x				
3	Xenoblade Chronicles	2010	Wii	x	x				
3	Xenogears	1998	PS1	x	x			x	
3	Xenosaga III	2006	PS2	x	x				

(*Continued* [*second half of columns*])

Boss Name	Battle Track 1 Title	Rock?	Sacred?	Battle Track 2 Title	Rock?	Sacred?	Battle Track 3 Title	Rock?	Sacred?
Orphan	Born Anew		x	Nascent Requiem					
Bhunivelze	Divine Love		x	Almighty Bhunivelze		x			
Ashera	Ashera the Creator			A Grasping Truth	x	x			
Ares	Duel with Ares		x						
Zeus	Zeus		x						
Zeus	Kratos vs. Zeus		x						
Baldur	[Untitled]		x						
Meta-God	Imbroglio								
YHWH	Final Battle		x						
Kagutsuchi	Last Boss Battle, After Transformation	x							
Luther Lansfield	Moody Goddess			Highbrow	x	x	Like Squashing Grape		x
Master Hand	Master Hand Fight								
Galeem and Dharkon	Galeem		x	Dharkon	x	x	Galeem/Dharkon		x
Mithos Yggdrasill	Mithos		x	Final Destination	x	x			
Zanza	Zanza	x	x	The God-Slaying Sword		x			
Deus	Awakening								
Wilhelm	Wilhelm			Promised Pain	x	x			

Criminal Worship – A Brief History of Catholicism in Japan

Christianity has a turbulent history in Japan and today comprises only 1.5 per cent of Japan's population – although it is the most populous religious group apart from Japan's endemic Shintoism (70.5 per cent) and culturally integrated Buddhism (67.2 per cent) (CIA 2023). Anti-Christian policies and rhetoric from the mid-seventeenth through the early twentieth centuries virtually eradicated the Christian presence in Japan. Before setting forth this history, two clarifications are necessary. The first clarification is that the historic footprint of Christianity in Japan is almost entirely Catholic – specifically Jesuit missionaries and converts thereof. While Protestantism has made some inroads into Japan after the Second World War, its presence has been historically negligible in Japan. The second clarification is that Christianity produced friction with Japan's political and social structures more than confronting its Shinto or Buddhist spiritual practices. In truth, Japanese governmental and philosophical authorities viewed Christianity more as a threat to social order than to Shintoism or Buddhism per se.

Kiri Paramore's monograph *Ideology and Christianity in Japan* thoroughly documents the history of Catholicism in Japan. There were two major outbreaks of anti-Christian discourse: the first when the Tokugawa shogunate outlawed Christianity and expelled Christian priests and missionaries, and the second from the mid-nineteenth century continuing through the Second World War (Paramore 2010, 1–2). Between these two periods of public suppression, a 'pervasive anti-Christian discourse' persisted which characterized Christianity as a 'western' and 'barbarian' intruder incompatible with Japanese ethics and civilization (4–5). The first wave of suppression began when Ieyasu Tokugawa forbade Christianity among his retainers, followed by outlawing Christianity across the shogunate in 1612 (repealed in 1873), expelling foreign priests and missionaries from Japan in 1614 and banishing Christian feudal lords in 1615 – mostly lords in western Japan who had been loyal to Ieyasu's erstwhile rival Hideyoshi Toyotomi (53–54). This effectively annihilated Christianity in Japan by the late 1630s, with the suppression of the Shimabara rebellion in Nagasaki prefecture signifying its last gasp in western Japan (55). Even after Christian presence in Japan had been thoroughly eradicated, anti-Christian written discourse continued as a means of social control, associating perceived social deviance with evidence of being a secret Christian (隠れキリシタン; 'hidden Christian'). The primary justification for the use of force and surveillance on socially deviant Japanese citizens accused of being secret Christians was that Christians worship Jesus, a criminal, necessitating Christianity's elimination to maintain law and order (57). Tokugawa officials thus successfully forbade Christianity as criminal worship.

As explained above, the anti-Christian backlash in Japan was not primarily doctrinal or religious, but 'focused on issues of political order and conservatism' (Paramore

2010, 7). Specifically, Tokugawa authorities used Christian foreigners as a convenient scapegoat with attacks 'aimed at legitimizing and buttressing the existing social order and the authority of the Tokugawa shogunate' (52–53). Anti-Christian writings such as the *Kiristhitan Monogatari* (キリシタン物語; 'Christian Story') dehumanized Catholic priests as 'long-nosed [...] with long fingernails and toenails, tall and dark-skinned with red noses and teeth longer than those of horses' (60). By extension to ordinary Japanese citizens, this characterization and many others like it justified discrimination towards any deviants thought to be influenced by Christianity (65). In this way, anti-Christian discourse proved an effective strategy for maintaining social hegemony as a precursor to the Japanese nationalism arising from the Meiji Restoration (1868). While Tokugawa officials used anti-Christian rhetoric to solidify Japanese national identity, post-Meiji nationalists initiated a second wave of anti-Christian discourse aimed at critiquing Christianity for its social egalitarianism. For example, Hakuseki Arai writes that Christians worshipping 'a Great King other than our own' threatens law and order 'by undermining the relationships between sovereign and subject, parent and child, husband and wife' (108). This critique, too, had precedent in the Tokugawa period's anti-Christian rhetoric; Shōsan Suzuki's novel *Hakirishitan* (破切支丹; 'crush Christianity') critiques Christianity for positioning God alone above all people, placing every person on equal status with one another rather than according to the five hierarchical relationships of Confucian philosophy (62). Echoing these sentiments at the turn of the twentieth century, University of Tōkyō philosopher Inoue Tetsujirō writes:

> If the masses and the aristocracy are loyal to their king and filial to their fathers, then there will be high moral standards. Therefore, if perchance there are teachings in the world [Christianity] that stand in opposition to this state of affairs, there is not the slightest need for our country to inquire into them.
>
> (144)

To these Japanese thinkers and authorities, Christianity was dangerous precisely because it envisioned all people as equals before one God.

Although Japanese thinkers heavily criticized Christianity for its perceived egalitarianism, they admired and emulated European and American nations' use of Christianity to promote imperialism and nationalism. The Meiji Restoration of 1868 and the following decades can be described as 'an attempt to replicate modern Western constructs of social control' (Paramore 2010, 132). The post-Meiji oligarchs of the late 1800s manufactured Japanese nationalism as a framework of total social control intended to emulate 'the intellectual/religious systems [... of] national cohesion and social control in European states' (3). Mitogaku (水戸学; 'Mito Learning') philosopher Aizawa Seishisai commended the use of religion to militarize the common people, arguing that the role of the masses during wartime is to serve as soldiers:

GENDER, RACE AND RELIGION IN VIDEO GAME MUSIC

> Employing witchcraft [Christianity] they [western nations] lead on the common people, uniting the hearts of the common people to the extent that they are capable of fighting [... in this way we will] turn the few into the many, and transform weakness into strength.
>
> (119)

In the project of constructing Japanese nationalism, Seishisai and Japanese officials desired to import religion's potential to weaponize common citizens, but without Christianity's egalitarian ideals. The solution? Reinvent Christianity's theology of one supreme deity within a framework directed towards the Japanese state itself. In the early 1800s, Seishisai and Yūkoku Fujita originated the nationalist concept of *sonnō jōi* (尊皇攘夷; 'worship the Emperor, expel the barbarians'), articulating a religious function of Japan's Emperor as a devotional symbol motivating the masses' loyalty to the Japanese state (118). *Sonnō jōi* was codified in 1890 by the Imperial Rescript on Education, which required all school students and staff to bow to the Emperor's seal, among many other similar policies (146). After Christian school-teacher Kanzō Uchimura refused to bow to the seal, anti-Christian discourse reignited in the media, and philosopher Inoue Tetsujirō proclaimed in an 1892 speech that Christianity and Japanese identity were 'inherently incompatible' (148). Echoing the rhetoric of the first wave of anti-Christian discourse, Tetsujirō declared:

> According to Christianity, beneath God all human beings are absolutely equal. There is not even a hierarchy between men and women. This is basically social egalitarianism. But in Japan and China we have from olden days had a custom of hierarchy between men and women. Scholars should follow this pre-existing custom.
>
> (151)

In Testujirō's argument, Christianity's anti-nationalist and egalitarian teachings rendered it irreconcilable with the philosophy of *sonnō jōi* required to establish an imperialist Japanese state (152).

After the Second World War and Emperor Hirohito's New Year's Rescript (covered in detail in Chapter 8), the cult of Emperor worship established by *sonnō jōi* and the Imperial Rescript on Education dissolved. As post-war Japan adopted a democratic constitution modelled after the United States, the objections from thinkers like Arai and Testsujirō that Japan was incompatible with Christianity's egalitarianism faded. As Article 14 of the Japanese constitution proclaims: 'All of the people are equal under the law and there shall be no discrimination in political, economic or social relations because of race, creed, sex, social status or family origin' (Prime Minister of Japan and His Cabinet 1946, n.pag.). In contemporary Japan, the very egalitarian outcome Shōsan Suzuki warned about has become codified in Japan's reconstructed national identity. The above attributions of gender egalitarianism and anti-nationalism to Christianity may strike readers as surprising – especially those familiar with Evangelical Protestantism in the twenty-first-century United States. For present purposes, it is sufficient to observe that Japanese anti-Christian discourse assumed Christian teachings entailed anti-nationalism and social egalitarianism and for that reason were deemed incompatible with Confucianism and the god-Emperor worship of *sonnō jōi*. The fall of the deified Emperor and absolute loyalty to the state associated with *sonnō jōi* and subsequent adoption of socially egalitarian ideals historically associated with Christianity well contextualize the god-slayer case study analyses of Chapters 7 and 8.

Song of the Saviour – Sonic Iconography in Lightning Returns: Final Fantasy XIII

The Final Fantasy series seems an unlikely candidate for a compelling theological critique of a traditional religious doctrine – yet that is precisely what *Lightning Returns: Final Fantasy XIII* (2013) presents. *Lightning Returns* invokes Christian terminology, symbolism and ideas from start to finish, affording a fascinating theological commentary from a Japanese cultural perspective. As foreshadowed by the historical context provided above, the iconography of *Lightning Returns* establishes a parallel between classical Christian attributes of God and the transcendent, inaccessible god-Emperor of imperial Japan. This cross-cultural, interfaith narrative commentary is no detached critique of foreign religious ideas but represents ongoing discourse in modern Japan with real social stakes. By critiquing the classical Christian doctrine of impassibility, *Lightning Returns* stages a narrative analogue to the post-war descent of Japan's god-Emperor Hirohito from remote inaccessibility to becoming a visible champion of social egalitarianism.

We last examined Lightning Farron in Chapter 3 as a model of alternative femininity within the *Final Fantasy* series. Here, in the finale of the 'Lightning Saga' trilogy, she is thrust reluctantly into a messianic role as saviour of the world Nova Chrysalia. After being suspended in crystal form for 500 years after the events of *Final Fantasy XIII-2* (2011), the God of Light Bhunivelze reanimates Lightning and appoints her as the saviour in the face of the oncoming apocalypse of the world. Lightning's task is to judge whose souls are worthy of salvation and guiding them to the new world formed after Nova Chrysalia's destruction. Throughout the game, citizens treat Lightning with differing attitudes ranging from exultant celebration to scepticism or antagonism. The Order of Salvation, based in the Luxerion Cathedral, is the institutional church worshipping Bhunivelze and the central governing power in Nova Chrysalia. On the other hand, the Children of Etro, branded heretics and zealots, view the saviour as a force of destruction and believe that salvation

211

comes through embracing death instead of eternal life in a new world. However, it is perhaps Lightning herself who believes least in the Order's cause, carrying out her mission reluctantly. As motivation, Bhunivelze claims to hold the soul of Lightning's sister Serah, promising to resurrect her in the new world as a reward for completing the mission. In order to ensure Lightning's compliance, Bhunivelze removed all emotion from her upon revival – after her trajectory to integrate her emotions in *Final Fantasy XIII*, Lightning now finds herself tragically incapable of feeling anything. To Bhunivelze, emotions are nothing more than inexplicable hindrances – a crucial point explored later in this chapter.

The Order of Salvation (救世院, *kyūseiin*, lit. 'salvation institution') and its religious practices and beliefs repeatedly reference Christianity – specifically, Roman Catholicism. Most striking is Lightning's title 'saviour', one of the most common devotional titles of Jesus Christ.[7] The central gospel of the Order is to place one's faith in Bhunivelze and trust completely in salvation for the next life rather than seeking present flourishing in Nova Chrysalia. This is a common external perception of Christian hope, an impression primarily drawn from Evangelical Protestantism and sometimes Roman Catholicism. The Luxerion Cathedral is closely modelled after Roman Catholic cathedral architecture in its overall shape, featuring Gothic spires and vaulted ceilings (Figure 7.2). The Order is headed by a high priestess, with a

FIGURE 7.2: Luxerion Cathedral (left) Bhunivelze's character model (right).

subordinate priesthood and enforcers of order and orthodoxy known as 'inquisitors' – doubtless referencing the infamous Catholic Inquisition – under her command. However, the clearest parallels to Christianity are exhibited by Bhunivelze himself, capitalized as 'God' in the English localization according to Christian grammatical convention. Several of Bhunivelze's attributes evoke the Christian god in particular. Bhunivelze is perfect in holiness, viewing humans' chaotic nature as impurities to be purged in the new world. He is considered omnipotent and nigh-omniscient, creator of the cosmos and all other gods – attributes notably absent in Shintoism's central deities Izanagi, Izanami and Amaterasu. Bhunivelze's design is modelled after the seraphim described in Isaiah 6 – though with one extra pair of wings (Figure 7.2). Additionally, Bhunivelze cannot experience or understand emotion, and he considers human emotion a weakness to be purged. This encodes Catholicism's classical theist doctrine of divine impassability that views God as eternally unaffected by anything external to himself, such that nothing or nobody can cause or prompt an emotional response from him. To be divine is to be free of human emotions, impassibility teaches. As Hope – Lightning's ally from *FFXIII* also revived by Bhunivelze and tasked with aiding Lightning – speculates about her lack of emotion: 'I think it's because you've been made something more than human. Something almost divine.' In Bhunivelze's order, divinity is incompatible with emotion – an observation key to the narrative's hermeneutic decoding. By game's end, Lightning chooses to reject Bhunivelze's so-called 'gift' and opposes his plan to destroy and recreate the world with only the souls of the saved, stripped of the emotions Bhunivelze views as imperfect. Lightning faces Bhunivelze in combat as the final boss of *Lightning Returns*, wielding her considerable, divinely bestowed powers against the supreme god of the gameworld.

It is fitting that the Order of Salvation, Lightning the saviour and Bhunivelze are sonically characterized with music invoking Catholicism. Several cues highlight the soundtrack's prominent use of sacred music topic traits. Some of these will be analysed below in greater detail, but it is worth surveying them together to observe patterns of how video game composers might employ sonic iconography.

1. 'The Ark' features soprano vocalise in a hymnic melody with a backing choir of accompanying female voices (Figure 7.3). The hymn evokes serene, transcendent affect through low-attack timbre and emphasis on higher treble pitches. The melody's motivic sequencing, motion in parallel thirds, and lilting triple metre at a slow tempo reinforce the sacred music topic. Note that the cue has limited emotional expressivity, except for a brief grandiose orchestral flourish just before its loop point. This is significant because 'The Ark' is heard in the headquarters of the same name, floating in the heavens above Nova Chrysalia, associating this music with Bhunivelze and Lightning the saviour in her emotionally repressed state. Lightning frequently discusses her emotionless experience with Hope while

GENDER, RACE AND RELIGION IN VIDEO GAME MUSIC

FIGURE 7.3: 'The Ark' hymn, musical transcription (above), 'A Sacred Oratorio', partial musical transcription (below).

in the Ark. As Hope is the only constant resident of the Ark, this music comes to be associated with seeing Hope – a detail that proves significant when the melody from 'The Ark' is featured in the final battle with Bhunivelze, who has possessed Hope's body, as he planned to do all along.

2. 'The Cathedral' is the cue underscoring Luxerion Cathedral, constituting the Order of Salvation's musical theme. Its sonic iconography is obvious, as the instrumentation consists almost entirely of magisterial organ sustained chords supported by touches of orchestral strings and bassoon. Here the music functions indexically, perhaps even diagetically – the organ is often heard during Catholic liturgy. While the instrumentation, tempo, timbre and harmonic rhythm support the sacred music topic in this track, the chord progressions sound quite out of place, evoking cognitive dissonance. Beginning with a Neo-Riemannian slide progression from D minor to D♭ major, the pair of chords transposes to G minor, then A minor. The B section cycles G minor, C major, E♭ minor, A♭ major – two Dorian-mode i-IV progressions in

mediant-related pairs. The implication of Dorian mode suggests the medieval church modes, characteristic of the sound of plainchant.

3. 'The Soulsong' is heard during the ritual of the same name within Luxerion Cathedral. Pointillistic harp and percussion textures are punctuated by swelling choir sustains on chords dissonant with the low-string drone. As Vanille wrestles with whether to complete or abort the Soulsong, a complex pair of choral chords resembling an A minor to A♭ major slide progression over a C bass pedal recalls 'The Cathedral'.

4. 'A Sacred Oratorio' is heard in the heart of Luxerion Cathedral, making the sacred meanings of the space abundantly clear (Figure 7.3). A viola presents a sombre chant-like melody in F Dorian mode, followed by male choir singing a close approximation of plainchant. The Latin lyrics speak of appealing to the God of light for salvation and eternal life, while the accursed will meet their end.[8] This is the aural equivalent of Luxerion's Cathedral's gothic architecture, firmly signifying Catholicism via Dorian-mode plainchant.

5. 'Divine Love' is the first of two themes heard in the final battle against Bhunivelze, which together constitute the focus of this chapter. The track's opening demonstrates a veritable tour de force of the sacred music topic's potential in video game soundtracks. In addition to epic orchestral music typical for RPG boss-battle music (further analysed in Chapter 8), the mixed choir presents a powerful unison punctuated by the orchestra in a combination reminiscent of Carl Orff's famous 'O Fortuna'. Motivically, the unison melody is related to the A section of 'Lightning's Theme', tying her agency to the fated duel. The Latin lyrics give voice to Bhunivelze's perspective speaking to Lightning, addressing her as a servant of God and bidding all creatures to worship and adore him now that the apocalypse has come.[9] A full-range choral glissando effect demonstrates the concessions the usually reserved sacred music style makes to the cue's dynamic, active orchestra. Throughout the remainder of the track, the choir supports the orchestration with downbeat hits or presenting a new, subdued melodic motive in the B section. Interestingly, this new theme sets the text instructing Lightning to fall prostrate before the all-encompassing love of Bhunivelze – a narratively significant detail analysed further below.

6. 'Almighty Bhunivelze' is a veritable masterpiece of sonic iconography that brings together the aforementioned analyses in a finale worthy not only of *Lightning Returns* but also the entire *FFXIII* trilogy (Figure 7.4). The six-and-a-half-minute track is too rich in compositional detail to describe in this space-limited format; however, several features are worth highlighting. The piece begins with rippling organ arpeggios – a gesture atypical for liturgical organ music – ushering in a rising string glissando and vocal fall. The introduction crescendo climaxes in a full choral unison singing the hymn melody from

FIGURE 7.4: Partial transcription of 'Almighty Bhunivelze' (opening). Transcription by the author.

'The Ark', now accompanied by pounding percussion and brass pulses before flourishing into an orchestral tutti. Though all pitches remain the same, the vocalise melody has been augmented into quadruple metre – though it is difficult for the ear to track with a constant rhythmic pulse emphasizing groupings of three eighth notes. The hymn is now set with Latin lyrics, which warn of the coming wrath and judgement of the omnipotent Bhunivelze.[10] The remainder of the composition is a theme and variations on the hymn from 'The Ark'. The choir presents variations of the hymn at 1:34, 2:46, 4:47 and 5:29; similarly, the organ and brass play the melody as a cantus firmus at 3:30. At 2:05 and 6:09, the soprano vocalise solo re-emerges as heard in 'The Ark', above the tempestuous orchestral texture, though rhythmically augmented in the former and processed by temporal phasing in the latter. But the cue's most jubilant climax arrives at 4:10, in a further transformation of the hymn suggesting a congregational anthem such as 'A Mighty Fortress is Our God'. A choral sweep leads into the track's loop point, solidifying the choir – and by extension, Bhunivelze's hymn – as the main musical agent of the piece. The track's coda features an organ solo that combines the Baroque toccata style with the hymn melody before diffusing musical energy in repeated Lydian plagal cadences.

Though tracks 1–4 are prime examples of sonic iconography, musically encoding Catholic identity into the in-game religion, it is 'Divine Love' and 'Almighty Bhunivelze' that fuels *Lightning Returns*' narrative and musical discourse on classical Christian theology.

Why does 'Almighty Bhunivelze' reprise the hymn from 'The Ark' so completely, taking it as the primary musical material in this extensive theme and variations composition? Perhaps it is because the Ark is Lightning's base of operations as the saviour – Bhunivelze's agent in Nova Chrysalia. Or perhaps it reflects the Ark's function of gathering souls, since Lightning's battle against Bhunivelze will determine the fate of those souls. Both reasons are likely intended – yet a third possibility is also musically encoded, providing a hermeneutic key to unlock the thematic message of *Lightning Returns*. Throughout the narrative, the Ark bears two additional associations – the location where Hope and Lightning converse, as well as where Bhunivelze placed her after awakening from crystallization. Both details support the same point: the placid, spiritual hymn communicates the loss of emotion experienced by both Hope and Lightning while in Bhunivelze's service. Bhunivelze views emotions as incomprehensible weakness fit only to be purged, as he does to Hope and Lightning. As Lightning complains to Hope on the Ark: 'Brave? I don't feel brave. I don't feel anything. No guilt, no courage, no fear.' Lightning, Hope and others frequently comment on Bhunivelze's inability to understand emotions, ensuring he never truly knows the hearts of his creations.

The pieces needed to decode the intricate semiotic web of *Lightning Returns* are now very nearly assembled. Before returning to decisive narrative, historical and musical observations, however, it is necessary to journey into Christian theology to understand the philosophical stakes inherent in *Lightning Returns*' portrayal of God, humanity and emotion.

The Most Human God – Impassibility and Divine Emotion in Christian Theology

In Christianity, 'theology' denotes the study of God's attributes. Omnipotence (ability to do all things), omniscience (knowledge of all truth), omnipresence (active in all space and time), aseity (necessary existence as the ground of all being) and trinity (three persons in one divine essence) are commonly ascribed attributes to the Christian God. Other attributes – such as simplicity, timelessness or immutability – are more heavily debated between theologians of various denominations. Impassibility – that God, in his transcendence, cannot experience pain, pleasure or emotion caused by or towards another being – is one such contested doctrine. With roots in the church fathers Ignatius of Antioch and Clement of Alexandria, divine impassibility was further developed in the writings of eminent theologians including Augustine, Anselm, Aquinas, Luther, Calvin and Leibniz. Though impassibility has adherents across Christianity's three major denominations (Orthodox, Catholic and Protestant), it is particularly associated with Catholicism for two reasons: 1) Catholicism affirms doctrinal commitment to classical theism to be considered orthodox, of which impassibility is a key component; and 2) the centre of gravity in the development of classical theism is Aquinas's *Summa Theologica*, a seminal text of Catholic theology.[11] On the other hand, impassibility has been observed to stand in tension or even contradiction with scriptures acknowledged within Christianity, particularly how God is portrayed in the portion adopted from the Jewish canon of scriptures, known to Christians as the 'Old Testament' and henceforth referred to as the 'Hebrew Bible' to acknowledge its historic origins (Leftow [2002] 2014, Section 2). God is said to be grieved by human actions (Gen. 6), burn with anger (2 Samuel 24), rejoice over the righteous (Zephaniah 3) and be moved to compassion by the cries of the oppressed (Exodus 3).[12] Classical theists typically understand such passages as anthropomorphic, pointing out that scriptures often speak metaphorically of God, including the language of God's face or hand. Still, critics wonder whether such responses are hermeneutically satisfactory, given the sheer volume of texts to be explained in this way. Appealing to metaphor is convenient – but even anthropomorphism and metaphor are communicative devices. What, then, is the deeper theological truth that these metaphors point to?

Though impassibility – and classical theism in general – dominated the theological mainstream until the nineteenth century, substantive challenges have since arisen (Leftow 2014). One seminal critique of divine impassibility is laid out in the writings of eminent twentieth-century German systematic theologian Jürgen Moltmann. God is love, Moltmann writes, as Christians all agree – but to love another opens one up to potential suffering via self-giving and self-sacrifice

(Moltmann 1980, 32). For what lover could claim to love the beloved, if nothing the beloved does could please or grieve the lover?

> A God who cannot suffer cannot love either. A God who cannot love is a dead God. He is poorer than any man or woman. [...] The living God is the loving God. The loving God shows that he is a living God through his suffering.
>
> (Moltmann 1980, 38)

God's love necessitates a relationship – for love cannot exist in isolation, with no other to love. For Moltmann, the doctrine of the trinity – that God's essence is not solitary but communal – entails that God's relationship with creation is not one of one-sided domination, but rather 'an intricate relationship of community' (Moltmann 1985, 2). God the Father loves God the Son and God the Spirit, is loved by each in turn and cooperates with each to love the third. This dynamic obtains not only within the Godhead but also extends from God to creation. 'God the Creator of heaven and earth is present *in* each of his creatures', writes Moltmann, 'and *in* the fellowship of creation which they share' (Moltmann 1985, 14, original emphasis). In other words, the same interpermeating love the triune God experiences is available between God and us, his creatures (Moltmann 1980, 157). This entails that God opens himself to grief and suffering on our account. Contrary to classical theists, for God to be capable of love entails the possibility of suffering (Moltmann 1973, 230). Indeed, it is precisely because of God's deep love for humanity that he can be grieved or injured by its actions (1973, 271). Unlike the anthropomorphisms of classical theism, this view takes seriously the Hebrew Bible's descriptions of the God whose spirit fills the prophets, travels with his people and suffers with them in exile (Moltmann 1980, 26–28). These narrative features lead Moltmann to conclude: 'God suffers with us – God suffers from us – God suffers for us' (Moltmann 1980, 4). Far from the detached deity of Plato, the God of the Hebrew Bible is involved, dynamic and relational.

How different a portrait from the impassible God of classical theism is set forth by Moltmann's theology! Where classical theism views God's grief or suffering in response to creatures' actions an impermissible weakness, Moltmann extols these as proof of God's perfect love. A faith whose core sacraments remember the crucified God should need no reminder of the potential sacredness of suffering. Though Christology (study of Jesus Christ) is outside the present inquiry's scope, God's participatory suffering brings added significance to that unmistakable Christian emblem, the cross. 'In the passion of the Son, the Father himself suffers the pains of abandonment', Moltmann writes, '[in] the death of the Son, death comes upon God himself' (1973, 192). The Christian concept of incarnation – and of *kenosis*, or self-emptying – elevates not only the suffering of humanity but also of all creation. As Moltmann writes: 'God also participates in the destiny of his own creation' by suffering with creatures, feeling their emotions and yearning for their flourishing (1985, 96–97). Joy, grief, yearning, anger, suffering – these are not foreign to God's experience after all, but rather part of the catalogue of divine emotion. Just as God the Son bears divine and human natures, God the Father through co-suffering with creation demonstrates his love as the most human God.

This analysis can at last articulate clearly the discursive parallel *Lightning Returns* forges between Japanese history and Christian theology. The impassable God of Christian classical theism parallels the transcendent, remote and inaccessible god-Emperor of *sonnō jōi* – and both are encoded in Bhunivelze, who remains invisible until the game's finale and has no direct relationship with his creatures. In imperial Japan, the deified Emperor constitutes the top of the nation's Confucian hierarchy, whose will is mediated to the common people only through the shogun and political officials as Japan's 'practical rulers' (Paramore 2010, 117). Moltmann's reclamation of divine emotion in turn parallels the post-war descent of Japan's god-Emperor from deified status, as codified in Article 1 of Japan's constitution: 'The Emperor shall be the symbol of the State and of the unity of the People, deriving his position from the will of the people with whom resides sovereign power' (Prime Minister of Japan and His Cabinet, 1946, n.pag.). The transcendent god becomes human, the agency is distributed to the common people and the ideals of Christian social egalitarianism, condemned by Tetsujirō, are made possible by a god who sympathizes – who exists in real relationship with his creatures.

Moltmann's theology should in no way be construed to offer the only or final word on divine emotion. Indeed, classical theists would certainly have objections and counterarguments to what is briefly sketched here. Nevertheless, Moltmann's refutation of impassibility provides a rigorous critique of the theological status quo that parallels the thematic message of *Lightning Returns*. These theological observations afford hermeneutic windows through which to decode the game's narrative and musical meanings.

Conclusion: Humanizing the Divine in 'Almighty Bhunivelze'

Bhunivelze, like the God of classical theism, is utterly transcendent – unable to experience joy or suffering in response to human actions. Yet Bhunivelze does not remain impassible through the game's end but experiences grief, anger and love for the first time after fusing with Hope, his vessel. Here the English- and Japanese-language versions of the game text differ. In English, Bhunivelze indwells Hope so that he may rule over the new, soulless humanity directly in the remade world. In Japanese, Bhunivelze merges with Hope in order to better understand his human creations by experiencing life as one. However, the influence of Hope's heart is greater than he anticipated, and in the game's final scene and battle, Bhunivelze develops an obsessive romantic fixation with Lightning, offering for her to become his consort in the new world. In both versions, Bhunivelze's emotions rampage in excess as the scene unfolds demonstrated through increasingly volatile exclamations and combat patterns. Upon his defeat, tears streaming down his face, Bhunivelze cries: 'I feel it! I feel grief! And pain! I feel anger!' The once-stoic Bhunivelze falls into a sea of chaos, raging with fresh emotions he cannot control. It appears Bhunivelze's fears were true – human emotion is unfit to mix with divinity.

Perhaps this conclusion would be correct – were it not for Lightning's example of healthy emotional integration. Throughout the game, Lightning connects emotionally with her former companions and the citizens of New Chrysalia, relearning how to feel genuinely and deeply. Through human relationship and experience, she retraces the developmental trajectory she underwent in *FFXIII*, going still further by embracing the emotional vulnerability that she had suppressed in herself since her childhood, represented by the mischievous child persona Lumina. Though raised by Bhunivelze to near-godhood as the saviour, Lightning attains full humanity through her own agency by the game's end. Lightning the saviour, with co-existing divine and human natures, parallels the incarnational state of Jesus Christ and the post-war humanization of Japan's Emperors. Lightning's defeat of Bhunivelze represents a rejection of the impassible God of classical theism and the inaccessible god-Emperor of *sonnō jōi* in favour of a saviour who understands humans in their suffering – one who can fully sympathize with humanity's weaknesses. Lightning's story teaches that divinity is compatible with humanity, exemplified through human emotions.

But what insight does music shed on the narrative themes of *Lightning Returns*, as well as its theological commentary? Much in every way. First, as observed in Chapter 3, music bears an especially close aesthetic relationship with emotional experience and expression (Robinson 2005). The concept of virtual agency encapsulates the particular capability of music to stimulate and express the thoughts and feelings of a human agent (Hatten 2018, 1). Virtual agency encodes Lightning's emotional development in 'Lightning's Theme' – and the same dynamic is present in *Lightning Returns*. 'Divine Love' first depicts Bhunivelze in his magisterial glory, combining orchestral grandiosity with choral hallmarks of the sacred music topic. The choral textures are measured and controlled, woven masterfully into the fabric of the broader orchestration. However, if 'Divine Love' is an oratorio of pristine transcendence, 'Almighty Bhunivelze' communicates uncontrolled passion and rage. Virtually every musical parameter in the track underscores this point. The texture is incredibly dense, frequently rendering individual layers impossible to distinguish in the soundtrack's mix. Its theme and variations form are rhapsodic and unpredictable, with only Bhunivelze's hymn providing continuity. Rhythmically, 'Almighty Bhunivelze' frequently frustrates metric expectations by juxtaposing two contrasting metres simultaneously (6/8 and 4/2 at 0:29; 6/8 and 4/4 at 4:46) or obscuring metre entirely (0:00–0:29, 1:02–1:34, 6:02–6:33). Timbrally, the cue employs a wealth of glissandi techniques, some orchestral and others electronic, smearing pitches together and heightening aural tension. These are too numerous to list, but a particularly salient example occurs at 4:09, precisely when a full choral proclamation of Bhunivelze's hymn should project a tone of stability and transcendence. Instead, a morass of aleatoric string glissandi and tubular bell strikes gradually crescendos until it overwhelms the hymn, undermining its projected tranquillity. This relationship generally holds throughout the track, with some accompanimental or percussive layer undermining the placid hymn texture. Though Bhunivelze's transcendent bliss is encoded via the vocalise melody from 'The Ark', the promise is proven vacuous by the tumultuous, dissonant orchestration that disrupts that peace.

The necessary elements are now in place to distil a robust interpretation that accounts for all narrative, musical and theological data. Analysing Bhunivelze's soundtrack through the lens of virtual agency reveals the change in the deity's emotional state as the battle progresses. 'Divine Love', heard in the battle's first three phases, depicts Bhunivelze omnipotent, transcendent and impassible. 'Almighty Bhunivelze', introduced in the final stage of the fight, communicates the unravelling of Bhunivelze's emotions as a consequence of becoming incarnate as Hope. The god's unleashed wrath exists in stark tension with the placid hymn, revealing the lie lurking beneath its serene soprano vocalise. The promise of a perfect, impassible creator is subverted time and time again by composer Mitsuto Suzuki's masterfully composed orchestration, suggesting that Bhunivelze's vision of an emotionless, soulless humanity is neither desirable nor sustainable. The clearest glimpse of Bhunivelze's musical identity – the exultant full-choral revelation of the hymn – simultaneously carries the most dissonant and repulsive affect, undercut repeatedly by aleatoric string glissandi and dense organ tone clusters. Whenever the voices of 'Almighty Bhunivelze' proclaim the deity's perfection and eternity, the discordant instrumental accompaniment communicates that their tranquil, transcendent texture is naught but a facade. Analogously, Moltmann concluded that the God of classical theism, unchanged in holiness and perfection, is not a good God. If God neither responds in pain nor pleasure to his creatures' actions, such a deity is not a loving God – and thus, no true God at all (Moltmann 1980, 38). Moltmann's insight parallels the unravelling of imperial Japan's prevailing philosophy of *sonnō jōi* – a god-Emperor removed from all public contact cannot truly unite the hearts and minds of the common people, but a human Emperor can lead modern Japan into a new, egalitarian era of harmonious peace. Or, as Lightning proclaims: 'The old world is dying, and your myths will die with it! In the new world, we won't need God!' The god-slayer trope in video games symbolizes the worldview-redefining descent of Japan's god-Emperor.

Analysing the encoding of Catholic music, theology and identity in *Lightning Returns* may give the impression that the game's only religious references are Christian ones – however, that conclusion would be misleading. In reality, Japan-produced video games speak first to their originating context in Japan, subsequently rippling out to other cultural contexts. *Lightning Returns* exhibits many narrative characteristics that more closely fit a Japanese context than a western one. For example, the reincarnation of souls from Nova Chrysalia onto Earth presupposes *rinne* (輪廻, lit. 'revolving around the wheel'), adapted from Buddhist Samsara, the cycle of death and rebirth. Bhunivelze – god of light, creation and order – and Etro/Lightning – goddess of death, darkness and chaos – are meant to exist in balanced harmony reflecting the Taoist concepts Yin and Yang. Finally, the post-credits scene depicting Lightning searching for her friends in modern-day Earth utilizes a common ending trope drawn from Nō (能; lit. 'talent') theatre and Japanese literature – though temporarily separated, friends and/or lovers will be eventually reunited in another life, time period or world.

This chapter explored the communicative potential of sonic iconography in video game music, facilitating semiotic connections to religious and theological ideas. *Lightning Returns: Final Fantasy XIII* weaves together narrative, cultural, visual and musical signifiers of Roman Catholic Christianity, presenting a powerful critique of the classical-theist doctrine of divine impassibility. Chapter 8 draws the sonic iconography of the sacred music topic into dialogue with a most unusual source – rock and roll music. In doing so, the descent of the god-Emperor theme introduced in this chapter will prove ever ubiquitous and salient in interpreting religious representation in Japanese video games.

NOTES

*   Standalone colour files of Figures 7.1 and 7.2, standalone illustration files of Figures 7.3 and 7.4 can be found under the Front Matter section for *Gender, Race and Religion in Video Game Music's* page on Intellect Discover.
1. Christian: 31.1 per cent, Muslim: 24.9 per cent, Hindu: 15.2 per cent, Buddhist: 6.6 per cent, folk religions: 5.6 per cent, Jewish: <1 per cent, other religion: <1 per cent, unaffiliated: 15.6 per cent (2020 est.)
2. Conversion rate defined as a person having changed from one religious affiliation to another, from religious to non-religious or from non-religious to religious at some previous point in

GENDER, RACE AND RELIGION IN VIDEO GAME MUSIC

that person's life. Inter-denominational change – such as Protestant to Catholic or Orthodox Jew to Reformed – was not counted in conversion rate.

3. 'God' is loosely defined here as an entity or class of beings within a gameworld that is of highest rank in terms of power, bearing a high degree of responsibility for determining and maintaining the structure of the present state of the gameworld. Note that this does not require that the god in question is the only being with that degree of power (as in the evil god and divine pantheon variants), is morally perfect or even good, nor that the god is transcendent or responsible for the creation of the gameworld. This definition is somewhat arbitrary, but patterned after the narrative usage of gods in video games.

4. Readers may be familiar with a common genre term 'Japanese RPG', or JRPG. I opt not to use this acronym, as the term is considered discriminatory and derogatory among Japanese game developers and is an archaic term reflecting a history of anti-Japanese vitriol among American game developers in the 2000s and early 2010s. Instead, I refer to such games as 'Japan-produced video games', 'RPGs produced in Japan' or similar descriptions (cf. Hayes 2023 for detailed coverage of this topic).

5. See Video 7.1, 'Thirty Years of God-Slaying in Video Game Music': https://www.youtube.com/watch?v=iKipYxStuCE. Accessed 3 June 2024.

6. See expanded version of Table 7.1 under the Front Matter section for *Gender, Race and Religion in Video Game Music's* page on Intellect Discover.

7. This particular connection to Christianity is intensified in the English localization. In Japanese, the term *kaihōsha* (解放者, 'liberator') does not have a particularly religious connotation nor connection to Christianity. However, this and other linguistic changes in the English localization make references to Christianity much more clear and intentional. In the Japanese original, Catholic associations are still communicated through other means such as the Order of Salvation's structure, architecture and musical score. The English localization's text has been enhanced to make its relevance to Christianity even clearer to players.

8. Latin: 'Omni dei luce ult | Salutaris Nostrum | Orate libero deus anima vitae aeterna | De maledictus fine | Ult beatitudine caros | Omni dei luce ult | Salutaris Nostrum.'

9. Latin: 'Servator Domini | Magnus Lumen sum numenus scantus | In precipito deacre vigor | Amor supremum et quod est deus | Sanctis sanctitis | Atrem lux fincus | Sanctis sanctitis | Sis at venturis | Lux nox ciata | Dei Bhunivelze est tuum se patris | Et tua clamors in precis ost | Teste mustus mundus | Adora deus sanctum.'

10. Latin: 'Deum volat cum ira | Omnipotens est ilius | Omnipotens Bhunivelze! | Ne in ira tua!' The complete lyrics are too lengthy to reprint in full here.

11. While many Orthodox and Protestant Christians would also affirm classical theism, these denominations lack the centralized structure of Catholicism, entailing less uniform doctrinal commitments across these denominations. Orthodox and Protestant theologians and congregations may thus experiment with a wider range of theological concepts outside of classical theism.

12. The reference list is non-exhaustive.

8

Battle Hymn of the God-Slayers: Troping Rock and Sacred Music in *Xenoblade Chronicles*

Introduction: The Human Voice of God

On 15 August 1945, the citizens of Japan heard the voice of their god speak for the first time. Not the voices of the elusive, uninvolved *kami* (神; 'god') of Shinto tradition, but rather the voice of the one on whom all of their nation's collective efforts for the past twenty years had been based. Japanese citizens had fought for him, endured difficult home front conditions for him and lost family members in his name. His was a constant household presence in the public consciousness – even as his person was thoroughly hidden from the ordinary citizen's eye. Japan's Emperor was considered fully divine and inaccessible to common folk, who owed him allegiance and veneration as his subjects. As both god and monarch, the Emperors functioned as the symbolic head of both the state and Japanese spirituality, infusing the people's loyalty and obedience to the Emperor with a significant religious dimension (Fisher 2012). This veneer of divinity was shattered with finality when Emperor Hirohito spoke to his people via radio in the Jewel Voice Broadcast (玉音 放送, *gyokuon hōsō*, lit. 'jewel sound broadcast'), marking the conclusion of the Second World War.[1] It is difficult to overstate how impactful hearing the Jewel Voice Broadcast would be to a Japanese citizen in 1945. The Emperors remained behind a veil of obscurity, and contact with the average subject was virtually non-existent – to hear the Emperor's human voice was quite literally worldview-shattering (Anon. 1945). As Japanese author Ōe Kenzaburō vividly recalls:

> [T]he Emperor as a god speaking to us in a human voice was beyond imagining in any reverie. The Emperor was a god, the authority of the nation, the organizing principle of reality. The military and the police, our system of social classes – the Emperor as a god was at the source of all things, and all the laws and systems under

our Constitution had erected hard, high barriers of reality to keep the Emperor at a distance from us.

(Kenzaburō 2002, 20)

As shocking as the mere fact of Hirohito's public address was, equally astonishing was the content of the Emperor's speech. One week after atomic bombs razed the cities of Hiroshima and Nagasaki, Japan's citizens feared hearing a message consistent with previous imperial messaging, ordering them to choose death over accepting defeat (Fisher 2012). Instead, the high-pitched, unassuming voice of Emperor Hirohito commended the very course of action previously considered unthinkable – surrender. Though the term 'surrender' was never used in order to save face, Hirohito accepted the Allies' joint declaration for unconditional surrender on behalf of the nation, shifting the tone from imperialist to pacifist: 'To strive for the common prosperity and happiness of all nations, as well as the security and wellbeing of our subjects, is the solemn obligation [...] which lies close to our heart' (Hirohito 1945, n.pag.). In the wake of the unprecedented destruction of populace and property from the bombings, Emperor Hirohito introduced a maxim quoted countless times in Japanese media during the reconstruction years and that remains central to Japanese culture to the present day: 'we have resolved to pave the way for a grand peace for all the generations to come by enduring the unendurable and suffering what is not sufferable' (Fisher 2012, n.pag.). The vision that Emperor Hirohito communicated radically reversed the course of Japan as a nation from one of nationalist superiority to peaceful, long-suffering humility. There is perhaps no other historical event as foundational to the making of modern Japan as this Jewel Voice Broadcast, when the revered Emperor Hirohito renounced his presumed divinity and the premise upon which the entire Japanese war effort was based.

On that day, Japan's god died in a very real and palpable sense. Western readers may wrestle with viewing Hirohito's broadcast through a religious lens, understanding it instead as of historical or political significance only. However, this response would overlook the considerable overlap between god and king, national and spiritual loyalty and the enmeshment of religious and cultural identities. As this chapter shall demonstrate, it is precisely this network of ideas that is frequently at play in the music and narratives of god-slayer games.

A Surprising Play of Opposites: Troping Rock and Sacred-Music Topics

This chapter continues the trajectory begun in Chapter 7, examining the god-slayer narrative trope and the music that most frequently characterizes its occurrences.

Whereas the previous chapter showcased the nuanced readings possible through the development of the sacred-music topic alone, this chapter explores the enrichment of meanings enabled by the conjunction of sacred music with other musical topics. Specifically, some god-slayer boss battle themes combine sacred-music topical features with ones from rock music in a surprising play of opposites, amplifying the music's semiotic potential. Analysing the troping of rock and sacred music unveils new depths of meaning from a fascinating case study, *Xenoblade Chronicles* (2010; remake 2020), recapitulating the themes of Japanese history, culture and religion with which this chapter began.

First, a conceptual review of musical topics focusing on their semiotic function is warranted. Music-topical features become convenient aural calling cards, quickly invoking a range of cultural and historical meanings to hearers. Raymond Monelle writes that musical topics strategically 'locate music in history and in culture', ensuring that musical communication is never devoid of meaning (Monelle 2006, 29). Robert Hatten defines a musical topic as triggering 'clear associations with styles, genres, and expressive meanings' – and thereby with real-world cultural associations (Hatten 2004, 2). In semiotic terms, topics import the range of meanings from one musical domain into another, creating 'fresh meanings' that transcend their individual components (Hatten 2014, 515). Monelle demonstrates the progression of hunting horn calls in music from indexical meaning, quoting contemporary horn calls in a piece to establish the setting of a hunt; to iconic meaning, in which originally composed music similar to the style of a horn call recalls associations with the hunt; and finally symbolic meaning, in which a set of musical conventions more broadly reminiscent of a hunting-horn call may be employed by composers to evoke a wide range of cultural associations related to the hunt, hunters and nobility in general. At the symbolic stage, the meanings carried by a musical topic may be quite diverse; Monelle lists manliness, nobility, youth, exoticism, nature, risk, morning and the woodlands as some of the many concepts related to the hunting-horn call topic (Monelle 2006, 95). It is when the musical topic enters firmly into the realm of symbolic signification that it becomes most malleable and versatile as a building block for constructing composers' unique, strategic meanings – as part of the shared palette for music-semiotic interpretation. As with the hunting horn, so too with other musical topics, including rock and sacred music.

Though many musical topics carry over to video game soundtracks from concert music and film, video game composers also develop topics more specific to the medium.[2] Video game music topics usually correspond to ludic functions, indicating a particular state of play – in Grasso's terms, the musical topics afford a certain range of gameplay actions. For example, the safety of towns, adventurousness of overworld travel, mysteriousness of dungeon exploration and intensity of combat are signalled by recognizable musical traits informing experienced players of their ludic significance. Although these topics may draw on pre-existing topical characteristics (e.g. *ombra* for dungeons, singing style and pastoral for towns, rock and roll for battle themes), they take on an independent life as a topic when consistently associated with gameplay states and drawn into an intertextual relationship with other music of similar ludic function. This is especially true of battle-music themes which bear a clear resemblance to other instances of the same type. The stylistic features of real-world rock music frequently serve as a foundation for a video game battle theme. It generally features a homophonic texture with distinct melody and accompaniment, utilizing typical rock instrumentation such as drum set, electric bass and/or electric guitar. Its melodies are typically rather active, with greater rhythmic syncopation and wider intervallic leaps, and its harmonic rhythm changes at a steady pace of roughly one chord per measure. Battle themes are generally in minor mode (as contemporary metal or hard rock often are), with loud dynamics and moderate to fast tempo (Baugh 1993, 28). Its expressive associations include adolescence and countercultural attitudes (Jackson 2000, 23), individual willpower and defiance of authority (Bleich et al. 1991, 251), passionate expression (Baugh 1993, 23), rebellious personality (Carpentier et al. 2003, 1653) and uniquely human experience of an individual (Jackson 2000, 11). Especially significant is the common thread of 'opposition to freedom-curtailing impositions by persons or institutions in power', placing the rock topic in marked tension with the sacred-music topic (Bleich et al. 1991, 351). While sacred music bespeaks tradition, devotion and organized religion, rock music emphasizes youth, rebellion and individual willpower.

The musical characteristics and cultural associations of the sacred-music topic were covered in detail in Chapter 7 and will not be rehashed in detail here. To summarize, the musical features and cultural associations contrast those of the rock topic on virtually every point. Where rock features loudness, sacred music maintains a soft, contemplative mood. While rock is defined by passion and excess, sacred music revels in solemnity and self-control. Point for point, the rock and sacred-music topics seem indelibly opposed to one another. Table 8.1 illustrates this thorough contrast between these two topics.

One further analytical tool adapted from the field of semiotics demonstrates the diametric opposition of rock and sacred music. The semiotician Algirdas Julien Greimas developed six modalities to measure the degrees and qualities of agency in literature, and music semiotician Eero Tarasti fruitfully applied these modalities to musical analysis (Tarasti 1994, 41–42). These analytical modalities excel in measuring semiotically significant changes in musical agency diachronically across a piece. Despite this precedent, Tarasti's implementation of Greimas's modalities has not gained widespread use in music semiotics, rendering each analysis utilizing

BATTLE HYMN OF THE GOD-SLAYERS

TABLE 8.1: Parameter comparison of rock and sacred-music topics and their semiotic associations.

Parameter	Rock Topic	Sacred Music Topic (Olga Sánchez-Kisielewska 2018)
Texture	Melody and accompaniment	Counterpoint or Homophony (98)
Instrumentation	Drum Set, Electric Bass, Electric Guitar	Solo Voice, Choir, Organ (138)
Melody	Active (syncopation, leaps possible)	Simple, stepwise (103)
Harmonic Rhythm	One chord per measure	One chord per beat (108)
Mode	Minor (when in video game battle themes)	Major (147)
Dynamic	Loud: *mf* to *ff* (Baugh 1993, 28)	Soft: *pp* to *mp* (128–129)
Tempo	Moderate to fast	'Exceedingly slow tempo' (126)
Expressive Meanings	Adolescence (Jackson 2000, 33) Counter-cultural attitudes (Ibid.) Individual willpower (Bleich 1991, 351) Defiance of authority (Ibid.) Passionate expression (Baugh 1993, 23) Rebelliousness (Carpentier 2003, 1653) Human experience (Jackson 2000, 11)	Archaism and ancient tradition (33) Ceremonial and liturgical order (156) United collective over the individual (94) Devotion (3) Solemnity and self-control (33, 45) Association with the divine (87) Spirituality and transcendence (57, 17)

them somewhat unique. This chapter understands the six modalities according to pairs of active or passive agency, grouped according to three axes – strategic vs. stylistic, diachronic vs. synchronic and change vs. stasis:

1. Strategic vs. Stylistic: Will (*vouloir*): a musical idea containing the developmental potential to serve as a hermeneutic premise for subsequent musical development, a musical idea that is unique, characteristic and strategic. Must

(*devoir*): a musical passage or figure that conforms or capitulates to conventional expectations (such as stylistic or tonal ones).

2. Diachronic vs. Synchronic: Can (*pouvoir*): a musical passage that exerts influence over other diachronic events in the same musical piece such as a key area modulation. Know (*savoir*): a musical passage with primarily synchronic significance, conveying meaningful information to the listener in the moment through strategic arranging of musical events.

3. Change vs. Stasis: Do (*faire*): a musical texture actively in flux and development, high in kinetic energy and a sense of instability and change between successive musical events. Be (*être*): a musical texture exhibiting homeostasis, stability and self-containment; a distinct isotopy not in the process of changing into another.

Table 8.2 summarizes Greimas's modalities in visual form.

These modalities are useful as parameters for evaluating music's degree of virtual agency in a quasi-quantitative manner, albeit in a necessarily subjective one. As mentioned in previous chapters, the virtual agency describes music's ability to 'simulate the actions, emotions, and reactions of a human agent' (Hatten 2018, 1). It is a virtual agency that enables listeners to hear and interpret music as possessing movement, agency, cultural or gendered character, development over time and emotional expressivity. Hatten's theory of virtual agency articulates what is typically described vaguely as the character of a musical passage or piece. Tarasti's modalities provide conceptual handholds for evaluating a topic's virtual agency – including the rock and sacred-music topics. When evaluating a passage of music using Greimas's modalities, Tarasti assigns a '+' sign to modalities that the passage exemplifies, with a double '+' sign for one that it exemplifies very strongly. A '–' (or double '–') sign means the music does not exemplify that modality – though

TABLE 8.2: A. J. Greimas's modalities as applied in musical semiotics (Tarasti 1994, 41–42).

Strategic vs. Stylistic	Diachronic vs. Synchronic Affect	Change vs. Stasis
Will (*vouloir*) Developmental potential to serve as hermeneutic premise, agential yearning	Can (*pouvoir*) Potential to effect change and influence over other events in the music	Do (*faire*) Kinetic energy, sense of change between successive musical events
Must (*devoir*) To capitulate to conventional expec-tations, such as tonal or stylistic ones	Know (*savoir*) To convey information through strategic arranging of musical events	Be (*être*) Establishing homeostasis or self-containment; a distinct isotopy

the '–' signs are usually not listed, since a single or double '+' in one modality entails a single or double '–' in its opposite. Following Tarasti's usage, I evaluate the rock topic as will++, can+ and do+ and the sacred-music topic as be++, know+ and must+. In other words, the rock topic's agency is one of maximum willpower and individuality, as shown by its cultural associations. It also conveys a high degree of kinetic energy and generally exhibits marked changes in harmonic progression and/or texture from section to section. By contrast, the sacred-music topic's virtual agency is primarily one of placid homeostasis and self-containment, as it invites congregational participants to contemplate their inward spiritual state. Chorales also emphasize the transmission of meaning – especially the theological meaning of a sacred text – and generally conform to conventional tonal and stylistic expectations. This is not to say that rock music does not have its own stylistic conventions (it does) or that sacred music does not innovate or defy conventional expectations (it also does). Rather, it means that sacred music signifies primarily via conformity to its conventional expectations, while rock music semiotically prioritizes individuality of expression and message. Both genres balance in a play between convention and innovation – but one's existence and value depends on its conformity, and the other on its individuality.

Once more, the rock and sacred-music topics are robustly opposed – thus, their combination in a single topical trope is highly surprising, with great potential for semiotic play, in both compositional design and listener interpretations. Now that the contrast between sacred-music and rock topics is clear, an important quantitative analytical point emerges from the longitudinal corpus study treated in Chapter 7. From that body of examples, 54% of god-slayer games ranked with a 2 or 3 in relevance exhibit sacred-music topic features, and 71% feature either sacred- or rock-topic features. Significantly, some games among those ranked with a 2 or 3 deliberately combine the two contrasting topics in an intriguing play of opposites. It should be noted that the combination – or musical trope – of rock and sacred-music topics is infrequent, occurring in approximately 16% of god-slayer games' final boss battle themes. Quantitative analysis of the data dispels the notion that troping rock and sacred music is a conventional means of scoring the struggle against a gameworld's god, as it is used only by a minority of video game music composers. Yet removal from the sphere of the conventional places the sacred-rock trope in the domain of the strategic, adding to the trope's semiotic significance. Video game composers may choose to employ this striking combination to achieve a richly meaningful result – one that enhances the process of interpretation and may support, nuance or contribute to the plot's thematic and narrative content.

A case study will illustrate the semiotic and narrative meanings potentially conveyed by this musical trope. A prominent example of this topical combination is the main theme of *Halo 2* (2004) juxtaposing plainchant and distorted electric-guitar-driven rock. The initial plainchant on neutral vocalise syllables outlines the Dorian medieval church mode, previously noted in Chapter 7 as a typical signifier of Catholic sacred music. Near the end of the chant phrase, a heavily distorted electric guitar enters, riffing improvisatorially on the primary leitmotif of the chant. This transitions out of the sacred music space into an energetic cinematic rock texture featuring a soaring electric guitar melody. Halfway through the track, a heavy drum set beat completes the quasi-metal topic. The electric guitar maintains the plainchant melody as its primary source material, developing it in the manner of one of Jimi Hendrix's virtuosic guitar solos. Not to be forgotten, the plainchant recapitulates at the cue's end, reminding listeners of the source of the guitar's melody. This time, however, the electric guitar joins the voices in melodic unison, encoding a fusion of sacred-music and rock-topic traits. The interplay of these two musical topics in *Halo 2*'s main theme is semiotically intentional, as their combined meanings are key to the game's narrative themes. The *Halo* series is suffused with symbolism reflecting a tension between science and religion throughout the narrative (Paulissen 2018, 5). The musical topics' union at the end of the track suggests that the Covenant Empire's theocratic religiosity and the Unified Earth Government's technologically driven militancy are perhaps not so incompatible in the end.

As effectively as the main theme of *Halo 2* illustrates the potential of combining sacred music and rock, a more powerful instance of both the sacred-rock musical trope and god-slayer narrative trope is *Xenoblade Chronicles*, which warrants and rewards deeper scrutiny. It is to the detailed musical analysis of *Xenoblade* that the remainder of the chapter turns.

A World with No Gods: Slaying God in Xenoblade Chronicles

Xenoblade Chronicles is at once like and unlike every other RPG. Its story is monumental and detailed, its cast members varied and lively and the fate of its world is placed in the hands of a young, teenage male protagonist – all hallmarks of the genre, especially for RPGs developed in Japan. Yet its expansive world was notable at the time of its release for adopting an open-world orientation (today, a staple in many, if not most, RPGs), for an extraordinary score composed by Yōko Shimomura (previously noted in Chapter 3 as the composer of *Final Fantasy XV*) and a dynamic and active combat system that belied the genre's presumed reliance on turn-based battles. It was also one of the first notable RPGs voiced in English entirely by British actors and dialects – another common practice today for voicing fantasy video games (MacDonald 2012). *Xenoblade*'s plot is too extensive to synopsize in any detail – however, brief remarks are in order to contextualize the narrative significance of the musical analysis to follow. The 100-hour epic narrative revolves around a god, a young man and a sword. The god is Zanza, the creator of the world Bionis who ordained a cycle in which all life dies, returns to nourish him and is then recreated. In addition to being the most powerful entity in Bionis, Zanza is worshipped by a cult of religious devotees and is initially transcendent, existing only in non-material form. Zanza is a prime candidate for the classic god-slayer narrative trope. The protagonist of the story is Shulk, an earnest young man researching the secrets of Bionis. As is the case for many RPG protagonists, Shulk compulsively protects all he comes across from danger, gathering a party of like-minded friends to aid him in his quest. The sword is the Monado, which grants its user an array of unique powers – perhaps most significantly the ability to foresee impending danger and change the future to avert that fate. Shulk wields the Monado throughout the game, eventually discovering Zanza as the mastermind behind the cycle of life and death and resolving to defy him in the game's final battle. *Xenoblade*'s story exemplifies the god-slayer trope in its purest form, as does its music during the battle with Zanza.

Xenoblade's battle themes typically exemplify a hard rock, metal-influenced topic conventional for many combat-driven video games. As the final boss, Zanza has a unique battle theme, 'Zanza the Divine', which is distinct from every other enemy's battle theme, as it initially lacks any rock elements. Rather, the track begins with a strong example of the sacred-music topic, instantiated both by textural style and instrumentation. The layering of recorded solo voice creates an effect reminiscent of choral music as the two melodic voices move in parallel perfect fifths – referencing the medieval Catholic sacred-music practice of organum, in which a melody is harmonized in strict parallel motion at a perfect interval. The use of organum to invoke the sacred-music topic and an association with ancientness or otherworldliness is not without precedent; Stefan Greenfield-Casas analyses the use of organum to a similar effect in association with the ancient entity Yunalesca in *Final Fantasy X* (2001) (Greenfield-Casas 2017, 14). Yet the sacred organum does not have the last word; a dramatic shift obliterates the static, otherworldly isotopy as a more conventional rock-topic battle theme shatters the calm – complete with drum set groove and distorted, power chord-style electric guitars reminiscent of the main theme of *Halo 2*. The transcription in Figure 8.1 demonstrates the highly salient contrast between sacred-music and rock topics in 'Zanza the Divine'.

Sacred-music and rock topics had alternated in the track's introduction, producing a marked juxtaposition. In the main section of the piece, however, the two topics are combined, producing an illustrative instance of the sacred-rock trope. In addition to the Phrygian-mode vocal melody, suggesting the medieval church modes, a layer of choral accompaniment enters approximately an octave above

GENDER, RACE AND RELIGION IN VIDEO GAME MUSIC

FIGURE 8.1: Partial musical transcription, 'Zanza the Divine'. Transcription by author.

the melodic voice. The choral layer is subtle but important – it is the only hint of collective singing in this track. This faint feature will prove to be key to later interpretation.

How do the rock and sacred-music features of the trope interact in this passage? Robert Hatten describes four axes of topical troping – compatibility, dominance, creativity and productivity – as helpful concepts to analyse the interaction of a trope's individual components (Table 8.3) (Hatten 2014, 515). First, 'compatibility' measures two topics' ability to fit together smoothly, such that maximal similarity may appear to be a single topic rather than a trope. Singing style and pastoral topics fit together very naturally, with little adjustment required; however, as has been noted, sacred-music and rock topics are much more incongruous. In such a

TABLE 8.3: Four axes for semiotic analysis of topical troping in music (Hatten 2014, 515).

Axis Name	Description
Compatibility	Evaluates how naturally a topic fits into its new environment, or two or more topics fit together. Ranges from similarity (high) to complementarity (balanced) to contradiction (low).
Dominance	Evaluates a topic's degree of salience or importance relative to others, based on hierarchical weight, temporal precedence, completeness, adherence to prototype, or prevailing influence.
Creativity	Evaluates a trope's ability to generate fresh semiotic meaning based on the novelty of the combination of topics troped. Greater originality generates more striking hermeneutic windows.
Productivity	Evaluates a trope's potential to serve as a premise for expressive discourse over the course of a piece or movement; productive tropes have high potential for subsequent musical development.

fusion, one or more of the topics involved in the trope will be curtailed to accommodate one or more of the others – leading to the next axis. 'Dominance' evaluates which component of the topical trope is most salient or important from a musical perspective – which topic is more complete, prominent or influential. Listener attention will tend to elevate one component of the trope over others. A march may be pastorally inflected, but it is still fundamentally a march; a learned-style fugue may contain elements of the hunt topic but still predominantly come across as a fugue. In the infrequent case that two or more components in a musical trope are evenly balanced, the result is of particular semiotic significance. Next, a trope's degree of 'creativity' involves its novelty and originality; if a trope of two topics is used very frequently, it loses its originality and becomes its own conventional topic. On the other hand, rarely combined topical features produce a meaningful fusion with considerable potential to signify complex networks of meaning to listeners. Two topics with a low degree of compatibility provide fertile ground for high creativity, as that particular combination is less likely to have previously occurred in the absence of a specific motivating context for the trope. The last of these four axes, 'productivity', measures a trope's potential to serve as the basis for further musical development over the course of a piece or movement – especially in regards to the music's semiotic meaning. As combinations of musical topics are typically highly marked, listeners expect them not to be singular occurrences, but rather providing a meaningful touchpoint for further compositional attention. The more striking the trope, the more its development inevitably attracts subsequent development as the composition unfolds.

As previously observed, the rock and sacred topics are not naturally compatible but contrast each other in every parameter. In 'Zanza the Divine', this tension may be observed by the sacrifices each topic must make in order for the two to coexist. The choral accompaniment adopts the rock topic's staccato articulation and slower harmonic rhythm, accenting the strong beats of the measure in a manner uncharacteristic of a sacred chorale. In turn, the rock topic has lost an active rock-style melody of its own, allowing the sacred topic to provide its melody instead. Concerning dominance, the rock topic is most prominent in the track's prevailing aesthetic, with the sacred topic's vocal instrumentation and Phrygian mode serving to inflect the rock battle theme with an archaic, magisterial flavour. In terms of creativity, the sacred-rock trope is highly marked due to its stark play of opposites, generating strong potential for semiotic meaning. As shown quantitatively, among the total corpus of god-slayer games, the sacred-rock trope is infrequent, adding to its significance whenever it does occur. The peculiar combination of rock and sacred-music topics appears uniquely motivated by the narrative god-slayer trope, creating a perfect musical depiction of rebellion against a divine power.

The last of Hatten's axes, productivity, must be evaluated in the context of the piece as a whole. The contrasting middle section of the track stages an expressive trajectory that reveals the high degree of productivity possessed by this instance of the sacred-rock trope. Initially, the rock elements drop out entirely, leaving the vocals accompanied by organ – the other signature sacred-music instrument. The music appears to reference and return to the lone sacred topic of the cue's opening, reasserting the initial stasis of the choral organum. Halfway through the section, however, the rock topic returns in a half-time groove, undergirding the dominant organ and vocals with an intermittent backbeat and increasing rhythmic drive. Closing the contrasting section, the rock groove that interrupted the introductory organum texture returns, looping into a repeat of the main section with its sacred-rock trope. It is now evident how the sacred-rock trope functions as a hermeneutic premise for the entirety of 'Zanza the Divine'; the sacred-music and rock topics – initially juxtaposed against each other – are joined in an unstable, low-compatibility trope. At first, the rock topic dominates, but it is in turn repelled and dominated by the sacred-music topic. Over the course of the contrasting middle, however, the rock elements gradually return until they become dominant once more. The topics' competition for dominance, looped continuously over the battle, musically encodes the struggle of Shulk's authority-defying willpower clashing with the magisterial and divine deity Zanza. Thus, the sacred-rock trope is semiotically productive as well.

Many final boss battles have multiple stages – so too does Zanza's battle and music. In the midst of Shulk and Zanza's desperate battle, Zanza assumes his ultimate divine form, against whom no mere mortal being could hope to compete. Yet Shulk, armed with the legendary Monado, has long since transcended merely mortal power. Channelling the combined power of his friends, Shulk's Monado metamorphoses into the True Monado, now bearing the Japanese kanji for kami on its hilt. Throughout the game, the Monado's hilt displayed the kanji for any type of being it had the ability to harm or destroy – the True Monado imparts Shulk the power needed to slay a god. In the titanic clash between divinity unleashed and god-slaying willpower, the battle music likewise changes to the aptly titled cue 'The God-Slaying Sword', displaying marked sacred-music characteristics in instrumentation and two-voice organum in its introduction (Figure 8.2).

The disappearance of rock elements in this battle theme poses these tracks' greatest hermeneutic question. Why would the composer dispel the rock half of the sacred-rock trope while Shulk continues to fight as defiantly as ever? Why undercut the carefully crafted battle for dominance between the sacred-music and rock topics? This development certainly seems interpretatively bewildering; if anything, one would expect the final phase of the battle to intensify its individualist rock-topic components, as the willpower represented by Shulk and his friends at last pushes through to victory. Yet three considerations reveal why these musical choices are provocatively appropriate, contributing to the climactic scene's overall thematic meaning. First, the vanishing rock elements symbolize how overpowering Zanza is in his full divinity, and how unlike all previous battles the climactic struggle is. In this – the gameworld's greatest conceivable struggle – there can be no hint of the mundane music fit for cleaning up low-level spiders and crabs. Accordingly, the

FIGURE 8.2: Partial transcription of 'The God-Slaying Sword', organum introduction. Transcription by author.

dominant sacred-music topic and cinematic, epic orchestration utterly transcend the game's conventional rock battle themes. Second, the singular identity of the game's final battle theme functions as a semiotic beacon, alerting players that the events about to occur are significant and meaningful. Whereas a recurrent battle theme prompts players to enter ludic autopilot – processing stimuli necessary for game-play but without much critical thinking towards the events' thematic significance – a different theme suggests that the battle is narratively, not just ludically, pivotal. This is not to say the musical shift's significance is only narrative – it also imparts ludic information signalling that this is the final stage of the battle, as all the rock compo-nents resembling the other battle themes have fallen away. Since the most striking trait of 'The God-Slaying Sword' is the prominence of its sacred-music elements, the shift suggests to attentive players that plot developments related to divinity will be key in interpreting the unfolding scene. Third, the track musically encodes Shulk's facing Zanza on equal ground, new god against old, rather than relying on merely human power as before. Shulk opposed Zanza previously as the embodiment of all that is human (rock topic); now, with his friends' aid, he confronts Zanza using a new mode of divinity (sacred-music topic).

Evidencing this interpretative move is a subtle – but semiotically marked – relationship between the two tracks. The melodic elements of 'Zanza the Divine' consisted primarily of solo voice, with the exception of a faint choral accompani-mental texture above the main melody. In 'The God-Slaying Sword', the accom-panimental choral voices are now firmly foregrounded in a chorale-like melody, suggesting the realization of Shulk's divine potential through the combined support of his friends. The significance of this development is apparent through the differ-ences in solo voice and choral singing within the domain of the sacred-music topic. Olga Sánchez-Kisielewska describes the choral manifestation of the sacred-music topic as 'anti-subjective', subsuming the individual voice into the unified collective (2018, 94). In a persuasive semiosis of *Final Fantasy X*, Greenfield-Casas interprets the chorale setting of the 'Hymn of the Fayth' in the game's climax as all Spira singing together, yearning for a new world (Greenfield-Casas 2017, 16–17). In Spira, as in religious congregations, the collectivism of choral singing can signify positively valenced unity in will or purpose in some situations even as it suggests negatively valenced suppression of individual will in other contexts. In 'Zanza the Divine', the melodic solo voice is emblematic of Zanza himself, a sole magisterial entity competing for dominance with the human individuality represented by rock elements. In 'The God-Slaying Sword', however, the dominant choral melody encodes the unified hopes of humanity, channelled through Shulk and the True Monado. The individualist rock topic therefore gives way to communal song, as all of Bionis's hopes for freedom from Zanza join Shulk in battle, imbuing him with the power to defy a god.

Shulk fells Zanza with his god-slaying sword, and the Monado offers to remake the world however Shulk desires, with him as its new god. As Zanza decided the shape and structure of Bionis and became its god, Shulk may create the new world in his own image. Yet Shulk refuses both divinity and the right to decide the form of the future world, casting aside the Monado after proclaiming: 'The future should be decided by each and every person in the world. And so what I – no, what we – wish for is a world with no gods!' The game's god-slaying narrative culminates in the abolition of the concept of deity itself. As with many god-slayer narratives, *Xenoblade Chronicles* ends in rebirth – the people working together to rebuild and transform the world into a paradise.

Descent of the God-Emperor: A Cultural-Historical Reading of the God-Slayer Trope

But how is the god-slayer trope to be interpreted? What cultural meanings does it convey, and why is it especially common in Japan-produced video games? It is tempting to read the god-slayer trope as an overtly antitheistic Japanese rejection of Christianity, in accordance with the waves of anti-Christian discourse detailed in Chapter 7. Yet that interpretative move would be too hasty, as there is a closer connection in Japan's recent history. A foundational dictum of semiotics insists that in order to decode what a particular sign may mean, an interpreter must evaluate the sign's probable meaning in its original context – in this case, Japanese history and culture. Building on the previous chapter's reading of *Lightning Returns* and this chapter's opening, the sociocultural hermeneutic key is by now a familiar one: the descent of imperial Japan's inaccessible, sovereign god-Emperor from divine to human status via the Jewel Voice Broadcast.

Greenfield-Casas analyses similar narrative and musical themes in another god-slaying RPG from Japan, *Final Fantasy X*. The soundtrack's iconic 'Hymn of the Fayth' plays multiple roles throughout the game's story. On the one hand, it does represent Spira's institutional religion, Yevon, especially in association with Yunalesca and Yu Yevon, two primary figureheads of the Yevon church. On the other hand, the hymn gestures at the simple, communal faith of Spira's people, particularly when sung in unison by the communal Ronso people and in six-part harmony by all of Spira (Greenfield-Casas 2017, 11, 16). The sacred-music associations of the hymn are neither wholly negative – representing a hegemony to be overthrown – nor wholly positive. Rather, the hymn and the game's other religious symbols are part of the domain of myth, which functions to connect the fictional gameworld to Japan's own history and culture. 'Myth in the context of *FFX*', writes Greenfield-Casas, 'disguises Japan's history – it presents a gamified

239

and mythicized simulation of the past' (23). Greenfield-Casas concludes that the protagonists' opposition to the Yevonite church and the deicide of Yu Yevon is a double allegory – first to the European Enlightenment, and through it to Japan's own experience of modernity (21). The present analysis furthers Greenfield-Casas's insight and argues that the ubiquitous god-slayer trope is a mythic retelling of one of the most formative moments in modern Japanese history – the Emperor's disavowal of divinity.

In the years leading up to the Second World War, Japan was one of the few remaining civilizations that believed its national leader was a god. Japan's 1889 Meiji Constitution declares the Emperor 'sacred', 'inviolable', 'heaven-descended', 'divine' and 'pre-eminent above all his subjects' (Haskin 1905, 51). *New York Times* correspondent Otto D. Tollschus described Japan's prevailing conception of its Emperors as 'deities superior to all others' whose 'descendants [the Japanese people] must likewise be superior to all other beings on earth' (1945, n.pag.). After the destruction of Nagasaki and Hiroshima ended Japan's participation in the war, the experience of military defeat compelled a collective rethinking of this cultural doctrine, as detailed in this chapter's introduction. In the post-war period of political, financial and societal reconstruction, Emperor Hirohito took two actions that have been called 'the most significant act by any Japanese Emperor' – the Jewel Voice Broadcast described at the beginning of this chapter and the New Year's Rescript following shortly thereafter (Trumbull 1958, n.pag.). First, the Jewel Voice Broadcast functioned as a direct inbreaking of the inaccessible, ineffable god-Emperor into everyday human history and affairs. Through the straightforward act of speaking to his subjects in a human voice, Emperor Hirohito dealt a lethal blow to the doctrine of royal divinity. The descent of the god-Emperor was brought to completion by a rapid public process of humanization in the following months, including multiple public appearances and goodwill tours (Trumbull 1958). Yet perhaps the most decisive catalyst for change came in the form of another speech – Hirohito's New Year's Rescript of 1 January 1946. The commemoration of a new year – when the nation was still wounded and torn apart by the War – brought with it a new national philosophy. Hirohito's public declaration brooked no ambiguity, describing the divinity of the Emperor as a 'false conception' and 'mere legends and myths' – an admission difficult to deny when spoken by the presumed deity himself (Hirohito 1946). Combining with Hirohito's astonishing remarks during the Jewel Voice Broadcast advocating for international peace and asking his subjects to endure the unendurable, the New Year's Rescript signalled a clear change in trajectory towards the Emperor's vision for a new Japan – one not based on the veneration of its deified Emperor. On that day, Japan's god died in a very real sense, leaving its people to reconstruct their whole religious and national reality.

Yet the now-human Hirohito also paved the road to modernity, 'the personification of a Japan that was able to rise from the ashes of war' (Goto 2014, n.pag.). In place of an unreachable, ineffable and divine Emperor, Hirohito the human walked among his people, shook their hands and demonstrated compassion for their concerns and troubles. The unassuming, modest Hirohito became a symbol beloved by all for his humanity – not the divinity previously ascribed. Rather than the acknowledgement of their Emperor's humanity representing Japan's shame, Hirohito's humility became the pillar of Japan's newfound strength. A particular anecdote serves to illustrate this point well. A widespread apocryphal parable depicts Hirohito's visit to a copper factory to meet its workers in person. When a workman approached to shake his hand – a boldness that would have been unconscionable before the war – Hirohito bowed first to the man, broadcasting humility unthinkable from a divine ruler (Trumbull 1958). The telling and retelling of Hirohito's act restored national dignity and signalled the way to a future without a god-Emperor. As in *Xenoblade Chronicles*, the task of constructing a new world fell to Japan's people without reliance on its god. Hirohito's influential New Year's Rescript anticipates this, borrowing utopian language from the earlier Meiji Charter Oath:

All classes, high and low, shall unite [...] All common people, no less than the civil and military officials, shall be allowed to fulfill their just desires so that there may not be any discontent among them [...] We wish to make this oath anew and restore the country to stand on its own feet again [...] We stand by the people and we wish always to share with them in their moment of joys and sorrows. The ties between us and our people have always stood upon mutual trust and affection. They do not depend upon mere legends and myths. They are not predicated on the false conception that the Emperor is divine and that the Japanese people are superior to other races and fated to rule the world.

(Hirohito 1946, 15)

Though the Meiji Restoration of 1868 has hitherto been discussed as a springboard for imperial Japan's nationalism, the creation of *sonnō jōi* and a renewal of anti-Christian discourse, it is also true that the Meiji Restoration, in its overarching quest to fashion Japan into a major world power in the image of western nations, instituted a number of egalitarian policies benefitting the common people. The Meiji-era reforms abolished feudal class privilege, established the 1889 Constitution, legalized Christianity, founded a national public education system and granted all male citizens the right to vote. It is to this spirit of democratic reform that Emperor Hirohito appealed, while specifically disavowing the cult of Emperor worship also formed during the Meiji era. The post-war 1946 Constitution makes this abundantly clear, proclaiming in its first article: 'The Emperor shall be the symbol of the State and of the unity of the People, deriving his position from the will of the people with whom resides sovereign power' (Prime Minister of Japan and His Cabinet 1946, n.pag.). To reiterate: the sovereign power of Japan derives from the will of the common people – not a sovereign divine Emperor. To suppress any room for possible misunderstanding, Article 4 decrees that the Emperor 'shall not have powers related to government' (Prime Minister of Japan and His Cabinet 1946, n.pag.). The death of Japan's god-Emperor elevated the Japanese populace to recreate the world in their own image.

The god-slayer trope is not one of nihilist deconstruction but of phoenix-like reconstruction. It is the entirety of *Final Fantasy X's* Spira united in harmony, singing the 'Hymn of the Fayth' and desiring a new and better world (Greenfield-Casas 2017, 16–17). In *Xenoblade Chronicles*, it is Shulk's wish to create a world with no need for gods. It is Japan's rebirth into modernity envisioned as myth – a mediatized analogue to the telling and retelling of the copper factory parable. God-slayer games fulfil the human craving for meaningful metanarrative – for interactive, playable parables, for the experience that one's actions find significance in a larger story (Newgren 2010, 138). As Rachel Wagner writes, video games are among the 'most powerful and poignant new modes of myth making today' (Wagner 2014, 110). Through cultural-historical semiosis, we see the god-slayer trope not as a rejection of the divine, but rather the embrace of all that is human. In the death of god – or rather, a particular conception of divinity – we find a resurrection of humanity undaunted by its limitations and finitude and instead empowered by them. And, as in *Lightning Returns* and *Xenoblade*, it is often music that serves as 'the bridge between our world and the gameworld' – the key to unlocking our own interpretative interactivity as listeners and players (Greenfield-Casas 2017, 32). This and the previous chapter have demonstrated using narrative, theological, sociocultural and musical analysis that the religious messages communicated through video games and their music are nuanced, complex ones. The meanings of the god-slayer narrative trope, invoking Catholic Christian musical and theological associations in Japan-produced video games, are not reducible to a clear East/West binary – it signifies in both socio-religious contexts at once. The critique of a stoic, impassable Christian God in *Lightning Returns* encodes a parallel renunciation of a remote, inaccessible god-Emperor mediated only through the shogun and other state officials. The quasi-Nietzschean, deicidal slaying of Zanza in *Xenoblade Chronicles* represents the dissolution of *sonnō jōi* – the ideological foundation of the Emperor worship cult and the Japanese imperialist state. And Lightning's and Shulk's wish to rebuild a world with no need for gods articulates Emperor Hirohito's egalitarian vision in the Jewel Voice Broadcast and subsequent New Year's Rescript. Just as the sound of Emperor Hirohito's voice reshaped his listeners' worldview, so too does video games' music exert a far-reaching influence on the beliefs of its players.

NOTES

*   Standalone illustration files of Figures 8.1 and 8.2 can be found under the Front Matter section for *Gender, Race and Religion in Video Game Music's* page on Intellect Discover.

1.   While *gyokuon* is etymologically composed of the *kanji* for 'jewel' or 'ball' (玉, commonly read as *tama*) and that of 'sound' or 'noise' (音, typically read as *oto*), the two together are idiomatically understood to refer to a beautiful sound (such as a musical instrument or voice) or, in a narrower range of meaning, the emperor's voice. Since emperors did not typically address the public before Hirohito, it is likely the 15 August 1945 broadcast that prompted the specific association between gyokuon and the emperor's voice. In other words, the Jewel Voice Broadcast was so impactful in Japanese public consciousness that this idiom came particularly to signify the emperor's voice speaking to common Japanese people.

2.   A non-exhaustive list of topics carrying over from concert music to video game music includes brass fanfares, military marches, the pastoral topical field, sacred music, singing style, waltz and heroic topics. Topics carrying over from film to video game music include the Feminine Romantic Cliché (Chapter 3), 'epic' cinematic sound, horror, the soaring topic (Atkinson 2019) and magical/supernatural. Topics with distinct applications in video game music include battle themes, main menu music, victory themes, overworld themes, game over screen music, combat initiation stingers and tutorial music.

Conclusion:
Enter the Real

'Game Over?' – Immersion, Interactivity,
Interpretation, Identity

Gender, Race and Religion in Video Game Music began with a bold promise: to set forth a robust answer to the question 'why do video games matter?' Although many compelling answers affirming video games' significance could be given, this book's answer could be summarized thusly: video games aesthetically encode identities that matter to real-world players. From gender and race to religion and mental health, video games communicate powerful meanings concerning many of society's most relevant topics. Music – alongside visuals, story and gameplay – is a crucial element that enhances video games' enjoyability, immersion, interactivity and meaning. Through the permeable magic circle of video games, music, like players themselves, brings real-world meanings into the gameworld. The music is never 'only' music, the game is never 'just' a game. Playing a video game entails playing with identity – the players, the characters and other human beings in the real world who may differ from the player. To listen to demographic representation in video game music is to hear the songs, the lives of others. The vocal agency of *Gris* journeys through the process of grief, narratively staging her eventual self-acceptance as a cracked, vulnerable and flawed human being. Noctis' unconventional musical theme reveals his alternative masculinity, and 'Aloy's Theme' represents her non-binary narrative role blurring conventionally feminine and conventionally masculine traits. *Super Mario Odyssey*'s faux-Mariachi betrays Nintendo's pan-Latin approach to Tostarena, while *Overwatch* exemplifies antiracist storytelling by neither exoticizing nor erasing its characters' core cultural identities. And the sonic iconography of the god-slayer trope in *Lightning Returns* and *Xenoblade Chronicles* encodes the descent of the god-Emperor – the most formative event in the making of modern Japan. Far from mere sonic wallpaper, video game music coordinates with its visual, narrative and ludic elements as an equal partner in the creation of meaning. And these multimedia stories, these playable parables – woven in the interpretative interactivity of video game semiosis – speak to the core of what it means to be human.

Every book leaves room for further research, whether taken up by myself or other ludomusicologists. Broadly speaking, these analyses model rigorous semiotic interpretation of video game music across a variety of genres, developers and decades, and I encourage other scholars to adopt a similar semiotic orientation applied to their research topics of choice. Proceeding from the presumption that musical choices are meaningful because they reward interpretative engagement, video games' musical meanings are ripe for semiotic harvest. More specifically, 'interpretative interactivity', 'racialized fantasy', my adaptation of Kendi's segregation-assimilation-antiracism framework and 'sonic iconography' are powerful theoretical concepts that will prove beneficial to other analyses of video game music. Similarly, the articulation of conventionally feminine and conventionally masculine musical traits in Chapter 2 may guide scholarship examining how other character themes present a characterization that conforms to, subverts or transcends gendered musical convention. This research leaves much untilled scholarly ground to others, including the musical construction of conventional femininity, conventional masculinity, alternative femininities and alternative masculinities in American- and European-produced video games and theorizing a musical semiotics of transgender, genderfluid, genderqueer and further non-binary gender expressions. Nor did my research take up musical representation of sexuality and identities relating to sexuality, which is equally deserving of scholarly attention. In cultural and racial representation, exploring the musical representation of Black and Middle Eastern communities is of vital importance, as well as other Latina/o or AAPI nationalities and musical strategies encoding White identity. In religious representation – generally underexplored in ludomusicology compared to gender, culture and race – the use of sacred music from Jewish, Muslim, Hindu, Buddhist and Shinto traditions (among many others) in video games needs theorizing. Lastly, on this non-exhaustive list, musical representation of Christianity – including Protestant and Orthodox Christianity – from the closer cultural proximity of American- or European-produced video games would likewise prove rewarding. All these topics and more would productively expand the study of demographic representation in video game music.

'New Game?' – Playing with Diversity

Much ink in popular and academic writing has been spilled in praise of the potential psychological, social and aesthetic benefits of video games. For Jane McGonigal, video games focus players' energy on achieving goals, providing psychological benefits that counteract depression (McGonigal 2010, 28). For Simon Penny, they are 'powerful inculators of behaviors' with lasting impact outside the game

(Penny 2004, 82). For Edward Castronova, games are 'becoming the most powerful source of personal meaning in the contemporary world' (Castronova 2007, 207). Marie-Laure Ryan describes video games' potential for weaving together immersion, interactivity and narrativity as 'total art' (Ryan 2015, 251, 259). Video games stand to inherit Janet Murray's vision of cyberdrama, which Murray predicts will become the 'most powerful representational medium yet invented' (Murray 1997, 284). For Celia Pearce, video games are the first medium to blur the 'boundary between author and audience so completely' (Pearce 2004, 153). To this chorus of voices, what more is there to add?

Drawing together the diverse (pun intended) threads of this book, let us briefly recapitulate Chapter 6's discussion of diversity. Recall that diversity, at its core, is the embrace of difference, rather than the erasure or exclusion of difference. Diversity is antithetical to discrimination in all its forms, including those thematized throughout the book. Hegemonic masculinity elevates itself over femininities and alternative masculinities – indeed, over any gender expression diverging from established norms. Racism creates a hierarchy from perceived ethnic and cultural differences, codified through racist policies and pseudo-science. And a religious or social institution may suppress and shun religious ideas it perceives as threatening or incompatible, as Tokugawa and post-Meiji officials did to Christianity in Japan. Diversity is an antidote in common for all of these cases – and video games, along with other works of media, participate in fostering cultures of diversity in the real world. Together with the music that in part comprises them, video games bear the potential to manifest representational diversity that counteracts monoculture in all its forms. Representational diversity, as distinct from quantitative equity, is concerned with the manner in which difference is portrayed – narratively, visually, ludically and musically. The messages video games and their soundtracks communicate may facilitate or frustrate representational diversity, shaping players' perceptions, beliefs and attitudes towards others who are different.

This emphasis on diversity is intentional, as it provides an alternative vision to another common proposal: 'empathy'. It has been popular to speak of video games as a means for fostering empathy – especially when virtual reality or other strong immersive factors are involved. For example, in a 2015 TED Talk, virtual reality storyteller Chris Milk claimed that VR devices are the 'ultimate empathy machine' (Bollmer 2017, 65), and empathy became a ubiquitous buzzword among journalists and game developers from 2015 to 2020 (Ruberg 2020, 55). The empathy craze in video game development and reception has been roundly critiqued, especially by queer scholars and indie game developers (Ruberg 2020, 59). One reason is that the rhetoric of empathy is ill-defined, used variously as an umbrella term meaning inhabitation, immersion, allyship, compassion, emotional understanding, perspective-taking and identification (Ruberg 2020, 63–64, 67; Schrier and Farber 2021, 203). More damningly, the rhetoric of empathy in video games falsely assumes that through an abbreviated, artificial and partial experience, total understanding of another's subjectivity is possible (Bollmer 2017, 64). The result of using video games as empathy machines is the commodification, appropriation and consumption of marginalized identities for the self-satisfaction of privileged players (Ruberg 2020, 61). Furthermore, when experiencing empathy becomes a prerequisite for acknowledging the Other, identities that cannot be transmitted or packaged for 'universal' consumption are deemed illegitimate (Bollmer 2017, 64).

These critiques of empathy lead Bollmer and Ruberg to nominate an alternative value for video games: radical compassion, an openness to and embrace of the Other despite intractable differences, 'refusing to assimilate the Other' into one's own subjectivity (Bollmer 2017, 74–75; Ruberg 2020, 68). Acknowledgement and embrace of the Other's difference without assimilation into one's own categories and values constitute a conceptual synonym to diversity and antiracism, as explored in Chapter 6. Representing diversity and difference well in video games preserves Otherness as something to embrace with openness and curiosity. Celebrating diversity is its own reward, a sufficient end unto itself. It is not consuming the difference of the Other in the name of 'empathy'. Attuning to diversity in video games means valuing encounters with musical Others as opportunities to stage radical compassion through the permeable magic circle of play. And perhaps, by understanding musical representation in video games, we will become more critical players, listeners, interpreters – and more compassionate members of an increasingly diverse world.

Appendix:
Audiovisual Media

21. 2008. Sony Pictures. Directed by Robert Luketic. 28 March 2008. Film.

Argo. 2012. Directed and Produced by Ben Affleck. 31 August 2012. Film.

Arms. 2017. Nintendo. Music composed by Atsuko Asahi and Yasuaki Iwata. 16 June 2017. Video game.

Avatar: The Last Airbender. 2005–2008. Nickelodeon. Directed by Michael Dante DiMartino and Bryan Konietzko. 21 February 2005–19 July 2008. Television.

Bejeweled 3. 2010. PopCap Games. Music composed by Peter Hajba, Alexander Brandon and Allister Brimble. 7 December 2010. Video game.

BioShock Infinite. 2013. Irrational Games. Music composed by Garry Schyman. 26 March 2013. Video game.

Captain Marvel. 2019. Marvel. Directed by Anna Boden and Ryan Fleck. 27 Feburary 2019. Film.

Catherine. 2011. Atlus. Music composed by Shoji Meguro. 17 February 2011. Video game.

Civilization IV. 2005. Firaxis Games. Music composed by Jeffery L. Briggs. 25 October 2005. Video game.

Civilization V. 2010. Firaxis Games. Music composed by Michael Curran and Geoff Knorr. 21 September 2010. Video game.

Civilization VI. 2016. Firaxis Games. Music composed by Geoff Knorr and Phil Boucher. 21 October 2016. Video game.

Chrono Cross. 1999. Square. Music composed by Yasunori Mitsuda. 18 November 1999. Video game.

Chrono Trigger. 1995. Square. Music composed by Yasunori Mitsuda. 11 March 1995. Video game.

Doctor Strange. 2016. Mravel. Directed by Scott Derrickson. 13 October 2016. Film.

Final Fantasy I. 1987. Square. Music composed by Nobuo Uematsu. 18 December 1987. Video game.

Final Fantasy II. 1988. Square. Music composed by Nobuo Uematsu. 17 December 1988. Video game.

Final Fantasy III. 1990. Square. Music composed by Nobuo Uematsu. 27 April 1990. Video game.

Final Fantasy IV. 1991. Square. Music composed by Nobuo Uematsu. 19 July 1991. Video game.

Final Fantasy V. 1992. Square. Music composed by Nobuo Uematsu. 6 December 1992. Video game.

Final Fantasy VI. 1994. Square. Music composed by Nobuo Uematsu. 2 April 1994. Video game.

Final Fantasy VII. 1997. Square. Music composed by Nobuo Uematsu. 31 January1997. Video game.

Final Fantasy VIII. 1999. Square. Music composed by Nobuo Uematsu. 11 February 1999. Video game.

Final Fantasy IX. 2000. Square. Music composed by Nobuo Uematsu. 7 July 2000. Video game.

Final Fantasy X. 2001. Square. Music composed by Nobuo Uematsu, Junya Nakano and Masashi Hamauzu. 19 July 2001. Video game.

Final Fantasy XII. 2006. Square Enix. Music composed by Hitoshi Sakimoto. 16 March 2006. Video game.

Final Fantasy XIII. 2009. Square Enix. Music composed by Masashi Hamauzu. 17 December 2009. Video game.

Final Fantasy XV. 2016. Square Enix. Music composed by Yoko Shimomura. 29 November 2016. Video game.

Ghost in the Shell. 2017. Directed by Rupert Sanders. 16 March 2017. Film.

God of War. 2018. Santa Monica Studio. Music composed by Bear McCreary. 20 April 2018. Video game.

Gris. 2018. Nomada Studio. Music composed by Berlinist. 13 December 2018. Video game.

Horizon Forbidden West. 2022. Guerrilla Games. Music composed by Joris de Man. 18 February 2022. Video game.

Horizon Zero Dawn. 2017. Guerrilla Games. Music composed by Joris de Man. 28 February 2017. Video game.

Journey. 2012. Thatgamecompany. Music composed by Austin Wintory. 13 March 2012. Video game.

Lightning Returns: Final Fantasy XIII. 2013. Music composed by Naoshi Mizuta, Mitsuto Suzuki and Masashi Hamauzu. 21 November 2013. Video game.

Ori and the Blind Forest. 2015. Moon Studios. Music composed by Gareth Coker. 11 March 2015. Video game.

Ouran High School Host Club. 2006. Bones Inc. Anime television series.

Overwatch. 2015. Blizzard Entertainment. Music composed by Derek Duke. 24 May 2016. Video game.

Overwatch 2. 2022. Blizzard Entertainment. Music composed by Derek Duke. 4 October 2022. Video game.

Madame Butterfly. 1915. Paramount Pictures. Directed by Sidney Olcott. 7 November 1915. Film.

Persona 5. 2016. Atlus. Music composed by Shoji Meguro. 15 September 2016. Video game.

Prince of Persia: The Sands of Time. 2010. Jerry Bruckheimer. Directed by Mike Newell. 9 May 2010. Film.

APPENDIX

Raji: An Ancient Epic. 2020. Nodding Heads Games. Music composed by Linos Tzelos. 18 August 2020. Video game.

Second Life. 2003. Linden Lab. 23 June 2003. Video game.

Silent Hill. 1999. Konami. Music composed by Akria Yamaoka. 23 February 1999. Video game.

Sim City. 1989. Maxis. Directed by Will Wright. 2 February 1989. Video game.

Spacewar! 1962. Programmed by Steve Russell. April 1962. Video game.

Super Mario Bros. 1985. Nintendo. Music composed by Koji Kondo. 13 September 1985. Video game.

Super Mario Odyssey. 2017. Nintendo. Music composed by Naoto Kubo, Shiho Fujii and Koji Kondo. 27 October 2017. Video game.

Super Mario World. 1990. Nintendo. Music composed by Koji Kondo. 21 November 1990. Video game.

Super Smash Bros. Ultimate. 2018. Nintendo. Music composed by Hideki Sakamoto and various arrangements. 7 December 2018. Video game.

The Last of Us Part II. 2020. Naughty Dog. Music composed by Gustavo Santaolalla. 19 June 2020. Video game.

The Legend of Zelda. 1986. Nintendo. Music composed by Koji Kondo. 21 February 1986. Video game.

The Legend of Zelda: Skyward Sword. 2011. Nintendo. Music composed by Hajime Wakai, Shiho Fujii, Mahito Yokoto and Takeshi Hama. 18 November 2011. Video game.

The Lord of the Rings Online. 2007. Standing Stone Games. 24 April 2007. Video game.

The Matrix. 1999. Warner Bros. Studios. Directed by the Wachowskis. 24 March 1999. Film.

The Sims. 2000. Maxis. Directed by Will Wright. 4 February 2000. Video game.

Tennis for Two. 1958. Programmed by William Higinbotham. 18 October 1958. Video game.

Xenoblade Chronicles. 2010, remake 2020. Music composed by Yoko Shimomura. 10 June 2010. Video game.

References

#Asians4BlackLives. 2020. 'Asians 4 Black Lives: Structural Racism is the Pandemic, Interdependence and Solidarity is the Cure'. *#Asians4BlackLives*. https://medium.com/@asians4blacklives/asians-4-black-lives-structural-racism-is-the-pandemic-interdependence-and-solidarity-is-the-cure-9162167d92e1. Accessed 26 February 2024.

Aang Aint White. 2008. 'Saving the World with Postage'. *Saving the World With Postage*, 11 December. http://aang-aint-white.livejournal.com/646.html. Accessed 26 February 2024.

Aarseth, Espen. 2004. 'Genre Trouble: Narrativism and the Art of Simulation'. In *First Person: New Media as Story, Performance, and Game*, edited by Noah Wardrip-Fruin and Pat Harrigan, 45–55. Cambridge, MA: MIT Press.

Anatone, Richard. 2021. 'Identity Crisis: Trauma, Memory Error, and Thematic Disassociation in the *FInal Fantasy* Series'. Paper presented at the *North American Conference on Video Game Music*, Virtual Conference, 12 June.

Anatone, Richard, ed. 2022. *The Music of Nobuo Uematsu in the Final Fantasy Series*. Bristol: Intellect.

Anderson, Eric. 2018. 'Inclusivity Masculinity Theory'. In *Unmasking Masculinities: Men and Society*, edited by Edward W. Morris and Freeden Blume Oeur, 38–44. Los Angeles: SAGE Publications.

Anderson-Barkley, Taylor and Kira Foglesong. 2018. 'Activism in Video Games: A New Voice for Social Change'. In *Woke Gaming: Digital Challenges to Oppression and Social Injustice*, edited by Kishonna L. Gray and Leonard David, 252–69. Seattle: University of Washington Press.

André, Naomi. 2006. *Voicing Gender: Castrati, Travesti, and the Second Woman in Early-Nineteenth-Century Italian Opera*. Bloomington: Indiana University Press.

Angles, Jeffrey. 2011. *Writing the Love of Boys: Origins of Bishōnen Culture in Modernist Japanese Literature*. Minneapolis: University of Minnesota Press.

Anon. 1945. 'Japan: The God-Emperor'. *Time* 45, no. 21, 21 May 1945: 35.

Atkinson, Sean. 2019. 'Soaring Through the Sky: Topics and Tropes in Video Game Music'. *Music Theory Online* 25, no. 2. http://www.mtosmt.org/issues/mto.19.25.2/mto.19.25.2.atkinson.php. Accessed 22 December 2023.

Atkinson, Sean. 2022. 'That Tune Really Holds the Game Together: Thematic Families in *Final Fantasy IX*'. In *The Music of Nobuo Uematsu in the Final Fantasy Series*, edited by Richard Anatone, 130–51. Bristol: Intellect.

Bailey, Kat. 2013. 'Lightning Returns: Carrying the Adventure Solo as Final Fantasy's 'First Female Protagonist'. *Engadget*, 18 January 2013. https://www.engadget.com/2013-01-18-lightning-returns-carrying-the-adventure-solo-as-final-fantasy.html#:~:text=Lightning%20 is%20Final%20Fantasy's%20first,her%20roots%20as%20an%20esper. Accessed 22 December 2023.

Bainbridge, William Sims. 2013. *eGods: Faith Versus Fantasy in Computer Gaming*. Oxford: Oxford University Press.

Balint, Peter and Patti Tamara Lenard. 2020. 'What is (the Wrong of) Cultural Appropriation?' *Ethnicities* 20, no. 2: 331–52. https://doi.org/10.1177/1468796819866498.

Barro, Robert, Jason Hwang and Rachel McCleary. 2010. 'Religious Conversion in 40 Countries'. *Journal for the Scientific Study of Religion* 49, no. 1: 15–36.

Barthes, Roland. 1977. 'The Death of the Author'. Translated by Stephen Heath. *Image, Music, Text*, 142–48. New York: Hill and Wang.

Battistella, Edwin L. 1990. *Markedness: The Evaluative Superstructure of Language*. New York: State University of New York Press.

Baugh, Bruce. 1993. 'Prolegomena to Any Aesthetics of Rock Music'. *Journal of Aesthetics and Art Criticism* 51, no. 1: 23–29. https://www.jstor.org/stable/431967. Accessed 26 February 2024.

Begbie, Jeremy. 2000. *Music, Theology and Time*. Cambridge: Cambridge University Press.

Begbie, Jeremy and Steven R. Guthrie, eds. 2011. *Resonant Witness: Conversations Between Music and Theology*. Grand Rapids: William B. Eerdmans Publishing Company.

Behm-Morawitz, Elizabeth and David Ta. 2014. 'Cultivating Virtual Stereotypes?: The Impact of Video Game Play on Racial/Ethnic Stereotypes'. *Howard Journal of Communications* 25, no. 1: 1–15. https://doi.org/10.1080/10646175.2013.835600.

Bellman, Jonathan. 1998. 'The Hungarian Gypsies and the Poetics of Exclusion'. In *The Exotic in Western Music*, edited by Jonathan Bellman, 74–103. Boston: Northeastern University Press.

Benne, Junae. 2017. 'Twintelle Brings Black Girl Magic to Nintendo'. *Black Girl Nerds*. https://blackgirlnerds.com/twintelle-brings-black-girl-magic-arms-nintendo/. Accessed 22 December 2023.

Bird, Sharon R. 2018. 'Welcome to the Men's Club: Homosociality and the Maintenance of Hegemonic Masculinity'. In *Unmasking Masculinities: Men and Society*, edited by Edward W. Morris and Freeden Blume Oeur, 14–23. Los Angeles: SAGE Publications.

Blackmer, Corinne E. and Patricia Juliana Smith, eds. 1995. *En Travesti: Women, Gender Subversion, Opera*. New York: Columbia University Press.

Bleich, Susan, Dolf Zillman and James Weaver. 1991. 'Enjoyment and Consumption of Defiant Rock Music as a Function of Adolescent Rebelliousness'. *Journal of Broadcasting and Electronic Media* 35, no. 3: 351–66. https://doi-org/10.1080/08838159109364130.

Blistein, Jon. 2021. 'Billy Porter Says Harry Styles Takes Wearing Dresses Too Lightly: "This Is My Life"'. *Rolling Stone*, 18 October. https://www.rollingstone.com/music/music-news/billy-porter-harry-styles-vogue-cover-fashion-1243781. Accessed 22 December 2023.

REFERENCES

Blizzard. 2021. 'Overwatch – Heroes'. https://overwatch.blizzard.com/en-us/heroes/. Accessed 2 June 2021.

Bollmer, Grant. 2017. 'Empathy Machines'. *Media International Australia* 165, no. 1: 63–76. https://doi.org/10.1177/1329878X17726794.

Bonds, Mark Evan. 2014. *Absolute Music: The History of an Idea*. Oxford: Oxford University Press.

Brito, Christopher. 2020. 'Bishop Blasts Trump for Staging Visit to Church after Protesters Were Tear-Gassed'. *CBS News*, 2 June. https://www.cbsnews.com/news/trump-st-johns-church-visit-staging-bishop-mariann-budde/. Accessed 22 December 2023.

Brock, André. 2011. '"When Keeping It Real Goes Wrong": Resident Evil 5, Racial Representation, and Gamers'. *Games and Culture* 6, no. 5: 429–52. https://doi-org/10.1177/1555412011402676.

Brooks, Dwight and Lisa Hébert. 2006. 'Gender, Race, and Media Representation'. In *The SAGE Handbook of Gender and Communication*, edited by Bonnie J. Dow and Julia T. Wood, 297–318. Los Angeles, CA: SAGE Publications.

Brown, Julie. 2000. 'Bartók, the Gypsies, and Hybridity in Music'. In *Western Music and its Others: Difference, Representation, and Appropriation in Music*, edited by Georgina Born and David Hesmondhalgh, 123–42. Berkeley: University of California Press.

Bruin-Molé, Megen de. 2018. 'Space Bitches, Witches, and Kick-Ass Princesses'. In *Star Wars and the History of Transmedia Storytelling*, edited by Sean Guynes and Dan Hassler-Forest, 225–40. Amsterdam: Amsterdam University Press.

Brunk, Conrad Grebel and James Young. 2012. *The Ethics of Cultural Appropriation*. Chichester: Wiley-Blackwell.

Brusuelas, Candice. 2018. 'Why Horizon: Zero Dawn is a Breakthrough for Feminist Gaming'. *Medium*. 17 July. https://medium.com/@cbrucewillis/why-horizon-zero-dawn-is-a-breakthrough-in-feminist-gaming-4164a1b6ed7e. Accessed 22 December 2023.

Burgess, Melinda C. R., Karen E. Dill, Paul S. Stermer, Stephen R. Burgess and Brian P. Brown. 2011. 'Playing with Prejudice: The Prevalence and Consequences of Racial Stereotypes in Video Games'. *Media Psychology* 14, no. 3: 289–311. http://www.tandfonline.com/doi/abs/10.1080/15213269.2011.596467. Accessed 22 December 2023.

Buschmeyer, Anna. 2013. 'The Construction of "Alternative Masculinity" Among Men in the Childcare Profession'. *International Review of Sociology* 23, no. 2: 290–309. http://www.tandfonline.com/doi/abs/10.1080/03906701.2013.804293. Accessed 22 December 2023.

Butler, Judith. 2011. *Bodies that Matter: On the Discursive Limits of Sex*. London: Routledge.

Byford, Sam. 2017. 'Nintendo's Yoshiaki Koizumi on Super Mario Odyssey and the Future of the Switch'. *The Verge*, 28 August. https://www.theverge.com/2017/8/28/16213402/nintendo-yoshiaki-koizumi-super-mario-odyssey-interview-gamescom-2017. Accessed 22 December 2023.

Campbell, Colin. 2017. 'Overwatch's Search for Diversity'. *Polygon*, 20 March. https://www.polygon.com/features/2017/3/20/14960924/overwatch-diversity-jeff-kaplan-interview-blizzard. Accessed 22 December 2023.

Campbell, Heidi and Gregory Price Grieve, eds. 2014. *Playing with Religion in Digital Games*. Bloomington: Indiana University Press.

Carabí, Angels and Josep María Armengol, eds. 2014. *Alternative Masculinities for a Changing World*. New York: Palgrave Macmillan.

Cardy, Simon. 2020. 'Overwatch Review (2020 Update)'. *IGN*, 19 May. https://www.ign.com/articles/overwatch-review-2020-update. Accessed 22 December 2023.

Carpentier, Francesca Dillman, Silvia Knoblock and Dolf Zillmann. 2003. 'Rock, Rap, and Rebellion: Comparisons of Traits Predicting Selective Exposure to Defiant Music'. *Personality and Individual Differences* 35: 1643–55. https://doi.org/10.1016/S0191-8869(02)00387-2.

Carr, Diane. 2007. 'The Trouble With Civilization'. In *Videogame, Player, Text*, edited by Barry Atkins and Tanya Krzywinska, 222–36. Manchester: Manchester University Press.

Castronova, Edward. 2005. *Synthetic Worlds: The Business and Culture of Online Games*. Chicago: University of Chicago Press.

Castronova, Edward. 2007. *Exodus to the Virtual World: How Online Fun is Changing Reality*. New York: St. Martin's Griffin.

Chalfant, Morgan. 2020. 'White House Compares Trump's Church Visit to Churchill'. *The Hill*, 3 June. https://thehill.com/homenews/administration/500977-white-house-compares-trumps-church-visit-to-churchill/. Accessed 22 December 2023.

Chan, Khee Hoon. 2017. 'The Uncomfortable Racial Stereotypes in ARMS and Videogames'. *Unwinnable*, 7 November. https://unwinnable.com/2017/11/07/the-uncomfortable-racial-stereotypes-in-arms-and-videogames/. Accessed 22 December 2023.

Chen, Wei-Huan. 2017. 'Fear of a Feminist Hero: Horizon Zero Dawn'. *Houston Chronicle*, 27 March. https://www.houstonchronicle.com/local/gray-matters/article/Fear-of-a-feminist-hero-Horizon-Zero-Dawn-11027667.php#:~:text=Aloy%20is%2C%20in%20other%20words,in%20a%20mainstream%20video%20game. Accessed 22 December 2023.

Cheng, William. 2014. *Sound Play: Video Games and the Musical Imagination*. Oxford: Oxford University Press.

Chhibber, Preeti. 2020. 'Raji Harnesses Hindu Stories, Creating a Grand Narrative'. *Polygon*, 2 October. https://www.polygon.com/2020/10/2/21494483/raji-an-ancient-epic-nintendo-switch-hinduism-india. Accessed 22 December 2023.

Choi, Yeomi, Janine Sakiko Slaker and Nida Ahmad. 2020. 'Deep Strike: Playing Gender in the World of Overwatch and the Case of Geguri'. *Feminist Media Studies* 20, no. 8: 1128–43. https://www.tandfonline.com/doi/full/10.1080/14680777.2019.1643388. Accessed 22 December 2023.

CIA. 2023. 'Japan'. *CIA: The World Factbook*, updated 13 June. https://www.cia.gov/the-world-factbook/countries/japan/#people-and-society. Accessed 28 June 2023.

Collins, Karen. 2008. *Game Sound: An Introduction to the History, Theory, and Practice of Video Game Music and Sound Design*. Cambridge, MA: MIT Press.

Collins, Karen. 2013. *Playing with Sound: A Theory of Interacting with Sound and Music in Video Games*. Cambridge, MA: MIT Press.

REFERENCES

Colp, Tyler. 2021. 'It's Tough to Defend Overwatch, but It's Still Unparalleled'. *Wired*, 29 May. https://www.wired.com/story/overwatch-five-years-comparison-lookback/. Accessed 22 December 2023.

Cone, Edward. 1974. *The Composer's Voice*. Berkeley: University of California Press.

Connell, Raewyn. 2005. *Masculinities*. Cambridge: Polity Press.

Cook, Karen. 2014 'Music, History, and Progress in Sid Meier's Civilization IV'. In *Music in Video Games: Studying Play*, edited by Kevin J. Donnelly, William Gibbons and Neil Learner, 166–79. New York: Routledge.

Copier, Marinka. 2005. 'Connecting Worlds: Fantasy Role-Playing Games, Ritual Acts and the Magic Circle'. In *Changing Views – Worlds in Play: Proceedings of the DiGRA 2005 Conference*. DiGRA. http://www.digra.org/dl/db/06278.50594.pdf. Accessed 22 December 2023.

Corbett, John. 2000. 'Experimental Oriental: New Music and Other Others'. In *Western Music and Its Others: Difference, Representation, and Appropriation in Music*, edited by Georgina Born and David Hesmondhalgh, 163–86. Berkeley: University of California Press.

Crawford, Garry and Victoria K. Gosling. 2009. 'More Than a Game: Sports-Themed Video Games and Player Narratives'. *Sociology of Sport Journal* 26, no. 1: 50–66. https://journals.humankinetics.com/view/journals/ssj/26/1/article-p50.xml. Accessed 22 December 2023.

Crenshaw, Kimberlé. 1989. 'Demarginalizing the Intersection of Race and Sex: A Black Feminist Critique of Antidiscrimination Doctrine, Feminist Theory and Antiracist Politics'. *University of Chicago Legal Forum*, no. 1: 139–67. http://chicagounbound.uchicago.edu/uclf/vol1989/iss1/8. Accessed 22 December 2023.

Cumming, Naomi. 2000. *The Sonic Self: Musical Subjectivity and Signification*. Bloomington: Indiana University Press.

Cumming, Naomi. 2001. 'Semiotics [semiology]'. *Oxford Music Online*, January. https://doi.org/10.1093/gmo/9781561592630.article.49388.

Dammann, Guy. 2015. 'Nobuo Uematsu: The Video Game Composer Shaking up Classical Music'. *The Guardian*, 7 April. https://www.theguardian.com/music/shortcuts/2015/apr/07/nobuo-uematsu-video-game-composer-shaking-classical-music. Accessed 22 December 2023.

D'Anastasio, Cecilia. 2017. 'Blizzard May Have Clarified Pharah's Controversial Background in *Overwatch*'. *Kotaku*, 19 May. https://kotaku.com/blizzard-might-have-clarified-pharahs-controversial-bac-1795377772. Accessed 22 December 2023.

Daniels, Shonte. 2017. 'Twintelle's Hair is an Act of Resistance'. *Paste Magazine*, 7 June. https://www.pastemagazine.com/games/arms/twintelles-hair-is-an-act-of-resistance/. Accessed 22 December 2023.

Dasgupta, Romit. 2013. *Re-Reading the Salaryman in Japan: Crafting Masuclinities*. London: Routledge.

de Wildt, Lars and Stef Aupers. 2017. 'Bibles and *BioShock*: Affording Religious Discussion on Video Game Forums'. *Chi Play*: 463–75.

Dehejia, Vidya. 2007. 'Hinduism and Hindu Art'. *The Met*, February. https://www.metmuseum.org/toah/hd/hind/hd_hind.htm. Accessed 22 December 2023.

Deloria, Philip Joseph. 2004. *Indians in Unexpected Places*. Lawrence: University Press of Kansas.

Demby, Gene. 2010. 'The Unbearable Whiteness of Bending'. *The American Prospect*, 30 June. https://prospect.org/article/unbearable-whiteness-bending./. Accessed 22 December 2023.

Department of Fair Employment & Housing. 2021. 'DFEH Sues California Gamign Companies for Equal Pay Violations, Sex Discrimination, and Sexual Harrassment'. 21 July. https://calcivilrights.ca.gov/wp-content/uploads/sites/32/2021/07/BlizzardPR.7.21.21.pdf. Accessed 22 December 2023.

Dewinter, Jennifer and Carly A. Kocurek. 2017. '"Aw Fuck, I Got a Bitch on My Team!": Women and the Exclusionary Cultures of the Computer Game Complex'. In *Gaming Representation: Race, Gender, and Sexuality in Video Games*, edited by Jennifer Malkowski and TreaAndrea M. Russworm, 57–73. Bloomington: Indiana University Press.

Dick, Alastair. 2001. 'Rāvanhatthā'. *Oxford Music Online*, edited by Neil Sorrell. https://doi.org/10.1093/gmo/9781561592630.article.51708.

Donlan, Christian. 2020. 'Raji: An Ancient Epic Review – A Gorgeous Adventure Through Architecture and Myth'. Eurogamer. 14 October. https://www.eurogamer.net/raji-an-ancient-epic-review-a-gorgeous-adventure-through-architecture-and-myth. Accessed 3 June 2024.

Downey, Jessica Thyst. 2018. 'Why Overwatch's Hero Diversity is Important to the Game'. *Dbltap*, 15 June. https://www.dbltap.com/posts/6091187-why-overwatch-s-hero-diversity-is-important-to-the-game. Accessed 22 December 2023.

Droumeva, Milena. 2018. 'From Sirens to Cyborgs: The Media Politics of the Female Voice in Games and Game Cultures'. In *Feminism in Play*, edited by Kishonna L. Gray, Gerald Voorhees and Emma Vossen, 51–68. Cham: Palgrave Macmillan.

Du Mez, Kristin Kobes. 2020. *Jesus and John Wayne: How White Evangelicals Corrupted a Faith and Fractured a Nation*. New York: Liverlight Publishing.

Dwyer, Colin. 2020. '"Black Lives Matter Plaza," Across from White House, Is Christened By D.C. Leaders'. *NPR*, 5 June. https://www.npr.org/sections/live-updates-protests-for-racial-justice/2020/06/05/870833518/black-lives-matter-plaza-across-from-white-house-is-christened-by-d-c-leaders. Accessed 22 December 2023.

Eck, Diana L. 2002. 'Darshan'. In *Religion, Art, & Visual Culture: A Cross-Cultural Reader*, edited by S. Brent Plate, 171–75. New York: Palgrave.

Elven, Julie. n.d. 'Credits & Industry Voices'. Professional Website. https://www.julieelven.com/credits. Accessed 22 December 2023.

Entertainment Software Association. 2017. '2017 Essential Facts about the Computer and Video Game Industry'. https://www.theesa.com/resource/2017-essential-facts-about-the-computer-and-video-game-industry/. Accessed 22 December 2023.

Entertainment Software Association. 2022. '2022 Essential Facts about the Video Game Industry'. https://www.theesa.com/resource/2022-essential-facts-about-the-video-game-industry/. Accessed 22 December 2023.

Eskelinen, Markku. 2001. 'The Gaming Situation'. *The International Journal of Computer Game Research* 1, no. 1. http://www.gamestudies.org/0101/eskelinen/. Accessed 22 December 2023.

REFERENCES

Eskelinen, Markku. 2004. 'Towards Computer Game Studies'. In *First Person: New Media as Story, Performance, and Game*, edited by Noah Wardrip-Fruin and Pat Harrigan, 36–44. Cambridge, MA: MIT Press.

Ewell, Philip. 2020. 'How We Got Here, Where To Next: Examining Assimilationism in American Music Studies'. *The University of Texas at Austin Butler School of Music*, 9 November. Virtual Presentation.

Ewell, Philip. 2023. *On Music Theory: And Making Music More Welcoming For Everyone*. Ann Arbor: University of Michigan Press.

Fahey, Mike. 2016. 'Hindu Leader Wants Blizzard To Drop Symmetra's Devi Skin From *Overwatch*'. *Kotaku*, 16 July. https://kotaku.com/hindu-leader-wants-blizzard-to-drop-symmetras-devi-skin-1783782164. Accessed 22 December 2023.

Fang, Jenn. 2018. 'Yellowface, Whitewashing, and the History of White People Playing Asian Characters'. *Teen Vogue*, 8 August. https://www.teenvogue.com/story/yellowface-whitewashing-history. Accessed 22 December 2023.

Fiore, Marissa. 2019. 'What's Happening to Overwatch and Its Diversity?' *HPCritical*, 26 July. https://www.hpcritical.com/all-post/2019/7/25/what-happened-to-overwatch-and-its-diversity. Accessed 22 December 2023.

Fisher, Max. 2012. 'The Emperor's Speech: 67 Years Ago, Hirohito Transformed Japan Forever'. *The Atlantic*, 15 August. https://www.theatlantic.com/international/archive/2012/08/the-emperors-speech-67-years-ago-hirohito-transformed-japan-forever/261166/. Accessed 22 December 2023.

Flood, Michael. 2014. 'Men's Antiviolence Activism and the Construction of Gender-Equitable Masculinities'. In *Alternative Masculinities for a Changing World*, edited by Àngels Carabí and Josep M. Armengol, 35–50. New York: Palgrave Macmillan.

Fordyce, Robbie, Timothy Neale and Thomas Apperley. 2018. 'Avatars: Addressing Racism and Racialized Address'. In *Feminism in Play*, edited by Kishonna L. Gray, Gerald Voorhees and Emma Vossen, 233–51. Cham: Palgrave Macmillan.

Fortescue, Adrian. 1910. 'Veneration of Images'. In *The Catholic Encyclopedia*, vol. 7. New York: Robert Appleton Company. https://www.newadvent.org/cathen/07664a.htm. Accessed 22 December 2023.

Frasca, Gonzalo. 1999. 'Ludology Meets Narratology: Similitude and Differences Between (Video)Games and Narrative'. *Ludology.org*. https://ludology.typepad.com/weblog/articles/ludology.htm. Accessed 26 July 2023.

Frasca, Gonzalo. 2004. 'Videogames of the Oppressed: Critical Thinking, Education, Tolerance, and Other Trivial Issues'. In *First Person: New Media as Story, Performance, and Game*, edited by Noah Wardrip-Fruin and Pat Harrigan, 85–94. Cambridge, MA: MIT Press.

Frazier, Jessica. 2014. 'Hinduism – Visual Art and Architecture'. In *The Oxford Handbook of Religion and the Arts*, edited by Frank Burch Brown, 350–57. Oxford: Oxford University Press. https://doi.org/ 10.1093/oxfordhb/9780195176674.013.024.

GENDER, RACE AND RELIGION IN VIDEO GAME MUSIC

Freedman, Alisa and Kristina Iwata-Weickgenannt. 2011. '"Count What You Have Now. Don't Count What You Don't Have": The Japanese Television Drama Around 40 and the Politics of Women's Happiness'. *Asian Studies Review* 35, no. 3: 295–313. http://www.tandfonline.com/doi/abs/10.1080/10357823.2011.602042. Accessed 22 December 2023.

Frith, Simon. 2000. 'The Discourse of World Music'. In *Western Music and Its Others: Difference, Representation, and Appropriation in Music*, edited by Georgina Born and David Hesmondhalgh, 305–22. Berkeley: University of California Press.

Frühstück, Sabine. 2011. 'After Heroism: Must Real Soldiers Die?' In *Recreating Japanese Men*, edited by Sabine Frühstück and Anne Walthall, 76–92. Berkeley: University of California Press.

Frühstück, Sabine and Anne Walthall, eds. 2011. *Recreating Japanese Men*. Berkeley: University of California Press.

Frushtick, Russ. 2016. 'Overwatch Review'. *Polygon*, 27 May. https://www.polygon.com/2016/5/27/11797672/overwatch-review. Accessed 22 December 2023.

Fülöp, Rebecca. 2012. 'Heroes, Dames, and Damsels in Distress: Constructing Gender Types in Classical Hollywood Film Music'. Ph.D. diss., University of Michigan, Ann Arbor. ProQuest Dissertations & Theses Global.

Gaijin Goombah. 2017a. 'Super Mario Odyssey's INSANE Japanese References! (pt -1)'. 18 November. https://youtu.be/Aqz4Ee9WyK0. Accessed 22 December 2023.

Gaijin Goombah. 2017b. 'Super Mario Odyssey's INSANE Japanese References (pt -2)'. 30 November. https://youtu.be/WIuoCqAWL9w. Accessed 22 December 2023.

Gamebyte. 2020. 'Representing the Myths, Stories & Culture of India in Raji: An Ancient Epic – A Developer Interview'. *Lara Jackson*, 20 September. https://www.gamebyte.com/representing-the-myths-stories-culture-of-india-in-raji-an-ancient-epic-a-developer-interview/. Accessed 22 December 2023.

Game Developer. 2020. 'Raji: An Ancient Epic & Crossing the Finish Line'. *Brandon Pham*, 17 December. https://www.gamedeveloper.com/business/raji-an-ancient-epic-crossing-the-finish-line. Accessed 22 December 2023.

GameZone 2012. '*Final Fantasy XIII* Japanese Release Date, the Lightning/Cloud Connection, and More', 4 May. https://www.gamezone.com/originals/final-fantasy-xiii-japanese-release-date-the-lightning-cloud-connection-and-more/. Accessed 22 December 2023.

Gandolfi, Enrico and Francesca Antonacci. 2020. 'Beyond Evil and Good in Online Gaming: An Analysis of Violence in "Overwatch" Between Demonization and Proactive Values'. *Journal of Virtual Worlds Research* 13, no. 1: 1–15.

Garcia, Janet. 2018. 'Super Mario Odyssey: Mario's Mexican Outfit is a Tired Stereotype'. *NerdMuch?* 20 October. https://www.nerdmuch.com/mexican-mario/. Accessed 22 December 2023.

Garcia, Janet. 2019. 'ARMs' Twintelle: Simultaneously Sexualized and Empowered'. *NerdMuch?* 15 January. https://www.nerdmuch.com/games/arms-twintelle/. Accessed 22 December 2023.

Geier, Caitlin. 2019. 'The Disappointing Lack of Female Body Diversity in Overwatch'. 10 May. http://www.caitlingeier.com/the-disappointing-lack-of-female-body-diversity-in-overwatch/. Accessed 22 December 2023.

REFERENCES

Gibbons, William. 2017. 'Music, Genre, and Natonality in the Postmillennial Fantasy Role-Playing Game'. In *The Routledge Companion to Screen Music and Sound*, edited by M. Mera, R. Sadoff and B. Winters, 412–27. New York: Routledge.

Gibbons, William. 2018. *Unlimited Replays: Video Games and Classical Music*. Oxford: Oxford University Press.

Gibbons, William and Steven Reale, eds. 2020. *Music in the Role-Playing Game*. New York: Routledge.

Gibson, William. 1984. *Neuromancer*. New York: Ace.

Glick, Peter and Susan Tufts Fiske. 1997. 'Hostile and Benevolent Sexism: Measuring Ambivalent Sexist Attitudes Toward Women'. *Psychology of Women Quarterly* 21, no. 1: 119–35.

González, Brittany. 2021. 'Blizzard and Overwatch Continue to Fail Black Women'. *Hotspawn*, 22 July. https://www.hotspawn.com/overwatch/news/blizzard-and-overwatch-continue-to-fail-black-women. Accessed 22 December 2023.

Gorbman, Claudia. 1987. *Unheard Melodies: Narrative Film Music*. Bloomington: Indiana University Press.

Gorbman, Claudia. 2000. 'Scoring the Indian: Music in the Liberal Western'. In *Western Music and Its Others: Difference, Representation, and Appropriation in Music*, edited by Georgina Born and David Hesmondhalgh, 234–53. Berkeley: University of California Press.

Goto, Shihoko. 2014. 'Hirohito's Long Shadow: Hirohito's Descendants Remain Committed to Japan's Traditional Values, Which Desperately Need Reform'. *The Wilson Quarterly* 38, no. 3. https://www.wilsonquarterly.com/quarterly/_/hirohitos-long-shadow. Accessed 22 December 2023.

Gramuglia, Anthony. 2020. 'Nintendo Missed a BIG Opportunity by Skipping Twintelle for Smash'. *CBR*, 9 June. https://www.cbr.com/nintendo-missed-big-opportunity-skipping-twintelle-smash/. Accessed 22 December 2023.

Grasso, Julianne. 2020. 'Video Game Music, Meaning, and the Possibilities of Play'. Ph.D. diss., University of Chicago, Chicago. ProQuest Dissertations & Theses Global.

Gray, Kishonna L., Gerald Voorhees and Emma Vossen, eds. 2018. *Feminism in Play*. Cham: Palgrave Macmillan.

Gray, Kishonna L. and Leonard David, eds. 2018. *Woke Gaming: Digital Challenges to Oppression and Social Injustice*. Seattle: University of Washington Press.

Greenbaum, Aaron. 2022. 'Horizon Forbidden West: The Strange Reasons Why the Sequel is Being Review Bombed'. *Den of Geek*, 23 February. https://www.denofgeek.com/games/horizon-forbidden-west-controversies-sequel-review-bomb-user-scores/. Accessed 22 December 2023.

Greenfield-Casas, Stefan X. 2017. 'Between Worlds: Music Allegory in *Final Fantasy X*'. M.Mus. thesis, The University of Texas at Austin, Austin TX. ProQuest Dissertations & Theses Global.

Groes-Green, Christian. 2012. 'Philogynous Masculinities: Contextualizing Alternative Manhood in Mozambique'. *Men and Masculinities* 15, no. 2: 91–111. http://journals.sagepub.com/doi/10.1177/1097184X11427021. Accessed 22 December 2023.

Haley, Susan and James O. Young. 2012. '"Nothing Comes from Nowhere": Reflections on Cultural Appropriation as the Representation of Other Culture'. In *The Ethics of Cultural Appropriation*, edited by Conrad Grebel Brunk and James Young, 268–89. Chichester: Wiley-Blackwell.

Hardgrave, Laura. 2015. 'Overwatch: Diversity in Gaming Done Right'. *Den of Geek*, 5 November. https://www.denofgeek.com/games/overwatch-diversity-in-gaming-done-right/. Accessed 22 December 2023.

Harrison, Rebecca. 2019. 'Gender, Race and Representation in the Star Wars Franchise: An Introduction'. *Media Education Journal* 62, no. 2: 16–19.

Haskin, Frederic Jennings. 1905. 'Japan's Divine Rulers: Emperor Held to Be Heaven-Descended and Sacred'. *The Washington Post*, 6 August. ProQuest Historical Newspapers: *The Washington Post*: 51.

Hatten, Robert. 1994. *Musical Meaning in Beethoven: Markedness, Correlation, and Interpretation*. Bloomington: Indiana University Press.

Hatten, Robert. 2004. *Interpreting Musical Gestures, Topics, and Tropes: Mozart, Beethoven, Schubert*. Bloomington: Indiana University Press.

Hatten, Robert. 2014. 'The Troping of Topics in Mozart's Instrumental Works'. In *The Oxford Handbook of Topic Theory*, edited by Danuta Mirka, 514–36. Oxford: Oxford University Press.

Hatten, Robert. 2018. *A Theory of Virtual Agency for Western Art Music*. Bloomington: Indiana University Press.

Hayes, Madsen. 2023. 'Yoshi-P is Right: It's Time to Retire "JRPG"'. *Inverse*, 1 March. https://www.inverse.com/gaming/jrpg-meaning-offensive-naoki-yoshida. Accessed 27 June 2023.

Heng, Geraldine. 2018. *The Invention of Race in the European Middle Ages*. Cambridge: Cambridge University Press.

Henriques, Donald Andrew. 2006. 'Performing Nationalism: Mariachi, Media and the Transformation of a Tradition (1920–1942)'. Ph.D. diss., University of Texas at Austin. ProQuest Dissertations & Theses Global.

Henry, Edward O. 2001. 'India, Subcontinent of'. *Oxford Music Online*. https://doi-org.libweb.lib.utsa.edu/10.1093/gmo/9781561592630.article.43272.

Herring, Cedric and Loren Henderson. 2015. *Diversity in Organizaitons: A Critical Examination*. New York: Routledge.

Hidaka, Tomoko. 2010. *Salaryman Masculinity: The Continuity of and Change in the Hegemonic Masculinity in Japan*. Boston: Brill.

Hilliard, Kyle. 2017. 'Arms' Creators on Twintelle's Popularity and the Strange Lore of the Game's World'. *Game Informer*, 7 June. https://www.gameinformer.com/b/features/archive/2017/06/07/-arms-creators-on-twintelles-popularity-and-the-strange-lore-of-the-games-world-luffy-one-piece.aspx. Accessed 22 December 2023.

Hillier, Brenna. 2011. 'Toriyama: Final Fantasy Leading Ladies' Looks Come Second'. *VG247*, 30 March. https://www.vg247.com/toriyama-final-fantasy-leading-ladies-looks-come-second. Accessed 22 December 2023.

REFERENCES

Hirohito. 1945. 'The Jewel Voice Broadcast'. Atomic Heritage Foundation, https://www.atomicheritage.org/key-documents/jewel-voice-broadcast. Accssed 22 December 2023.

Hirohito. 1946. 'Text of Hirohito New Year Rescript'. *New York Times*, 1 January: 15.

Hodge, Daniel White. 2010. 'Role Playing: Toward a Theology for Gamers'. In *Halos and Avatars: Playing Video Games with God*, edited by Craig Detweiler, 163–75. Louisville: Westminster John Knox Press.

Holland, Samantha. 2004. *Alternative Femininities: Body, Age and Identity*. Oxford: Berg Publishers.

Holt, Kris. 2020. 'Blizzard Releases an "Overwatch" Soundtack That Covers all 21 Maps'. *Engadget*, 13 July. https://www.engadget.com/overwatch-soundtrack-maps-in-game-event-152515487.html. Accessed 22 December 2023.

Hourihane, Colum, ed. 2017. *The Routledge Companion to Medieval Iconography*. London: Routledge.

Huang, Yunte. 2010. *Charlie Chan: The Untold Story of the Honorable Detective and His Rendezvous with American History*. New York: W. W. Norton.

Huizinga, Johan. 1949. *Homo Ludens: A Study of the Play-Element in Culture*. Kettering: Angelico Press.

Hynes-Tawa, Liam. 2021. 'Tonic, Final, Kyū: Tonal Mappings in the Meiji Period and Beyond'. *Analytical Approaches to World Music 9*, no. 1: 1–54. https://iftawm.org/journal/oldsite/articles/2021a/Hynes-Tawa_AAWM_Vol_9_1.pdf. Accessed 22 December 2023.

Jackson, Travis A. 2000. 'Spooning Good Singing Gum: Meaning, Association, and Interpretation in Rock Music'. *Current Musicology* 69: 7–41.

Jander, Owen, John Barry Steane, Ellen T. Harris, Gerald Waldman and Elizabeth Forbes. 2001. 'Mezzo-soprano'. *Oxford Music Online*, January. https://doi.org/10.1093/gmo/9781561592630.article.18571.

Jenkins, Henry. 2004. 'Game Design as Narrative Architecture'. In *First Person: New Media as Story, Performance, and Game*, edited by Noah Wardrip-Fruin and Pat Harrigan, 118–30. Cambridge, MA: MIT Press.

Jenkins, Jack. 2020. 'Ahead of Trump Bible Photo Op, Police Forcibly Expel Priest From St. John's Church Near White House'. *Religion News Service*, 2 June. https://religionnews.com/2020/06/02/ahead-of-trump-bible-photo-op-police-forcibly-expel-priest-from-st-johns-church-near-white-house/. Accessed 22 December 2023.

Johnson, Todd M. 2004. 'Demographic Futures for Christianity and the World Religions'. *Dialog: A Journal of Theology* 43, no. 1: 10–19.

Jones, Camden. 2020. 'Smash Bros Ultimate DLC Could (and Should) Introduce its First Black Character'. *ScreenRant*, 10 June. https://screenrant.com/smash-bros-ultimate-arms-dlc-fighter-black-twintelle/. Accessed 22 December 2023.

Juul, Jesper. 2005. *Half-Real: Video Games Between Real Rules and Fictional Worlds*. Cambridge, MA: MIT Press.

Juul, Jesper. 2008. 'The Magic Circle and the Puzzle Piece'. In *Conference Proceedings of the Philosophy of Computer Games*, edited by Stephan Günzel, Michael Liebe and Dieter Mersch, 56–67. Postdam: Potsdam University Press.

Kain, Erik. 2019. '"Gris" Review: More Than Just a Pretty Coat of Paint'. *Forbes*, 3 January. https://www.forbes.com/sites/games/2019/01/03/gris-review-more-than-just-a-pretty-coat-of-paint/?sh=662b1a741564. Accessed 22 December 2023.

Kaplan, Jeff. 2017. 'Overwatch: How Blizzard Created a Hopeful Vision of the Future'. *DICE Summit*, 22 February. https://youtu.be/5-mh2hJDaGQ. Accessed 22 December 2023.

Kendi, Ibram Xolani. 2019. *How to Be an Antiracist*. New York: One World.

Kenzaburō, Ōe. 2002. 'The Day the Emperor Spoke in a Human Voice'. Translated by John Nathan. *World Literature Today* 76, no. 1: 19–23. https://www.jstor.org/stable/40157002. Accessed 22 December 2023.

Kessler, David. n.d. 'The Five Stages of Grief'. *Information Website*. https://grief.com/the-five-stages-of-grief/. Accessed 22 December 2023.

King, Helen. 2013. *The One-Sex Body on Trial: The Classical and Early Modern Evidence*. London: Routledge.

King, Jade. 2021. 'Overwatch 2 Needs to Treat Its Queer Characters with More Respect'. *The Gamer*, 9 April. https://www.thegamer.com/overwatch-2-needs-to-treat-its-queer-characters-with-more-respect/. Accessed 22 December 2023.

Kokonis, Michalis. 2014. 'Intermediality Between Games and Fictions: The "Ludology vs. Narratology" Debate in Computer Game Studies: A Response to Gonzalo Frasca'. *Film and Media Studies* 9, no. 1: 171–88. https://doi.org/10.1515/ausfm-2015-0009.

Kress, Gunther. 2010. *Multimodality: A Social Semiotic Approach to Contemporary Communication*. New York: Routledge.

Kübler-Ross, Elisabeth and David Kessler. [1969] 2014. *On Grief and Grieving: Finding the Meaning of Grief Through the Five Stages of Loss*. New York: Scribner.

Lacina, Dia. 2019. 'Overwatch's Latest Gay Hero is Great, But Let's Not Praise Blizzard Just Yet'. *Paste*, 9 January. https://www.pastemagazine.com/games/overwatch/overwatchs-latest-gay-hero-is-great-but-lets-not-p/. Accessed 22 December 2023.

Laing, Heather. 2007. *The Gendered Score: Music in 1940s Melodrama and the Women's Film*. Burlington: Ashgate.

Lamerichs, Nicholle. 2021. '[Game Theory] Beauty and Melancholy in Gris'. 22 February. https://nicollelamerichs.com/2021/02/22/game-theory-gris-and-grief-in-games/. Accessed 22 December 2023.

Lawver, Bryan. 2019. 'Overwatch's Idea of Diversity Could Use Some Work'. *ScreenRant*, 25 July. https://screenrant.com/overwatch-diversity-sigma-bare-feet-problem/. Accessed 22 December 2023.

Lee, Jonathan G. 2016. 'The Insight: Is Overwatch Blizzard's Star Wars?' *The New York Videogame Critics Circle*, 11 July. https://nygamecritics.com/2016/07/11/the-insight-is-overwatch-blizzards-star-wars/. Accessed 22 December 2023.

REFERENCES

Leftow, Brian. (2002) 2014. 'Immutability'. *Stanford Encyclopedia of Philosophy*, [1 July] 5 August. https://plato.stanford.edu/entries/immutability/. Accessed 22 December 2023.

Lehman, Frank. 2013. 'Hollywood Cadences: Music and the Structure of Cinematic Expectation'. *Music Theory Online* 19, no. 4. https://www.mtosmt.org/issues/mto.13.19.4/mto.13.19.4.lehman.html. Accessed 26 September 2021.

Longreads. 2016. 'Playing with History: What Sid Meier's Video Game Empire Got Right and Wrong about "Civilization"'. 26 October. https://longreads.com/2016/10/26/what-sid-meiers-video-game-empire-got-right-and-wrong-about-civilization/. Accessed 22 December 2023.

Loughry, Sarah. 2018. 'Video Game Vocalist- Julie Elven'. Cubebrush, 4 September. https://cubebrush.co/blog/gaming-vocal-artist--julie-elven. Accessed 22 December 2023.

Loveridge, Sam. 2017. 'Horizon Zero Dawn – The Feminist Action Game We've Been Waiting For'. *The Guardian*, 31 January. https://www.theguardian.com/technology/2017/jan/31/horizon-zero-dawn-the-feminist-action-game-weve-been-waiting-for. Accessed 22 December 2023.

Lutgendorf, Philip. 2002. 'All in the (Raghu) Family'. In *Religion, Art, & Visual Culture: A Cross-Cultural Reader*, edited by S. Brent Plate, 187–92. New York: Palgrave.

MacDonald, Keza. 2012. 'Xenoblade Chronicles Review'. *IGN*, 3 April. https://www.ign.com/articles/2012/04/03/xenoblade-chronicles-review. Accessed 22 December 2023.

Majewski, John. 2021. 'What Do Players Learn From Videogames?' *The Public Historian* 43, no. 1: 62–81. https://online.ucpress.edu/tph/article/43/1/62/116376/What-Do-Players-Learn-from-Videogames-Historical. Accessed 22 December 2023.

Malaby, Thomas. 2007. 'Beyond Play: A New Approach to Games'. *Games and Culture* 2, no. 2: 95–113. https://doi.org/10.1177/1555412007299434.

Malkowski, Jennifer and TreaAndrea M. Russworm, eds. 2017. *Gaming Representation: Race, Gender, and Sexuality in Video Games*. Bloomington: Indiana University Press.

Mandujano-Salazar, Yunuen Ysela. 2017. 'It is Not That I Can't, It is that I Won't: The Struggle of Japanese Women to Redefine Female Singlehood Through Television Dramas'. *Asian Studies Review* 41, no. 4: 526–43. https://www.tandfonline.com/doi/full/10.1080/1035782 3.2017.1371113. Accessed 22 December 2023.

Marks, Tom. 2016. 'Civ 6's Music Evolves Alongside Your Cities, and It's One of Its Best Features'. *PC Gamer*, 30 September. https://www.pcgamer.com/how-civilization-6s-music-evolves-through-the-eras/. Accessed 22 December 2023.

Martens, Todd. 2020. 'Discover the Joy of a Game That Transports You into the Mythologies of Ancient India'. *Los Angeles Times*, 10 September. https://www.latimes.com/entertainment-arts/story/2020-09-10/discover-the-joy-of-a-game-that-transports-you-into-the-mythologies-of-ancient-india. Accessed 22 December 2023.

Martino, Shannon. 2021. 'Might, Culture, and Archaeology in Sid Meier's Civilization'. *Near Eastern Archaeology* 84, no. 1: 32–43. https://www.journals.uchicago.edu/doi/10.1086/713340. Accessed 22 December 2023.

Mason, Michele M. 2011. 'Empowering the Would-be Warrior: Bushidō and the Gendered Bodies of the Japanese Nation'. In *Recreating Japanese Men*, edited by Sabine Frühstück and Anne Walthall, 68–90. Berkeley: University of California Press.

Mateas, Michael. 2004. 'A Preliminary Poetics for Interactive Drama and Games'. In *First Person: New Media as Story, Performance, and Game*, edited by Noah Wardrip-Fruin and Pat Harrigan, 22–33. Cambridge, MA: MIT Press.

McAlpine, Fraser. 2017. 'The Japanese Obsession with Girl Bands – Explained'. *BBC*, 30 June. https://www.bbc.co.uk/music/articles/84fd62c3-f5a4-49e6-9e3e-6f5217c1448c. Accessed 14 August 2020.

McClary, Susan. 2002. *Feminine Endings: Music, Gender, and Sexuality*. Minneapolis: University of Minnesota Press.

McGee, Jade. 2022. 'The Onna-Musha: Japan's Fearsome Warrior Woman'. *History Guild*. https://historyguild.org/the-onna-musha-japans-fearsome-warrior-women/. Accessed 1 November 2022.

McGonigal, Jane. 2010. *Reality is Broken: Why Games Make Us Better and How They Can Change the World*. New York: Penguin Books.

McLelland, Mark. 2020. 'Bishōnen'. *Japanese Media and Popular Culture (University of Tokyo)*, 25 April. https://jmpc-utokyo.com/keyword/bishonen/. Accessed 19 June 2023.

McMillen, Andrew. 2017. 'The Sleeper Autistic Hero Transforming Video Games'. *Wired*, 12 July. https://www.wired.com/story/the-sleeper-autistic-hero-transforming-video-games/. Accessed 22 December 2023.

McMillan, Emily. 2018. 'Annual Game Music Awards 2017 – Audio of the Year.' *VGM Online*, 8 February. http://www.vgmonline.net/awards2017audio/. Accessed 3 June 2024.

MCV/Develop. 2017. 'Behind the Music of Horizon Zero Dawn'. 26 May. https://www.mcvuk.com/development-news/behind-the-music-of-horizon-zero-dawn/. Accessed 22 December 2023.

Media Action Network for Asian Americans (MANAA). 2010. 'M. Night Shyamalan Misses the Point'. 30 March. http://manaa.blogspot.com/2010/03/m-night-shyamalan-misses-point.html. Accessed 22 December 2023.

Messerschmidt, James W. 2018. *Hegemonic Masculinity: Formulation, Reformulation, and Amplification*. Lanham: Rowman & Littlefield Publishing.

Mol, Angus A. A. and Aris Politopoulos. 2021. 'Persia's Victory: The Mechanics of Orientalism in Sid Meier's Civilization'. *Near Eastern Archaeology* 84, no. 1: 44–51. https://www.journals.uchicago.edu/doi/10.1086/713527. Accessed 22 December 2023.

Mol, Angus A. A., Aris Politopoulos and Csilla E. Ariese-Vandemeulebroucke. 2017. '"From the Stone Age to the Information Age": History and Heritage in Sid Meier's Civilization VI'. *Advances in Archaeological Practice* 5, no. 2: 214–19. https://www.cambridge.org/core/product/identifier/S2326376817000092/type/journal_article. Accessed 22 December 2023.

Moltmann, Jürgen. 1973. *The Crucified God*. Translated by R.A. Wilson and John Bowden. New York: Harper & Row Publishers.

Moltmann, Jürgen. 1980. *The Trinity and the Kingdom*. Translated by Margaret Kohl. Minneapolis: Fortress Press.

REFERENCES

Moltmann, Jürgen. 1985. *God in Creation*. Translated by Margaret Kohl. San Francisco: Harper & Row Publishers.

Monelle, Raymond. 2006. *The Musical Topic: Hunt, Military and Pastoral*. Bloomington: Indiana Universty Press.

Moniuszko, Sara M. 2020. 'Harry Styles Responds to Criticism Over "Vogue" Cover Ballgown: "Bring Back Manly Men"'. *USA Today*, 2 December. https://www.usatoday.com/story/entertainment/celebrities/2020/12/02/harry-styles-talks-vogue-cover-dress-criticism-racial-justice/3794226001/. Accessed 22 December 2023.

Montfort, Nick. 2004. 'Interactive Fiction as "Story," "Game," "Storygame," "Novel," "World," "Literature," "Puzzle," "Problem," "Riddle," and "Machine"'. In *First Person: New Media as Story, Performance, and Game*, edited by Noah Wardrip-Fruin and Pat Harrigan, 310–18. Cambridge, MA: MIT Press.

Moon, Krystyn R. 2004. *Yellowface: Creating the Chiense in American Popular Music and Performance, 1850s–1920s*. New Brunswick: Rutgers University Press.

Morioka, Masahiro. 2013. 'A Phenomenological Study of "Herbivore Men"'. *Review of Life Studies* 4: 1–20.

Morris, Edward W. and Freeden Blume Oeur, eds. 2018. *Unmasking Masculinities: Men and Society*. Los Angeles: SAGE Publications.

Muncy, Julie. 2017. 'Super Mario Odyssey, Like Nintendo's Best Games, Is a Surrealist Triumph'. *Wired*, 26 October. https://www.wired.com/story/super-mario-odyssey-review/. Accessed 22 December 2023.

Murray, Janet. 1997. *Hamlet on the Holodeck: The Future of Narrative in Cyberspace*. New York: The Free Press.

Murray, Janet. 2004. 'From Game-Story to Cyberdrama'. In *First Person: New Media as Story, Performance, and Game*, edited by Noah Wardrip-Fruin and Pat Harrigan, 2–11. Cambridge, MA: MIT Press.

Napier, Susan. 2011. 'Where Have All the Salarymen Gone? Masculinity, Masochism, and Technomobility in Densha Otoko'. In *Recreating Japanese Men*, edited by Sabine Frühstück and Anne Walthall, 154–76. Berkeley: University of California Press.

Newgren, Kevin. 2010. 'BioShock to the System: Smart Choices in Video Games'. In *Halos and Avatars: Playing Video Games with God*, edited by Craig Detweiler, 135–48. Louisville: Westminster John Knox Press.

Nickelodeon Asia. 2005. 'Everything You Ever Wanted to Know About Avatar: The Last Airbender Answered by the Creators, Mike & Bryan!' *NickSplat*, 12 October. https://web.archive.org/web/20071217111256/http://www.nicksplat.com/Whatsup/200510/12000135.html. Accessed 22 December 2023.

Nietzsche, Friedrich. 1974. *The Gay Science*. Translated by Walter Kaufmann. New York: Vintage.

Nintendo. 2022. 'Top Selling Title Sales Units – Nintendo Switch'. 30 June. https://www.nintendo.co.jp/ir/en/finance/software/index.html. Accessed 22 December 2023.

Nintendo UK. 2017. 'Super Mario Odyssey – Luncheon Kingdom Showcase With Yoshiaki Koizumi (Nintendo Switch)'. 23 August. Video, 18:22. https://youtu.be/6UE7gj7wbug. Accessed 22 December 2023.

Nomada Studio. n.d. 'Gris'. Product Website. https://nomada.studio/. Accessed 22 December 2023.

Omi, Michael and Howard Winant. 2015. *Racial Formation in the United States*. New York: Routledge.

Palacios, Alejandro. 2018. 'Super Mario Odyssey: How to Represent a Culture, the Italian Plumber Way'. *Medium*, 5 September. https://medium.com/@alejandropalacios_98575/super-mario-odyssey-how-to-represent-a-culture-the-italian-plumber-way-41469560c367. Accessed 22 December 2023.

Paramore, Kiri. 2010. *Ideology and Christianity in Japan*. London: Routledge.

Pargman, Daniel and Peter Jakobsson. 2008. 'Do You Believe in Magic? Computer Games in Everyday Life'. *European Journal of Cultural Studies* 11, no. 2: 225–44. https://doi.org/10.1177/1367549407088335.

Park, Michael K. 2015. 'Race, Hegemonic Masculinity, and the "Linpossible!": An Analysis of Media Representations of Jeremy Lin'. *Communication & Sport* 3, no. 4: 367–89. https://doi.org/10.1177/2167479513516854.

Pasaribu, Rouli Esther. 2020. 'Freeter, Arafo, House Husband: Shifting Values of Hegemonic Masculinity and Emphasized Femininity in Four Japanese Television Dramas'. *IZUMI* 9, no. 1: 48–57. https://ejournal.undip.ac.id/index.php/izumi/article/view/29419. Accessed 26 February 2024.

Pascoe, Cheri Joe. 2018. 'Look at My Masculinity! Girls Who Act Like Boys'. In *Unmasking Masculinities: Men and Society*, edited by Edward W. Morris and Freeden Blume Oeur: 329–92. Los Angeles: SAGE Publications.

Paulissen, Jarell. 2018. 'The Dark of the Covenant: Christian Imagery, Fundamentalism, and the Relationship Between Science and Religion in the Halo Video Game Series'. *Religions* 9, no. 126: 1–12. https://doi.org/10.3390/rel9040126.

Pearce, Celia. 2004. 'Toward a Game Theory of Game'. In *First Person: New Media as Story, Performance, and Game*, edited by Noah Wardrip-Fruin and Pat Harrigan, 143–53. Cambridge, MA: MIT Press.

Pearlman, Steven Ray. 1988. 'Mariachi Music in Los Angeles'. Ph.D. diss., University of California Los Angeles. ProQuest Dissertations & Theses Global.

Pease, Bob. 2000. *Recreating Men: Postmodern Masculinity Politics*. London: SAGE Publications.

Pease, Bob. 2014. 'Reconstructing Masculinity or Ending Manhood? The Potential and Limitations of Transforming Masculine Subjectivies for Gender Equality'. In *Alternative Masculinities for a Changing World*, edited by Angels Carabi and Josep Armengol, 17–34. New York: Palgrave Macmillan.

Penny, Simon. 2004. 'Representation, Enaction, and the Ethics of Simulation'. In *First Person: New Media as Story, Performance, and Game*, edited by Noah Wardrip-Fruin and Pat Harrigan, 73–84. Cambridge, MA: MIT Press.

REFERENCES

Phillips, Winifred. 2014. *A Composer's Guide to Game Music*. Cambridge, MA: MIT Press.

Plate, S. Brent, ed. 2002. *Religion, Art, & Visual Culture: A Cross-Cultural Reader*. New York: Palgrave.

Poblocki, Kacper. 2002. 'Becomig-State: The Bio-Cultural Imperialism of Sid Meier's Civilization'. *Focaal – European Journal of Anthropology* 39: 163–77.

Pradeep, K. 2017. 'Phad and the Portable Temple'. *The Hindu*, 9 September. https://www.thehindu.com/society/history-and-culture/phad-and-the-portable-temple/article19645174.ece. Accessed 22 December 2023.

Prime Minister of Japan and His Cabinet. 1946. 'The Constitution of Japan'. https://japan.kantei.go.jp/constitution_and_government_of_japan/constitution_e.html. Accessed 22 December 2023.

Ramey, Lynn T. 2014. *Black Legacies: Race and the European Middle Ages*. Gainesville: University Press of Florida.

Requena-Pelegrí, Teresa. 2014. 'Fathers Who Care: Alternative Father Figures in Annie E. Proulx's The Shipping News and Jonathan Franzen's The Corrections'. In *Alternative Masculinities for a Changing World*, edited by Angels Carabi and Josep Armengol, 115–30. New York: Palgrave Macmillan.

Reynolds, Margaret. 1995. 'Ruggiero's Deceptions, Cherubino's Distractions'. In *En Travesty: Women, Gender Subversion, Opera*, edited by Corinne E. Blackmer and Patricia Juliana Smith, 132–51. New York: Columbia University Press.

Rezeanu, Cătălina-Ionela. 2015. 'The Relationship Between Domestic Space and Gender Identity: Some Signs of Alternative Domestic Femininity and Masculinity'. *Journal of Comparative Research in Anthropology and Sociology* 6, no. 2: 9–29.

Robbins, Emmet. 1982. 'Famous Orpheus'. In *Orpheus: The Metamorphoses of a Myth*, edited by John Warden, 3–23. Toronto: University of Toronto Press.

Roberts, Rebecca. 2014. 'Fear of the Unknown: Music and Sound Design in Psychological Horror Games'. In *Music in Video Games: Studying Play*, edited by K. J. Donnelly, William Gibbons and Neil Learner, 138–65. New York: Routledge.

Robbins, Emmet. 1982. 'Famous Orpheus'. In *Orpheus: The Metamorphoses of a Myth*, edited by John Warden, 3–23. Toronto: University of Toronto Press.

Robinson, Jenefer. 2005. *Deeper than Reason: Emotion and Its Role in Literature, Music, and Art*. Oxford: Oxford University Press.

Rodgers, Daniel. 2020. 'Just How Revolutionary is Harry Styles' Vogue Cover?' *Dazed*, 19 November. https://www.dazeddigital.com/fashion/article/51147/1/harry-styles-vogue-december-cover-dress-gender-fluid-gucci-tyler-mitchell. Accessed 22 December 2023.

Rosselli, John. 2001. 'Castrato'. *Oxford Music Online*, January. https://doi.org/10.1093/gmo/9781561592630.article.05146.

Ruberg, Bonnie. 2020. 'Empathy and Its Alternatives: Deconstructing the Rhetoric of "Empathy" in Video Games'. *Communication, Culture and Critique* 13, no. 1: 54–71. https://doi.org/10.1093/ccc/tcz044.

Ryan, Marie-Laure. 2015. *Narrative as Virtual Reality 2: Revisiting Immersion and Interactivity in Literature and Electronic Media*. Baltimore: Johns Hopkins University Press.

Said, Edward Wadie. 1978. *Orientalism*. New York: Vintage Books.

Saladin, Ronald. 2019. *Young Men and Masculinities in Japanese Media: (Un-)Conscious Hegemony*. Singapore: Palgrave Macmillan.

Salen, Katie and Eric Zimmerman. 2004. *Rules of Play: Game Design Fundamentals*. Cambridge, MA: The MIT Press.

Sam, Jordan Hugh. 2020. 'Stand By Me: Sounds of Queer Utopias and Homosexual Panic in *Final Fantasy XV*'. Paper presented at the *North American Conference on Video Game Music*, Virtual Conference, 14 June.

Sánchez, Kate. 2018. 'Latinx in Gaming: "Overwatch"'. *But Why Tho?* 16 October. https://butwhytho.net/2018/10/16/latinx-in-gaming-overwatch/. Accessed 22 December 2023.

Sánchez-Kisielewska, Olga. 2018 'The Hymn as a Musical Topic in the Age of Haydn, Mozart, and Beethoven'. Ph.D. diss., Northwestern University.

Schrier, Karen and Matthew Farber. 2021. 'A Systematic Literature Review of "Empathy" and "Games"'. *Journal of Gaming & Virtual Worlds* 13, no. 2: 195–214. https://doi.org/10.1386/jgvw_00036_1.

Schut, Kevin. 2013. *Of Games & God: A Christian Exploration of Video Games*. Grand Rapids: Brazos Press.

Scott, Suzanne. 2017. '#Wheresrey? Toys, Spoilers, and the Gender Politics of Franchise Paratexts'. *Critical Studies in Media Communication* 34, no. 2: 138–47. http://dx.doi.org/10.1080/15295036.2017.1286023.

Scott, Suzanne. 2019. *Fake Geek Girls: Fandom, Gender, and the Convergence Culture Industry*. New York: New York University Press.

Seidler, Victor Jeleniewski. 2014. 'Moving Ahead: Alternative Masculinities for a Changing World'. In *Alternative Masculinities for a Changing World*, edited by Angels Carabi and Josep Armengol, 219–32. New York: Palgrave Macmillan.

Shaw, Adrienne. 2010. 'Identity, Identification, and Media Representation in Video Game Play: An Audience Reception Study'. Ph.D. diss., University of Pennylvania, Philadelpha. University of Pennsylvania ScholarlyCommons.

Sheehy, Daniel Edward. 2006. *Mariachi Music in America: Experiencing Music, Expressing Culture*. New York: Oxford University Press.

Shimomura, David. 2017. 'Video Game Journos and Giving Mario a Pass'. *Unwinnable*, 30 October. https://unwinnable.com/2017/10/30/video-game-journos-and-giving-mario-a-pass/. Accessed 22 December 2023.

Sims, David. 2019. 'A Change for Rotten Tomatoes Ahead of Captain Marvel'. *The Atlantic*, 4 March. https://www.theatlantic.com/entertainment/archive/2019/03/rotten-tomatoes-captain-marvel-review-ratings-system-online-trolls/584032/. Accessed 22 December 2023.

REFERENCES

Singman, Brooke. 2020. 'Trump Responds to Milley Apology for Lafayette Square Photo Op'. *Fox News*, 12 June. https://www.foxnews.com/politics/trump-responds-to-milley-apology-for-lafayette-square-photo-op. Accessed 22 December 2023.

Smith, Jennifer. 2020. 'Worldbuilding Voices in the Soundscapes of Role Playing Video Games'. Ph.D. diss., University of Huddersfield, Huddersfield, UK. The University Repository.

Smith, Jennifer. 2021. 'Voices, Combat, and Music: Identity, Camaraderie, and Relationships in *Final Fantasy XV*'. *Journal of Sound and Music in Games* 2, no. 2: 42–62. https://doi.org/10.1525/jsmg.2021.2.2.42.

Smith, Luke. 2008. '*FFXII* Interview: Nomura, Kitase, Hashimoto and Toriyama'. *1UP*, 7 June. https://web.archive.org/web/20110805002459/http:/www.1up.com/news/ffxiii-interview. Accessed 22 December 2023.

Smith, Raven. 2021. 'Harryween and the Problem With Boys in Dresses'. *Vogue*, 3 November. https://www.vogue.com/article/harry-styles-harryween-boys-in-dresses. Accessed 22 December 2023.

Society for Music Theory. 2020. 'Executive Board Response to Essays in the Journal of Schenkerian Studies Vol. 12'. 28 July. https://societymusictheory.org/announcement/executive-board-response-journal-schenkerian-studies-vol-12-2020-07. Accessed 22 December 2023.

Sorrell, Neil. 2001. 'Sāraṅgī'. *Oxford Music Online*. https://doi.org/10.1093/gmo/9781561592630.article.24581.

Spooner, Brian. 1988. 'Weavers and Dealers: The Authenticity of an Oriental Carpet'. In *The Social Life of Things: Commodities in Cultural Perspective*, edited by Arjun Appadurai, 195–235. Cambridge: Cambridge University Press.

Square. 1994. *Final Fantasy VI*. Music composed by Nobuo Uematsu. Video game. Meguro: Square.

Square. 2004. *Final Fantasy IX*. Music composed by Nobuo Uematsu. Video game. Meguro: Square.

Square. 2006. *Final Fantasy XII*. Music composed by Nobuo Uematsu. Video game. Meguro: Square.

Square. 2009. *Final Fantasy XIII*. Music composed by Nobuo Uematsu. Video game. Meguro: Square.

Square. 2016. *Final Fantasy XV*. Music composed by Nobuo Uematsu. Video game. Meguro: Square.

Square Portal. 2015. 'Controversial, Groundbreaking and Iconic – Claire Farron From Final Fantasy XIII'. https://squareportal.net/2015/03/09/controversial-groundbreaking-and-iconic-claire-farron-from-final-fantasy-xiii/. Accessed 22 December 2023.

Square Portal. 2016. 'Listen to "NOCTIS" from Final Fantasy XV Soundtrack'. https://squareportal.net/2016/09/07/listen-to-noctis-from-final-fantasy-xv-soundtrack/. Accessed 22 December 2023.

Starkey, Brando Simeo. 2019. 'After Three Years, It Makes No Sense There are No Black Female Characters in Overwatch'. *Andscape*, 22 February. https://andscape.com/features/after-three-years-it-makes-no-sense-there-are-no-black-female-characters-in-overwatch/. Accessed 22 December 2023.

Starkey, Daniel. 2016. 'How Overwatch Became a Rarity: The Troll-Free Online Shooter'. *Wired*, 30 May. https://www.wired.com/2016/05/overwatch-the-rare-positive-shooter/. Accessed 22 December 2023.

Stop AAPI Hate. 2021. 'National Report (Through September 2021)'. 18 November. https://stopaapihate.org/national-report-through-september-2021/. Accessed 22 December 2023.

Substance 3D. 2020. 'Raji: An Ancient Epic – Enter the Realm of Indian Mythology'. 2 July. https://magazine.substance3d.com/raji-an-ancient-epic-enter-the-realm-of-indian-mythology/. Accessed 22 December 2023.

Summers, Alicia and Monica K. Miller. 2014. 'From Damsels in Distress to Sexy Superheroes: How the Portrayal of Sexism in Video Game Magazines has Changed in the Last Twenty Years'. *Feminist Media Studies* 14, no. 6: 1028–40. https://doi.org/10.1080/14680777.2014.882371.

Summers, Timothy. 2016. *Understanding Video Game Music*. Cambridge: Cambridge University Press.

Swann, Peter. 2017. 'Horizon: Zero Dawn is the Feminist Game We Need, but Not the One We Deserve'. *Comiscverse*, 28 March. https://comicsverse.com/horizon-zero-dawn-feminist-game/. Accessed 22 December 2023.

Tabata, Hajime. 2016. '*FFXV* Revealed! Tabata Insider Info'. Xbox On, 13 April. https://youtu.be/ipTGqVSXwRg. Accessed 22 December 2023.

Tarasti, Eero. 1994. *A Theory of Musical Semiotics*. Bloomington: Indiana University Press.

Tassi, Paul. 2020. '"The Last of Us Part 2" Is Getting Predictably User Score Bombed On Metacritic'. *Forbes*, 21 June. https://www.forbes.com/sites/paultassi/2020/06/21/the-last-of-us-part-2-is-getting-predictably-user-score-bombed-on-metacritic/?sh=4363087b5c25. Accessed 22 December 2023.

Taylor, T. L. 2007. 'Pushing the Borders: Player Participation and Game Culture'. In *Structures of Participation in Digital Culture*, edited by Joe Karaganis, 112–30. New York: SSRC.

Taylor, Timothy. 2007. *Beyond Exoticism: Western Music and the World*. Durham, NC: Duke University Press.

Thapliyal, Adesh. 2020. 'How "Raji: An Ancient Epic" Falls into the Indian Far-Right's Trap'. *Vice*, 27 October. https://www.vice.com/en/article/m7ajbv/raji-ancient-indian-epic-far-right-hindu-nationalism. Accessed 22 December 2023.

The Catholic Encyclopedia. 1910. 'Christian Iconography'. Transcribed Michael C. Tinkler. New York: Robert Appleton Company. https://www.newadvent.org/cathen/07625a.htm. Accessed 22 December 2023.

The Opportunity Agenda. 2011. 'Social Science Literature Review: Media Representations and Impact on the Lives of Black Men and Boys'. https://www.opportunityagenda.org/sites/default/files/2018-04/2011.11.30%20-%20Report%20-%20Media%20Representation%20and%20Impact%20on%20the%20Lives%20of%20Black%20Men%20and%20Boys%20-%20FINAL.pdf. Accessed 22 December 2023.

Themperor Somnium. 2021. 'Gris's Sky Temple: Sacred Spaces in Video Games'. 15 February. https://youtu.be/Fp_S4juSnX8?si=bp7VE9bArBLRGmA_. Accessed 3 June 2024.

Thompson, Ryan. 2020. 'Operatic Conventions and Expectations in *Final Fantasy VI*'. In *Music in the Role-Playing Game: Heroes & Harmonies*, edited by William Gibbons and Steven Reale, 117–28. New York: Routledge.

Tollschus, Otto D. 1945. 'The God-Emperor: Key to a Nation: The Problem of Japan is the Status of the Emperor who Rules his People as a Divinity'. *The New York Times*. 18 August.

https://www.nytimes.com/1945/08/19/archives/the-godemperor-key-to-a-nation-the-problem-of-japan-is-the-status.html. Accessed 7 June 2024.

Totilo, Stephen. 2015. 'How Anita Sarkeesian Wants Video Games to Change'. *Kotaku*, 26 February. https://kotaku.com/how-anita-sarkeesian-wants-video-games-to-change-1688231729. Accessed 22 December 2023.

Travén, Marianne. 2016. 'Voicing the Third Gender – The Castrato Voice and the Stigma of Emasculation in Eighteenth-Century Society'. *Études Épistémè* 29: 1–15. https://doi.org/10.4000/episteme.1220.

Treitler, Leo. 1993. 'Gender and Other Dualities of Music History'. In *Musicology and Difference: Gender and Sexuality in Music Scholarship*, edited by Ruth A. Solie, 23–45. Berkeley: California University Press.

Treitler, Vilna Bashi. 2013. *The Ethnic Project: Transforming Racial Fiction into Ethnic Factions*. Redwood City: Stanford University Press.

Trumbull, Robert. 1958. 'A New Role for the "Son of Heaven"'. *The New York Times*. 14 September. https://www.nytimes.com/1958/09/14/archives/a-new-role-for-the-son-of-heaven-emperor-hirohito-of-japan-is-no.html#:~:text=is%2Dno.html-,A%20New%20Role%20for%20the%20'Son%20of%20Heaven'%3B%20Emperor,nation%20groping%20for%20new%20standards. Accessed 22 December 2023.

Turtiainen, Riikka, Usva Friman and Maria Ruotsalainen. 2020. '"Not Only for a Celebration of Competitive Overwatch but Also for National Pride": Sportificating the Overwatch World Cup 2016'. *Games and Culture* 15, no. 4: 351–71. http://journals.sagepub.com/doi/10.1177/1555412018795791. Accessed 22 December 2023.

Tzelos, Linos. 2021. Private email correspondence with Thomas B. Yee. 16 September.

Uematsu, Nobuo. 2002. 'Beyond Final Fantasy: Sound'. Bonus DVD to *Final Fantasy* X PAL Release. Video interviews, 3:48.

UNESCO. 2012. 'Arirang, lyrical folk song in the Republic of Korea'. https://ich.unesco.org/en/RL/arirang-lyrical-folk-song-in-the-republic-of-korea-00445. Accessed 22 December 2023.

Van Elferen, Isabella. 2016. 'Analyzing Game Musical Immersion: The ALI Model'. In *Ludomusicology: Approaches to Video Game Music*, edited by Michiel Kamp, Tim Summers and Mark Sweeney, 32–52. Sheffield: Equinox Publishing Ltd.

Van Elferen, Isabella. 2020. 'Ludomusicology and the New Drastic'. *Journal of Sound and Music in Games* 1, no. 1: 103–12. https://doi.org/10.1525/jsmg.2020.1.1.103.

van Klyton, Aaron. 2016. 'All The Way From … Authenticity and Distance in World Music Production.' *Cultural Studies* 30, no. 1: 106–28. https://doi.org/10.1080/09502386.2014.974642.

Villarreal, Benjamin J. 2017. '"The World Could Always Use More Heroes": Why Overwatch Matters'. *First Person Scholar*, 6 December. http://www.firstpersonscholar.com/the-world-could-always-use-more-heroes/. Accessed 22 December 2023.

Vinzant, John. 2020. 'Sed Non Eodem Modo: Comparing Ludomusicology to Nineteenth-Century Musikwissenschaft'. Paper presented at the *North American Conference on Video Game Music*, Virtual Conference, 14 June.

Vocum Personae. 2015. 'A Bastion of Masculinity: Gender Dynamics Within Heavy Metal'. https://vocempersonae.wordpress.com/2015/05/03/a-bastion-of-masculinity-gender-dynamics-within-heavy-metal/. Accessed 8 April 2020.

Vrtačič, Eva. 2014. 'The Grand Narratives of Video Games: Sid Meier's Civilization'. *Teorija in Praska* 51, no. 1: 91–105.

Wagner, Rachel. 2014. 'Gaming Religion? Teaching Religious Studies with Videogames'. *Transformations: The Journal of Inclusive Scholarship and Pedagogy* 25, no. 1: 101–11. https://www.jstor.org/stable/10.5325/trajincschped.25.1.0101. Accessed 22 December 2023.

Ward, Alex. 2020. 'US Park Police Said Using "Tear Gas" in a Statement was a "Mistake." It Just Used the Term Again'. *Vox*, 5 June. https://www.vox.com/2020/6/5/21281604/lafayette-square-white-house-tear-gas-protest. Accessed 22 December 2023.

Warren, Michael. 2020. 'Trump Risks Potential Backlash From Evangelicals With 'Tone-Deaf' Bible Photo-Op'. *CNN*, 3 June. https://edition.cnn.com/2020/06/03/politics/trump-evangelicals-church-protests/index.html. Accessed 22 December 2023.

Webster, Andrew. 2016. 'Overwatch and the New Wave of Friendly Online Shooters'. *The Verge*, 31 May. https://www.theverge.com/2016/5/31/11821148/overwatch-blizzard-multiplayer-first-person-shooter. Accessed 22 December 2023.

Wheeler, André. 2020. 'Harry Styles Wore a Dress on the Cover of Vogue – and US Rightwingers Lost It'. *The Guardian*, 16 November. https://www.theguardian.com/lifeandstyle/2020/nov/16/harry-styles-vogue-cover-dress. Accessed 22 December 2023.

Williams, Hayley. 2020. 'How Horizon Zero Dawn Moves Beyond the Strong Female Character'. *Kotaku*, 3 August. https://www.kotaku.com.au/2020/08/how-horizon-zero-dawn-moves-be-yond-the-strong-female-character/. Accessed 22 December 2023.

Willis, Dre. 2016. 'Overwatch: A Step in the Right Direction for Diversity in Gaming'. *Geeks of Color*, 28 September. https://geeksofcolor.co/2016/09/28/overwatch-a-step-in-the-right-direction-for-diversity-in-gaming/. Accessed 22 December 2023.

Xataka México. 2017. 'Nintendo elimina al Mario "mexicano" de la portada de Super Mario Odyssey', 1 August. https://www.xataka.com.mx/videojuegos/nintendo-elimina-al-mario-mexicano-de-la-portada-de-super-mario-odyssey. Accessed 22 December 2023.

Yee, Thomas B. 2018. 'Replies to Ravasio, Noble, and Kluth'. *American Society for Aesthetics Graduate E-Journal* 10, no. 1. https://asageorg.wordpress.com/2019/05/15/replies-to-ravasio-noble-and-kluth-yee/. Accessed 22 Decemeber 2023.

Zimmerman, Eric. 2004. 'Narrative, Interactivity, Play, and Games: Four Naughty Concepts in Need of Discipline'. In *First Person: New Media as Story, Performance, and Game*, edited by Noah Wardrip-Fruin and Pat Harrigan, 154–64. Cambridge, MA: MIT Press.

Zimmerman, Eric. 2012. 'Jerked Around by the Magic Circle – Clearing the Air Ten Years Later'. *Game Developer*. https://www.gamedeveloper.com/design/jerked-around-by-the-magic-circle--clearing-the-air-ten-years-later. Accessed 26 July 2022.

About the Author

Some composers found their love of music hearing Brahms or Beethoven – Thomas B. Yee (b. 1992) discovered his from the beeps and boops of the Super Nintendo. Thomas composes transformative Holocaust Remembrance opera (*Eva and the Angel of Death*) and concert pieces remixing live performance with the chiptune aesthetics of retro video game soundworlds. Thomas's research analyses the representation of gender, race and religion in video game music and the compositional innovations of Japanese 8-bit era video game composers. Thomas B. Yee is assistant professor of instruction in theory and composition at the University of Texas at San Antonio School of Music, USA.

Index

#

#BlackLivesMatter 131–32, 164, 166, 195

#WheresRey? 50

A

A Composer's Guide to Game Music 12

Aerith 60, 68

affective zone 10, 27–28

ALI model 11

Aloy 111–17, 120–24, 245

Anatone, Richard 66–67

antiracism 166–69, 173, 186, 245–46

arafō (アラフォー) 83, 86–87, 89

Ashe 73, 88

assimilationism 167–69, 171, 178–79, 186, 246

Atkinson, Sean 12, 71, 116

aural skills 34–35

authenticity 140, 143–45, 151

Avatar: The Last Airbender 129–30

B

Bartz 65–66

Berlinist 41

Bhopa 154

Bhunivelze 211–13, 215, 217, 220–23

bisnōnen (美少年) 70

bushidō (武士道) 64–65, 93

C

cadence

Picardy-Aeolian 55–56, 68

Captain Marvel 106–07

castrati 117

Cecil 64–65

Celes 66–67

Cheng, William 9–10

Christianity

Bible 195–96

evangelicalism 84, 195, 211

expulsion from Japan 208, 247

iconography 198–99

in Japan 208–11

Roman Catholicism 178, 212, 214

see also sacred music

chromaticism 49, 52, 54, 57, 65

Chrono Cross 32–37

Civilization series

Civilization IV 170–71

Civilization V 172–73

Civilization VI 173–81

classical music 12, 168–69

Cloud Strife 68, 87, 163

Collins, Karen 9, 25, 31

Connell, Raewyn 55, 82, 95, 118

conventional (music) 100

Cook, Karen 170–71, 179

Critical Race Theory 168

cultural appropriation 137, 145–46

D
damsel in distress 109–11, 121
darshan 156–57
de Man, Joris 115–16
diegetic 9, 10, 38
    supra-diegetic 11
    meta-diegetic 30
diversity 146–47, 180–83, 247–48
    and equity 188–90
divine attributes 218
    classical theism 218, 220–21
    impassibility 213, 218–21
doxxing 106

E
Elferen, Isabella van 11–12
Elven, Julie 114–17, 121–22
emotion
    divine 220
    empathy 114, 247–48
    expression 91
    integration 90, 96, 221
    suppression 95–96, 213
Esports 183
Ewell, Philip 132, 168
exoticism 141, 143–45, 169, 172–73, 245

F
Fach vocal classification 115
fantasy defence 130–31, 136, 158–59
femininity (conventional) 47–48, 246
    alternative 81–84, 86–87, 246
    hegemonic (Japan) 86
    emphasized 65, 83, 90
    musical conventions 51, 54, 56–57
    subversion 74, 88, 120–21
Feminine Romantic Cliché (FRC) 56–57, 89
feminism 109, 111–12
    musicology 50–52, 101
film music 29, 51, 56–58

Final Fantasy series (*FF*)
    Final Fantasy I 53
    Final Fantasy II 53
    Final Fantasy III 53–54
    Final Fantasy IV 64–65
    Final Fantasy V 65–66
    Final Fantasy VI 66–67, 201
    Final Fantasy VII 68–69
    Final Fantasy VIII 69–70
    Final Fantasy IX 70–71
    Final Fantasy X 71–72, 233, 239–40, 242
    Final Fantasy XII 72–73
    Final Fantasy XIII 87–89
    Final Fantasy XV 92–100
    Lightning Returns: Final Fantasy XIII
        211–17, 220–23, 245
Floyd, George 131–32, 164, 166, 195

G
Game Sound 9
Gamergate 106, 124
Garnet 71
gender 47
    egalitarian representation 100–01
    gender and sex terminology 47–48
    markedness of 54–55
    player demographics 111
    social construction 52
    third 117–18, 120–21, 245
Gibbons, William 12
Gillis, Ariana 122
god-slayer
    narrative trope 200–03, 239, 242, 245
    musical trope 203, 227, 231
Grasso, Julianne 10, 27–28, 227
Great Masculine Renunciation (fashion) 80
Greenfield-Casas, Stefan 233, 238–40
Greimas' modalities 230
grief 39, 42, 114, 245
    stages of 39

INDEX

Gris 37–43, 245
guitarrón 140–41
guzheng (古筝) 176

H

Hamauzu, Masashi (浜渦正志) 74, 87
Hatten, Robert 54, 100, 185, 227, 234–36
heavy metal 69
Hebrew Bible 218–219
Hirohito (Emperor) 225–26, 240–41
Hollywood Production Code 56
Homo Ludens 2–3
homohysteria 95
homosociality 94
Hope Estheim 91, 213, 217, 220
Horizon Forbidden West 111, 121–23
Horizon Zero Dawn 111–17
How to Be an Antiracist 166
Huizinga, Johan 2
hybridity 145
hypermasculinity 69 *see also* masculinity

I

iconography 198
identity 2, 14, 16, 26, 30–31, 92–93, 124, 135,
   156, 182, 197, 245
      gender 47, 55, 79, 82
      master category 133, 197
      musical continuity 41–42
Ideology and Christianity in Japan 208–11
idol (アイドル) 57
immersion 24–26
Inazō, Nitobe 64, 93, 95–96
India
      architecture 152–53
      Hindu temple 157
      religious traditions 156–57
      video game industry 152
interactivity 6, 9, 24–26 *see also* interpretative
   interactivity

interpretation 14–15, 28
      multiplicity of 15, 30 *see also* interpreta-
         tive interactivity
interpretative interactivity 28–31, 242,
   245–46
intersectionality 135–36

J

Japan
      alternative femininities and masculinities
         83, 99, 102
      Confucian social order 209
      conventional gender 86
      corporate culture 94–95
      emperor 210, 220, 240–42, 245
      Equal Employment Opportunity Law 85
      iconography 138–139
      Japan-produced video games 16–17,
         202, 223, 239
      masculinity 64
      see also bushidō and *sararīman*
      music industry 57
      music (traditional) 142, 150
      post-war reconstruction 210,
         240–42
      Shinto, Buddhist traditions 208,
         225
Jewel Voice Broadcast 225–26, 239–41
Journey 27–28, 37

K

kabuki (歌舞伎) 142
karōshi (過労死) 94
Kendi, Ibram X. 133, 165–69, 190, 246
Kessler, David 39
Koizumi, Fumio (小泉文夫) 150
koto (琴) 142, 185
Knorr, Geoff 180
Kübler-Ross, Elisabeth 39
Kubo, Naoto 140, 149–50

L

Lacqueur, Thomas 118
Leia (Princess) 48–49, 56
leitmotif 11, 120
Lenna 66
Lightning Farron 84–92, 211–13, 217–23
Locke 67
ludic dialectic 183
ludology 5–7, 13
ludomusical narrativity 10, 27–28
ludomusicology 9

M

magic circle 3, 14, 24, 245
mariachi 140–42, 147–48
markedness 54–55
masculinity (conventional) 47–48, 246
    alternative 81–83, 93–98, 245–46
    hegemonic 55, 64–65, 80–83, 94, 101–02, 135–36, 247
    inclusive 94
    musical conventions 51, 55–56, 101
    subversion 97, 120–21
McClary, Susan 50–52, 101
methodology 14–16, 201–02
    hermeneutic of hope 165–66
mezzo-soprano 40–41, 116, 119–22
Min Min 163–64
minimalism 50
mode
    Aeolian 122
    Dorian 50, 65, 214–15
    Locrian 155–56
    Lydian 12, 72, 116, 217
min'yō (民謡) 142–43, 148–49
miyakobushi (都節音階) 142, 150–51, 185–86
    Phrygian 233
Moltmann, Jürgen 218–20, 222
Monelle, Raymond 227
multimodality 13, 15–16

N

nanpa (ナンパ) 70
nanshoku (男色) 70
narrative 7–8
    ludic 38–39
    musical 29–30, 36–37, 149–50, 238
narratology 7–8, 13
Neo-Riemannian 214
New Year's Rescript 210, 240–42
Nietzsche, Friedrich 200
Nintendo Entertainment System (NES) 53
Noctis Lucis Caelum 92–100, 245

O

objectification (sexual) 96–97, 110
onna-musha (女武者) 85
orientalism 135–36, 169
Orpheus 23, 32
Overwatch 181–87, 245

P

Paramore, Kiri 208
pentatonic scale 38
Phillips, Winifred 12–13
play 2–3
Playing with Sound 9, 25
pop-ballad (style) 66, 69–72

Q

queer sexuality 79, 107, 182, 246
Quinn, Zoe 106

R

race 134–35
    and ethnicity 132–33
    hegemony 168
    pseudo-science 135, 173
    terminology 133
racialized fantasy 131, 136–40, 158–59, 246
racism 132, 134, 166–69, 247

INDEX

radical compassion 248

Raji: An Ancient Epic 152–5

ravanhatta 154–56

representation 2, 15, 31, 246
    gender 50–52, 101–02, 124
    racial 130–32, 158–59, 163–65, 182–83
    religious 198

religion
    demographics 197
    in video games 198

review bombing 106–07, 122–24

Rey (Skywalker) 49–50

Rinoa 69–70

Romantic (style) 49, 54, 58, 90

Rosa 65, 91

ryōsaikenbo (良妻賢母) 66, 86

S

sacred music (Christian) 199, 203
    organum 233 *see also* topic, musical

Said, Edward 135–36

Sakimoto, Hitoshi (崎元仁) 74, 87

sankyoku (三曲) 142

sararīman (サラリーマン) 91, 93

Sarkeesian, Anita 106, 109, 187

second woman 119–20

segregationism 167–69, 172–73, 186, 246

self-acceptance 42

semiotics 13–14, 25–26, 238
    gender 119
    music 30–31, 227, 246
    politics 196

sengyōshufu (専業主婦) 66, 85

sexism 110, 123–24

shakuhachi (尺八) 142

shamisen (三味線) 142

Shimomura, Yōko (下村陽子) 74, 98, 232

shinobue (篠笛) 142, 151

Shulk 233, 236–39, 242

Smith, Jennifer 99

social justice 16, 131–132, 163–69, 182

sonic iconography 199–200, 245–46

sonnō jōi (尊皇攘夷) 210, 220–22, 241

soprano 40–41, 57

sōshokudanshi (草食男子) 83

Sound Play 9–10

Squall 69

Star Wars (franchise) 48–50

stereotype 137, 146–48, 151, 169

Stop AAPI Hate 134

strategic (music) 100

Styles, Harry 79–80

Summers, Timothy 11, 27, 67

Super Mario series 109
    Super Mario Odyssey 136–143, 147–51, 245

Super Nintendo Entertainment System (SNES) 54

Super Smash Bros. series 163
    Super Smash Bros Ultimate 163–64

T

Terra 66–67, 88

tetrachord 150

The Last of Us Part II 107

The Legend of Zelda series 109

theme, musical
    character 52–54, 59–60
    event 53
    location 53, 184
    terrain 170–72

Tidus 71–72

Tifa 68–69

topic, musical 54, 227–28
    heroic 55–56, 65, 67–68, 88
    hunt 227
    Indianism 144, 169
    martial 116
    mechanistic 116
    pastoral 71

topic, musical *(Continued)*
 rock 228, 231
 sacred music 203, 214–15, 228, 232–38
 soaring 12, 116
 transcendent 116
 video-game specific 227–28
travesti 119–20
tresillo 147
trope (musical topics) 184, 231
 four axes 185, 234–36
Trump, Donald 84, 107–08, 195–96
Twintelle 163–64
two-sex theory 118
Tzelos, Linos 154–56, 158

U
Uematsu, Nobuo (植松 伸夫) 26, 57–58, 74, 87
Understanding Game Music 11
United States
 academic music studies 168–69
 social context 16, 133, 195, 211
 video game player demographics 111

Unlimited Replays 12
ushinawareta jūnen (失われた十年) 85

V
Vaan 73
vihuela 140–41
virtual 4, 14, 24
virtual agency 60, 91, 221–22, 230–31

W
whitewashing 129–30, 169
Williams, John 49
world music 145, 169

X
Xenoblade Chronicles 232–39, 242, 245

Y
yellowface 129
Yuna 60, 72

Z
Zanza 233, 236–39
Zidane 70–71

www.ingramcontent.com/pod-product-compliance
Lightning Source LLC
Chambersburg PA
CBHW080742050525
25994CB00029B/8